VOLUME **B** **1790 TO 1877**

A HISTORY *of* US

CONCISE EDITION

Front Cover

"Drummer" Jackson, a former slave, served as a drummer in the 79th United States Colored Troops during the Civil War.

398–401 *Atlas of North America*. H. J. de Blij, editor-in-chief. New York: Oxford University Press, 2005.

ISBN-13: 978-1-60153-182-7

Printed by Bradford & Bigelow, Newburyport, MA, USA, August 2020.

VOLUME **1790 TO 1877**

B

Joy Hakim

A HISTORY *of*
US

CONCISE EDITION

Editors of the K^{12} Concise Edition

John Holdren and Patricia O'Connell Pearson

Concise Edition Volume B Staff and Contributors

Allyson Jacob, Kay McCarthy, Jill Tunick *Text Editors*
Suzanne Montazer *Creative Director, Print and ePublishing*
Stephanie Shaw Williams *Print Visual Designer*
The Quarasan Group, Inc. *Interior Design and Composition*
Kim Barcas, Carol Leigh *Cover Designers*
Meredith Condit, Charlotte Fullerton *Picture Editors*
Jean Stringer *Rights Manager*
David Swanson *Cartographer*
Jay White *Contributing Instructional Designer*
Susan Raley *Senior Manager, Editors*
Candee Wilson *Senior Project Manager*

Maria Szalay *Senior Vice President, Product Development*
John Holdren *Senior Vice President, Content and Curriculum*
David Pelizzari *Vice President, Content and Curriculum*
Kim Barcas *Vice President, Creative*
Laura Seuschek *Vice President, Instructional Design and Evaluation & Research*
Aaron Hall *Vice President, Program Management*

Lisa Dimaio Iekel *Senior Production Manager*
John Agnone *Director of Publications*

About K12 Inc.

K12 Inc., a technology-based education company, is the nation's leading provider of proprietary curriculum and online education programs to students in grades K–12. K^{12} provides its curriculum and academic services to online schools, traditional classrooms, blended school programs, and directly to families. K12 Inc. also operates the K^{12} International Academy, an accredited, diploma-granting online private school serving students worldwide. K^{12}'s mission is to provide any child the curriculum and tools to maximize success in life, regardless of geographic, financial, or demographic circumstances. K12 Inc. is accredited by CITA. More information can be found at www.K12.com.

A Note from the Author

In this second volume of the concise edition of *A History of US* I once again find myself awed by the American achievement. Perhaps no era offers so much in the way of idealism, good sense, hard work, and thoughtless nastiness, as the years that go from George Washington to Abraham Lincoln to the missed opportunity known as Reconstruction. This book, abridged by my friends at K^{12}, retains the major stories from the original edition; if you want to read more, the complete ten volumes are still available.

—Joy Hakim

Contents

PART 1

THE NEW NATION

PART 2

GOING PLACES

PART 3

THE ROAD TO WAR

PART 4

CIVIL WAR AND RECONSTRUCTION

PART 1

the NEW NATION

The Father of Our Country

George Washington served as president from 1789 to 1797. This famous portrait was painted by Gilbert Stuart in 1796. ▼

George Washington was 57, and he was home, at Mount Vernon, the place he loved most. Before, when his country asked, he had left the comforts of his Virginia estate for the harshness of war. Then he left again to spend four hot months in Philadelphia, where he was needed to see a constitution written. Now, he was being asked to leave once more.

It was April 14, 1789, and Charles Thomson rode to Mount Vernon with a letter for George Washington.

Thomson—who was Irish-born—had been secretary of the Continental Congress from its beginnings in 1774. That congress was out of business. The new constitution had changed things. The confederation was finished; now there was a union of states and a new congress of the United States.

The letter that Thomson carried told George Washington that he had been elected president of that union. He had been elected

George Washington's Mount Vernon plantation comprised five working farms on 8,000 acres of land fronting the Potomac River. Washington and his family lived at the Mansion House Farm. ▼

unanimously—and that was important; it would not happen with any other president. It meant the government could get started without fighting over a leader. The letter said Washington was expected in New York for his inauguration. That city was to be the capital until a new one could be built.

Of course, Washington must have been proud. Martha, his wife, must have been proud of him. But he hated to leave her and Mount Vernon, especially in April. Cherry trees were in bloom; so were daffodils and tulips, and so, too, the dogwood trees, whose white blossoms floated like a layer of lace in the midst of the green woods. Washington was a farmer. In April he was thinking about spring crops and all the chores that had to be done on his big plantation.

But he did what his sense of duty told him to do: what he felt was best for his country. He agreed to be president. Two days later he wrote in his diary: "About ten o'clock I bade farewell to Mount Vernon, to private life, and to domestic felicity, and with a mind oppressed with more anxious and painful sensations than I have words to express, set out for New York."

It took eight days to make the 235-mile journey. It would have been faster, but in each town citizens greeted their president-elect with a parade, or a bonfire, or fireworks, or speeches, or a ceremonial dinner, or a chorus, or sometimes all those things.

Yet he was always gracious. Waving from his carriage, he saw many faces he remembered from Revolutionary War battlefields or from Valley Forge. As he approached Philadelphia he got out of his

▲ Martha Washington

Felicity is happiness.

"The Electors Shall Meet..."

The Constitution says:

Each State shall appoint, in such manner as the Legislature thereof may direct, a number of Electors, equal to the whole number of Senators and Representatives to which the State may be entitled in the Congress.... The Electors shall meet in their respective States, and vote by ballot for two persons....The person having the greatest number of votes shall be the President....

Those electors, known as the Electoral College, do the actual voting for president. That's why, sometimes, the results of the popular vote and the presidential vote aren't the same.

▲ Washington arrives in New York for his inauguration as the first president of the United States. Thousands of people gathered to cheer his arrival.

Abigail Adams, wife of John Adams (who became George Washington's vice president), wrote about the new country's leader: "He is polite with dignity, affable without familiarity, distant without haughtiness, grave without austerity, modest, wise, and good."

In his inaugural address on April 30, 1789, Washington talked of preserving "the sacred fire of liberty," and of the "republican model of government" as an "experiment entrusted to the hands of the American people."

carriage, mounted a white horse, and rode toward the city. The parade of horsemen that followed him grew longer and longer.

When he finally arrived in New York—rowed across the Hudson River from New Jersey on a barge decorated with streamers—church bells rang, cannons roared, and people cheered until they were hoarse.

Ever modest, Washington thanked the crowd and said, "After this is over, I hope you will give yourselves no further trouble, as the affection of my fellow citizens is all the guard I want."

Six days later they were still cheering. It was the day of his inauguration—April 30, 1789. Washington wore a plain brown suit made of American cloth, stood on the balcony of Federal Hall overlooking Wall Street, bowed to the great crowd below, put his hand on his heart, and took the oath as president.

Afterwards, he and the members of Congress walked up Broadway to spired, stately St. Paul's Episcopal Church. There, under a blue-sky ceiling, the new president prayed for guidance, for the young republic, and for himself.

A Revolution in France

While George Washington was president, other nations were ruled by kings, emperors, and tsars (zars). Remember, the birth of the United States was a world-shaking event. We were the first modern nation to form a people's government, to write our own constitution, and to elect our own leaders.

Most Americans in the 18th and 19th centuries knew a lot about kings and didn't want one in the United States. King Louis XVI and Queen Marie Antoinette were the rulers of France in 1785, when Thomas Jefferson arrived as America's ambassador. France's King Louis XVI didn't eat alone. Three hundred and eighty-three men, including nobles, waited on him and presented each morsel of his food in a splendid, ceremonial fashion. It took four people just to serve the king a glass of water.

In a letter to George Washington, Jefferson wrote, "I was much an enemy to monarchy before I came to Europe. I am ten thousand times more so since I have seen what they are."

It cost the French people a great deal of money to pay for all the pleasures of their king and queen. Taxes were very high. Supporting the royal family was making the people poor.

The French people knew all about the American Revolution; they decided to have one of their own. The French Revolution began on July 14, 1789, when angry citizens stormed a horrid old prison called the Bastille (ba-STEEL or bas-TEE-yuh). The king and the nobles had been putting political prisoners in the Bastille and forgetting them there. After the revolution, the key to the Bastille was sent to President Washington.

The French people wanted to form a democratic government. But their revolution got off track. The king and queen were executed. Some brutal leaders began killing people and couldn't seem to stop. When the French Revolution turned nasty, many French people wanted to leave their country. Some of those people came to America.

The storming of the Bastille on July 14, 1789, marked the beginning of the French Revolution. ▼

About Being President

Precedent (PRESS-ih-dent) and *president* (PREZ-ih-dent)—they sound similar, but their meanings aren't the same. Say them aloud and hear the difference.

President Washington appointed a cabinet of advisers, including Thomas Jefferson and Alexander Hamilton. ▼

No one could tell George Washington how to be president. No one had done the job before. Washington knew that whatever he did would set a precedent. That means he would be the example and other presidents would follow his lead.

The Constitution outlined the basic tasks of the president, but it didn't go into details. George Washington had to decide many things himself.

As always, he did his very best. He didn't want the president to be like the English king, but he did think it important that the president be grand. He wanted people to look up to the president and respect and admire him.

So Washington acted with great dignity and rode about in a fine canary-yellow carriage pulled by six white horses whose coats were shined with marble dust, whose hoofs were painted black, and whose teeth were cleaned before every outing.

When President Washington held official receptions he wore velvet knee breeches, yellow gloves, silver buckles on his shoes, and a sword strapped to his waist. He used his coach to tour the country.

As president he was head of the executive branch of our three-branch government. (The other two branches are the legislative, which is Congress, and the judicial, which is the courts.) Washington knew he couldn't make all the decisions of the executive branch by himself. So he appointed advisers. Most of those helpers were called secretaries: secretary of state, secretary of the treasury, and so on. Altogether, they were known as the "cabinet."

Washington picked the very best people he could find. To help with foreign affairs, he picked an American who had been Virginia's governor and had lived in France and knew a lot about foreign nations. Can you guess who he was? Well, George Washington named Thomas Jefferson as his secretary of state.

You can't run a country without money. Since the days of the Revolution, when the states first united, they had had money problems. Washington needed a good man as a financial adviser. He named Alexander Hamilton as secretary of the treasury. Hamilton organized the nation's monetary system. Some people think that Alexander Hamilton was the best secretary of the treasury ever.

To head the army and navy, Washington chose his old friend Henry Knox. He was the general in charge of artillery during the Revolutionary War. Washington named him secretary of war in charge of national security.

John Adams, who had been elected George Washington's vice president, was also a cabinet member. Washington completed the cabinet when he appointed Virginia's governor, Edmund Randolph, as attorney general.

▲ James Madison, who wrote much of the Constitution and Bill of Rights, assisted President Washington with his speeches.

When he needed help writing a speech, President Washington turned to a congressman who had one of the finest minds in American history: James Madison. (And when Congress wished to address the president, guess who wrote the message? James Madison. So Madison was writing and answering the same messages!)

Altogether, Washington had about 350 people help him manage the new government. That was only about 100 more people than he supervised at his plantation home, Mount Vernon.

Almost as soon as the new government got started, something happened that Washington hadn't expected. His two top advisers argued with each other. They really argued. Jefferson and Hamilton had ideas that clashed. They found it hard to compromise.

Both were brilliant men. Both were Patriots who wanted to do their best for their country. They just disagreed on what was best. Did they ever disagree! In fact—this is interesting—political parties in America developed because of that disagreement.

The country didn't begin with parties like today's Democrats and Republicans. The Founding Fathers—the men who wrote the Constitution—didn't realize that parties would develop. Washington didn't like the idea at all. He called them "factions" and warned against them. "The spirit of party," said the president, "agitates the community with ill-founded jealousies and false alarms."

But people just don't think alike. That's what makes politics—and life—interesting. James Madison understood that. Madison knew that it was dictators who usually try to force all people to think alike. Dictatorships are one-party governments.

Madison believed that in a democracy factions should be encouraged. He thought the more the better. He said they would balance each other and then no one group could become too strong and take control of the government.

The Whiskey Rebellion

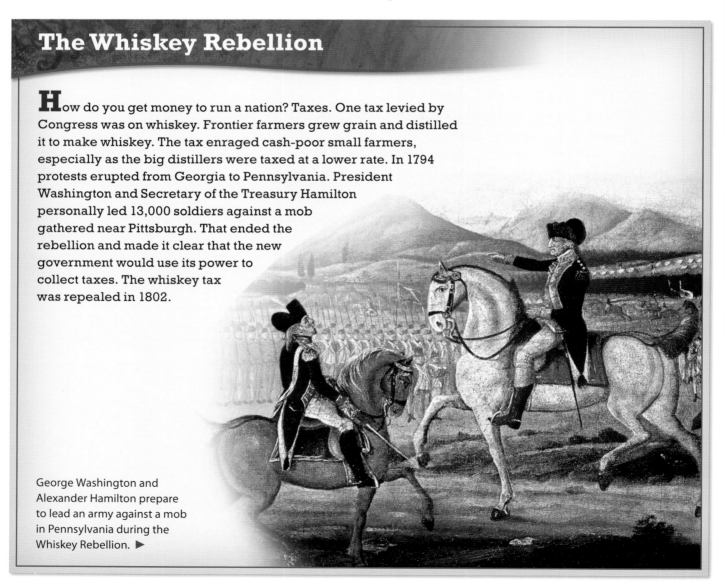

How do you get money to run a nation? Taxes. One tax levied by Congress was on whiskey. Frontier farmers grew grain and distilled it to make whiskey. The tax enraged cash-poor small farmers, especially as the big distillers were taxed at a lower rate. In 1794 protests erupted from Georgia to Pennsylvania. President Washington and Secretary of the Treasury Hamilton personally led 13,000 soldiers against a mob gathered near Pittsburgh. That ended the rebellion and made it clear that the new government would use its power to collect taxes. The whiskey tax was repealed in 1802.

George Washington and Alexander Hamilton prepare to lead an army against a mob in Pennsylvania during the Whiskey Rebellion. ▶

The Parties Begin

Those two opposites—Jefferson and Hamilton—had ideas that needed balancing. They helped found the country's first political parties. They respected, but didn't understand, each other. "Mr. Jefferson," wrote Hamilton, "is at the head of a faction decidedly hostile to me and…dangerous to the union, peace, and the happiness of the country." Jefferson replied that Hamilton's ideas "flowed from principles adverse to liberty, and…calculated to undermine and demolish the Republic."

Whew! Those are strong words. "Dangerous," "hostile," "adverse to liberty"—did they really mean it? These were men who had built the country together. What was going on?

To put it simply, they disagreed about power and who ought to have it. It was that old conflict that had kept everyone arguing when the Constitution was being written.

Jefferson and Hamilton were both concerned about liberty and about power. How do you balance the two? How do you guarantee freedom? How do you create a government that can keep order and make sure that government doesn't oppress people? How strong should the government be?

The Sense of America

Hamilton published an attack on Jefferson saying that he was disloyal to the Constitution. Jefferson wrote a letter to President Washington answering that charge.

No man in the United States, I suppose, approved of every title in the constitution; no one, I believe, approved more of it than I did… my objection to the constitution was that it wanted a bill of rights, securing freedom of religion, freedom of the press, freedom from standing armies, trial by jury, and a constant habeas corpus act. Colonel Hamilton's was that it wanted a King and House of Lords. The sense of America has approved my objection, and added a bill of rights, not the King and Lords.

▲ Thomas Jefferson

Alexander Hamilton ▼

One meaning of *mass* is "a great many people." *The masses* came to mean "the workers and ordinary folk in a country."

Hamilton believed the government should be strong. If the government was to work for all the people, instead of just those with the loudest voices, it needed to be powerful. Hamilton thought that government should be run by aristocratic leaders; that is, by the prosperous, well-educated citizens who he thought had the time and talents to best run a country. He feared the masses. He said they sometimes acted like sheep, mindlessly following a leader.

Hamilton didn't think himself part of the masses. Although he had been poor as a boy, he became rich and well educated.

But Hamilton was also wary of the rich. He thought they often acted out of self-interest—that means they did what was good for themselves. Hamilton knew the government needed checks and balances so no group could gain control.

"Give all power to the many," wrote Hamilton, "and they will oppress the few. Give all power to the few, they will oppress the many. Both therefore ought to have power, that each may defend itself against the other."

Thomas Jefferson feared powerful government. It was justice and liberty for the individual that concerned him. He saw a strong, centralized government as an enemy of individual liberty. Jefferson had been in Europe and had seen kings in action: he hated monarchies. He feared a king-like president.

Jefferson had faith in ordinary people. He thought they could govern themselves—if they were educated. And so he wrote a plan for public schools and colleges. He wanted an amendment to the Constitution that would provide for free education. (He didn't get his amendment, and his plan for education in Virginia was turned down in the General Assembly.)

Because of the differences in ideas, it became clear that political parties were needed. Hamilton's followers formed the "Federalist Party." Jefferson's followers were called "Democratic-Republicans," or sometimes just Republicans.

Now this is confusing, so pay attention. The Federalists and Republicans were not like our Democrats and Republicans—but they were the beginnings of today's party system. This is what is confusing: Jefferson's Republican Party was not like today's Republican Party. Actually, it was the parent of today's Democratic Party. (The modern Republicans got started later with a president named Abraham Lincoln.)

Jefferson said, "The many!"
Hamilton said, "The few!"
Like opposite sides of a penny
Were those exalted two.
If Jefferson said, "It's black, sir!"
Hamilton cried, "It's white!"
But, 'twixt the two, our
Constitution started working right.
—Stephen Vincent Benét

▲ In the young United States, people often gathered in coffee houses and taverns to read newspapers and discuss important issues.

Jefferson and Hamilton were both good men, and the ideas of each have been important in our country. On most issues (but not all), Hamilton was a "conservative" and Jefferson a "liberal." Have you ever heard people argue about conservatism and liberalism? Well, if you haven't, you will. These words have had very different meanings at different times. That argument almost tore the country apart in 1800, and it continues today. But we need Hamiltonians, we need Jeffersonians, and we need to have them work together. Which is just what has always happened in America. That is not true in many other nations.

In some countries, people who speak out against the government are put in jail or even killed. Members of the losing party are thrown out of the country or even killed. That doesn't happen in America. Here, since the time of President George Washington, winners and losers have always agreed to work together—as Thomas Jefferson and Alexander Hamilton did. What does that mean for you? Do you have to be afraid of being on the side of the losing party? Can you speak out for an unpopular cause? Of course you can—you're an American.

Money, Money, Money, Money

Lots of people argue about money, so you may not be surprised to learn that Hamilton and Jefferson did that, too. They had different visions of the way they wanted the United States to grow. Hamilton wanted to encourage business and industry. Jefferson hoped to keep America a nation of farmers and landholders.

But the world was changing, and, whether Jefferson liked it or not, cities and factories were on their way. So was a *money economy*.

In early America, most people were self-sufficient farmers and had little use for money. They bartered—traded—for what they needed. About the time when the United States became a nation, we were turning into a *capitalistic* society.

Capital is money, or any goods or assets that can be turned into money. If your family owns a house or car that can be sold for cash, that is part of your family's capital, along with any money you have in the bank and in your pocket.

Hamilton wanted to encourage businesses, like this tin shop where workers are making plates, cups, and other items to be sold. ▼

If you want to start a business you will probably need to borrow money to do so, (Most businesses are started that way.) You will need *credit*. Credit is borrowing power. The bank, or whoever lends you the money, needs to be convinced you will pay back the loan. They need to be sure your credit is good. Sometimes you have to promise to give them your house or car if you can't pay back the loan. The house (or whatever the bank believes has value) is called your *collateral*.

Governments need to borrow money, too. One way they do that is by issuing government bonds. A *bond* is a written promise to pay the amount loaned plus interest. (*Interest* is a charge for borrowing money. Charging interest is one way banks make their money.) You can buy a government bond. You will be lending money to your government and you will earn interest, too.

Just like people, some governments pay their debts promptly and have good credit. Some governments *default* on their bonds. That means they don't pay what they owe. Then they

Jefferson envisioned a country of independent farmers and landholders. ▼

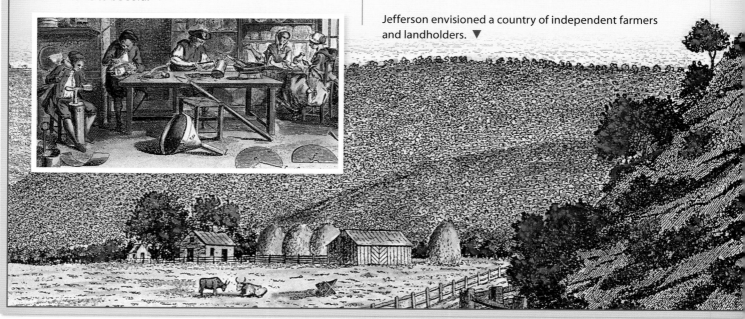

▲ The first American bank, Philadelphia's Bank of the United States, cost so much to construct that the builders had to finish the sides in brick instead of marble.

◄ Under the new Constitution, the government began minting coins.

have difficulties the next time they want to borrow money.

The Congress of the Articles of Confederation had borrowed from citizens and from other nations in order to fight the Revolutionary War. The debt was huge and it was not being paid off properly. The bondholders were not getting interest payments. They could not get their money back for their bonds.

Some Americans thought that was all right. They thought it was unfair for the new nation to be stuck with the debts of the old government. Some people suggested that the new United States government ignore those old debts.

Many former soldiers and farmers and everyday citizens had lent the government money. That made them *investors*. They held government bonds. There were rumors that the government would not pay the debt. Many of those investors sold their bonds for much less than their *face* (promised) value. Some people who held $100 government bonds sold them for $25. They thought they were lucky to get anything for them.

The people who bought the bonds were *speculators*. They were taking a chance. Many of the speculators were wealthy, so they could afford to take a chance.

That was the situation when Alexander Hamilton became secretary of the treasury. The government debt was $64.12 million. It would be very difficult to pay that enormous amount of money.

Jefferson and Madison believed the new government should not be responsible for the mistakes and debts of the old. They didn't want to see speculators get rich.

Hamilton disagreed. He said, "States, like individuals, who observe their engagements, are respected and trusted, while the reverse is the fate of those who pursue an opposite conduct." But Hamilton couldn't get Congress to pay the debt. Jefferson, who never liked conflicts, said, "I think it necessary to give as well as take in government like ours." So he invited Madison and Hamilton to dinner and "encouraged them to consider the thing together." If Madison would stop protesting payment of the debt, perhaps Hamilton could use his influence to put the capital of the nation on Virginia's Potomac River. Hamilton agreed.

When Hamilton stepped down as treasury secretary in 1795, the debt had been paid and people wanted to buy U.S. government bonds because they knew they could trust the new nation. They would soon admire its new capital on the banks of the Potomac.

The United States developed a form of capitalism called *free enterprise*. "Free" doesn't mean there are no business regulations. You wouldn't want that. For example, if ingredients weren't listed on food packages, you'd never know what was inside—until you got sick. But in our free enterprise system, the aim has always been to keep government rules at a minimum.

A Capital City

The nation's capital didn't land on the banks of the Potomac right away. First it was in New York, but that wasn't right. Then it was moved to Philadelphia in 1790. But Philadelphia wasn't right, either.

Each state wanted the capital city for itself. Which state would get it?

There was a sensible answer: a new city would be built and it would not be in any state—then there would be no state jealousy. It would have its own piece of land in a special place to be known as the "District of Columbia." (I don't have to tell you who that was named after, do I?)

The capital was called the Federal City. George Washington picked the site for it on the Potomac River. It seemed a good choice—right in the middle of the country. (Middle of the country? Yes, in 1790.) Congress approved.

Now the city needed planning. Thomas Jefferson had visited and studied cities and gardens in Europe. He was fascinated by architecture and landscape design. He had many ideas for the new city. But professionals were needed to set to work.

Benjamin Banneker and Andrew Ellicott survey the new capital city that would become Washington, D.C. ▼

To begin, the land needed surveying. Major Andrew Ellicott was appointed to do the job. He chose Benjamin Banneker as his assistant. Banneker, who was 60, set up a field observatory tent with a hole in its top. For the next three months, during the cold winter, he spent almost every night lying on his back in the tent looking at the sky through a six-foot-long instrument called a "zenith sector." By observing the stars, he made calculations that Ellicott then used in his survey of the 10-square-mile city-to-be. Banneker, a self-taught surveyor, astronomer, and mathematician, also used the star data to predict the weather and movement of planets for an almanac that he published.

In L'Enfant's grand plan for Washington, big avenues cut diagonally across a square grid of streets. Today, that pattern makes driving around very complicated.

The man who actually planned the Federal City was another genius. Pierre-Charles L'Enfant (lahn-FAHN) studied art and engineering in Paris and then came to America and fought in the Revolutionary War. After that, he helped plan a New York dinner party for 6,000 people! It was a grand party to celebrate New York's ratifying of the Constitution, and it was a great success.

L'Enfant's first big architectural job came when he redesigned New York's old City Hall and turned it into a headquarters for the new government. It was named Federal Hall. But it was as the designer of the new nation's capital that he became famous. L'Enfant put a broad, grassy mall in the center of the city-to-be. Then he laid out rectangular city blocks and cut through them with broad, spoke-like avenues. He decided that

Benjamin Banneker, the son of a freed slave, had wide-ranging interests. He studied mathematics and astronomy. He accurately predicted an eclipse, calculated the cycles of locust plagues, and wrote a scientific paper on bees. From 1792 to 1802 he published a popular almanac. A public-spirited citizen, he suggested that the new cabinet have a minister of peace as well as a minister of war. He worked for free public education and an end to capital punishment. He was a vigorous opponent of slavery. A Quaker opposed to slavery wrote that Banneker's achievements showed that *the powers of the mind are disconnected with the colour of the skin.*

Benjamin Banneker was the first black man to receive a presidential appointment—but he still could not vote.

▲ President Washington inspects the construction of the presidential mansion. The second president, John Adams, would be the first to live there.

Notice these words: *capitol* for the building and *capital* for the city. How will you remember which is which? Well, one way to do it is to think of the round dome on top of the Capitol and think of the letter *o*, which is round.

the House of Congress, called the "Capitol," was to be on a hill (Capitol Hill) overlooking the mall and the Potomac River. From the President's House there would be another view of mall and river. It was a splendid design.

A contest was announced to find the best plan for the President's House. One person who entered the contest put a false name on his entry. He was an amateur architect (a man who loved to design buildings), but he didn't want the judges to know his real name. Can you guess who it was? The secret competitor was Thomas Jefferson. He didn't win the competition. James Hoban, an Irishman, won and became architect of the White House.

Another contest was announced. This was for the Capitol. Some strange entries arrived: a bridge builder whose bridges collapsed sent a design. So did a carpenter who seemed to like windowless rooms. The winning entry came from William Thornton, who was born in the British Virgin Islands and had studied to be a doctor in Edinburgh, Scotland. George Washington said Thornton's design combined "grandeur, simplicity, and convenience."

It took forever to build the Capitol. Other architects were soon adding their ideas to the winning entry: Frenchman Etienne Hallet was one; Thomas Jefferson was another; English-trained Benjamin Henry Latrobe was yet another. The Capitol was still under construction when our 16th president took office. (His name was Abraham Lincoln.)

From its beginnings, the U.S. government looked for people with good ideas and didn't worry about their differences. It was appropriate that a Frenchman, an African American, a Scotsman, an Englishman, and an Irishman all helped to make our nation's capital beautiful.

▲ A new dome for the Capitol was under construction at the time of Abraham Lincoln's inauguration in 1861.

The Census

In 1790 the United States took its first census. It counted all its citizens. We've been doing that every 10 years since 1790.

Almost 4 million were counted in 1790—3,929,214, to be exact. Of those, 697,681 were slaves. No one counted the Indians.

In 1790, most Americans—95 percent—lived on farms. Just 3 percent of America's citizens lived in the six largest cities: Philadelphia, New York, Boston, Charleston, Baltimore, and Salem. And those who lived in the city often had chickens, a cow, and a vegetable garden.

All the big cities in early America were ports. Shiploads of new people—immigrants—were sailing into those ports almost every day. Most of those immigrants cleared farmland or helped build more new cities. And they had children, lots of children. So it was no surprise when each new census showed huge population gains. In 1790 there were fewer than 4 million Americans. By 1890 there were 63 million Americans. What is the population today?

▲ Immigrants and their descendants contributed to the rapid growth of the American population.

The Adams Family Moves to Washington

Our second president, John Adams (right), said that "the affectionate participation and cheering encouragement" of his wife, Abigail Adams (below), was his "never-failing support." ▶

Our second president was the first president to live in the new capital. He was John Adams, that solid thinker from Massachusetts who helped convince Thomas Jefferson to write the Declaration of Independence.

The Federal City was still being built when John Adams moved in. A few weeks later his wife, Abigail, headed south. She got lost in the woods trying to find Washington.

Now you may remember that Abigail Adams was a strong woman who liked to write letters and who said what was on her mind. In a letter to her daughter she described the new city:

Woods are all you see, from Baltimore until you reach the city, which is only so in name…there are buildings enough, if they were compact and finished, to accommodate Congress and those attached to it; but as they are, and scattered as they are, I see no great comfort for them.

Despite all those woods, the president and his wife didn't have enough wood for their fireplaces, and there was no one to cut it. John Adams wouldn't have slaves, there weren't many laborers in the new city, and wood was very expensive. Abigail complained that they couldn't afford wood on the president's salary and that the President's House was damp. (There were no furnaces then; fires in the fireplaces kept houses warm and dry.)

Still, Abigail found many things to admire.

Upstairs there is the oval room, which is designed for the drawing-room, and has the crimson furniture in it. It is a very handsome room now; but, when completed, it will be beautiful…. [The city] is a beautiful spot, capable of every improvement, and, the more I view it, the more I am delighted with it.

The Federal City was not far from George Washington's home at Mount Vernon. The first president watched as the new city and the second president got settled. Then, in 1799, something terrible happened. George Washington got sick. It happened suddenly. Doctors were called. They bled the nation's hero. It wasn't the right thing to do. (Although it seemed right then.) Washington died just two weeks before the start of the new century. Americans were shocked and grieved, and could hardly imagine their country without this founder.

Abigail Adams went to Mount Vernon to help share Martha Washington's grief.

Henry Lee, who had fought with Washington, spoke at his funeral. He said what citizens everywhere were thinking. He said Washington was "first in war, first in peace, first in the hearts of his countrymen."

Everyone agreed that the nation's new home—the muddy and unfinished Federal City—should be named Washington to honor its first president.

In 1902, President Theodore Roosevelt officially changed the name of the Executive Mansion to the White House, although people had been calling it that for quite some time. The White House has been home to every American president except George Washington, and he approved the act that led to its construction. Sometimes it is known by its address: 1600 Pennsylvania Avenue.

"I die hard, but I am not afraid to go," said George Washington on his deathbed in 1799. The whole country mourned (below, the memorial procession in Philadelphia). Many Americans saw Washington almost as a god or saint, which embarrassed him greatly. ▼

About President Adams

John Adams was a great man, but he was just passable as president. Now that is my opinion; you are free to disagree. Some historians do. Adams was a fine person—honorable and thoughtful. So was his wife, Abigail, and so, too, was their brilliant son John Quincy. Benjamin Franklin, who was pretty good at judging people, said Adams "was always an honest man, often a wise one, but sometimes and in some things, absolutely out of his senses."

What did Franklin mean? Was John Adams crazy? No, he wasn't crazy, it just seems that sometimes he got carried away with his own ideas and forgot about reality. He had a hard time appreciating ideas that were different from his. Do you know anyone like that?

Sometimes when you study history it seems as if people in the past were all greater than people now. But they didn't look that way to the people who knew them. Ben knew John. He knew his good points and his weak ones. And Adams had plenty of both.

John Adams was brave and intelligent, and he loved his country. When he was young, and the country needed help breaking away from England, he was a strong leader and a fine thinker. Then he went off to Europe, where he served his country well as a diplomat in France, Holland, and England.

Adams believed in representative government—what people called "republicanism"—but he didn't think much of democracy. Like Alexander Hamilton, he thought the educated and the aristocratic should govern; he didn't trust the mass of people.

John Adams was a complicated man. Perhaps he was just too independent to be a good politician.

John Adams thought the best thing he did as president was to keep the United States out of war. He may have been right.

You see, France was fighting England. France had been America's best friend during the Revolutionary War, so the French thought the United States should side with them now against England. Some Americans agreed. Others remembered the old ties with England and wanted to back

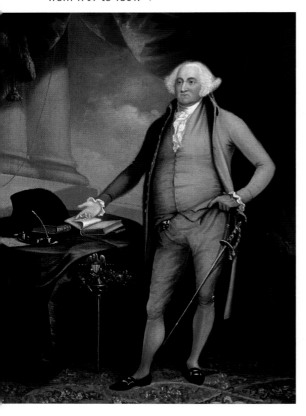

John Adams served as president from 1797 to 1801. ▼

▲ Under President John Adams, the United States did not go to war with either France or England, but French aggression led to several conflicts at sea. Here, the USS *Constellation* captures a French frigate in the Caribbean.

England. President Adams wouldn't let our nation take sides; he kept the United States neutral.

That made the French angry. They captured some American ships and took the sailors prisoner. That made a lot of Americans angry, especially Alexander Hamilton, who wanted to enter the war on England's side—even though England was also capturing American ships. John Adams had to fight Hamilton and other people in his own party. He did. He kept America out of war.

He tried to do something else and failed. He tried to stop some of the nasty political fighting between the Federalists and the Democratic-Republicans. He couldn't do that. Like Alexander Hamilton, John Adams was a Federalist. He believed in a strong central government.

As you know, the Democratic-Republicans wanted as little government as possible. They had faith that people could govern themselves. They believed in democracy. They called the Federalists "monarchists," which wasn't quite fair.

People in the two parties got very, very angry at each other. If children acted the way the country's leaders were acting, their parents would tell them to stop being silly, make up, and be friends. But each side was scared for the nation. Most of the Federalists really seemed to believe that if the Democratic-Republicans were elected the country was doomed. The Republicans believed that the Federalists had already messed everything up.

A "Great Beast"?

Once, at a dinner, Hamilton got angry at a Jeffersonian. Thomas Jefferson had faith that ordinary people could govern themselves, but when Hamilton heard that idea he pounded the table with his fist and said what he thought. *"Your people, sir,"* he said, *"your people is a great beast!"* And that was just what Hamilton, Adams, and the Federalists seemed to believe. Adams and the Federalists believed that human nature needs to be controlled. Jefferson and the Democratic-Republicans believed human nature needs to be set free. There is truth in both views.

CHAPTER 7

Alien and Sedition: Awful and Sorry

Now the Federalists did something that was bad—dreadfully bad. In 1798, the Federalist Congress passed laws called Alien and Sedition acts, and President Adams signed them. (The Constitution says the president must either sign or veto—reject—all laws passed by Congress.)

There were three Alien acts—all were mean-spirited. One made it difficult for aliens—foreigners—to become U.S. citizens. Another said the president could throw anyone he wanted out of the United States, if he thought them dangerous. (President Adams never used that power.) The acts were aimed at the French, many of whom were fleeing France's revolutionary upheavals.

As you know, England and France were at war. The Federalists admired the English. (Thomas Jefferson and the Democratic-Republicans admired the French.) The Federalists acted as if the French were all villains. Religious prejudice was at work, too. Most people in the young United States were Protestants. Most French people were Catholics. Unfortunately, some Americans wanted to keep Catholics out of the country. They supported the Alien acts.

The Alien acts were bad enough, but the Sedition Act may have been worse. It made it a crime to criticize the government.

Some people got arrested for doing just that. Some were newspaper editors. One was Ben Franklin's grandson. Another was Congressman Matthew Lyon of Vermont. Lyon had come to this country from Ireland, at age 15, as an indentured servant.

Lyon was an independent guy, wild, with a real temper. You probably would not have liked him. He was called "The Spitting Lyon" because he once spat in the face of Connecticut's representative, Roger Griswold. Another time he had a fight—with fists and sticks—right on the floor of Congress.

Lyon attacked President Adams with words. It was in a Vermont newspaper, the *Rutland Gazette*. He said the president was trying to act like a king. He said Adams should be sent "to a mad house." Well, because of the Sedition law, it was Lyon who got sent away—to jail!

In 1789, the United States got its first Roman Catholic bishop: John Carroll. (John Carroll was related to Charles Carroll of Maryland, who was the only Roman Catholic to sign the Declaration of Independence.) Some Americans feared the French Revolution would send a wave of French Catholics to the United States. That was why a number of people supported the Alien Act. They were motivated by religious prejudice.

This 1798 cartoon shows Matthew Lyon and Roger Griswold slugging it out in Congress. Speaker of the House Jonathan Dayton (in the big chair) looks on, apparently amused. The British had a tradition of poking fun at their politicians in cartoons.

All this happened in the country where people had fought for free speech and a free press. Thomas Jefferson was talking about the Alien and Sedition acts when he wrote to a friend, "I know not which mortifies me most, that I should fear to write what I think, or my country bear such a state of things."

Article I of the Bill of Rights says: *Congress shall make no law respecting an establishment of religion, or prohibiting the free exercise thereof; or abridging the freedom of speech, or of the press; or the right of the people peaceably to assemble, and to petition the Government for a redress of grievances.*

Abridging means "cutting" or "limiting." A book that is abridged has been shortened.

A Free Press?

Thomas Adams, the editor of the *Boston Independent-Chronicle*, attacked the Alien and Sedition acts and was thrown in jail. He continued to publish his newspaper from his jail cell. Across the top of the paper was printed, "A free press will maintain the majority of the people." Next to it was the note, "This was originally written by John Adams…when the British excises [customs duties], stamp acts, land taxes, and arbitrary power threatened the people with poverty and destruction."

Thomas Jefferson deeply opposed the Alien and Sedition acts. Later, when Jefferson became president, he was visited by a famous German scientist, Baron Alexander von Humboldt. In the president's office the baron noticed a newspaper article that attacked the president viciously. "Why is this libelous journal not suppressed?" the baron asked. "Why do you not fine the editor, or imprison him?" Jefferson smiled, and said, "Put that paper in your pocket, baron, and if you hear the reality of our liberty, the freedom of the press, questioned, show them this paper and tell them where you found it."

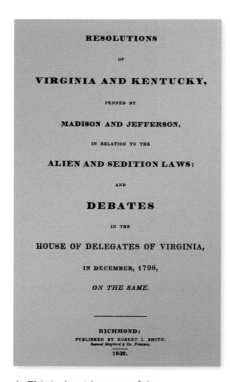

▲ This is the title page of the resolutions, drafted by James Madison and Thomas Jefferson, which declared that Kentucky and Virginia considered the Alien and Sedition acts to be unconstitutional and thus would not obey them. The Kentucky and Virginia resolutions opened up the important question of whether states had the right to declare federal laws to be unconstitutional. Although the Alien and Sedition acts were not repealed, when the hated laws expired, they were not renewed.

The term *checks and balances* is often used to describe our three-branch government. It means just what it says.

Congress and the president had done something the Constitution said they couldn't do. They were abridging freedom of speech and of the press. What could be done?

If Congress were to pass Alien and Sedition acts today, the Supreme Court would declare them unconstitutional. But the Supreme Court was just getting organized during Adams's term as president. The justices didn't even stay in one place; they rode around the country listening to cases. The court wasn't very strong.

No one was quite sure what to do. The legislatures of two states—Virginia and Kentucky—passed "resolves" (today they are called *resolutions*) declaring the Alien and Sedition laws unconstitutional. Jefferson wrote the Kentucky Resolutions; Madison wrote the Virginia Resolutions. They argued that if a state believed a law unconstitutional, it had the right to say so and not obey the law.

What Jefferson and Madison and most Americans wanted was to get rid of those awful Alien and Sedition laws. But just imagine if each state had the right to declare laws unconstitutional. Things would get very strange in this 50-state country.

Massachusetts replied to Virginia and Kentucky with its own resolutions. Massachusetts said that the states had agreed to the Constitution and were bound by that agreement. It was not up to the states, said Massachusetts, to say if a law was unconstitutional or not.

Is this getting complicated? Stick with it: it is very important. The Constitution was a great beginning, but there were things to be worked out. It took time to get the engine of government operating properly. It was not until 1803 that the Supreme Court first claimed the right to decide if a law is unconstitutional. That made a difference. It helped make our government work well.

The men who wrote the Constitution were afraid of power—political power. So they set up a government with three parts—the executive, legislative, and judicial branches—that were supposed to be equal partners to balance and check each other.

But at first the Supreme Court didn't seem to know what it was to do. It was no check or balance at all. The court was so weak it was even hard to get good people to serve as justices. Then President Adams made a brilliant choice. He appointed John Marshall as chief justice of the Supreme Court.

Something Important: Judicial Review

Virginia was ruled by an aristocracy. It was an aristocracy of mind as well as money. A poor boy with talent could make his way in Virginia. John Marshall was such a boy. Born in a log cabin on Virginia's frontier, he was the eldest of 15 children. His father was a farmer who helped George Washington survey some land. Washington became a family friend.

Their friendship helped young John, but he would have succeeded anyway. He was friendly, cheerful, fun to be around—and he had a good brain and used it.

John Marshall had hardly any formal schooling: his parents were his teachers. They taught him well, and he studied and read on his own. When the Revolutionary War began his father enlisted. John went with him. He was popular in the army; someone with a merry nature was needed, especially during the terrible winter at Valley Forge. John was 22, tall, gangling, and good at athletics. He was known as "Silverheels," because he was a fast runner.

After the war, when his brothers and most of his friends headed west, John Marshall went the other way, to Williamsburg, where, for about six weeks, he attended lectures on the law by Thomas Jefferson's mentor, George Wythe. But, mostly, he learned law by studying on his own. When he opened a law office in Richmond he didn't have enough money to buy law books. It didn't matter; he had ability, ambition, and that easygoing, not-stuck-up nature.

Aristocracy means "government by a privileged class." Usually aristocrats are wealthy and powerful, but some people talk of an aristocracy of talent. In a letter to John Adams, Thomas Jefferson wrote, "I agree with you that there is a natural aristocracy among men. The grounds of this are virtue and talents."

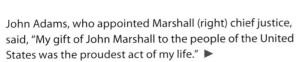

John Adams, who appointed Marshall (right) chief justice, said, "My gift of John Marshall to the people of the United States was the proudest act of my life." ▶

As a young congressman, John Marshall voted against the Sedition Act and against his own Federalist Party. That took courage. He was chief justice of the Supreme Court for 34 years. He made the Supreme Court powerful and the judiciary an equal third branch of the government.

In 1799, Marshall was elected to Congress as a member of the Federalist Party. The following year, President Adams named him secretary of state. The year after that he became chief justice of the U.S. Supreme Court. The Supreme Court met in the basement of the Capitol, because, although Pierre L'Enfant had planned a site for the Court, nothing had been built there yet.

But fancy rooms weren't any more important to John Marshall than fancy clothes. What he cared about was the way the United States was governed. He believed that a strong government would help protect the rights of all the people. He tried to make the federal

▲ John Marshall got little formal legal training. He learned law by practicing it—by taking on cases and arguing them in local courts such as the one pictured here. He argued only one Supreme Court case before he became chief justice—and he lost. Ironically, in that case he based his argument on the idea of states' rights. Once he got to the Supreme Court, he spent much of his effort in striking down attempts to strengthen state power.

government stronger than the state governments. He tried to make the Supreme Court strongest of all. In 1803, in a very important Supreme Court case called *Marbury v. Madison*, Marshall said the Court could throw out any law passed by Congress if the Court thought that law was unconstitutional. "It is emphatically the province and duty of the judicial department to say what the law is," wrote Chief Justice Marshall in that very important case.

Marbury v. Madison began a process called "judicial review." It gave the Supreme Court the power to decide if a law passed by Congress meets the requirements of the Constitution.

But who really cares if a law is constitutional or unconstitutional, if Congress wants it? Well, imagine that tomorrow Congress passes a law saying you can't criticize the president. Suppose your mother does that and she goes to jail. That actually happens in some countries. In those countries people are even afraid to talk to their friends. It happened here in 1798 with the Sedition Act.

Judicial review protects all of us. It helps guarantee our freedoms. Judicial review made the Constitution stronger. It made the Supreme Court powerful. It made the Court a real check and balance to the two government branches.

We Americans have always cared about our freedoms, especially the freedoms guaranteed in the Bill of Rights. John Marshall made sure those rights would be protected—even from Congress and the president.

John Marshall and Thomas Jefferson were cousins. But these two brilliant, remarkable Virginians couldn't stand each other. Each thought the other was not to be trusted. Their dispute was all about ideas. These were men who cared deeply about their ideas.

Marshall believed the purpose of the government was to protect "life, liberty, and property." (How did Jefferson define the purpose of government? Remember, it was "life, liberty, and....")

John Marshall and his cousin, Tom Jefferson, did agree on one thing: the Alien and Sedition acts. Neither liked them. Most of the country didn't like them, either. When John Adams ran for a second term he was defeated. Many people think it was because of his support of the Alien and Sedition acts. The great Federalist Party never achieved power again.

Judicial means "judges and court"; you know what review means. *Judicial review* means the review of laws by the courts. Thomas Jefferson didn't like the idea of judicial review; he thought it made the Court too powerful. A few legal scholars agree with him. Supreme Court justices are appointed, not elected. They hold office for life. Can you see problems if some not-very-good justices are appointed and they live for a long time?

Meet Mr. Jefferson

The election of 1800 was a tie. Democratic-Republicans Thomas Jefferson and Aaron Burr each got 73 votes. (Federalists John Adams and Charles Pinckney got 65 and 64 votes, respectively.) It was up to the House of Representatives to break the tie. After an all-night session and 36 ballots they were still deadlocked. Alexander Hamilton persuaded some of his Federalist colleagues that a vote for Jefferson was "the lesser evil." Jefferson became president and Burr vice president (and Burr nurtured a grudge against Hamilton). That messy election led to the passage, in 1804, of the 12th Amendment, which called for separate ballots for president and vice president.

On a morning in March 1801, Thomas Jefferson sat down to breakfast at his usual seat at the end of a long table at Conrad and McMunn's boardinghouse in Washington, D.C., where he paid $15 a week for a room and three meals a day.

The morning was cold and it was a special day, so someone offered him a seat near the fireplace. "No, thank you," said Jefferson, who would accept no favors. He meant to be a democratic president, a man of the people.

It was later that very day that he walked up the hill to the Capitol and was sworn in as the third president of the United States. Afterwards, in a quiet voice, he read his inaugural address.

Most of those listening were surprised by what he said. They expected something strong and startling from the man who had defied England with his great Declaration. Jefferson had spent the past years fighting the Federalists and Federalist ideas. Now he stood before them and said, "Let us unite with one heart and one mind. Every difference of opinion is not a difference of principle.... We are all Republicans—we are all Federalists." It was an appeal for unity and good will. It set the tone for his presidency.

What was it about this man that made him so special? He was not a soldier. He was not a good orator. He was shy. He didn't pretend to be anything he was not.

Thomas Jefferson once said, "If a nation expects to be ignorant and free, in a state of civilization, it expects what never was and never will be." Jefferson's presidency, from 1801 to 1809, is known as the Age of Jefferson. ▼

◄ President Jefferson did not care for pomp; he rode horseback without a guard.

Perhaps it was that Jefferson looked for the good in people. He appealed to the best instincts in his countrymen and countrywomen—and they knew it. He was, himself, a combination of the best the country had: his father was a farmer, his mother came from the Virginia planter aristocracy. From them he got a superb education and learned responsibility, good manners, and to be generous.

Jefferson wanted a government that would interfere as little as possible with people's lives. He cut taxes, reduced the size of the military, and balanced the budget.

On New Year's Day and the Fourth of July the President's House was open to any citizen who wanted to meet the president. On ordinary mornings, if you had business to do with the government, you could stop by. Jefferson issued orders to his staff that all visitors—farmers and gold-braided diplomats—should receive the same courtesy. There was to be no favored treatment in a democracy. But when everyone was left to find his or her own seat at the president's table, there was so much pushing and shoving that, finally, seating charts had to be made.

When he had someplace to go, President Jefferson rode on horseback, without a guard—he had no use for the elegant presidential coach.

A Big Cheese

People liked President Jefferson. One group of Massachusetts Baptists liked him so much they decided to make a cheese for him—a *"mammoth cheese,"* as it was called. It weighed 1,600 pounds. It took three weeks to get the cheese to Washington, D.C. The cheese must have come in handy. It arrived in 1801 and was so enormous that in 1805 they were still serving it at presidential receptions.

He chose his friend James Madison to be secretary of state and Swiss-born Albert Gallatin (GAL-uh-tin) as secretary of the treasury. As you know, many people say that Federalist Alexander Hamilton was the best secretary of the treasury ever. Well, others say the same of Republican Albert Gallatin. Gallatin said that the national debt was more dangerous to America than the risk of foreign aggression. The debt and the military budget had risen during John Adams's presidency. Gallatin reduced the military budget and cut the debt almost in half.

Jefferson believed he was involved in a revolution. He believed he was taking the nation back to the democratic spirit of 1776. Actually, he didn't change things as much as he thought he did. The country he led was in no danger of becoming a monarchy. George Washington and John Adams had enjoyed riding in a fancy coach, but they were Republicans; they cherished this people's government.

And the Federalists—who had predicted terrible things from the man they screamingly described as a radical—were surprised. They had forgotten that Jefferson was a gracious country gentleman with fine taste and a belief in the goodness of men and women. The nation didn't fall apart under a Democratic-Republican administration.

But when Thomas Jefferson went shopping and bought a huge piece of land for the nation, some people thought it extravagant.

Radical means "from the root." It comes from radix, the Latin word for "root." A political radical wants to change things from the bottom up.

Economic Arguments

As you know, Jefferson and Hamilton often disagreed. Though both were concerned about paying off the nation's debts, their ideas about taxation differed.

There was, for instance, the matter of protective tariffs. (A *tariff* is a tax on imports or exports. A *protective tariff* is a tax on foreign goods, making those goods more expensive than products made in the United States.) Hamilton was in favor of taxing citizens. Hoping for an industrialized society, he supported high protective tariffs (to "protect" American manufacturers).

Jefferson was opposed to taxing citizens heavily. Favoring an economy based on agriculture, he worried about farmers' expenses. He wanted all goods available at the best price possible.

The two leaders also fought over the issue of banks. Hamilton, a supporter of a strong central government, believed a Bank of the United States was needed to hold the government's funds and to pay its bills. Jefferson, who feared a too-powerful national government, supported regional and state banks.

Jefferson bought all the land that France claimed in North America. That land—the French called it Louisiana because their king was named Louis—went from the Mississippi River to the Rocky Mountains and maybe beyond. No one was sure how far it went. Jefferson spent $15 million on the Louisiana Purchase (which amounts to about four cents an acre). With that purchase he doubled the size of the country, and he did it peacefully. It was a great bargain, although at the time many thought it worthless and unneeded.

If President Jefferson hadn't bought that land, those of you who live in Missouri and Iowa and Nebraska, and a lot of other states, might all be speaking French today.

The Louisiana Purchase happened in 1803. That is a date to remember. The Mississippi was no longer controlled by a foreign power.

Once the United States purchased the Louisiana Territory, someone had to find out what it had bought. How big was the territory, what was it like, and where did it end? Jefferson sent an expedition to investigate.

▲ Jefferson had wanted to buy only New Orleans so that American merchants could use the port duty-free. Then the French foreign minister offered to sell the entire territory of Louisiana. Americans James Monroe and Robert Livingston signed the purchase agreement on behalf of the United States.

A Fatal Duel

In 1804 a duel took place. With pistols. Today, dueling is against the law. Then, people with arguments sometimes tried to shoot out their differences.

Aaron Burr was angry at Hamilton because Hamilton had supported Thomas Jefferson for president instead of Burr. Yes, Jefferson was Hamilton's rival, but Hamilton knew Jefferson would make a better president than Burr. Besides, he couldn't stand Burr, who had once been a Federalist and then switched to the Democratic-Republican Party. Hamilton, in a letter to John Adams, said that Burr was *"unprincipled both as a public and private man…I feel it a religious duty to oppose his career."*

But it was Burr who challenged Hamilton to a duel. There are several different stories of that duel, but there is no arguing about the outcome: Burr's shot killed Alexander Hamilton. And everyone agrees that Hamilton was a man of rare talent and integrity who loved his country. His death was a tragedy for the nation.

▲ Aaron Burr and Alexander Hamilton prepare to duel.

Meriwether and William— or Lewis and Clark

President Jefferson asked Meriwether Lewis to be his secretary. That didn't make much sense. Lewis was a terrible speller. Clearly, Jefferson had another reason for having Lewis around. He wanted to train him for an exploring mission. Thomas Jefferson was filled with curiosity about the West. He wanted to know about its land and its plants and animals; he wanted to know about the Indians who lived there. Are you ever curious about space and distant galaxies? The West was as unknown in 1803 as much of outer space is now.

Meriwether Lewis was born in Virginia's wooded piedmont. He became a captain in the Virginia militia. As a soldier he learned the ways of the Indians and how to survive in the wilderness. Lewis was a dreamer and a thinker, and, like Thomas Jefferson, a careful observer who loved the land and its birds and animals.

Just as we train astronauts today for voyages into the unexplored world, so, too, did President Jefferson see that Meriwether Lewis was trained in the scientific methods of the day. Lewis learned to gather seeds and identify bones. Benjamin Rush—one of the most famous scientists in America—taught him how to preserve bird and animal specimens. Lewis's mother had medical skills; from her he learned to take care of himself and others.

William Clark was to be his partner in command. Together they prepared for a very difficult expedition. They chose men who were used to living in the wild. They trained them until they were tough and disciplined. When a man fell asleep on guard duty, he was whipped. You can be sure he wouldn't fall asleep again.

Some people say it was the best-organized exploration of all time. I'm not going to go that far, but it was pretty terrific. Meriwether Lewis and William Clark knew what they were about. They explored that big unknown land that the United States had just bought from France—the territory of Louisiana—and they even crossed the Oregon Country. They went all the way from the Mississippi River to the

▲ President Thomas Jefferson chose Meriwether Lewis (above, right) and William Clark (above, left) to lead an expedition into the unknown western lands that the United States bought from France. Their bold expedition went from the Mississippi River all the way to the Pacific Ocean and back.

▲ The young Shoshone woman Sacajawea acted as a translator and guide for Lewis and Clark.

Pacific Ocean and back. It was dangerous country, with unexpectedly high mountains, difficult deserts, fierce animals, and wary Indians. They had prepared for danger, but they weren't quite prepared for the beauty: for the colors of wildflowers, the brilliance of sunsets on snowy mountain peaks, the sweet smell of prairie grass.

If only we could have been with them. They saw a world that would soon be gone forever. They saw birds and animals no white or black men had seen before—they saw woolly mountain goats and big-horn sheep and bright-plumed western woodpeckers. They dug up the bones of a 45-foot dinosaur. Wherever they went they took careful notes, made maps, wrote down vocabulary lists of Indian words, and collected samples of strange plants and animals. They added 200 species to the world's list of known plants. The Native Americans taught them to use some of those plants as medicines, some as foods.

If ever you need a partner for an adventure, try to find someone with abilities different from your own. Someone not like you but whom you respect and enjoy. Lewis and Clark were not alike. That was what made them such a great team; their abilities complemented each other.

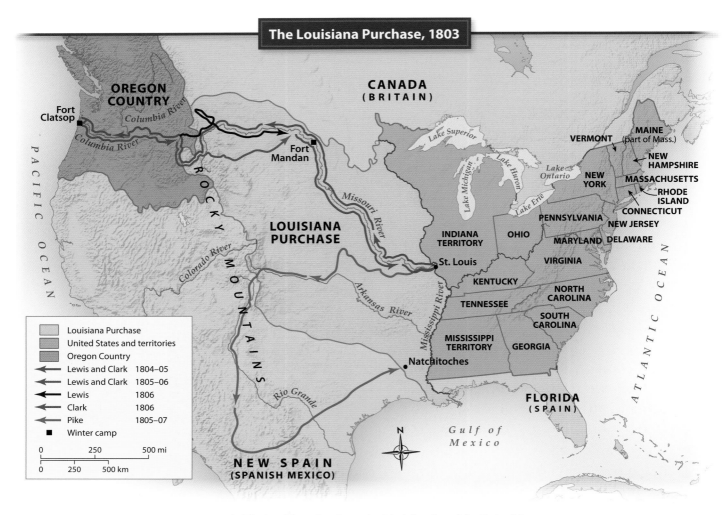

The Louisiana Purchase, 1803

Legend:
- Louisiana Purchase
- United States and territories
- Oregon Country
- Lewis and Clark 1804–05
- Lewis and Clark 1805–06
- Lewis 1806
- Clark 1806
- Pike 1805–07
- ■ Winter camp

0   250   500 mi

0   250   500 km

▲ The Louisiana Purchase doubled the size of the United States.

As long ago as the days of de Soto and Verrazzano and John Smith, explorers had been looking for a water route across North America—a Northwest Passage. Lewis and Clark's expedition was the last official attempt to find that Northwest Passage—until the 20th century, when submarines found it under the ice of the far north.

Meriwether Lewis was a quiet, shy man. He liked being in the wilderness, away from civilization. He liked science and was a fine thinker, but sometimes he was moody.

William Clark was a happy, good-natured, talkative person. He loved nature and the outdoors, but he also liked to be around people. Clark knew how to draw maps, and the actual maps he drew on that journey are now at Yale University. Like Lewis, he had been a soldier and was a Virginian. Clark was 34 that spring of 1804 when they headed out into the unknown West. Lewis was four years younger.

President Jefferson wanted to know all about the Native Americans who inhabited the land; he wanted Lewis and Clark to establish friendships with the Indians and prepare for trade with them. Treasury Secretary Albert Gallatin asked that they find out whether "that country is susceptible of a large population," which is an old-fashioned way of asking: Can lots of people live in the West?

Lewis and Clark went up the Missouri River on a 55-foot flatboat and two narrow canoes. The boat held 21 bales of gifts for the Indians: beads, ribbons, mirrors, cooking pots, and tools, as well as food and supplies for the expedition. They moved slowly, mapping, exploring, and hunting as they went. They wrote about their many adventures in the daily journals they kept for the president. (You can find copies of the journals of Lewis and Clark in most libraries.)

They knew that the source of the Missouri River would be found in mountain streams. So they were prepared to climb mountains. On the other side of the mountains they thought they would find new rivers leading to the Pacific. Well, they were right—sort of. They found mountains, but not the kind of mountains they expected. They were used to the time-worn Appalachians. They weren't prepared for the awesome, towering Rocky Mountains. They called them the "stone mountains." And the

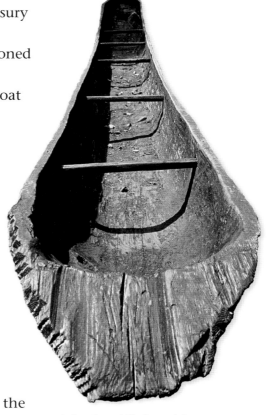

▲ Lewis and Clark used dugout canoes, each made from a single tree trunk, as they moved up the Missouri River.

The President's Instructions

Here is part of the instructions Jefferson sent to Meriwether Lewis:

The object of your mission is to explore the Missouri River…and communicate with the water of the Pacific Ocean. Beginning at the mouth of the Missouri, you will take observations of latitude and longitude at all remarkable points on the river.… Your observations are to be taken with great pains and accuracy, to be entered distinctly and intelligibly for others as well as yourself to comprehend.…

Other objects worthy of notice will be: the soil and face of the country, its growth and vegetable productions…the animals of the country generally, and especially those not known in the U.S.; the remains and accounts of any which may be deemed rare or extinct; the mineral productions of every kind…volcanic appearances; climate as characterized by the thermometer, by the proportion of rainy, cloudy, and clear days, by lightning, hail, snow, ice, by the access and recess of frost, by the winds prevailing at different seasons, the dates at which particular plants put forth or lose their flowers, or leaf, times of appearance of particular birds, reptiles, or insects.

Rivers flow from their source to their mouth. The *source* of a river is its beginning portion—usually a mountain stream.

The *mouth* of a river is the place where it flows into another river or into the ocean.

▲ The men of the Lewis and Clark expedition had never seen towering mountains like the Rockies. (This view of Lander's Peak in Wyoming was painted by Albert Bierstadt about 60 years after Lewis and Clark's explorations.)

rivers going west weren't where they thought they would find them. They had to cross deserts to get to them.

That wasn't all. They were surprised by rattlesnakes, bears, and mountain lions. But there were unexpected pleasures, too. They feasted on beaver tails, buffalo humps, and deer and elk steaks. They were stunned by the endless herds of buffalo. They captured four black-and-white magpies, put them in cages, and sent them back down the river with other bird, animal, and plant specimens for President Jefferson. Meriwether Lewis thought the caged birds were "butifull."

Lewis and Clark captured to send back to President Jefferson black-billed magpies, just one of over 300 species of plants and animals they identified for the scientific community. ▼

A man named York was an important member of the Lewis and Clark team. York was Clark's black slave. He was taller than six feet and an excellent swimmer, hunter, and trapper. The Indians were awed by York; most had never seen a black man before. Indian warriors often painted their bodies with charcoal. It was a mark of success in battle. So when they saw strong, charcoal-skinned York, they thought him the mightiest of men. York trekked, hunted, and risked his life for the expedition. (When they returned home, York asked for his freedom. Clark would not grant it.)

Even with all their training, Lewis and Clark might not have been successful—at least, they might not have gotten to the West Coast—if it hadn't been for a woman, an Indian woman named Sacajawea (sak-uh-juh-WE-uh). They met her when they built a camp and settled down for the winter in present-day North Dakota. Sacajawea was 16 and married to a Frenchman. She was about to have a baby; everyone was excited about that. When the baby was born she named him Jean Baptiste, for his father, but called him Pompey.

In the spring, when Lewis and Clark were ready to start out again, they hired Sacajawea's husband as a translator of Indian languages. Sacajawea came along with her baby strapped to her back. (Years later, Pompey became a well-known western guide.) But it was Sacajawea who turned out to be the helpful one; her no-good husband was lazy.

After following the Missouri River to its source, Lewis and Clark finally realized that there was no way to cross the continent by water.

▲ There are more statues of Sacajawea than of any other woman in American history. This one stands on the grounds of North Dakota's state capitol in Bismarck.

Lewis and Clark, with Sacajawea, York, and others on the Lower Columbia River where it approaches the Pacific Ocean ▼

▲ An unexpected happy reunion took place when Lewis and Clark met with the Shoshone, the tribe from which Sacajawea had been kidnapped as a child.

By now it was late summer. They had to get out of the mountains before winter; otherwise they might freeze or starve, and that would be the end of President Jefferson's exploration team.

They needed horses in order to continue. Would Indians sell them horses? Things didn't look good. Then some Shoshones came to their camp. (*Shoshone* means "valley dweller.") As soon as Sacajawea saw the Shoshone leader, she burst into tears. It was her brother, Ca-me-ah-wait. When she was a child, Sacajawea had been kidnapped from this very tribe. The white men had brought her home.

Ca-me-ah-wait was so happy that he hugged Meriwether Lewis. Lewis and Clark got their horses.

Pikes Peak

In 1806, a young army officer named Zebulon Montgomery Pike headed west from St. Louis on an exploring mission. It was the same year Lewis and Clark returned from their trip. They had gone northwest; Pike went southwest.

Traveling along the Arkansas River into Colorado, he came upon a towering mountain that loomed straight up from the level plain. Pike tried to climb it but failed.

Zebulon Pike wrote about his adventures. People were fascinated with his account, especially with his description of an enchanting—and rich—little Spanish town named Santa Fe. The mountain Pike never climbed was named Pikes Peak in his honor. American traders began itching to get to Santa Fe, that rich Spanish town. Soon, traders were loading their wagons and heading west on a route called the Santa Fe Trail.

A Monumental Journey

Almost three decades before Thomas Jefferson sent Lewis and Clark on their expedition, Spanish explorers were charting the West. On July 29, 1776, two Catholic friars and eight other men set out to find a way across New Spain from Santa Fe (in New Mexico) to Monterey (on the coast of California).

They were "without noise of arms," which means they didn't have guns. They were taking a chance, but Silvestre Veléz de Escalante, who was 25 and kept a diary of their journey, said guns "usually terrify the tribes." This expedition, said Spanish-born Escalante, was in God's hands. Francisco Atanasio Dominguez, 36 and Mexican-born, agreed.

With leather bags stuffed with necessities, 10 pack mules carrying supplies to trade with the Indians, and 20 head of cattle to eat en route, the small band headed northwest, following the Rio Grande, the Chama, the Navajo, the Dolores, the Gunnison, and the Colorado rivers. They were traveling through Indian territory—then unknown to Europeans—and were expected to explore and map as they went.

In early September, still in Colorado, they were met by "about eighty Yutas all on good horses...we concluded that they traveled together...to find out whether any more Spanish people were following us." Because the party was so small, and without guns, they were no threat to the Indians, who rode on.

The explorers headed into Utah, along the Green River, across semidesert, following trails blazed by buffalo. They now had an Indian guide. On September 17, Dominguez and Escalante were exploring the ruins of an old pueblo in Utah.

As they went on, the Spanish explorers met and dealt peacefully with Comanches, Hopis, Utes, Lagunas, Yutas, Sabuaganas—more than a dozen different Indian peoples—most of whom had never seen men like them before.

When they reached the valley of the Great Salt Lake (near what is now Provo, Utah), they were enchanted with the land they saw. "This is the most pleasing, beautiful and fertile site in all New Spain," Escalante wrote to Spain's King Carlos III. "It alone is capable of maintaining a settlement with as many people as Mexico City." (Mexico City in 1776—with 100,000 people—was larger than Boston, New York, and Philadelphia combined.)

With the weather turning freezing cold, they turned back. On January 2, 1777, "we arrived at the Villa de Santa Fe." The next day Dominguez and Escalante gave their diary to the governor. It included amazingly accurate maps useful to others who came later.

They didn't make it to Monterey, but they did explore more than 2,000 miles of land, more than Daniel Boone had explored in his whole lifetime. And they did it peacefully, "without noise of arms." Today, in Utah, you will find a national monument, a town, and a river all named Escalante. And you'll know why.

◀ Sunset Arch at Escalante National Monument, Utah

CHAPTER 11

A Powerful Orator, and the Great Tekamthi

At the very time that Meriwether Lewis and William Clark were crossing the Rocky Mountains, a group of Indians was gathered on the other side of the continent, at Buffalo Creek, in the state of New York. They were Iroquois of the Seneca tribe, and their leader was the powerful orator Sagoyewatha.

During the Revolutionary War, the Iroquois had been divided. Some had fought on the American side, but others, like Sagoyewatha, had fought bravely for the British. Because Sagoyewatha wore a red English jacket in battle, the Americans called him Red Jacket.

The six Iroquois nations are the Cayuga, the Mohawk, the Oneida, the Onondaga, the Seneca, and the Tuscarora.

Sagoyewatha Speaks

Here is part of what Sagoyewatha said to the Christian missionaries who came to convert his people:

Friends and Brothers…we have listened with attention to what you have said.…

There was a time when our forefathers owned this great island… from the rising to the setting sun. The Great Spirit had made it for the use of Indians. But an evil day came upon us. Your forefathers crossed the great water and landed on this island. Their numbers were small. They found friends and not enemies. They told us they had fled from their own country for fear of wicked men and had come here to enjoy their religion.…

We took them to be friends. They called us brothers. We believed them.… At length their numbers had greatly increased. They wanted more land; they wanted our country. Our eyes were opened and our minds became uneasy. Wars took place.…

Brothers, …you have now become a great people, and we have scarcely a place left to spread our blankets. You have got our country but are not satisfied; you want to force your religion upon us.…

You say there is but one way to worship and serve the Great Spirit. If there is but one religion, why do you white people differ so much about it?…

Brothers, we…also have a religion which was given to our forefathers and has been handed down to us.… Brothers, we do not wish to destroy your religion or take it from you. We only want to enjoy our own.…

▲ In youth Red Jacket was called Otetiani, meaning "prepared" or "ready." As chief, he took the name Sagoyewatha—"He Causes Them to Be Awake." This may have referred to his skill as a speaker.

At war's end Chief Red Jacket did not flee to Canada, as many Iroquois did. He stayed behind and was made to sign a treaty that gave much Indian land to the new nation.

Now the Iroquois were being asked to give up their religion. Some preachers had come from Boston to convert the Indians to Christianity. The Senecas listened politely to the ministers. Then Sagoyewatha/Red Jacket replied. In his strong voice, he argued eloquently for the Indians' right to keep their way of life and practice their own religion.

Most Americans didn't care about what happened to Red Jacket and his people. The Iroquois had lost most of their land and power. Things would get worse for them. They were going to be pushed west and then pushed again. There would be promises and treaties and they would all be broken. The new Americans wanted Indian land and they didn't know a fair way to share it. The Indians would lose most of their land. No one realized that in 1805, which was when Red Jacket spoke—though perhaps some understood that the Native Americans would not give up their land easily. Terrible Indian wars lay ahead.

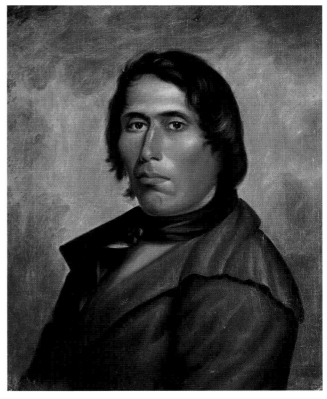

"We gave them forest-clad mountains, valleys full of game," said Tekamthi (known as Tecumseh). "In return they gave us…rum and trinkets and a grave." ▼

The land west of the Mississippi seemed so vast that President Jefferson thought it would take thousands of years to fill. Jefferson said there was "land enough for our descendants to the thousandth and thousandth generation." He did not know—nor did anyone else in 1805—that within a 100 the land west of the Appalachians would be filled with farms and cities.

Always the white men told the Indians that if they just moved once more they would be secure. If they just signed a treaty, they would have land and would not have to move again. And some of the Indians believed them. But Tekamthi did not.

Tekamthi, a leader of the Shawnee people, had met the white men who were coming into his land—the land of Kentucky and Ohio. He respected the brave men like Daniel Boone, but others he grew to hate. For they killed his

▲ The Prophet, Tenskwatawa—his name means "The Open Door"

father and took his land and made promises they did not keep. He wanted the white men to go back—over the mountains—and leave the hunting lands of the West for the Indians. He would make the white men go. He would do it by uniting the Indian tribes into a mighty league. For help, Tekamthi turned to his brother, Tenskwatawa, a shaman, a religious leader called "The Prophet," renowned for his wisdom. The brothers told the Indians to stop drinking the white men's liquor—that it only made them weak. And the tribesmen stopped. The brothers also told them to go back to Indian ways and to be proud of their heritage. And the Indians did that, too.

Tekamthi traveled far to reach other tribes: he went to the land the white men called New York and then to lands west of the great Mississippi. Everywhere he gathered followers. Tekamthi said he did not want to fight the white men; he wanted to share the land, but if the whites would not share, he would fight.

The whites called him Tecumseh and knew he was powerful. William Henry Harrison, who had been appointed governor of the Indiana Territory, was worried about Tecumseh. Most of the Indiana

Osceola

He would come to be called Asi-yo-ho-lo. The white men who heard it said *Osceola*. When he was a boy of six, or perhaps seven, the great Tecumseh came to his village on the Tallapoosa River in Alabama. The boy, a Creek of the Tallasee tribe, must have been mightily impressed. Tecumseh had come to persuade the tribes to forget their rivalries. He preached a message of strength in unity. But the Creek did not hear.

Some, who lived and farmed as the whites did, were called White Sticks. The others, who still maintained their Indian ways, were Red Sticks. The White Sticks wanted to cooperate with the Americans; the Red Sticks wanted to drive them away. Soon there would be civil war between these groups. It was a disaster for both groups of Indians. Never again were the Creeks powerful.

Asi-yo-ho-lo, with his mother and what was left of the Tallasee tribe, headed south. They crossed the border into Spanish Florida.

The Indians who lived in Florida were called Seminoles. The Creek boy and his tribespeople were welcomed by the Seminoles. They settled in fertile north Florida. The boy grew to love his new home. Like Tecumseh, he stood out among the others. But he carried with him anger at White Stick Creeks and at white men. You will hear more about Osceola.

▲ Osceola's mother had a second husband, a white man named Powell. Osceola (above) is sometimes called Powell. That's a mistake; his father was Native American.

▲ A U.S. force under General William Henry Harrison defeats Native Americans under Tecumseh's brother Tenskwatawa, The Prophet.

Territory, by treaty, was supposed to be Indian land. But white settlers were moving in. Harrison was afraid that Tecumseh was too powerful, that the Indians would endanger the white settlers.

In 1811, when he knew Tecumseh was far away visiting tribes in Alabama, Harrison marched to the Shawnee camp on the banks of the Tippecanoe River. The Prophet was in charge. He knew nothing of military leadership; he thought his belief in the Great Spirit would be enough. The Prophet told his followers that God would make the bullets bounce off their chests. He may have believed that. When Harrison and his army were just a mile away from the Indian village, The Prophet and his men attacked.

Bullets did not bounce off their chests. Indians died. Actually, two of Harrison's soldiers died for every Indian killed. But the Shawnee village was destroyed and the Shawnee hearts went with it.

Harrison claimed a great victory at Tippecanoe. It made him a national hero. His nickname became "Old Tippecanoe."

The tribes would no longer unite behind Tecumseh. In 1813, Tecumseh fought with the British against the Americans and was killed in battle. White men moved into the Indiana Territory. The treaties with the Indians were forgotten.

The Revolutionary War Part II, or the War of 1812

▲ The French physician for whom the guillotine is named intended it to be a swift and merciful form of execution.

George Washington warned Americans to stay out of foreign quarrels. Unfortunately, England and France wouldn't let us do that. It would have been nice if they had left our infant nation alone. This country needed a few years to grow up without having old friends pick on us. But that wasn't to be. And so we went to war. This is how it came about.

As you know, soon after our revolution, France had a revolution of its own. At first, everyone thought the French Revolution would be like the one in America—but it got out of hand. The winners of the revolution began chopping off the heads of the losers—really—with a head-chopping machine called a guillotine (GHEE-yuh-teen).Then a powerful French general named Napoleon Bonaparte came to power.

Napoleon Bonaparte, Emperor of France from 1804 to 1815 ▶

▲ The British navy captured American ships and forced American seamen to work on British ships, a practice called *impressment.*

Napoleon tried to conquer most of Europe, and England declared war on France.

Americans had a hard time trying to figure out what was going on across the ocean. News traveled slowly. We tried to stay out of the European war; we tried to stay neutral, but neither England nor France respected nations that were neutral.

Both countries captured American ships and took American sailors as prisoners. The British sea captains forced the American sailors to work on British ships. Naturally, that made people in this country angry.

There was something else that made Americans angry with England. England had never cleared out of the forts it held in the territories west of the Appalachian Mountains. (England was supposed to leave after the Revolutionary War.) Many English men and women seemed to believe that someday America would again be part of the British Empire.

▲ James Madison served as president from 1809 to 1817.

Capturing ships and holding territory—those are two pretty good reasons for fighting. There was a third reason that wasn't so good. Many Americans wanted Indian land. But the English in their western forts had become friends and protectors of the Indians.

Americans were divided. Most New Englanders did not want to get involved in another war with England. (England controlled the seas, and New England depended on its sea trade.) Most westerners, and some southerners, wanted to go to war. Scholarly James Madison, who was 63 and president, was cautious. But in Congress and across the land, a new generation of leaders was taking the place of the men who had fought in the Revolution. These new leaders had been youngsters when the Constitution was written.

They didn't remember the long, hard battles of the Revolutionary War. They were eager to fight. Henry Clay, from Kentucky, was one of the new leaders; Andrew Jackson, of Tennessee, was another. Those who wanted to go to war were called "war hawks." They finally convinced President Madison that the nation's honor was at stake. In 1812 war was declared against Great Britain.

The War Hawks thought they could march to Canada and take all that land from England. Henry Clay boasted that the Kentucky militia could do it all by itself. When it came to the sea, however, he thought differently. So did most Americans. They believed the famous English navy would easily outfight them. Were they surprised! Canada didn't fall to the American forces—the Americans fought poorly in Canada—but the little American navy won some surprising victories against the big British navy, and no one in the world expected that.

But the War of 1812 (which really should be called the War of 1812 to 1815, because that was how long it lasted) started slowly. Then the war in Europe—the one between England and France—ended.

Old Ironsides

In 1812, the British royal navy had 1,017 warships. The U.S. Navy had 18. In the War of 1812, the *Constitution* took on the British frigate HMS *Guerrière* and, in a famous battle, destroyed her. Cannonballs from the *Guerrière* kept bouncing off the sides of the *Constitution*. After that, she was often called *"Old Ironsides."*

The ship was actually made of wood, with thin copper sheathing to keep ship's worms away. The *Constitution's* hull was 25 inches thick, with live oak—said to be the toughest wood in the world—at its center.

The USS *Constitution* battles the HMS *Guerrière* in August 1812. ▼

◀ Today, you can visit the restored USS *Constitution* in Boston Harbor. The ship is the oldest commissioned naval vessel afloat anywhere in the world.

In 1830, when a Boston newspaper reported that the USS *Constitution* was to be scrapped, lots of people were upset. The newspaper was wrong, but Oliver Wendell Holmes didn't know that. He sat down and wrote a poem called *"Old Ironsides."* The poem was soon reprinted all over the nation, making the *Constitution* even more famous than before.

In 1844, the ship embarked on a round-the-world voyage that included visits to 25 foreign ports for diplomatic, scientific, and business affairs. She was seen as a symbol of the United States; her name added to that image. Today the *Constitution* is still a commissioned warship and the world's oldest still afloat. She is docked in Boston and visited by nearly a million people a year.

Napoleon lost. That was terrible for the United States. It meant the English could now send more soldiers to America. They did. In 1814 they sailed an army into Chesapeake Bay, landed redcoats, whipped American troops at Bladensburg (five miles from Washington, D.C.), and then marched on, heading for the nation's capital.

By that time there were hardly any American soldiers in the city—they'd all fled—and those residents who were still around were keeping quiet about it behind their shuttered windows. The British commander, Major General Robert Ross, had orders to "destroy and lay waste" the towns he captured. Ross, however, was prepared to negotiate with Washington's leaders: if they paid ransom he might spare the city. But there weren't any leaders to be found.

So the general sent his soldiers to burn Congress's home—the Capitol—but it was so well built they had a hard time of it. They piled up chairs and books and drapes and torched them. Finally, much of the building went. Then they headed toward the President's House.

James Madison wasn't at home. (He had been at Bladensburg; now he was off somewhere consulting with his generals. He was courageous, but when it came to military leadership he was a dud.) It was his wife, Dolley, who was the indomitable member of the family. She was in the President's House getting ready to have dinner with

British soldiers watch as the Capitol and the President's House burn in Washington. ▼

When the Madisons returned to the capital, Dolley said, "We shall rebuild Washington. The enemy cannot frighten a free people." ▼

▲ First Lady Dolley Madison is credited with saving many valuables as invading British troops approached the President's House. Among the items saved was the Gilbert Stuart portrait of George Washington.

friends. Dolley was advised to flee, but, before she did, the First Lady took important papers, silverware, and red velvet drapes, and had them loaded onto a wagon. She got out just before the British arrived. The British toasted the king with the president's Madeira wine and ate Dolley's dinner—the wine was still chilled and the meats laid out handsomely. After dinner the British set a bonfire inside the President's House.

From there they carried their torches to the Treasury and were disappointed to find no money inside. They burned that building and they burned the Library of Congress, too.

The British soldiers were now eager to march on—to Baltimore. They hated that place. With its 45,000 inhabitants, it was the fourth-largest city in the States. But it was Baltimore's private sailing ships that made them angry. Privateers from Baltimore had

During the War of 1812 the British burned the Library of Congress and all its books. In order to start a new library, the nation bought 6,487 books from Thomas Jefferson for $23,950 (which was much less than they had cost Jefferson).

The President's House as it looked after the British burned it in 1814 ▶

The War of 1812–1815

CANADA
(BRITAIN)

Lake Superior

Lake Michigan

Lake Huron

ILLINOIS
TERRITORY

MICHIGAN
TERRITORY

Thames River
(1813)

Lake Ontario

Lake Erie

York (Toronto)
(1813)

Plattsburgh
(1814)

Lake
Champlain

St. Lawrence River

MAINE
(part of Mass.)

VERMONT

NEW
HAMPSHIRE

NEW YORK

Boston

MASSACHUSETTS

RHODE ISLAND

New York City

CONNECTICUT

Put-in-Bay
(1813)

Tippecanoe
(1811)

OHIO

INDIANA
TERRITORY

Ohio River

PENNSYLVANIA

Baltimore
(1814)

NEW JERSEY

DELAWARE

Washington, DC
(1814)

MARYLAND

VIRGINIA

Norfolk

KENTUCKY

Mississippi River

TENNESSEE

NORTH
CAROLINA

Wilmington

SOUTH
CAROLINA

MISSISSIPPI
TERRITORY

GEORGIA

Charleston

Savannah

New Orleans
(1815)

Pensacola

FLORIDA
(SPAIN)

Gulf of
Mexico

ATLANTIC OCEAN

N

United States and territories
United States victory
British victory
British blockade

0   150   300 mi
0   150   300 km

▲ American and British forces fought
for control of cities including
Washington, D.C.; Baltimore; and
New Orleans as well as for control
of Canada and the West.

been capturing and sinking British ships. No mercy was to be shown at Baltimore.

But the British didn't know that something was happening at Baltimore that was changing the mood of despair. Major General Samuel Smith had taken charge of the city and put Baltimore's citizens to work. It wasn't easy for him to get the rich merchants to agree to sink their own ships in the harbor to make a barrier to keep out the English, but Smith convinced them that it was better than losing everything if the city fell. Trenches were dug, cannons put in place, and the citizen militia—which had performed miserably at Bladensburg—was drilled and drilled again. A letter printed in the *Evening Post* said, "White and black are all at work together. You'll see a master and his slave digging side by side. There is no distinction, whatsoever."

Baltimore harbor was guarded by big, star-shaped Fort McHenry. Major George Armistead commanded that fort. Early in the war, Armistead went to Mary Pickersgill, a well-known Baltimore flag maker, and ordered an American flag "so large the British will have no difficulty seeing it at a distance." She and her 13-year-old daughter sewed a huge flag, 42 feet by 30 feet, with 15 stripes and 15 stars. Armistead raised it over the fort.

The English ships couldn't miss it when they sailed into the harbor. They were soon approached by a small ship of truce. Francis Scott Key, a Washington lawyer who had fought at Bladensburg, had been sent to rescue William Beanes, a much-loved doctor who had been taken hostage by the British. Key had letters from British prisoners of war saying they were being well treated—that got Dr. Beanes released. But the two men and the truce ship had to wait with the British until the fighting was over.

The battle began on a Sunday. The British admiral, Sir George Cockburn (pronounced CO-burn), could see that the ships sunk in the harbor prevented him from sailing right up to the city. He would have to capture Fort McHenry if he wanted Baltimore.

That night, rockets and bombs lit the starless sky like fireworks. The rockets were real whiz-bangers with fire-spouting tails. The

▲ The flag that flew over Fort McHenry and inspired "The Star-Spangled Banner"

The Last Battle

Do you know what the word *irony* means? It has to do with things not being as they seem to be. There was a big irony in the War of 1812. It was about a battle fought at New Orleans on January 8, 1815: big battle, big American victory, big irony.

The Americans lost 13 men at New Orleans, and about 60 were wounded. More than 2,000 British soldiers were killed, wounded, or missing. The hero of that astounding battle was little known. He was General Andrew Jackson. So what was the irony?

A peace treaty had been signed a few days earlier in Europe, but the news hadn't reached New Orleans. No one knew the war was over. All those men—on both sides— died fighting a war that was already history.

The Battle of New Orleans took place days after a treaty ending the war was signed. ▼

English had learned about rockets in India; they used them to frighten their enemies. The rockets were terrifying but not very dangerous (unless one hit you directly).

It was the cannons on the British ships that were dangerous. Some of their shells had a range of two miles—nothing in the batteries at Fort McHenry could match that. Were the Americans scared? Well, the all-night bombardment certainly didn't make them feel good. Early in the morning, a British force set out to do battle. But something happened that they hadn't expected. Their commander, General Robert Ross, was killed. Confusion set in.

While British ships were lobbing shells on one side of the Baltimore peninsula, British infantry—foot soldiers—marched up the other. They were supposed to coordinate an attack. But there was a communications foul-up. The infantry turned back, and the navy didn't know. Sailors fought to protect soldiers who weren't there.

Meanwhile, the bombing of Fort McHenry went on—and on—for 25 hours. Francis Scott Key, on the truce ship, watched the "rockets' red glare" and listened to "bombs bursting in air." And then it stopped. It was very dark and very quiet, and it was raining so hard no one could tell what had happened. Had the fort been captured? No one knew until, finally, "by the dawn's early light," Key saw Mrs. Pickersgill's "broad stripes and bright stars," and realized— the fort had held! The British hadn't been able to scare, or beat, the Americans.

They turned around and sailed away. Francis Scott Key found words spinning in his head. They became a poem he called "The Defense of Fort McHenry." It could be sung to the tune of an old British drinking song. Friends published his poem in Baltimore. Soon it was republished in town after town. Baltimore's heroism inspired the young nation.

If Baltimore had fallen, where might the British have marched next? Philadelphia had readied its militia. Now there was jubilation. People were soon singing Key's words, and someone gave them a new name. It was "The Star-Spangled Banner."

Was the War of 1812 worth it? Well, it made the British realize they had really lost their colonies. It made them respect the United States. It made us Americans realize we could not have Canada. It made our nation grow up. It made Americans feel proud. After all, we had fought off the most powerful nation in the world—twice.

Our National Anthem: "The Star-Spangled Banner"

In the first stanza, old Dr. Beanes is speaking. He is asking Francis Scott Key some questions. He uses a few unusual words: *ramparts* are high walls that surround a fort. *Perilous* means "dangerous." *O'er* is the poet's way of saying "over."

> Oh! say can you see, by the dawn's
>   early light,
> What so proudly we hailed at the twilight's
>   last gleaming?
> Whose broad stripes and bright stars,
>   through the perilous fight,
> O'er the ramparts we watched were so
>   gallantly streaming.
> And the rockets' red glare, the bombs
>   bursting in air,
> Gave proof through the night that our flag
>   was still there.
> Oh! say, does that star-spangled banner
>   yet wave
> O'er the land of the free and the home of
>   the brave?

Does the flag still wave? Has the fort held? In the second stanza, poet Key answers the questions. More words: *foe* is enemy; *towering steep* are other words for those steep walls—the ramparts.

> On the shore, dimly seen through the mist
>   of the deep,
> Where the foe's haughty host in dread
>   silence reposes.
> What is that which the breeze, o'er the
>   towering steep,
> As it fitfully blows, half conceals, half
>   discloses?
> Now it catches the gleam of the morning's
>   first beam,
> In full glory reflected, now shines on
>   the stream:

▲ Francis Scott Key sees the American flag still flying above Fort McHenry in the dawn's early light.

> 'Tis the star-spangled banner, Oh! long
>   may it wave
> O'er the land of the free and the home of
>   the brave!

We're skipping the third stanza—which is not often sung. The fourth stanza is about hope for America's future. It is usually sung a bit more slowly than the others.

> Oh! thus be it ever, when freemen shall
>   stand Between their loved homes and
>   the war's desolation.
> Blest with victory and peace, may the
>   Heav'n-rescued land
> Praise the Power that hath made and
>   preserved us a nation.
> Then conquer we must, for our cause it is just.
> And this be our motto—"In God is our trust."
> And the star-spangled banner in triumph
>   doth wave
> O'er the land of the free and the home of
>   the brave.

That Good President Monroe

James Monroe reminded some people of George Washington. He was another tall, courtly Virginian and so honest that Thomas Jefferson said you could turn his soul inside out and "there would not be a spot on it."

When Monroe became our fifth president, in March 1817, he was already being called the "last of the Revolutionary farmers." Washington, Adams, Jefferson, and Madison were all unusual farmers: each loved and understood the land, each revered book learning, and each believed it was his duty to serve his country. James Monroe was the same kind of man.

People liked him. It made them feel good to have a president who was handsome and kindly, who had fought bravely as a soldier in the Revolutionary War, who had studied law with Thomas Jefferson, and who had served in the Virginia General Assembly when the Constitution was ratified.

Monroe wore knee pants and silver buckles on his shoes, even though those styles were old-fashioned by the time he was president. He was tall and gangly, with wide-set gray eyes and a large nose. He had been raised in a privileged home where he was trained to be a leader and to help others.

Some important things happened during his presidency. One important thing was that the United States got Florida from Spain. (That is especially important if you happen to live in Florida.) Spain— such a mighty country in Columbus's time—had become weak.

Slaves had been fleeing to Spanish-held Florida, where they lived in all-black villages or in biracial Seminole communities. Suppose you were a slave and willing to risk the dangers of running away. If you lived in Virginia, or Maryland, or Kentucky, you would probably head north and try to make it to Canada. But if you lived in South Carolina, or Georgia, or Alabama, you wouldn't have much chance of escape if you went north. If you headed the other way, and were lucky, you might just get to Florida. There, the Seminole Indians would protect you. You can see why the Southern slave owners hated the Seminoles. And they were angry with the Spaniards for not making the Seminoles return their runaways.

▲ James Monroe served as president from 1817 to 1825. "Our country is like a new house," said Monroe. "We lack many things, but we possess the most precious of all—liberty!"

At Monroe's swearing-in for his second term as president the band played "Hail to the Chief"—the first time that song was played for a president. "Hail to the Chief" was the work of two Scotsmen: the composer, James Sanderson, wrote the tune to accompany lines from a poem by the famous writer Sir Walter Scott.

In 1817, Secretary of War John C. Calhoun sent General Andrew Jackson into Florida. Jackson was on Spanish soil; he was only supposed to capture runaway slaves, but he did more than that. He had learned to fight as the Indians fought. He burned villages and destroyed crops. He captured, killed, and humiliated the Seminoles. His White Stick Creek Indian allies fought with him. More than half his soldiers were Creeks. It was the First Seminole War. Osceola, who was now 14, was taken prisoner (but later released).

Some Americans were upset. They thought Jackson had gone too far. The Spaniards were really upset. John Quincy Adams was President Monroe's secretary of state. He offered Spain a deal. He said the United States would pay Spain $5 million for Florida. (Spain could still hold Texas and California and other western regions.) The Spaniards signed John Quincy Adams's treaty. They had no choice; Spain was too weak to fight. General Andrew Jackson was named governor of the new U.S. territory: Florida. It was 1821.

Lots of people in the United States couldn't wait to move to Florida. But what about the Seminoles? They had to make way for the white settlers. They were forced to move south to an inland reservation on sandy, barren land where crops hardly grew at all. Soon many were starving. The young man, Osceola, went south with the others. He was now a military chief, a *tustenugee*, a kind of policeman.

▲ Runaway slaves in the Deep South often sought protection with the Seminole Indians.

◄ Seminoles attack an American fort during the Seminole Wars. In the end, the Seminole were forced off their lands and onto a barren reservation.

President James Monroe discusses the policy that would come to be known as the Monroe Doctrine, which remains a part of American foreign policy. ▶

As the power of the United States grew, the Monroe Doctrine became more and more important. But when Monroe first made his speech, a lot of people in Europe sneered at the idea of this upstart new country telling them what to do in South America. What really kept most European nations away was fear of the mighty British navy.

▲ John Quincy Adams was president from 1825 to 1829. He wrote, "My life has been…marked by great and signal successes which I neither aimed at nor anticipated."

Florida wasn't the only place where Spain lost out. Spain and Portugal could no longer control their colonies in South and Central America. One by one they had revolutions. They became independent nations. As soon as that happened, other European countries began to look greedily at those new Latin-American nations. James Monroe and John Quincy Adams decided something needed to be done to keep Europe out of the Americas.

In December 1823 President Monroe gave a speech to Congress. He said that the American continents were closed to other nations. He told the European countries that they were not welcome to look for colonies in this hemisphere. The United States will not interfere in Europe's affairs, said Monroe, so Europe should keep its hands off America. That speech is very famous. What he said is called the "Monroe Doctrine." It has been American policy since the days of James Monroe.

The years that Monroe was president have been called an "Era of Good Feelings." Most things were going well in the country. The old fight between the Hamiltonian Federalists and the Jeffersonian Republicans seemed to have died down.

But it is hard to have people and politics without having arguments, and, before long, people were fussing about politics again. And now there were new parties and new arguments.

John Quincy Adams wanted to be president…and so did Andrew Jackson. Their election battle in 1824 was hot-tempered. When Adams won and became our sixth president, Jackson's supporters were very angry. They believed Jackson had been cheated out of the presidency. (He wasn't.) They weren't interested in extending the era of good feelings. Now there was an era of political grouchiness.

A Day of Celebration and Tears

On the Fourth of July, 1826, John Quincy Adams was still president. Do a little arithmetic and you'll see that day was the 50th anniversary of the signing of the Declaration of Independence.

On July 4, 1826, the two men most responsible for the Declaration—Thomas Jefferson and John Adams—were still alive. They had been good friends when the Declaration was written. Later, they became political enemies: one a Federalist, the other a Republican. And then, after both retired, a friend of each visited John Adams in Massachusetts. "I love Thomas Jefferson and I always shall," said Adams. "That is enough for me," said Jefferson, when he heard of the remark. He sat down and wrote Adams a letter. And so began a correspondence—a series of remarkable letters about their ideas, and memories, and hopes—letters that you can find in the library.

As that 50th Independence Day approached, Americans were especially proud of those Founding Fathers and of the great Declaration. They were pleased that John Adams's son was president. Celebrations were planned across the nation.

The mayor of Quincy, Massachusetts, wrote to John Adams and asked him to take part in a special ceremony. But Adams was 91 and not feeling well. In Washington, D.C., the citizens were also planning a celebration. Washington's mayor wrote to Thomas Jefferson and asked if he would participate. But Jefferson was 83 and ailing. He wrote back saying he wished he could come, but he was not well enough.

Finally, when the Fourth of July came, Thomas Jefferson lay in his bed at Monticello. He asked, "Is it the Fourth?" and soon breathed no more.

In another bed, on that same day, this one in Quincy, Massachusetts, John Adams whispered, "Thomas Jefferson survives," and then he was dead.

Messengers on horseback set out from Massachusetts, carrying the sad news south. Messengers were already on their way north from Virginia with their sad news. They met in Philadelphia, the city where young Adams and young Jefferson had worked together on the great Declaration. There, in the shadow of Independence Hall, the couriers exchanged their messages.

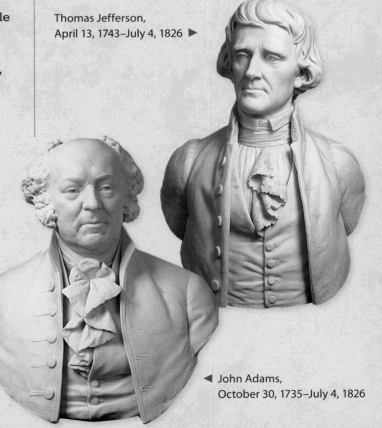

Thomas Jefferson,
April 13, 1743–July 4, 1826 ▶

◀ John Adams,
October 30, 1735–July 4, 1826

Old Hickory

There is something you might have noticed about the first six presidents: they were all from Virginia or Massachusetts. There is something else, too. They were all aristocrats. They had been born into successful, prosperous families. That gave them the time and opportunity to be well educated. John Adams and his son John Quincy Adams were both Harvard graduates. James Madison went to the College of New Jersey (Princeton). Thomas Jefferson and James Monroe attended the College of William and Mary. Only George Washington was not a college man; still, he was well read…and rich. Now how do you think you would feel if you were living in 19th-century America in Tennessee and you were poor? Do you think you would have a chance to be president?

After Andrew Jackson was elected the seventh president, you would know you had a chance. If Andy Jackson could be president, then any white male born in the United States could be president.

Jackson was born in 1767 in a log cabin on the border between North and South Carolina. His parents were poor Scotch-Irish farmers. The Scotch-Irish were people who had moved from Scotland to Northern Ireland to the United States. Andrew's dad died just before he was born; his mother had to move with her three sons into her sister's home. There were 11 children in the house, and you know how kids are. It was a noisy place. Andy soon learned to speak out, and wrestle, and make the older boys respect him. He also learned to read.

The birthplace of President Andrew Jackson in Waxhaw, South Carolina ▼

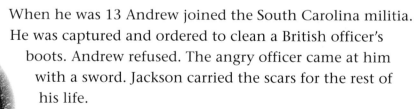

When he was 13 Andrew joined the South Carolina militia. He was captured and ordered to clean a British officer's boots. Andrew refused. The angry officer came at him with a sword. Jackson carried the scars for the rest of his life.

Andrew's older brother was killed fighting in that Revolutionary War. Andrew and another brother were taken to a military prison, where they got smallpox. His second brother died. Then his mother died. At 14 Andrew Jackson was an orphan. "I felt utterly alone," he said.

He learned to take care of himself. He had to. He was a fighter with an explosive temper who liked to have a roaring good time. Sometimes he drank and gambled. But he learned from his mistakes. People were attracted to him. He was smart and honest and fun to be around. But what should he do with his life? He tried being a schoolteacher, but that didn't work out. Then he studied law and became a lawyer. That got him started in politics. When he was 21 he was appointed attorney general for the region that would soon become Tennessee. By the time he was 30 he owned two large plantations near Nashville.

Andrew Jackson was a man of action, a born leader who was always doing things and going places and changing the world he lived in. He served in Congress; he was a judge, a general, and a military hero. "He came into national party politics like a cyclone from off the western prairies," wrote a professor named Woodrow Wilson (who would become president himself). Jackson formed a new political party: the Democratic Party.

▲ Andrew Jackson built his rural home, called the Hermitage, near Nashville, Tennessee. Today, you can visit the restored house and plantation museum.

Andrew Jackson was shot in the arm during a battle. The army doctor wanted to amputate his arm. Jackson decided to get a second opinion. He went to a Cherokee medicine man, who saved his arm.

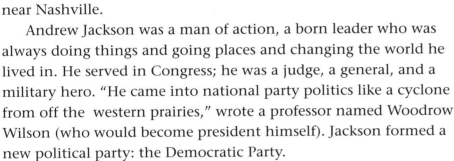

◄ Andrew Jackson appealed to ordinary people. His election changed the American political landscape.

▲ Elections in the new republic were rowdy affairs (as shown in this painting by George Caleb Bingham, titled *The County Election*). Voting wasn't by secret ballot. You spoke out your choice, or raised your hand, and everyone knew your vote.

But when Harvard University gave an honorary degree to Andrew Jackson, John Quincy Adams was so horrified—he was a Harvard graduate and thought his school was disgracing itself—that he refused to attend the ceremony. JQA called Jackson "a barbarian and savage who can scarcely spell his own name." That "barbarian and savage" became an astonishingly popular president.

He was tall and lean and stood straight as the barrel of a rifle. His eyes were blue, bright blue. His thick hair was the color of sand, although it turned silver long before he became president. His soldiers called him "Old Hickory," because they said he was strong as a hickory tree. In his portrait you can see a kind face. It was also a sad face. His wife, Rachel, whom he loved dearly, died just before his inauguration.

What an inauguration it was! The people—ordinary people—had elected one of their own to be president. They wanted to be there to see him take office. They wanted to celebrate with him.

And so they did. Some came from 500 miles away. It seemed to people in Washington as if everyone in the West had come to town for the big day. And they all wanted to get into the White House—at the same time. They poured in through the doors in their buckskin clothes and muddy boots, and they climbed on the satin chairs and

Andrew Jackson was the first common man elected president, and the common people celebrated his inauguration. ▼

▲ Andrew Jackson, who served as president from 1829 to 1837, promoted the idea of government by the people.

Andrew Jackson's democracy was only for white males. It would be many years before blacks, Indians, Asians, and women were allowed to vote. However, Jackson's presidency paved the way for all peoples.

broke glasses and spilled orange punch and pushed and shoved each other. President Jackson had to go out a back door to get away from the mob. Finally someone thought to bring buckets of punch onto the lawn and that got the crowd out of the President's House.

Some people remembered President Washington's receptions, where men wore gloves and silver buckles and talked softly. Those were the good old days; how comfortable they seemed. This modern world of Andrew Jackson and his friends would be the end of the United States, some said. That old Federalist, Chief Justice John Marshall, swore in President Jackson. It was said that Marshall would just as soon have sworn in the devil.

Mobs would take over; life would be awful—so the aristocratic leaders thought. But it didn't happen. Andrew Jackson did change the presidency—it was never the same again. Most people think he made it stronger.

It helped that he had good manners, natural manners. People who thought they would be angry at him ended up being charmed. For many of the earlier presidents, democracy had meant government for the people. During the Jacksonian Era, democracy meant government *by* the people. "Let the people rule," was his motto. And, ever since Andrew Jackson's time, we have.

The Spoils System

When Jefferson became president he replaced a lot of government employees (who were Federalists) with people from his own party (Democratic-Republican). He started something. Andrew Jackson went farther than anyone before. "To the victor belongs the spoils," said a senator. And so it was called *the spoils system*. It was a way of rewarding party workers but not a great way to run an efficient government. (A Civil Service Commission, established in 1871, has helped create a core of professional government workers. But the spoils system still persists.)

Naming Presidents

I'm sure you can name the first seven presidents. You know them all. Yes, you do.

Of course you know number one: the man who was said to be "first in war, first in peace, and first in the hearts of his countrymen."

The second president had a wife named Abigail. They were New Englanders, from Massachusetts. The second president was an important man at the Continental Congress in 1776. He helped persuade the best writer there to write a declaration telling the British to go home.

The man who wrote that famous declaration was president number three. He was the most versatile of the Founding Fathers. That means he could do many different things and do them all well. He wrote the Virginia Statute for Religious Freedom and founded the University of Virginia.

President four was a good friend of president three. He was called the "Father of the Constitution." He wrote the Bill of Rights. His wife's name was Dolley.

President number five was the last Virginia president to wear knee pants and buckles on his shoes. An important policy—called a *doctrine*—bears his name. That doctrine told Europe's nations to keep their hands off the two American continents.

President number six was the son of president two. They were the first father and son to be presidents.

Number seven was a general who won some big battles. He was a man of the people, but he didn't seem to think that Native Americans or slaves were Americans.

Those first seven were outstanding. Now come the next eight, who were not. (Most people think that the president after that—number 16—was the best of all.) I'm going to list those next eight presidents and just tell you a few things about each of them.

President number eight: Martin Van Buren (1837–1841)
Van Buren was the first president who was born a citizen of the United States. (The other presidents were all subjects of the British king when they were born.) Van Buren helped turn the old Democratic-Republicans into the modern Democratic Party. He was a good friend of Andrew Jackson, but he was never as popular as the general. Van Buren didn't get reelected. Eight years later he tried again as head of a new party, the Free Soil Party. It had an important cause: to keep slavery out of the western territories.

▲ Martin Van Buren

President number nine: William Henry Harrison (1841)
Harrison, who defeated The Prophet at Tippecanoe, was an aristocrat and the son of a Virginia governor. Harrison's campaign managers made him sound like an old log-cabin boy who came up the hard way. (He hadn't.) They made his opponent—Van Buren—sound like the aristocrat. (He wasn't.) It worked—Harrison was elected. Old Tippecanoe (that was his nickname) gave the longest inaugural address in history. In bitterly cold weather, he spoke for nearly two hours and caught a cold. It developed into pneumonia, and that was the end of William Henry Harrison. He was the first president to die in office. He was chief executive for only 31 days.

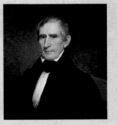

▲ William Henry Harrison

President number 10:
John Tyler (1841–1845)
When William Henry Harrison ran for the presidency, his election campaign slogan was "Tippecanoe and Tyler too." John Tyler, the vice-presidential candidate, was *Tyler* too. He was the first vice

▲ John Tyler

president to take office because of the death of a president. Tyler and Harrison were elected as members of the new Whig party. The Whigs were those who didn't like Andrew Jackson. (Many of them were former Federalists.) But Tyler fought with the leaders of the party, and after he had been in office five months they said he was no longer a Whig.

President number 11:
James Knox Polk (1845–1849)
President Polk, who was from Tennessee, said, "I am the hardest working man in the country." His hard work paid off: the Oregon and California territories became part of the United States while Polk

▲ James K. Polk

was president, and Iowa, Texas, and Wisconsin became states. He fought a war with Mexico. He ruined his health from overwork while in office. He died of exhaustion only three months after his term was over.

President number 12:
Zachary Taylor (1849–1850)
Taylor was a brave, patriotic general who was called "Old Rough and Ready" by his troops because he was plain and unassuming—in fact, downright messy. He owned slaves, but he didn't want

▲ Zachary Taylor

slavery to spread into the western territories. Taylor, an intelligent man, might have been a good president, but he died in office after serving only 16 months.

President number 13:
Millard Fillmore (1850–1853)
Millard Fillmore was a New Yorker and the second vice president to take over after a president died. Fillmore sent Commodore Matthew Perry to Japan to open trade between the two nations. Fillmore

▲ Millard Fillmore

installed the first kitchen stove in the White House. The first bathtub in the White House was installed by his wife, Abigail Fillmore. ("What an extravagance," said some people.)

President number 14:
Franklin Pierce (1853–1857)
Franklin Pierce was a New Hampshire man and, although a Northerner, he did not object to slavery. Two months before Pierce was inaugurated, his 11-year-old son, Bennie, was killed in a

▲ Franklin Pierce

train accident. The Pierces were sad all the rest of their lives. Pierce was not a strong president.

President number 15:
James Buchanan (1857–1861)
James Buchanan of Pennsylvania was the only bachelor president. His inauguration was the first to be photographed. In his time the arguments about slavery grew fierce. He didn't do

▲ James Buchanan

anything to try to make things better. In fact, he didn't do much of anything as president.

PART 2

GOING PLACES

Yankee Ingenuity: Cotton and Muskets

Ingenuity (in-juh-NEW-uh-tee) means inventiveness—finding a way to get things done.

Back in colonial times, Americans raised most of the food they ate and made most of what they wore. They spun their own yarn, wove their own cloth, and stitched their own clothes. They dipped candles and built tables and chairs. Wealthy colonists who wanted fancy dishes, fine cloth, elegant furniture, or handsome books sent to England for them. Most manufactured goods were made in England; raw materials came from the colonies.

It was a system that worked well. America provided lumber, pitch, tobacco, cotton, and grains. England took those raw materials and turned them into usable products that could be sold around the world.

Most people in early America lived on self-sufficient farms. They produced most of their own food, clothing, and simple household goods. They sold their surplus to people in towns or cities as well as to England. ▶

During the American Revolution the system stopped. Wham! Suddenly there was no place to send raw materials and no supply of fine goods. What did the colonists do? They used their heads. They looked for new markets for their raw materials. Their ships sailed to faraway places: to Spain, to China, to India, and to Turkey.

After the war the new United States began trading with England again. But American society was changing. We were now a democracy with a strong and growing middle class. It wasn't only the very rich who wanted to buy things. Ordinary people wanted them, too.

In England something was happening that could make that possible. That something was an "industrial revolution." Let me explain. It is the end of the 18th century, and if you want a new shirt this is what you have to do:

▲ A spinning wheel twists raw fiber—such as cotton, wool, or flax—into yarn or thread.

Take some wool, or flax, or cotton, and sit down at a spinning wheel. Try wool. You have to turn that sheep's wool into yarn. That takes carding (combing) and then spinning. It is a slow process. Since you've been working all winter, you do have a supply of yarn. How about dipping the yarn in indigo (blue) dye? Now, unless you plan to knit your shirt, you're still not ready to make it. You need to sit at a loom and weave the yarn into cloth. When you've done that, then, finally, you can get a pair of scissors, cut out a pattern, and sit back with your needle and thread and start sewing. Do you now see why you have only two shirts—one for everyday and one for church?

Here is Elizabeth Fuller's diary for a few days in 1791:

Aug 16. I picked blue wool. Aug. 17. I broke blue wool. Aug. 19. I carded blue wool. Ma spun.

And here is what Lucy Larcom had to say (you'll read more about Lucy in a minute):

I think it must have been at home, while I was a small child, that I got the idea that the chief end of woman was to make clothing for mankind.... I suppose I have to grow up and have a husband, and put all those little stitches into his coats and pantaloons. Oh, I never, never can do it!

Well, something was happening in England that was changing that made-at-home way of making things. It was a revolution—an

Samuel Slater designed this spinning frame from an English model. He installed it at his mill in Pawtucket, Rhode Island, in 1790. ▼

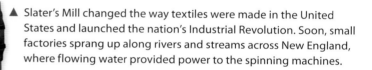

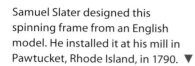

▲ Slater's Mill changed the way textiles were made in the United States and launched the nation's Industrial Revolution. Soon, small factories sprang up along rivers and streams across New England, where flowing water provided power to the spinning machines.

industrial revolution (although no one called it that for a while). It was a new system of organizing work, based on new ideas in science and technology and business.

Things once made at home were being made faster, and sometimes better, in factories. Tasks were divided in new ways. People began working in teams, and that was much more productive than working alone. It was machinery that made it all possible. Americans wanted some of those machines.

The English weren't about to share their new knowledge. They wanted to be the only ones with the machinery that made factories possible. They wanted to keep the Industrial Revolution in England. They wouldn't let anyone who worked in a cotton factory leave England.

Some Americans offered a big reward to anyone who could build a cotton-spinning machine in the United States. Samuel Slater, a young apprentice in a cotton factory in England, had a remarkable memory. He memorized the way the machines were built. Then he ran off to London. In London he pretended to be a farm worker. He didn't tell anyone he had worked in a cotton mill. It was 1790 when he sailed for America; he brought the key to the Industrial Revolution with him.

Slater built a small factory next to a waterfall on the Blackstone River at Pawtucket, Rhode Island. (Moses Brown and William Almy were his partners. They provided the money.) Waterpower turned the machines that spun cotton fibers into yarn. Soon there were spinning mills beside many New England streams. (Women working on hand looms in their homes wove Slater's yarn into cloth.)

Now that factories could turn cotton into yarn—quickly and easily—you can see there would be a great demand for raw cotton. Anyone who could grow cotton would make a lot of money. Cotton grew very well in the southern states.

The cotton that grew in the coastal region was easy to use. It was called "long-staple cotton" and it had seeds that fell right off the cotton bolls. But the tidewater coastal lands were in poor shape. There wasn't much good land left. People didn't practice scientific farming.

When Sam Slater came to Providence, he boarded with a Quaker family, the Wilkinsons. Hannah Wilkinson was the eldest daughter, and she and Sam fell in love and were married. Some years later, Hannah became famous in her own right: she developed fine cotton sewing thread—the kind you buy on spools—which she made from the fine cotton yarn that Sam manufactured.

◄ Seeds must be removed from cotton seedpods before the fiber can be spun.

Increasing demand for raw cotton led to more and bigger cotton plantations, and more slave labor, in the South. ▼

▲ The cotton gin made short-staple cotton profitable, which led to an increased demand for slave labor. Here, slaves haul and gin cotton.

▲ Eli Whitney's cotton gin combed the seeds from cotton, increasing a worker's output of clean cotton from one pound a day to 50.

They often destroyed land by growing the same crops year after year. Then, when the land was no longer productive, they moved on.

Short-staple cotton was the only cotton that would grow inland. However, short-staple cotton has lots of dark seeds, and those seeds stick to the cotton bolls. You can't spin cotton that is full of black seeds. It took a worker all day to remove the seeds from just one pound of cotton. If only there were an easy way to get rid of those seeds....

Eli Whitney heard all about that problem when he came to Savannah, Georgia, to take a job as a teacher. Whitney, a New Englander with an inventive mind, had just graduated from Yale College. It took him very little time to come up with a simple machine that removed seeds from cotton. He called it a "cotton engine"—the name was soon shortened to *cotton gin*. Instead of taking all day to remove seeds from a pound of cotton, a worker with a cotton gin could clean 50 pounds of cotton in a day—and clean it better than he ever could by hand.

The invention of the cotton gin, in 1793, did something that no one expected: it encouraged slavery.

The South had been having economic problems. Slavery wasn't as useful as it had been in the early colonial days. Tobacco had used up the soil. There wasn't enough work for the slaves. Many slaves were set free because owners no longer wanted to feed and house them. Thomas Jefferson and the other Founders thought slavery might gradually disappear.

Eli Whitney's cotton gin changed things—really changed things. If you could grow a lot of cotton you could get rich. So Southerners looked for land to grow cotton and workers to plant and harvest it. Slaves became very valuable again. Whitney didn't mean it, but his invention helped turn the American South into a slave empire. It made the South into a land of cotton. It kept it rural.

At the same time, the North was becoming urban and industrial. It began in earnest after 1810, when a Boston businessman named Francis Cabot Lowell took a trip to England. While he was there he visited a cloth-making factory. (Remember, in the United States cloth had to be made on hand looms.) Lowell was able just to look at the

Cotton Production in 1790 and 1820

1790 (3,000 bales of cotton)

1820 (300,000 bales of cotton)

= 1,000 bales of cotton

▲ Francis Cabot Lowell built his textile factory in Waltham, Massachusetts, a few miles west of Boston.

In the 18th century, only the very wealthy wore cotton clothes. Factories changed things. They could turn out products quickly and efficiently. They made goods affordable. Because of people like Eli Whitney, Sam Slater, and Francis Lowell, most Americans were soon wearing cotton.

English power looms and understand the way they were built. No one believed that could be done. When he came home to America he built a factory that was even better than those in England. Lowell's factory had machines for both spinning and weaving. He took cotton fibers and turned them into finished cloth—all in the same building. Even in England, no one had done that.

Once you get started with machines and technology, one invention seems to lead to another. In the old days most things were made from start to finish by one worker. A musket, for instance, was made by a gunsmith who would make guns one at a time. No two muskets were exactly alike. If a musket broke you had to find a gunsmith to repair it. Think what that means on a battlefield.

Eli Whitney began making muskets with interchangeable parts. In a factory one person could make all the stocks and another all the barrels. The parts from one musket would fit every other musket. It was very efficient. It had another big advantage. Can you see what it was?

Suppose a part broke. If parts are interchangeable you can fix a musket by taking parts from another musket. Think of the advantage of that on a battlefield. It was a simple idea—like the cotton gin—but it changed industry. Eli Whitney wasn't the first to design interchangeable parts. But when he showed his muskets to a group of politicians that included President John Adams and Vice President Thomas Jefferson, he made the idea popular.

Slater, Lowell, and Whitney helped bring the factory system to America. There were big advantages to the system, but disadvantages, too. The skilled craftsman, who took pride in his work and used his mind as well as his hands, became rare. Unskilled workers could now do things that only artisans had been able to do in the past.

Factory goods cost much less than handcrafted goods. That meant that ordinary people could afford things they had never been able to buy before. That made life better for most people. But not for everyone.

Work in the factories was mind-dulling. Workers did the same task, over and over and over. "What can be expected of a man who has spent 20 years of his life in making heads for pins?" asked a Frenchman who visited some factories.

The air in the cotton mills was full of tiny, almost invisible cotton fibers that got into your lungs (and sometimes led to cancer or other ailments). Those new spinning machines and looms were big and powerful and had no safety devices. If a worker's hand slipped, she might lose it. The noise was deafening—some workers actually went deaf. Factory lighting was usually poor—that didn't help your eyesight.

Child workers carry heavy loads of clay in a brickyard. Employers cut costs by paying children less than they paid adults. ▼

Some of the workers in the factories were children. Some were as young as seven years of age. How would you like to work in a factory instead of going to school? Sounds good to you? Well, children often worked 10 or more hours a day.

Lucy Larcom was a real girl. When she was little, a neighbor called Aunt Hannah, who kept a small school, taught her to read. They sat together near the kitchen fireplace. As Aunt Hannah twisted the thread on her spinning wheel, she pointed out words in the spelling book with a pin. Lucy was quick to learn. Soon Aunt Hannah taught her to read the stories in the Bible. Then Lucy went to school. Lucy loved school; she wanted to go on, to learn more, but...*alas, I could*

According to the law in Massachusetts, children were allowed to work only nine months a year so that they could go to school for the other three months.

not go. The little money I could earn—one dollar a week…was needed by the family. Lucy went to work in a factory.

Francis Lowell hired young farm women for his factory. Lowell housed them in dormitories and saw that they lived well and got fair salaries. But other factory owners took advantage of workers, especially women and children. They paid them poorly and made them work long hours.

Some mill owners built mill villages. They provided whole families with jobs, houses, schools, churches, and stores. It sounded good— and sometimes it was—but it gave the owners control of the workers' lives. Then they could do almost anything they wanted. Mill owners in Pawtucket lengthened the workday *and cut wages* at the same time. (The women weavers led a "turnout." It was one of the nation's first strikes.)

Those factory workers were taking part in two revolutions. The first was that Industrial Revolution; Slater and Lowell had helped bring it from England to America. The second, which was related, was a market revolution. That means the United States was going from a self-sufficient *farm economy* (where most families took care of their own needs, and rarely used money), to a capitalist *market economy*, based on jobs and money (where people earned wages and bought goods in markets and stores). These revolutions were just getting under way when Andrew Jackson became president. Once they got going they moved quickly and broadly. Revolutions do that—they change more than anyone ever expects.

Women working in textile factories played an important role in bringing the Industrial Revolution to the United States. ▶

Building Roads and Canals

One thing leads to another: if you start making cloth, thousands of yards of it, you can't keep it all in New England. You have to send it to other markets.

If your ships go to China and bring back fine goods, you can't keep all those goods in Salem or Boston. If you grow grain in New Jersey, or forge iron in Pennsylvania, or make guns in Connecticut, you need to find ways to get your products to people who want to buy them. If you live in the West, you want to send your grain, furs, and cattle to eastern markets. How do you get your goods to market? How can you get cloth from Boston to Buffalo?

In the first half of the 19th century, roads were no answer. Picture this: ruts, holes, mud, stones, and when you come to a river—no bridge. Now you have an idea of the roads.

What was needed was modern transportation. Americans—who were becoming known all over the world for their ingenuity—soon came up with some answers. They were canals, steamboats, railroads, and improved roads.

Let's start with the new roads. Actually they were pretty terrible— but in the 19th century they seemed exciting, and much better than

Helping the Coachman

In 1774 Dr. Josiah Quincy, the president of Harvard College, took a week to get from Boston to New York by stagecoach:

We reached our resting place at night, if no accident intervened, at 10 o'clock, and, after a frugal supper, went to bed with a notice that we would be called at three which generally proved to be half-past two, and then, whether it snowed or rained, the traveler must rise and make ready, by the help of a horn lantern and a farthing candle, and proceed on his way over bad roads, sometimes getting out to help the coachman lift the coach out of a quagmire or rut.

▲ Before the mid-1800s, most roads in the United States were unpaved, rutted, rocky, and often muddy.

the existing roads, which were usually just dirt paths. Do you know what *corduroy* is? Well, it is a cotton cloth with ridges and valleys. Some roads were made of round logs placed next to each other. They were called "corduroy roads." Can you see why? What would it be like to ride on a corduroy road? Plank roads, made by placing flat wooden planks next to each other, were better but not great. They quickly rotted away.

Road building was a new science. (The ancient Romans knew how to make good roads, but their skill was forgotten until the end of the 18th century.) No one knew how to build good roads, so they experimented. Often the new roads wore out or washed away almost as soon as they were built. Still, some very useful roads did get finished. The best were macadam roads, built with a new process developed in Scotland (by a man named McAdam) using crushed stones and clay as a base and asphalt or tar on top.

About 1806, some people with big ideas decided that we needed a road that would go across the country—well, at least from the East Coast to the Mississippi, which seemed across the country to most Easterners then. (Remember, the Louisiana Purchase was made in 1803.

In Maryland, a crew lays the first macadam road in the United States. John McAdam's process layered crushed stone and clay with tar on top. ▼

▲ The National Road caused controversy over the role of the federal government, but it opened the way for mail delivery and freight hauling between the eastern United States and the West.

Hardly anyone knew what was beyond St. Louis.) That very long road was called the National Road and was to be paid for by the federal government. Does that sound like a good idea? Well, it didn't seem that way to everyone. It caused a whole lot of controversy.

The people in the West wanted it—they really wanted it. But many Easterners said, "Why should our tax money go for a road out to that wilderness?" In the South, people were shouting about states' rights. They didn't think the national government should pay for roads. If that happened, even states that the road didn't go anywhere near would have to help pay for them. President James Monroe said it was unconstitutional. But finally the National Road was begun. By 1818 it stretched from Cumberland, Maryland, to Wheeling in western Virginia. Then powerful Senator Henry Clay got involved. He wanted to see the road extended, and it was. By 1833 it went to Columbus, Ohio; by 1850 it was at Vandalia in central Illinois.

Some people called the National Road the Cumberland Road.

In 1815, a committee report for the North Carolina legislature said that more than 20,000 inhabitants had left the state during the previous 25 years. Most had moved west.

The intersection of two roads could be a busy meeting place for covered wagons heading west, local farm wagons, people on horseback and on foot, and even livestock. ▶

Over its wilderness route passengers squeezed shoulder to shoulder in hard-backed, leather-seated stagecoaches. That was a lot better than walking, which is what many did alongside their packed wagons. The road carried all kinds of traffic: mule-drawn carts heaped with farm produce; big, horse-drawn vans stuffed with bales of southern cotton going to northern mills; northern factory products heading south; and wagonloads of immigrants, still speaking foreign tongues, bound west to destinations they could not even imagine.

Before the National Road was built it took four weeks to travel from Baltimore to St. Louis. On the road, if you traveled without stopping, you could make it in four *days*. One traveler (his name was Charles Fenno Hoffman), who went the whole way on horseback, wrote this:

> *It appears to have been originally constructed of large round stones, thrown without much arrangement on the surface of the soil, after the road was first levelled. These are now being ploughed up, and a thin layer of broken stones is in many places spread over the renovated surface…. It yields like snow-drift to the heavy wheels which traverse it…. There is one feature, however, in this national work which is truly fine, I allude to the massive stone bridges which form a part of it.*

Renovated means restored or made new.

New roads made it easier for Americans to travel and to buy and sell goods. Some of the roads were built by private companies. The company would put sharp sticks—called pikes—on a movable rod that blocked the entrance to the road. To get on the road you had to pay a toll; the gatekeeper then turned the pikes.

Roads were expensive to build and maintain—there had to be a better and cheaper way to move goods and people.

Some people thought canals were the answer. Ben Franklin, back in 1772, wrote, "Canals are quiet and very manageable." George Washington believed that canals were the wave of the future. He invested in the Patowmack Canal system (near Washington, D.C.) and in the Kanawha Canal. Investors thought that canal would be like a major highway, taking goods and people from Virginia's James River across the Appalachian Mountains to the Ohio River. But the Kanawha Canal was never completed.

In New York, DeWitt Clinton decided a canal could be built from Albany to Buffalo, which meant from the Hudson River to Lake Erie. It would be named the Erie Canal. Look at a map. That was to be some canal! A canal, by the way, is a big ditch. That's what some people called this one: "Clinton's Ditch." Many people thought it a crazy project. It would cost a lot of money and would be very difficult to build. The Erie Canal would have to traverse 360 miles, most of it through the wilds of New York State. There were steep hills to climb. Boats would have to get over those hills. To raise the boats, locks would be needed. A lock is like an elevator for water and boats.

The first bicycles were seen at the beginning of the 19th century. In 1813 a celeripede (suh-LER-ih-peed) appeared in America. It had two wheels but had to be pushed with your feet, like a kiddie car. True bikes came in the 1830s, but with the pedals on the rear wheel and the seat over that wheel.

▲ The celeripede did not have pedals or brakes, so its usefulness was limited and its popularity short lived.

Usually an ordinary household on or near the turnpike maintained the tollgate. On the Cumberland Road, for "every score of sheep, or every Dearborn, Sulky, Chair or Chaise with one horse," the toll was 6 cents, while "every Chariot, Coach, Coachee, Stage, Phaeton or Chaise with two horses and four wheels" had to pay 12 cents. Just like subway-fare dodgers today, some folks tried to avoid paying tolls. They were called "shunpikers"—which is where our word *piker* (meaning "cheapskate") comes from.

▲ The Erie Canal allowed barge traffic between New York City and the city of Buffalo on the shores of Lake Erie. The canal reduced the time and cost of shipping and travel and spurred western settlement.

▲ Mules or horses walked along a towpath to pull the barges in the canal.

When Thomas Jefferson heard of the project he said to a canal booster, "Why, sir, you talk of making a canal of 350 miles through the wilderness—it is little short of madness to talk of it at this day!" No question about it, it was a very ambitious project. But that didn't stop DeWitt Clinton or the many Americans who wanted to build the canal. It was 1817 when they set to work.

Thousands of laborers were needed. Ireland was having economic problems—people in Ireland were hungry. Canal workers got 50 cents a day and all the meat they could eat. That sounded good to many Irishmen, especially to those who'd just arrived in this country.

It was planned that horses or mules would pull most of the boats on the Erie Canal. No, the animals didn't have to swim. Workers built a towpath next to the canal. Boats were attached to ropes and towed by the horses.

Somehow it all got built. It was four feet deep and 40 feet wide. It was a manmade river; it was an engineering marvel! You could ride on a barge from the Atlantic Ocean, up the Hudson River, across the Erie Canal, and on to the Great Lakes. On the canal there were 83 locks to raise and lower you, your boat, and the water you were floating in.

They didn't call it the "Big Ditch" anymore; now it was called the "Grand Canal" and sometimes "Clinton's Wonder." DeWitt Clinton, who was now Governor Clinton, took the first ride from Buffalo to New York City. It had taken eight years to dig the Erie Canal. Clinton's trip took nine days. When Clinton got to New York City he dumped a barrel of Lake Erie water into the Atlantic Ocean. Then there was a grand parade; church bells rang and people cheered.

Everyone could ride the canal. There were fancy passenger boats that served fine meals on linen tablecloths. There were flatboats with people, cargo, and animals jammed together. There were ordinary rafts. You could go on a slow boat, at two miles an hour, and pay a penny and a half a mile. Or you could whiz along at four miles an

Vessels on the Erie Canal ranged from elegant passenger boats with fine dining to open flatboats crowded with people, cargo, and animals. ▼

Towns such as Lockport, pictured here, grew up along the Erie Canal. ▶

hour and and pay 5 cents a mile. Towns grew up around the canal; it made life better for people.

Before the canal was built, it cost $100 to ship a ton of grain from Buffalo to New York. By 1855 it only cost $8 on the Erie Canal. People packed their belongings and took the Erie Canal west; they moved to places like Indiana, Michigan, and Wisconsin. They went east, too; the canal helped make New York the country's largest city. Before long there was a canal frenzy throughout the nation. But no other canal was as successful, or as long, as the Erie Canal.

A Popular Song

Canal laborers sang as they worked. Soon everyone was singing a song called "The Erie Canal."

I've got a mule and her name is Sal,
Fifteen miles on the Erie Canal.
She's a good old worker and a good old pal,
Fifteen miles on the Erie Canal.
We've hauled some barges in our day,
Filled with lumber, coal, and hay,
And we know every inch of the way
From Albany to Buffalo.

CHORUS

Low bridge! Everybody down.
Low bridge! We're a-coming to a town.
You'll always know your neighbor,
You'll always know your pal
If you've ever navigated on the Erie Canal.

We'd better get on our way, old pal,
Fifteen miles on the Erie Canal.
You can bet your life I'd never part with Sal,
Fifteen miles on the Erie Canal.
Get us there, Sal, here comes a lock;
We'll make Rome 'fore six o'clock.
One more trip and back we'll go,
Right back home to Buffalo.

(Repeat CHORUS)

Teakettle Power

Think about blowing a whistle. It takes lung power to do it. With that same power you can blow up a balloon or push a toy sailboat in the bathtub. Early in the 18th century it seemed to occur to several people that boiling water—steam—produced the same effect and might be used as a source of power.

Have you heard a teakettle blow a whistle? Have you ever seen a teakettle blow off its spout? Steam is powerful stuff. Picture a huge boiler filled with water that is boiling furiously. The steam that it makes can move a boat or a train.

Some people—those with curious minds—began to think of ways to do that. Some Englishmen started the process, but quite a few Americans worked on the problem. William Henry, John Stevens, and John Fitch were American inventors—each built a steamboat—but each had some bad luck and the country wasn't quite ready for their ideas.

It was ready when Robert Fulton came along. Fulton was an artist, a good one, who had studied painting in London. Fulton was also an inventor.

◄ Scottish inventor James Watt made a workable steam engine in the late 1700s. Robert Fulton and others built on Watt's work to revolutionize transportation.

▲ Robert Fulton's steamboat, the *Clermont*, makes its way on the Hudson River in New York in 1813.

In 1807, Fulton's steamboat, the *North River*, steamed up the Hudson River the 150 miles from New York City to Albany. It made that voyage in 32 hours, and that seemed astonishingly fast.

Before the steamboat, boats floated down a river on the river's current. There was no easy way they could go upriver against the current.

Fulton's boats were soon chugging up the Mississippi at 10 miles an hour (easily). By 1820 there were 60 steamboats on the Mississippi; by 1860, there were about a thousand.

Steamboats were efficient, fast, fun, and—dangerous! If steam is trapped in a boiler and for some reason can't get out, the boiler will explode. That happened to a number of steamboats. They blew their lids and killed people when they did.

The same thing happened when steam power took to the rails. Now that was a good idea! Take a steam engine and have it pull a set of wagons rolling on a track. Hold on to your hat: we're going to whiz at 20 miles per hour. As steam engines improve, trains will go faster and faster.

◄ A steamboat race on the Mississippi River in 1866

But talk about dangerous! Besides exploding, the engines jump their tracks, and trains crash into each other. The trains are called "iron horses" and "teakettles on tracks." The engines are made of iron and have tall smokestacks and fireboxes. Passenger cars look like stagecoaches, and, like fancy coaches, are painted with bright designs. Because the cars are wide open, the colorful paint is soon covered with soot, and so are the passengers. And soot isn't the only thing the riders have to worry about: the engines give off sparks that fall on their clothes and get into their hair. On the first train in New York, passengers are kept busy putting out fires in each other's clothing.

But soon the design is improved, and the passenger car becomes a long, enclosed room with an aisle down the center and seats on either side. The first steam engines were fired with wood, but coal was found to produce a hotter flame. Either way, a fireman is kept busy lifting wood or shoveling coal to keep the fire blazing and the water boiling.

When the Baltimore & Ohio Railroad opens 13 miles of railroad track in 1830, horses are used to pull carriages on wheels. On a track, one horse can pull as heavy a load as 10 horses off the track. But the railroad's directors are not satisfied. They are forward thinkers. They want to try a new steam engine. British engineers who come and look at the track say sorry, the Baltimore & Ohio track has too many curves for a steam engine. No engine can stay on that track, they say. Peter Cooper thinks differently. He is a Baltimore inventor and he owns an iron foundry. Later, he wrote, "I had naturally a knack at contriving, and I told the directors that I believed I could knock together a locomotive that would get around that curve."

The early 1800s were years of fast growth. New words and expressions appeared in the language at that time—they were hurry-up expressions:

> like greased lightning
> quick as a wink
> in a jiffy
> like a house afire
> shake a leg
> lickety-split

Early trains offered faster travel than anything on roads, but passengers were exposed to soot, cinders, and sparks from the iron engines, not to mention the threat of explosions and crashes. ▼

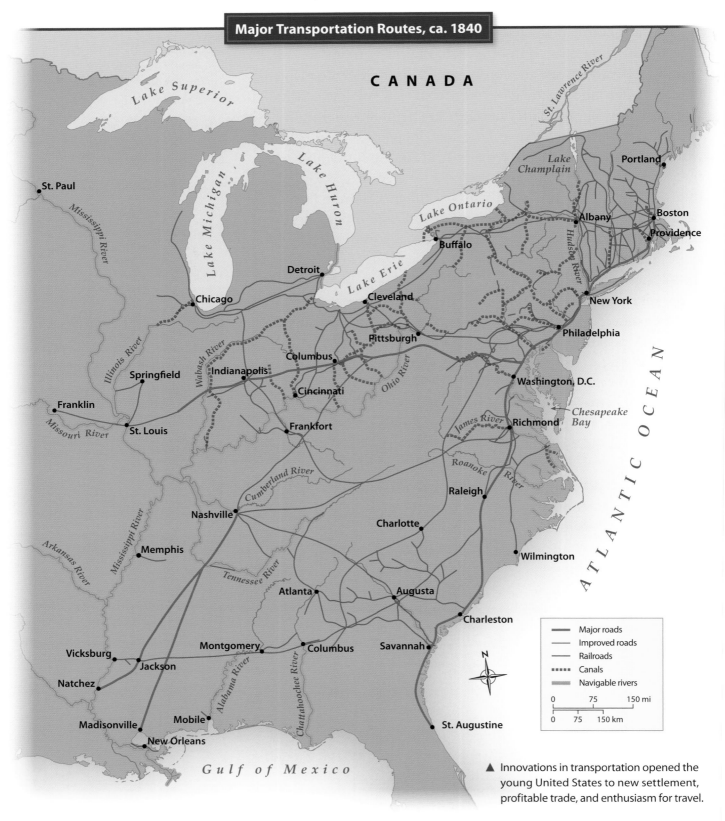

Major Transportation Routes, ca. 1840

CANADA

Lake Superior

Lake Michigan

Lake Huron

Lake Ontario

Lake Erie

Lake Champlain

St. Lawrence River

Hudson River

St. Paul

Portland

Albany

Boston

Providence

Buffalo

Detroit

Cleveland

New York

Chicago

Pittsburgh

Philadelphia

Columbus

Illinois River

Wabash River

Springfield

Indianapolis

Cincinnati

Ohio River

Washington, D.C.

Franklin

Missouri River

St. Louis

Frankfort

James River

Richmond

Chesapeake Bay

Cumberland River

Roanoke River

Raleigh

Nashville

Charlotte

Arkansas River

Mississippi River

Memphis

Tennessee River

Wilmington

Atlanta

Augusta

Charleston

Vicksburg

Montgomery

Columbus

Savannah

Jackson

Chattahoochee River

Alabama River

Natchez

Madisonville

Mobile

New Orleans

St. Augustine

Gulf of Mexico

ATLANTIC OCEAN

N

Legend
- Major roads
- Improved roads
- Railroads
- Canals
- Navigable rivers

0   75   150 mi

0   75   150 km

▲ Innovations in transportation opened the young United States to new settlement, profitable trade, and enthusiasm for travel.

Which is just what he did. He found a small engine, took the barrels from two muskets (for pipes) and some other odds and ends and built a little steam locomotive he named *Tom Thumb*, after the children's fairy tale. Then he invited the directors for a ride. "We started—six on the engine, and thirty-six on the car. It was a great occasion.... We...made the passage to Ellicott's Mills in an hour and twelve minutes."

Tom Thumb worried a Baltimore stagecoach company. They didn't want competition from iron engines. So they challenged the owners of the train to a race. Their best horse-pulled railcar against *Tom*. Well, the horse was soon in the lead; then the engine built up power and pulled ahead. It was way ahead when an engine belt slipped out of place. The steam pressure fell and the train came to a stop. The people in the horse-drawn train laughed as they galloped by. They wouldn't laugh for long. Trains were the future.

Canals had a problem: they froze in winter. Stagecoaches and horse-pulled trains had problems, too: they were small and couldn't carry heavy freight. Besides, horses get tired and need replacing. Trains could be used year round. They could carry very heavy loads. By 1840, more than 3,000 miles of track had been laid.

By 1850 there were almost 9,000 miles of track in America; by 1860—the year before the Civil War—there were 30,000 miles of track. Traveling by train, at an unbelievable 30 miles an hour, you could go from New York to Chicago in only two days.

> *When I hear the iron horse make the hills echo with his snort like thunder, shaking the earth with his feet, and breathing fire and smoke from his nostrils (what kind of winged horse or fiery dragon they will put into the new Mythology I don't know), it seems as if the earth had got a race now worthy to inhabit it.*
> —Henry David Thoreau, *Walden*

◄ The *Tom Thumb* locomotive races a horse-drawn railcar.

Technology (tek-NOL-uh-jee) is the use of scientific ideas for practical purposes.

Cities and Progress

It was a head-over-heels affair. The whole country was caught in its web. It was technology that had captured us. We Americans, in the 19th century, became fascinated with machines and scientific advances. We watched as they changed our old ways, and, mostly, we liked what was happening.

We fell in love with speed—with locomotives and steamboats and clipper ships.

We fell in love with American inventions—with John Deere's steel plow, Cyrus McCormick's reaper, Elias Howe's sewing machine, Charles Goodyear's vulcanized rubber, and Samuel Morse's electric telegraph.

We fell in love with indoor plumbing. And many of us fell in love with city life.

Back at the end of the 18th century—in 1790, when the first census was taken—95 percent of all Americans lived on farms. By 1820, 93 percent of Americans lived on farms or in rural villages. By 1850,

▲ Throughout the second half of the 19th century, the firm founded by Currier and Ives produced popular lithographic prints tinted with watercolor. This print is titled *Progress of the Century*.

it was 85 percent. Slowly, we were on the way to becoming an urban nation. Where do you live? Where do most Americans live today?

In 1790, only two cities—New York and Philadelphia—had 20,000 or more people. By 1860 there were 43 American cities of at least that size and another 300 cities with more than 5,000 inhabitants.

New York, according to the poet Walt Whitman, was "million-footed." But that was only when New Yorkers hopped on one foot. A million people lived in New York. Philadelphia had 500,000. Cincinnati, known as the "Queen City of the West," had 160,000. New Orleans, "Queen of the South," had 169,000.

What were all those people doing in cities?

Most were working—making things, or teaching, or selling, or preaching. Many were new immigrants who stayed only a short time before they went off to look for opportunity elsewhere. They moved and then moved again; Americans were a restless people, always searching for a better life.

We Americans became famous all over the world for "know-how." People in this country learned to use their hands and heads to make things, and make them well. In the 19th century the United States was becoming an industrial nation. Industry was helping cities grow.

▲ When this lithograph of Broadway was made in 1836, about 300,000 people lived in New York City. Just 30 years later, the city was home to a million people.

Castle Garden in New York City, at the southern tip of Manhattan Island, was the main arrival station for European immigrants from 1855 to 1890. ▼

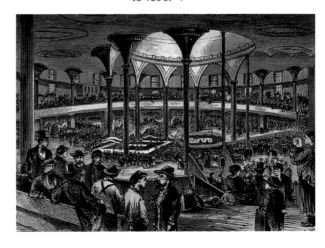

▲ The enormous Astor House Hotel in New York City opened in 1836.

If you've never been in a city before (and many 19th-century Americans had not), it's a mighty exciting place. Why, just look at that building over there—it must be six stories tall. You can get a stiff neck looking up that high! Do you think there is any danger it will topple over? It's the handsomest building in town—and it's a hotel. Step inside and you'll be in a big lobby, where trees grow in pots.

They say that some American hotels even have vertical railroads inside. (City folk call those vertical railroads "elevators.")

Boston's Tremont House, built in 1829, is the finest hotel in the country. It has eight "bathing rooms" in the basement. Cold water comes into the baths from rooftop tanks that collect rain. Now listen to this: the Tremont House basement has eight water closets (someday they'll be called toilets) for the 200 to 300 guests.

New York's Astor House Hotel, built in 1836, has running water above the first floor. (It is the first public building to try that.)

And in New York, A.T. Stewart's Department Store, six stories high and built of white marble, has 400 clerks and big glass windows to show the splendid merchandise sold inside. It is a new idea—a store that sells almost everything you could want. People visit New York just to see Stewart's store. Soon cities all over the land have their own versions of Stewart's and the Astor House.

Of course, every city has a newspaper; some have five or six or more. Newspapers are changing the nation. In 1830 there are

This is the city and I am one of the citizens,
Whatever interests the rest interests me, politics, wars, markets, newspapers,
schools,
The mayor and councils, banks, tariffs, steamships, factories, stocks, stores,
real estate and personal estate.

—Walt Whitman, from *Song of Myself*

1,000 newspapers in America. Mostly they are sold by yearly subscription—at about $8 a year. That's a lot of cash; most people can't afford to read a paper. That is, until 1833, when Benjamin Day publishes a newspaper, the *New York Sun*, that sells for a penny. Two years later he is selling nearly 20,000 copies of the *Sun* every day—and lots of advertising, too. James Gordon, newly arrived from Scotland, soon follows with the even more successful *New York Herald*, and Horace Greeley with the *New York Tribune*.

By 1840 the nation has 138 daily papers and 1,141 weeklies. Readership is growing at an even faster rate than population. Now, everyone seems to be a newspaper reader.

Some people complain that the penny papers are vulgar and trashy, but there are newspapers for every taste. They are wildly popular and help spread information and democracy, too. (Everyone can afford to read them, not just the rich.) They are part of the excitement of city life.

Farm life is quiet; city life is not. In America you can have your choice.

But building cities quickly means there is little time for planning—and that sometimes leads to trouble. Have you ever heard adults talk about the "good old days"? Well, they weren't as good as some people think.

▲ The front page of the first issue of the first penny newspaper, the *New York Sun*, published on September 3, 1833

Growth of American Cities, 1790–1840

CHAPTER 18 Cities and Progress **91**

Crime was an awful problem in the 19th century. Most American cities didn't have uniformed police, but they did have street gangs, pickpockets, and robbers.

There just weren't enough rooms for all those people who were moving in; the cities were overcrowded—and dirty. Boston had a good sewage system, but most cities didn't.

Wastewater from baths and sinks went into open street gutters. Pigs roamed city streets, and so did rats. Chicago had almost no indoor plumbing (until after 1860). No one understood the importance of cleanliness, so disease was a terrible problem. Whole neighborhoods were sometimes wiped out by cholera and other deadly diseases.

And then there was fire. Most city buildings were wooden and built close together. If a fire was ignited—*whoosh*—a city could burn down.

It was December of 1835, and cold; New York's fire hydrants were all frozen. So the city's firemen could do nothing but watch when a fire got started. Soon most of New York was ablaze—700 buildings turned to ash. That happened in more than one city.

For all that, America's cities were full of good surprises. An Englishwoman visiting

Tenements, such as this one on Mulberry Street in New York City, were overcrowded, dirty, and dangerous. ▼

Homeless people had to pay a fee to spend the night in a crammed, unhealthy shelter. ▼

▲ A terrible fire destroyed much of New York City in December 1835.

America in 1834 (her name was Harriet Martineau) was amazed to hear a concert of Mozart's music in Cincinnati, Ohio. A few years earlier, she was told, the only sounds there were "the bellow and growl of wild beasts."

Most Americans were sure they were in the best possible place in all the world. They knew that if the farm or city where they lived didn't work out, they could move on: to a new city sprouting in the wilderness, or to a new frontier. America's land was so vast that much of it was still unmapped. That added to its allure. It seemed limitless, and so did the opportunities it offered. Those new cities were fascinating, but it was land of their own that most Americans wanted.

The Richest Man in America

▲ John Jacob Astor went from fur trader to financier.

John Jacob Astor arrived in Baltimore from Germany with seven flutes. If he could sell them, he thought, they would get him started in the New World. They did. When he died, 64 years later (in 1848), he was the richest man in America and he owned a whole lot of Manhattan Island (which is the center of New York City).

Astor started by selling furs and musical instruments, and soon had a shop in New York. Besides that, he was buying and selling goods to Indians at frontier outposts. He began importing guns, ammunition, and wool. That wasn't all; he acquired a fleet of ships and sent some of them off to China. He controlled most of the Pacific Coast fur trade. He created a trade network linking Britain, New England, the Pacific Coast, and East Asia—and he did it long before others thought globally. Then Astor began buying real estate. He was soon called "the landlord of New York," and he became super-rich. He said he was sorry he hadn't bought all of New York.

What was he like? He was tight. It took the artist John James Audubon six trips to see him before Astor would pay the $1,000 he had promised for Audubon's masterpiece, *Birds of America.* He told Audubon he didn't have any cash. But he did found some libraries, and he gave money to colleges and a few other worthy causes.

John Jacob Astor's Pacific Fur Company established the first permanent settlement in the Oregon country in 1811. Astoria, named for Astor, sits near the mouth of the Columbia River. ▼

Life in the Mills

No people had ever inhabited a land that offered so much to so many. Most Americans lived on farms, got up early in the morning, and went cheerfully to work: milking cows, feeding chickens, building houses, growing crops, and raising children. Ten children was not unusual for a 19th-century American family. However, big as they were, families were smaller than they had been in the 18th century. They would continue to get smaller. No one was quite sure why. One thing was clear: for most people, life was good in America. The air was pure, the streams full of fish, the woods full of game, and the meadows full of wildflowers. Besides, we were a free people, working for ourselves.

Well, most of us were. Two groups were not. There were the slaves, who sometimes worked from sunup to sundown and only rarely for themselves. Free people were beginning to have guilty feelings about slavery. A few people—abolitionists—were working to end the horrors of black slavery. (You'll read more about them later.)

There was another group—also enslaved—but not by law or skin color. They were slaves of factory, mine, and mill. Their lives were horrible. They had no fresh air to breathe. They went into the mills as children. Often, they died in their thirties. They were almost without hope. Hardly anyone knew they existed.

◄ Miners dig and load coal into an underground mule-drawn cart in Pennsylvania during the 1860s.

Then, in 1861, an article appeared in the most important magazine of the day: the *Atlantic Monthly*. The article, called "Life in the Iron Mills," was unsigned. It created a sensation. Everyone began talking about it—but no one suspected that the writer was a shy, unmarried, 30-year-old woman. Her name was Rebecca Harding.

Harding lived in Wheeling, Virginia. (Soon Wheeling and the surrounding area would break away from Virginia and become West Virginia.) Wheeling was an Ohio River town, on the border between North and South. Some people there kept slaves and believed in slavery, but most did not. It was a border in other ways, too. The rough-and-tumble frontier was just spitting distance away. Not far off—in the other direction—were the planter societies of Virginia and Maryland.

Thirteen thousand people lived in Wheeling. Some were wealthy and prosperous; their gorgeous homes lined the riverfront. Rebecca lived in one of those grand houses on the river. But it was the commonplace folk of Wheeling she wrote about in the article that stunned all those who read it. She wrote of people whose lives were so different from those in the big houses they might as well have lived in a different galaxy.

Pollution in mill towns such as Scranton, Pennsylvania, pictured here, poured from the huge chimneys and smokestacks of the mills where the townspeople labored. ▼

Wheeling was an iron-mill town. Ironworkers dragged themselves to work that lasted 14 hours a day, six days a week. They went into the mill at age 9 or 10, and left when they died.

Rebecca Harding wrote of the ironworkers and their town—it was her town, too. She described the smoke that

▲ Steelworkers at the Bessemer Steel plant in Pittsburgh, Pennsylvania, 1875

rolls sullenly in slow folds from the great chimneys of the iron foundries, and settles down in black, slimy pools on the muddy streets. Smoke on the wharves, smoke on the dingy boats, on the yellow river,—clinging in a coating of greasy soot to the house-front, the two faded poplars, the faces of the passers-by.… Smoke everywhere! A dirty canary chirps desolately in a cage beside me. Its dream of green fields and sunshine is a very old dream—almost worn out, I think.

In a country where the idea of pollution was still unknown, where sunshine and clear air were believed to be nature's gifts to all, Harding's description was startling.

She was just beginning. She went on to tell of the people who worked in the hot furnace of a mill:

Masses of men, with dull, besotted faces bent to the ground, sharpened here and there by pain or cunning; skin and muscle and flesh begrimed with smoke and ashes; stooping all night over boiling cauldrons of metal…breathing from infancy to death an air saturated with fog and grease and soot, vileness for soul and body.

Rebecca Harding told the story of a young ironworker: Hugh Wolfe. Hugh was fictional, but he might have been real. He was talented—he made statues of men and women out of the refuse from the iron mill, and he dreamed of life as an artist. Hugh's poor, homely cousin, Deborah, wanted to make his dream come true. So she stole money and gave it to Hugh. He got caught and sent to prison, where he died, not yet 20.

People wept when they read the story and learned—often for the first time—of the wage slaves who tended the scalding pots of liquid metal that became the iron and steel needed to build the railroads and machines the nation was demanding.

Did her story help those workers? Probably not, for no one then knew how to smelt iron, or dig minerals, or make steel without hard, horrible, backbreaking labor. No one wanted to do that kind of labor. No one should have had to do it. The carbon monoxide vapors from the burning coal destroyed people's lungs. The liquid metal spilled, hardened, and flew off as accidental bullets. A visitor to nearby Pittsburgh described that mill town as "Hell with the lid taken off." Someday the problem would be partly solved by machines. But in the 19th century no one knew that. Harding's story made some people of her time aware of the horror of millwork.

> A *strike* is a work stoppage to protest low wages or bad working conditions.
>
> *Labor unions* are organizations of workers.
>
> A *rogue* (rohg) is a villain.

Striking Times

It was a snowy day in March 1860 when the women shoemakers of Lynn, Massachusetts, went on strike. The weather didn't discourage them. They took out their parasols, put on their hoop skirts, marched behind the Lynn city guard and its brass band, and sang. Most of the town turned out to watch and sing with them.

Two weeks later the strike was still under way and the women had a chowder party to keep up their spirits (with dancing and kissing in the party). But when one of their bosses said he had persuaded some women to come back to work, the strikers weren't amused. They kicked the boss out of the party and had the band play the "Rogue's March."

The striking women were serious about their goal: higher wages. Some people (especially employers) didn't like the idea of labor unions or strikes, but strikes were judged legal by Chief Justice Lemuel Shaw of the Massachusetts Supreme Court in 1842.

Women in Lynn, Massachusetts, strike for better conditions. In some factories, women worked 16-hour days and earned $1 a week. ▶

Working Women and Children

CHAPTER 20

*W*omen *in early America didn't work.*

Do you believe that? Some people do. They think working women are a new phenomenon. Well, people who believe that don't know their history. Women have always worked in America. They just didn't always work for wages.

How about American men? Have they always worked? Of course. But they didn't work for wages, either. In the old days, most men and women worked on farms, for themselves, and didn't see much cash. If they had extra crops, they sold or bartered them for goods they couldn't produce themselves.

Some American men and women were indentured servants or slaves, and of course they didn't work for themselves, and they usually didn't get wages either. A few people, however, were paid cash or wages for their work: craftspeople (blacksmiths, shoemakers, furniture makers, printers, etc.), teachers, and ministers.

In Europe those cash-paying jobs had almost always belonged to men. America was different. From the beginning there was a labor shortage. If a blacksmith wanted to teach his daughter his craft, he could do it in America. Some American women were blacksmiths and shoemakers and coopers (barrel makers). Some were teachers. The traditional churches would not ordain women as ministers, but on the frontier—where preachers were in short supply—women were often called to preach.

When factories began to open in America, women filled the factories. There was an unfortunate reason for that. Women were willing to work for lower wages than men.

> A *phenomenon* (fuh-NOM-uh-non) is a fact or event, especially one that you can see for yourself. Usually that event is uncommon or remarkable.

Women and girls formed a large part of the workforce in America's early factories, such as this mid-19th-century textile mill. ▶

In 1820, half of the nation's industrial workers were children under 10 years of age.

In this New York City factory, children worked long hours assembling paper boxes. ▼

There was another group that worked for still lower wages: children. Nineteenth-century factories were filled with children—boys and girls who almost never got a chance to play.

Do you sometimes complain about school? Well, you might stop complaining after you read what factory life was like for some 19th-century children. This description was written by Herman Melville in 1855. (You'll hear more about Melville in a few chapters.) Melville needed some paper (he was a writer), so he got on his horse and went off to a paper factory.

When he arrived, this is what he saw: "At rows of blank-looking counters sat rows of blank-looking girls, with blank, white folders in their blank hands, all blankly folding blank paper...."

The women in this mid-19th-century factory are binding books. ▼

Those girls didn't have a choice. They had to work.

Slave children didn't have a choice, either. "I was only seven years old when I was sent away to take care of a baby," said Harriet Tubman who, when she grew up, became famous for helping slaves run away to freedom.

One mornin' after breakfast I stood by the table waiting [to clear the table]; just by me was a bowl of lumps of white sugar.... I never had anything good; no sweet, no sugar, and that sugar, right by me, did look so nice, and my Missus's back was turned to me so I just put my fingers in the sugar bowl to take one lump, and maybe she heard me for she turned and saw me. The next minute she had the rawhide down [to whip Harriet]...I ran and I ran and I ran.

I Am Well Which Is One Comfort

Mary Paul grew up in northern Vermont and went to work in the Lowell, Massachusetts, textile mills while still in her teens.

Lowell mill girls worked six days a week, 12 hours a day. Bells rang them to work, meals, and bed. Mary wrote often to her father to tell of her experiences and get news from home:

Dear Father, I am well which is one comfort. My life and health are spared while others are cut off. Last Thursday one girl fell down and broke her neck which caused instant death. She was going in or coming out of the mill and slipped down it being very icy. The same day a man was killed by the [railroad] cars. Another had nearly all of his ribs broken. Another was nearly killed by falling down and having a bale of cotton fall on him. Last Tuesday we were paid. In all I had six dollars and sixty cents paid $4.68 for board [rent and food].... At 5 o'clock in the morning the bell rings for the folks to get up and get breakfast. At half past six it rings for the girls to get up and at seven they are called into the mill. At half past 12 we have dinner are called back again at one and stay till half past seven.

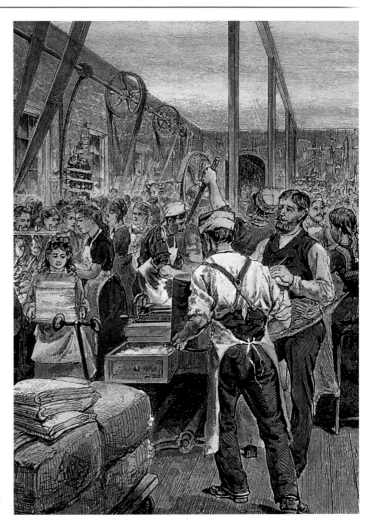

Busy textile mills were often crowded, noisy, and hazardous places to work. ▶

Making Words

The Indian whose name was Sequoyah had talent. When he was small, he was able to draw amazing pictures of birds and horses and people. When he grew to manhood he became a silversmith and made fine jewelry: earrings, bracelets, and necklaces for the Indian men and women and sturdy silver pieces to hang around the necks of their horses.

We don't know if he was happy as a silversmith; we do know that—once he saw something the white men could do—he became a different man. What he saw seemed too astounding to be believed.

A white man would take words, turn them into shapes, and scratch them on a slate or draw them on a piece of paper. Then another man could look at those shapes and say the first man's words. Was it magic?

Sequoyah could draw pictures of things he could see. But you can't see words. You can't touch words. How can they be pictured? Sequoyah was determined to find out.

Sequoyah was a Cherokee, a member of a proud nation of hunters, warriors, and farmers who seemed to do everything well. But no Cherokee could write his own language, because reading and writing were unknown to the Indian tribes. Indian stories and speeches were remembered and retold by orators, or storytellers, or singers. Sequoyah knew that often in retelling, words are changed. He thought the words of some of the great Indian leaders needed to be remembered just as they were first said. Would the white man's idea work with Indian words?

◀ Cherokee scholar and tribal leader Sequoyah displays his printed Cherokee alphabet. Finding a way to write down the Cherokee language, Sequoyah said, was "like catching a wild animal and taming it." Almost all Cherokees became literate in a few years.

Sequoyah, being a Cherokee, had confidence. He believed he could find a way to write his people's words. But how was it to be done?

Suppose you didn't know how to read or write English or any other language; how would you begin to create a written language? Sequoyah thought up a logical system. He made marks stand for sentences. Soon he had so many marks and so many sentences he was lost. He knew he could never remember them all. Then he tried making marks for words. Then there were too many word marks to remember. Finally he made marks for sounds— and he knew he had a good system. He came up with 86 Cherokee syllables and a system of 86 symbols to stand for them. That sounds like a lot of characters to learn, compared to the English alphabet of 26 letters. But it works very well for Cherokee.

▲ It took Sequoyah 12 years to develop his Cherokee alphabet.

Now figuring all this out took him a long time. His wife, Sarah, was angry because he wasn't making his beautiful silver jewelry. His family was becoming poor. His friends told him he was being foolish; some thought the symbols were dangerous witchcraft. They tried to get Sequoyah to stop. This is what Sequoyah said:

> *If our people think I am making a fool of myself, you may tell our people that what I am doing will not make fools of them. They did not cause me to begin and they shall not cause me to give up.*

Sequoyah was a determined man who knew he had something important to accomplish. If his friends couldn't understand that, well, he was sorry, but he wouldn't give up. But some Cherokees were so frightened they destroyed all his work. He had to start again. It took him 12 years to develop his written Cherokee language.

When his system was finished, in 1821, he taught it to his daughter. She was six. Then he invited his friends to visit. He sent his daughter across a field, beyond shouting distance. Then he asked a visitor to say some words—any words—and he made marks on a slate. The visitor took the slate to the child: she said the words!

▲ When they saw the benefits of a written language, most Cherokees learned to read.

▲ The front page of the first edition of the *Cherokee Phoenix*, published February 21, 1828

The giant redwood trees, called sequoias, and Sequoia National Park, in California, are named for Sequoyah, the Cherokee who devised a written language.

The Indians tried it over and over again. Each time the child said the exact words.

Could it be trickery? Or witchcraft? Some Cherokees were still fearful. Sequoyah taught his nephew and other children. Try as they might, the visitors could never fool the children.

Now people were convinced. Sequoyah's wife was proud of him. The chiefs wanted to write the speeches of the great leaders—and Sequoyah did that. Then they learned they could "speak at a distance," by writing letters. They called the letters "talking leaves." Soon the Cherokees were printing a newspaper.

The problem with the Indians, said many white men and women, was that they were "savages" and "uncivilized." By that they meant that the Indians did not do and think as the white people did. But the Cherokees confounded the whites. Many of them did live as the whites did. Some Cherokees married white people. Some combined the two ways of life. They cleared the land, built big farms, planted apple and peach orchards, raised cattle and hogs, and lived in beautiful plantation homes. Some lived in European-style houses. Many owned slaves. Missionaries moved into Cherokee territory and converted some of the Indians to Christianity. They built schools. The Cherokees formed a government, wrote a constitution, and built a capital city with broad avenues and solid buildings. They became very prosperous. But the wealthier the Cherokees became, the more anxious other people were to have their land.

That Cherokee land stretched across the mist-covered southern Appalachian Mountains in a semicircle that reached from Kentucky to Alabama. Mostly the Indians built their farms and villages in the mountain foothills, where the land was fertile and the creeks brought abundant water. The immigrants who were pouring into the country from Scotland and Ireland and Germany wanted that same fertile land.

After all, that was why they had come to the New World. They had been told there was land enough for everyone. But the land in the East was all taken. They would have to go to the frontier if they wanted land.

That was when they discovered a problem: most of that frontier belonged to the Indians. "Why should the Indians have so much?" they asked. "Isn't there enough land for everyone?"

So they pushed west. Some of them put up their cabins on Indian land. Many wanted to live peacefully with the Indians. Some didn't. In Europe they had read that the Indians were ruthless savages. Many believed that. A few hated Indians just because they were different. Some attacked and killed Indians. The Cherokees didn't know which white people were friendly and which ones weren't. They just knew their land and lives were being threatened, so they went on raids and killed white people and burned their cabins and farms. The settlers didn't know which Indians could be trusted and which ones were killers, so they went on raids and killed Indians and burned their homes and fields. Life on the frontier was terrifying— and very dangerous.

Slavery seems to have been part of Cherokee ways as far back as anyone could remember. At first the slaves came from enemy tribes, and then a few slaves were whites; gradually, more and more of them were blacks.

The Cherokees formed a government, represented by the Seal of the Cherokee Nation. John Ross, pictured here, was an important Cherokee leader who resisted efforts to resettle his people. ▼

▲ Not only Cherokees, but also many other Native Americans, including these Mandan villagers, were killed by smallpox and other diseases to which they had no immunity.

Many settlers died, but mostly it was the Indians who were losing out. The white people's diseases, weapons, and numbers were too much to withstand. Anyone could see that the tribes were being destroyed. Some leaders, like George Washington and James Madison, tried to find ways to protect the Indians. It wasn't easy to do. Jedidiah Morse (who wrote the first American geography book) said that all Indians should live west of the Mississippi. Most white Americans—including Thomas Jefferson and Andrew Jackson—agreed. They all thought the Indians would be safe there and could live in peace. (They couldn't see into the future and know that settlers would take that western land, too.)

The Cherokees didn't want to move. They loved their land.

Congress passed an Indian Removal Act (in 1830). That law made it legal for the president to move the tribes west. President Jackson was eager to do so. In his seventh Annual Message to Congress, he said that the Indians would be moved to reserved lands west of the Mississippi River. "The pledge of the United States has been given by Congress that the country destined for the residence of this people shall be forever 'secured and guaranteed to them.'"

Meanwhile, gold was discovered on Cherokee land in Georgia, and gold hunters came by the thousands. They brought their guns with them. The Cherokees had no choice. Even though they had their own nation and were governing themselves, they had to go.

The Georgia government divided up the Cherokee land. They held a lottery and gave the land to white settlers. Soldiers helped those settlers move into beautiful Cherokee homes. They took the Cherokee farms and orchards. President Jackson said there was nothing he could do about it. The truth was, he didn't want to do anything about it.

A Time to Weep

It was called the "Trail of Tears." And it was a trail, a long trail west, that people were forced to walk. As they went they wept, because they didn't want to go. They didn't want to leave their homes, their farms, their hunting grounds, the land of their fathers and mothers.

The people who wept were Native Americans. They were being forced to move by white soldiers with guns, and by a president, Andrew Jackson, who was famous as an Indian fighter.

One group was stubborn. It was the Cherokees, and they refused to move west. They refused to give up their land. They appealed to the government. Two congressmen, Henry Clay and Daniel Webster, said the Indians were right: their land was their land and no one else's. In 1832 Clay ran for president against Andrew Jackson (who was seeking a second term). The Cherokees prayed that Clay would win—everyone seemed to think he would—but he didn't. Jackson was popular. He was a man of the people, a man of the frontier, in many ways a good president. Most U.S. citizens agreed that the Indians should move west. They approved of Jackson's Indian policy. But sometimes the majority is not right.

The case of the Cherokees was argued before the Supreme Court. Court cases are named for those who are on opposite sides in the conflict. This case was called *Worcester v. Georgia*. The *v* is for *versus*,

The U.S. military forced the Cherokee Indians from their homes in 1838. Thousands died on the westward journey along the Trail of Tears. ▼

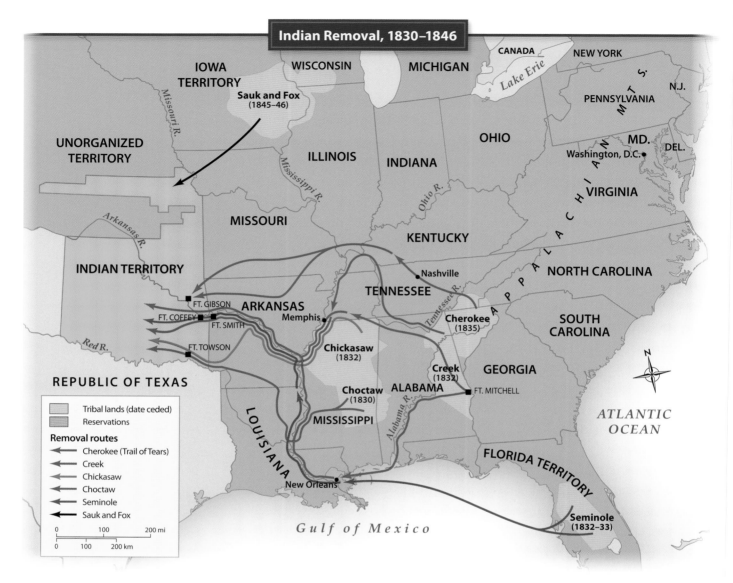

Indian Removal, 1830–1846

CANADA
NEW YORK
IOWA TERRITORY
WISCONSIN
MICHIGAN
Lake Erie
Sauk and Fox (1845–46)
PENNSYLVANIA
N.J.
UNORGANIZED TERRITORY
ILLINOIS
INDIANA
OHIO
MD.
DEL.
Washington, D.C.
Missouri R.
Mississippi R.
Ohio R.
VIRGINIA
Arkansas R.
MISSOURI
KENTUCKY
INDIAN TERRITORY
NORTH CAROLINA
Nashville
FT. GIBSON
ARKANSAS
TENNESSEE
Tennessee R.
FT. COFFEY
FT. SMITH
Memphis
Cherokee (1835)
SOUTH CAROLINA
Red R.
FT. TOWSON
Chickasaw (1832)
Creek (1832)
GEORGIA
REPUBLIC OF TEXAS
Choctaw (1830)
ALABAMA
FT. MITCHELL
ATLANTIC OCEAN
LOUISIANA
MISSISSIPPI
Alabama R.
New Orleans
FLORIDA TERRITORY
Gulf of Mexico
Seminole (1832–33)

Legend:
- Tribal lands (date ceded)
- Reservations

Removal routes
- Cherokee (Trail of Tears)
- Creek
- Chickasaw
- Choctaw
- Seminole
- Sauk and Fox

0   100   200 mi
0 100 200 km

▲ Thousands of Native Americans were forced from their homes in the Southeast and Northwest. They were sent to reservations in what is now Oklahoma.

which is Latin and means "against," or "opposed to." It was Georgia (then the largest of the 27 states) against Worcester.

Worcester (say WUSS-ter) was a man named Samuel Worcester. He was a Congregational minister, a missionary, who had come to the Indian territory to teach school and to preach Christian doctrine.

Georgia passed a law saying all white men in the Indian portion of the state needed to be licensed. The law was really meant to get rid of the preachers who were taking the side of the Cherokees. No one would give Sam Worcester a license.

Worcester was arrested—twice. In order to stay out of jail, he moved to nearby North Carolina and continued his work from there. His wife and children stayed in Georgia. Then his baby died. When he came home to be with his wife Worcester was arrested again. He was tried, found guilty, and sentenced to four years in prison at hard labor. He appealed his case to the Supreme Court.

The old man who was chief justice of the Supreme Court could remember British times and the Indian treaties of the old days. He was a man with a mind as straight as an Indian's arrow. Do you know his name? (Hint: he was Thomas Jefferson's cousin.) The great chief justice wrote a famous opinion in *Worcester v. Georgia*. (A justice's written words are called an *opinion*.) That opinion is still read and cited as a statement of fairness on human rights.

It went beyond the case of Samuel Worcester. The court ruled on the issue of Indian ownership of their own land and their right to govern themselves. Great Britain, said the chief justice,

> *considered [the Indians] as nations capable of maintaining the relations of peace and war; of governing themselves…and she made treaties with them, the obligation of which she acknowledged.*

Falling Trees—and Hills Bare of Bear

Frenchman François André Michaux (FRON-swah ON-dray me-SHO) spent years in America studying its trees and flowers. He is known as the "father of American forestry." Michaux was horrified by the waste of oak, hemlock, and cypress. Homes and factories and steamboats and railroads were burning forests as fuel. Timber was scarce in the East, and so were native grasses; they had been destroyed by overgrazing.

Farmers had to send to England for clover and timothy grass seed to sow for their cattle to eat. A few people, like Michaux, worried about nature and the environment, but most Americans thought the land was endless and its resources endless, too. They weren't, of course. Before the end of the 18th century, just about all the original forest east of the Appalachian Mountains had been cut and burned.

In 1800, Daniel Boone returned to Kentucky (he'd been away for 20 years) and was depressed by what he found. When he had lived there, he said, "you could not have walked more than a mile in any direction without shooting a Buck or a Bear. Thousands of Buffalo roamed the Kentucky hills and land that looked as if it never would become poor. But when I [returned]…a few signs only of Bear were to be seen. As to Deer I saw none."

Settlers in Savannah, Georgia, cut down many trees for lumber. ▼

Now here is the important part:

The Cherokee nation, then, is a distinct community, occupying its own territory…in which the laws of Georgia can have no force, and which the citizens of Georgia have no right to enter, but with the assent of the Cherokees themselves.

The most famous of all chief justices (yes, it was John Marshall) had a whole lot more to say, but you get the idea. The Cherokees had won the right to their own land. (And to decide if Sam Worcester could teach and live on that land.) The Supreme Court said that *the Indians have a present right of possession.* In other words, it was unconstitutional to push the Indians from their land.

Only it didn't matter. The president—Andrew Jackson—refused to enforce the law. Our American system of checks and balances failed.

People in Georgia wanted Indian land. (I don't want to pick just on Georgia. The same thing happened in many other states.) So the Indians of the eastern woodlands went west. Some fought before they went. The Sauk and Fox in Illinois fought especially hard, but their cause was hopeless.

The Choctaws were first; they moved in 1831. Three years later the Chickasaws trudged west. The Creeks signed a treaty that said "they shall be free to go or stay, as they please." It didn't matter. In 1836 they were sent west—some with chains around their necks.

The Cherokees set out in 1838. They left their homes and walked west, against their wishes. They went from their lush, fertile mountain lands to a region beyond the Mississippi that few people wanted (at the time). They walked—the children, their parents, and the old people—on hot days and cold. They walked in rain and windstorm. Often there was not enough food; often there was no shelter. Always there was sadness, for one of every four of them died during the cruel march.

The government said the new land would be theirs forever. But when the white people moved west they forgot their promises to the Indians. They took their land again, and again, and again.

The Second Seminole War

The Indian Removal Act of 1830 stated that all Indians east of the Mississippi could be moved west to reserved Indian lands. When land-seeking settlers, called "homesteaders," had filled up the fine country in northern Florida, they began pushing their way south onto the land reserved for the Indians. Most whites said the Seminoles must move.

But then the Seminoles learned that the U.S. government intended that they move west and live with the White Stick Creeks. Remember, many of the Seminoles had been Red Sticks and viewed the White Sticks (who lived like white Americans) as their enemies. The Seminoles, led by Osceola, decided to resist.

Osceola and his men attacked plantations and ambushed soldiers. They wrecked the sugarcane industry. They crushed the American army troops sent to stop them.

As more lives were lost, Americans grew sick of the war. Osceola and his men were tired as well.

And Osceola had caught malaria.

Then one day, the Seminoles raised a white flag of truce. They wished to exchange prisoners. When the Seminoles arrived for the meeting, however, army troops overwhelmed them and captured Osceola. Osceola's capture under a white flag of truce outraged most American citizens. John Ross, a respected Cherokee peacemaker, wrote to the secretary of war protesting "this unprecedented violation of that sacred rule…of treating with all due respect those who…presented themselves under a flag of truce."

Osceola's malaria grew worse, and he died in prison. Most of the Seminoles who were left went west to the Indian territory. Some still refused to go. In 1842 the government gave up; about 300 Seminoles remained in Florida. In the end, no one won the Seminole War.

▲ Native American Seminole chief Osceola is seized at Fort Peyton, Florida, during a conference in October 1837.

◀ A band of Seminoles prepares to ambush approaching U.S. troops.

CHAPTER 23

Riding the Trail to Santa Fe

Americans were moving west. In 1821, Missouri became a state. In September of that year, William Becknell led four men west from Old Franklin, Missouri, "for the purpose of trading for horses and mules and catching wild animals of every description." Becknell and his companions had goods loaded onto mule backs. They planned to trade with Indians. They weren't having much luck when they met a group of Mexicans who urged them to go to Santa Fe. Mexico had just become independent of Spain; perhaps the new governor would let them into the territory.

Becknell reached Santa Fe in November, quickly sold everything he had for Spanish silver dollars, packed the coins in bulging rawhide bags, and was back in Missouri 48 days later. He brought a message from Governor Facundo Melagres of New Mexico. American traders were now welcome in Mexican territory, said the governor. That was all that merchants in the states had to hear. Their wagons were soon cutting deep ruts in a trail west. It was called the Santa Fe Trail.

Traders scout the vast wilderness ahead of them as they journey west. ▼

We are caraing on a smart Trade with St. tefee, wrote a Missouri merchant (and poor speller) in 1824. Becknell went back that same year. This time he piled $3,000 worth of trade goods into huge, heavy wagons. And he blazed a southern cutoff that avoided the steep mountain passes. It was a journey of more than 800 miles—through a long, waterless desert region—but, with water and food in his wagons, Becknell made it. He also made a 2,000 percent profit on his merchandise. When American merchants learned that, they began pouring into Santa Fe. Some New Mexicans—especially those who had been Americans but were now Mexican and liked the gracious, leisurely life—urged the governor to stop the trade. It was too late. There was no stopping the Americans.

Mostly it was men who traveled the Santa Fe Trail. They went in big caravans. They didn't plan to settle. They were going to get rich, or for adventure, or to see new lands. Some of them did all those things. Their heavy wagons were pulled by teams of mules or oxen and were filled with cotton cloth, tin cups, socks, mirrors, cutlery, ribbons, buttons, glassware, ink, hats, gloves, and silk shawls. They brought the food that they ate on the trail, and that included cattle, chickens, and hogs. They slept in tents, or in the open air, or under the wagons.

It was a tough journey from Missouri to New Mexico, and it took over a month. The traders faced blazing heat, fierce thunderstorms, maddening mosquito attacks, rattlesnakes, long thirsty stretches, and, sometimes, when they were invading Indian territory, ambush. But most of the traders were young and loved the adventure of it all.

Mexico had a freedom revolution in 1821. The Spanish government was kicked out and the country became independent. In 1824 Mexico adopted a constitution that made it a republic.

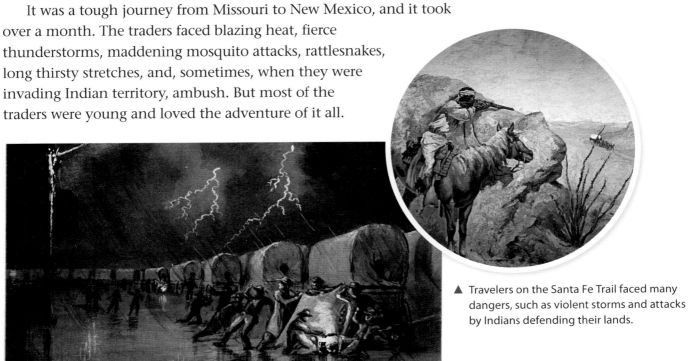

▲ Travelers on the Santa Fe Trail faced many dangers, such as violent storms and attacks by Indians defending their lands.

▲ Mountain men, as they were called, were tough and self-sufficient.

The caravans were filled with a mixture of characters. One letter writer told of a wagon train that had men of "seven distinct nations, each speaking his own native tongue." They included a talkative Frenchman who threw his hands around "with curious gesticulations," two "wanderers from Germany," two Polish exiles of "calm eccentricity," a Creek and a Chickasaw Indian, and Americans who "were mostly backwoodsmen, who could handle the rifle...."

Only a few American women had traveled the Santa Fe Trail in 1846 when Susan Magoffin headed west from Missouri. She was 18, newly married, pregnant, and very much in love. She was excited by the adventure. *Oh this is a life I would not exchange for a good deal!* she wrote from her tent on the trail. *There is such independence, so much free uncontaminated air.... I breathe free without that oppression and uneasiness felt in the gossiping circles of a settled home.*

Susan's husband was a wealthy trader in charge of a big wagon train. Susan traveled in a carriage with a servant. Still, it wasn't an easy trip for a proper American girl who wore long dresses buttoned to her neck. It was hot on those open plains. Magoffin was a good sport. She pitched in and fed the chickens, cooked meals, sewed, wrote in her diary, made notes on the wild flowers and animals, gathered berries, and settled arguments.

Whatever happened—and a lot did happen—she tried to keep her cheerful spirit. When the rains came and her bed was an island in the tent, she pretended it was a boat. When thunder and lightning raged and the tent collapsed, she made the best of it.

A Mournful Memory

For the white settlers, the journey west held excitement and promise. They believed they were the front line of a new nation (and they were). But it was an old world to the Native Americans, and they were losing it (and they soon knew that). Here are words, spoken in 1854, by the great Chief Seattle:

▲ Chief Seattle

There was a time when our people covered the land as the waves of a wind ruffled sea covers its shellpaved floor, but that time long since passed away with the greatness of tribes that are now but a mournful memory. I will not dwell on, nor mourn over, our untimely decay, nor reproach my paleface brothers with hastening it, as we too may have been somewhat to blame.

When the carriage crashed down an embankment, Susan was hit on the head, knocked out, and almost killed. Somehow, she made the best of that, too.

When the Magoffins hit the trail, they took 14 wagons, 2 horses, 11 mules, and 200 oxen. Susan made the trip from Independence to Santa Fe several times; she died of yellow fever at age 27.

Susan Magoffin filled her diary with details, especially of people. The Indians and the Mexicans were fascinated with her and the clothes she wore.

> *A parcel of Indians are around the tent peeping in at me and expressing their opinions. It is a novel sight for them. These are the Pueblos or descendants of the original inhabitants—the principal cultivators of the soil—supplying the Mexican inhabitants with fruits, vegetables, etc.*

▲ On the trail west, Susan Shelby Magoffin wrote in her diary, "Oh, this is a life I would not exchange for a good deal!... There is such independence."

Albert Bierstadt's *Emigrants Crossing the Plains* (painted in 1867) ▼

When she finally reached Santa Fe, she wrote:

What a polite people these Mexicans are...this morning...a little market girl...came in and we had a long conversation on matters and things in general, and I found that though not more than six years old she is quite conversant in all things. On receiving her pay she bowed most politely, shook hands with a kind "adios" and... also a promise to return tomorrow.

While Susan Magoffin was traveling the Santa Fe Trail, her brother-in-law James Magoffin was on a secret mission for President James K. Polk. James Magoffin went into Santa Fe ahead of an American army and persuaded the New Mexican governor (who happened to be his brother-in-law) not to fight. Then Colonel Stephen Watts Kearny, of the U.S. Army, arrived and captured New Mexico without spilling any blood. New Mexico became U.S. territory. Some of the Spanish-speaking New Mexicans were furious. They felt they were being taken over by foreign invaders. And

they were. (They didn't seem to remember what *they* had done to the Indians.) But many New Mexicans were happy to be under U.S. rule.

U.S. control didn't change life a whole lot in Santa Fe. It did make things easier for the Santa Fe traders. They didn't have to fill out the long, tiresome papers the Mexican officials had demanded.

In 1866 (which was after the Civil War), trail traffic hit its peak. That year, 5,000 freight wagons headed west from Missouri. Stagecoaches were making regular runs on the trail, too. By then, railroad trains had already chugged into eastern Kansas. When their tracks reached New Mexico, in 1879, the Santa Fe Trail was history.

◄ Charles Russell, an American artist, chronicled the West in more than 2,000 paintings and sculptures.

The New Americans Are Called Immigrants

It is 1846 and a disease—a blight—has destroyed Ireland's potato crop. There is almost nothing to eat for most of the Irish. It is hard for us to imagine people starving to death, but that is happening in Ireland. It is called the Great Potato Famine. In addition, a "poor law" in Ireland is taxing small farmers much more than it taxes the rich. Between 1847 and 1854, 1.6 million Irish come to the United States.

Germany is having problems, too. New factories are putting people out of work, cities and villages are filled with poor people, German farmers aren't doing well, and a freedom revolution fails. Then a rumor spreads through Germany: America is going to close its doors. Immigrants will no longer be allowed. It is just a rumor—it isn't true—but it starts a panic. Many Germans pack their bags and hurry off to the land of freedom and opportunity.

In China there are few jobs. In America railroads need building. So, beginning in the late 1840s, boatloads of Chinese come, work on the railroads, and stay.

All these people are ambitious, or they wouldn't have made the big journey to the "New World." They are the kind of people who don't mind moving—and moving again once they arrive in America.

Between 1845 and 1860, more immigrants come to this country in proportion to the total population than at any other time in our history. (Be sure you understand: there will be a larger number of immigrants later, but there will also be a much larger total population.) They come from Germany, China, Ireland, India, Norway, Sweden, Finland, Poland, Russia, Italy, Greece, Ethiopia, Morocco, Japan, and Turkey.

Have you ever heard of the Isle of Man? It is near England. People from the Isle of Man are called "Manx." Manx come to the United States. Most of the immigrants come from northern Europe, but wherever there is a nation, there is usually someone who sets out for America.

Rich, successful people don't leave their homelands. Why should they? The people who come to America are mostly poor, or troubled, or persecuted, or kidnapped, or adventuresome. Some of them stay in the East, where the ships leave them, but many travel on—to the West. In America, those rag-tag, adventuresome people will show the world the power of opportunity.

Chinese immigrants arrive in San Francisco. ▼

Pioneers: Taking the Trail West

Their ancestors had hugged parents and grandparents, wiped away their tears, and set out for a New World.

Now another generation of men, women, and children was heading out toward a little-known world. They, too, were leaving parents and grandparents—often never to see them again. They were heading west. For some it would be a great adventure; some would not live to finish the journey. They were going for the reasons that usually make people move: because they wanted a better life for themselves and their children, or because they were adventurous or restless.

They went in trim, wooden-wheeled wagons pulled by oxen or mules. The wagons were called "schooners," named after the fast two-masted ships that sailed out of New England's ports. These were prairie

In the 19th century, wave after wave of pioneers moved west, seeking land. ▶

◄ Mountain men tracking on the Great Plains

schooners, and they weren't fast. But, when the wind blew over the prairies and filled the canvas that roofed the wagons, they seemed almost to be sailing across the waves of prairie grass.

They called themselves "emigrants" because they were leaving the United States. The pioneers (for that is what we call them now) were going west to places they had heard about from wandering mountain men, or from traders, or from newspaper articles (many of which were written by people who had never left home).

They went due west. They were heading for foreign lands—Mexican California, or the territory of Oregon. (Oregon was claimed by England and the United States.)

It was a depression that got many of them started. A depression is a time of economic hardship when money seems to disappear and jobs do, too. In 1837, the United States entered a terrible depression. In New York and Philadelphia and Baltimore, thousands had no jobs. Banks closed and people lost their savings. The price of corn and wheat fell below the cost of growing it. Many farmers who had borrowed money to buy farming equipment and seeds couldn't pay back the loans, so they lost their farms.

Mountain Men

Some people like danger and adventure, some like to be free of civilization, and some like to live by their wits. It was those special people who headed west. One group was known as the "mountain men." They headed into the unexplored West—to the Rocky Mountains and beyond—to trap beaver for the fur market. Instead of buying furs from the Indians, as most American fur traders did, they lived as the Indians lived and trapped and hunted furs themselves. They lived with grizzly bears, rattlesnakes, mountain lions, blizzards, floods, and drought. They wore their hair long and wore rough buckskin clothes. The mountain men and the Indians were sometimes the best of friends. Often they were mortal enemies.

It is a 2,000-mile walk, over plains and mountains, from Missouri to Oregon. The pioneers set out in early spring and, if they make it on schedule, arrive before the winter snows.

Many families buried loved ones along the trail. ▼

What could they do? They could sell whatever they had left and use the money to head west (where land was free and fertile and opportunity seemed to be waiting). And, in 1843, that was just what some people began to do. They went west on the Oregon Trail.

Many of them never made it. They weren't prepared for the hard, hard journey: for rain that soaked through the canvas cover of the prairie schooner, for biting cold and burning heat, for hunger and accidents and disease. They brought the disease with them from the East. It was called "cholera" (KOL-er-uh), and it had come from Europe with the immigrants. It went west, as they did, and it was a killer. The trails became lined with graves; mothers and fathers buried their children—sometimes children buried their parents.

But they began the trip with optimism; they were looking for adventure.

Wagon ruts lead toward Chimney Rock in Nebraska. ▼

▲ Eager pioneers on the Oregon Trail

Most were young—many of the mothers and fathers were still teenagers—and they added children as they went west. One in five of the women is said to have been pregnant on some part of the journey. Their babies were born in the hard-floored schooners, or in tents, or in the out-of-doors. Their children would remember the fun and the freedom of the trip. Martha Morrison went west to the Oregon Territory in 1844, when she was 13.

> We did not know the dangers we were going through. The idea of my father was to get on the coast: no other place suited him, and he went right ahead until he got there…. We went down the river Deschutes in an open canoe, including all the children; and when we got down there was no way to get to the place where my father had determined to locate us, but to wade through the tremendous swamps. I knew some of the young men that were along laughed at us girls, my oldest sister and me, for holding up what dresses we had to keep from miring; but we did not think it was funny.

Deschutes, in French, means "falls" or "rapids." The Deschutes River was filled with rapids and was very dangerous.

Nine miles out of Independence the wagon trains cross the Missouri state line and are in land guaranteed to the Indians. (Later the Indian treaties will be forgotten, and this will be Kansas .) Thirty-two more miles and the road forks. A small hand-lettered sign points northwest and says, "Road to Oregon." Those who take the other branch are going southwest, on the Santa Fe Trail.

For most pioneers, the journey west began in St. Louis. (The pioneer family might have already traveled from the East Coast on the Erie Canal, and then overland, and then down the Ohio River and on across the Mississippi.) St. Louis, where the Missouri River meets the Mississippi, was now the gateway west. Pioneers who had money could take a steamboat from St. Louis, up the Missouri River, and head for a "jumping-off" town, like Independence, Missouri, or Council Bluffs, Iowa. There they could buy supplies and team up with other emigrants. Francis Parkman, who had come from Boston, described Independence in 1846:

The town was crowded. A multitude of shops had sprung up to furnish the emigrants and Santa Fe traders with necessaries for their journey; and there was an incessant hammering and banging from a dozen blacksmith's sheds, where the heavy wagons were being repaired, and the horses and oxen shod. The streets were thronged with men, horses, and mules. While I was in the town, a train of emigrant wagons from Illinois passed through, to join the camp on the prairie, and stopped in the principal street. A multitude of healthy children's faces were peeping out from under the covers of the wagons.

Usually, only the smallest children and the sick got to ride in the wagons. There was no room for anyone else. The wagons weren't as big as the heavy Conestogas the Pennsylvania Dutch used back East. The prairie schooners had to be lightweight so they wouldn't exhaust the oxen on the long pull ahead. Besides, there was so much to take that the schooners were always filled.

Pretend you are leaving home—perhaps forever. What will you take with you? You need food for your trip: flour, beans, bacon, coffee, dried fruit, sugar, salt, and vinegar. Sheep, goats, cows, and chickens will come along. You will need clothes. Your mother packs pants, shirts, dresses, and some cloth to make clothes for you children as you grow. Into the wagon go pots, pans, water kegs, teakettles, and chamberpots to use along the way, and axes, plows, and saws for the new life that is ahead of you. There are books: a Bible, schoolbooks, and storybooks. Your parents are musical: your father has brought his violin (he calls

Blacksmiths in "jumping-off" towns outfitted and repaired wagons and shod the horses, mules, and oxen. ▼

▲ Prairie schooners were designed to be lightweight to spare the oxen and make the trip as fast as possible.

it a fiddle); your mother has packed a harmonica. In the evening, around the campfire, they entertain the others. There is still more in the wagon: a favorite family portrait, a mirror, and a rocking chair. There are guns, medicines, and spare parts for wagon repairs. You have brought a hoop and some marbles; your sister has brought a doll; the baby, a rattle.

When the oxen are exhausted and lie dying by the trail, your parents will sell the plow, the axe, the books, and the teakettle, get two mules for them and be lucky. The cows will be gone—eaten when there was no game to be shot. The portrait and the rocking chair are gone also, left under a tree, perhaps for Indians to find. As you climb into the Rockies everything that adds unnecessary weight must be left behind—your lives may depend on that.

"Another Fine Cow Died This Afternoon"

Amelia Stewart was born in Boston. That was where she met Joel Knight, who had come from England and was studying to be a doctor. They got married and a few years later headed west, to Iowa. In 1853, after 16 years in Iowa, they packed their goods in a covered wagon and headed west again. By now they had seven children. Amelia Knight kept a diary of their five-month journey. The actual diary, in her handwriting, can be found at the University of Washington library. Here is some of it.

Wednesday, July 27th—Another fine cow died this afternoon. Came 15 miles today, and have camped at the boiling springs, a great curiosity. They bubble up out of the earth, boiling hot. I have only to pour water on my tea and it is made. There is no cold water in this part....

Monday, August 1st—Still in camp, have been washing all day, and all hands have had all the wild currants we could eat. They grow in great abundance along the river. There are three kinds, red, black, and yellow. This evening another of our best milk cows died. Cattle are dying off very fast all along the road. We are hardly ever out of sight of dead cattle on this side of Snake River. This cow was well and fat an hour before she died. Cut the second cheese today....

Friday, August 5th—We have just bid the beautiful Boise River, with her green timber and rich currants, farewell, and are now on our way to the ferry on the Snake River. Evening— traveled 18 miles today and have just reached Fort Boise and camped. Our turn will come to cross some time tomorrow. There is one small ferry boat running here, owned by the Hudson's Bay Company. Have to pay three dollars a wagon. Our worst trouble at these large rivers is swimming the stock over. Often after swimming half way over

the poor things will turn and come out again. At this place, however, there are Indians who swim the river from morning till night. There is many a drove of cattle that could not be got over without their help. By paying them a small sum, they will take a horse by the bridle or halter and swim over with him. The rest of the horses all follow and by driving and hurrahing to the cattle they will almost always follow the horses, sometimes they fail and turn back.

Monday, August 8th—We have to make a drive of 22 miles, without water today. Have our cans filled to drink. Here we left, unknowingly, our Lucy behind, not a soul had missed her until we had gone some miles, when we stopped a while to rest the cattle; just then another train drove up behind us, with Lucy. She was terribly frightened and said she was sitting under the bank of the river, when we started, busy watching some wagons cross, and did not know we were ready.... It was a lesson for all of us.

▲ Women washed, sewed, cooked, and cared for children as they traveled west.

Friday, August 12th—Lost one of our oxen. We were traveling slowly along, when he dropped dead in the yoke.… I could hardly help shedding tears, when we drove round this poor ox who had helped us along thus far, and had given us his very last step.

Thursday, August 18th—Commenced the ascent of the Blue Mountains. It is a lovely morning and all hands seem to be delighted with the prospect of being so near the timber again, after the weary months of travel on the dry, dusty sage plains, with nothing to relieve the eye. Just now the men are hallooing till their echo rings through the woods. Evening—Traveled 10 miles today and down steep hills, and have just camped on the banks of Grand Ronde River in a dense forest of pine timber—a most beautiful country.

Friday, August 19th—Quite cold morning, water frozen in the buckets. Traveled 13 miles, over very bad roads, without water. After looking in vain for water, we were about to give up as it was near night, when husband came across a company of friendly Cayuse Indians about to camp, who showed him where to find water, half mile down a steep mountain, and we have all camped together with plenty of pine timber all around us…we bought a few potatoes from an Indian, which will be a treat for our supper.

The last entry in Amelia's diary came on Saturday, September 17th; they were in Oregon.

A few days later, my eighth child was born. [*Never, in the diary, had she mentioned being pregnant.*] After this we picked up and ferried across the Columbia River, utilizing skiff, canoes, and flatboat to get across, taking three days to complete. Here husband traded two yoke of oxen for a half section of land with one-half acre planted to potatoes and a small log cabin and lean-to with no windows. This is the journey's end.

Wagon trains faced tremendous danger in crossing rivers. ▼

Getting There

The pioneers didn't go west alone. That would have been foolish. The journey was too dangerous. They traveled in groups of wagons, and they called them "wagon trains."

They met in Independence, or one of the other jumping-off towns. Sometimes they didn't even know each other when they began the trip. Before long, the wagon train seemed like a big family. Often the pioneers made plans to settle together. Just as the people who traveled on the *Mayflower* made a compact that gave them rules and leaders, so, too, the wagon communities wrote their own constitutions and had laws, courts, and officers.

Jesse Applegate's group did just that. He was one of the leaders of the first big wagon train to Oregon. It must have looked like

The trip west began by organizing a wagon train. Some wagon trains had as many as 1,000 pioneers and all their animals and belongings. ▼

an enormous parade—with wagons, cattle, chickens, dogs—and more than 1,000 pioneers. (About 600 of them were children.) It was a well-organized trip. Baptiste Charbonneau was a guide. Remember Charbonneau? He was Pompey, Sacajawea's baby, now grown up. Here is Jesse Applegate, in 1843, describing a day on the trail:

▲ Good guides and wagon masters were crucial for a successful journey.

> It is four a.m.; the sentinels on duty have discharged their rifles—the signal that the hours of sleep are over; and every wagon and tent is pouring forth its night tenants, and slow-kindling smokes begin to rise.... From six to seven o'clock is a busy time; breakfast is eaten, the tents struck, the wagons loaded, and the teams yoked. There are 60 wagons. They have been divided into 15 divisions or platoons of four wagons each. The women and children have taken their places [in the wagons]. The pilot stands ready to mount and lead the way. Ten or fifteen young men are ready to start on a buffalo hunt....
>
> It is on the stroke of seven that the clear notes of the trumpet sound in the front; the leading division of wagons moves out of the encampment and the rest fall into their places...the wagons form a line three quarters of a mile in length; some of the teamsters ride upon the front of their wagons, some walk beside their teams; scattered along the line companies of women and children are taking exercise on foot; they gather bouquets of rare and beautiful flowers that line the way.

The pioneers walk all day with a stop for lunch. As the sun is setting, the wagons halt and cluster together.

> It is not yet eight o'clock when the first watch is to be set; the evening meal is just over.... near the river a violin makes lively music, and some youths and maidens have improvised a dance; in another quarter a flute gives its mellow and melancholy notes to the still air.... It has been a prosperous day; more than twenty miles have been accomplished.

Wagons had to be rafted or ferried across deep rivers, which could take up a month or more of travel time. ▶

Twenty miles, a fine day! Usually a wagon train does well to make 15 miles a day. How about doing some arithmetic? It is about 2,000 miles from Missouri to the West Coast. If you walk 2,000 miles and you average 15 miles a day, how many days will it take to get to your destination? Now turn those days into months.

After you get that answer you can add a month for river crossings, wagon repairs, a snowstorm, a much-needed rest, and a day for the birth of a baby. If those are your only delays you will be very lucky.

A Woman Alone

Janette Riker was on her way to Oregon with her father and two brothers. They were in Montana—it was September 1849—and the men went off hunting. They never returned. Riker was on her own. She knew she couldn't cross the mountains alone, and winter was coming, so she took tools from the wagon and built a hut for herself. Then she put the wagon's stove inside, along with provisions, and blankets, and a load of firewood she had chopped. Because she had no meat, she killed an ox, butchered and salted it, and prepared for Montana's long, cold winter. It soon came. Wolves and mountain lions sniffed outside her shelter, but she didn't budge from the hut until a spring thaw flooded her out. Then she moved back into the wagon. Finally, Indians found her and were so astonished that she had survived—on her own—that they took her west, where she wanted to go.

▲ Wolves were just one hazard Janette Riker faced during the long, cold winter.

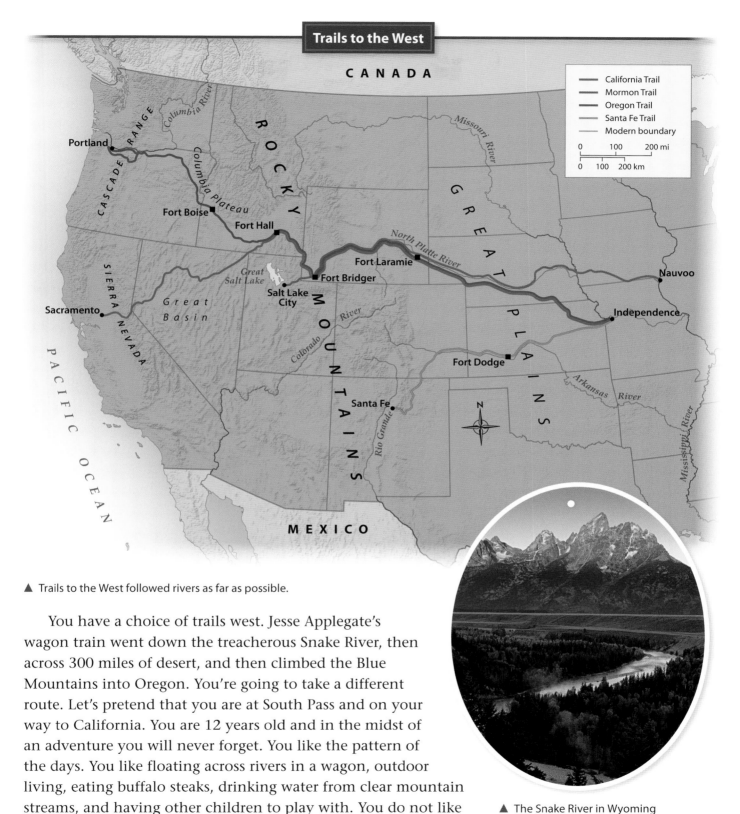

Trails to the West

CANADA

Legend:
- California Trail
- Mormon Trail
- Oregon Trail
- Santa Fe Trail
- Modern boundary

0   100   200 mi
0 100 200 km

Portland

CASCADE RANGE

Columbia River

Columbia Plateau

ROCKY

Fort Boise

Fort Hall

SIERRA NEVADA

Great Salt Lake

Fort Bridger

Fort Laramie

North Platte River

GREAT

Missouri River

Nauvoo

Sacramento

Great Basin

Salt Lake City

MOUNTAINS

Colorado River

Independence

PLAINS

Fort Dodge

Arkansas River

PACIFIC OCEAN

Santa Fe

Rio Grande

N

Mississippi River

MEXICO

▲ Trails to the West followed rivers as far as possible.

You have a choice of trails west. Jesse Applegate's wagon train went down the treacherous Snake River, then across 300 miles of desert, and then climbed the Blue Mountains into Oregon. You're going to take a different route. Let's pretend that you are at South Pass and on your way to California. You are 12 years old and in the midst of an adventure you will never forget. You like the pattern of the days. You like floating across rivers in a wagon, outdoor living, eating buffalo steaks, drinking water from clear mountain streams, and having other children to play with. You do not like

▲ The Snake River in Wyoming

▲ Windstorms could damage a covered wagon and spook horses, mules, or oxen.

the mosquitoes, the pounding rainstorms, buffalo hump soup, the day there is no water to drink, the sadness when a horse stumbles and your best friend's father is killed. But, all in all, it has been a good trip—so far.

At South Pass you are halfway to California; there is excitement in the wagon train. The air is clear and the climb is gradual. The pass is like a roadway between mountains. At your feet are yellow violets, purple larkspur, and a few stalks of that red flower called Indian paintbrush. The birds here are as colorful as the wildflowers: you spot mountain bluebirds and yellow tanagers. High overhead a bald eagle circles. It is August, but you can see snow and ice on top of the mountains. You don't realize how high above sea level you are. You also don't realize what is ahead of you. Your parents don't either.

The pass is full of game: pronghorn, elk, bison, and bighorn sheep with great curving horns. Your father kills an elk and everyone celebrates and feasts around the campfire.

Pioneer men hunted for food to feed their families during the journey. ▶

▲ In William Tylee Ranney's *Advice on the Prairie,* painted in 1853, a mountain man advises a group of travelers about what to expect as their wagon train proceeds west.

You come down from the Rockies in high spirits. The Utah desert discourages you a bit, but the Humboldt River with its grassy banks cheers you again.

Soon the Humboldt turns foul. People and animals who drink it become sick. Then the river ends. Just plain ends. There is nothing but desert and burning sun. No one has ever heard of a river just ending. The Humboldt does.

Now there are 65 miles to walk with no water at all. Sixty-five miles littered with skeletons of mules, oxen, and people.

Do you wish you hadn't come? Some people go crazy—really crazy; they lose their minds under the beating sun of the desert.

▲ The skeletons of horses, cows, mules, oxen, and sometimes people littered the trails west.

The California Trail follows the Humboldt River for about 350 miles— much of it pleasant, with water, grass, and game for food. Then the Humboldt sinks beneath the desert in an area called the Humboldt Sink. From there to the Truckee River there is no water. In 1848 pioneers found another route to California. It went along the Carson River to Lake Tahoe and was a bit easier than the Truckee Route, 25 miles to the north.

Mount Whitney, at 14,505 feet above sea level, is part of the Sierra Nevada, a rugged, craggy range. It is just 84 miles from Death Valley, the lowest point in the United States, at 282 feet below sea level. Wagon trains headed for California had to cross either the Sierra Nevada or Death Valley. ▼

▲ Death Valley is the hottest, driest, lowest place in North America, with temperatures as high as 134°F and an average of just two inches of rain per year.

It isn't over when you reach the Truckee River. The mountains ahead will make the Rockies seem easy, even though they are not as tall. The Sierra Nevada are real rocky mountains. Made of granite they are, and, when the snows come, almost impossible to climb.

Of course, you can avoid them. You can go down to Death Valley. But I wouldn't suggest that.

Religious pioneers make their way on the trail to the Great Salt Lake of Utah. ▼

In 1844 the first wagons made it all the way—pulled up one side of the steep Sierra Nevadas with ropes and pulleys and let down on the other side the same way. After that the pioneers started flowing west, like a river.

In 1845, 3,000 pioneers traveled west on the Oregon and California trails. During the following two years, more than 5,000 religious pioneers left the United States and headed for the valley of the Great Salt Lake. They set up communities in a land they called Deseret. It was soon to be known by its Indian name: *Utah*.

Remember how the Pilgrims came to America so they could practice their religion in peace? Well, 200 years later, other religious pioneers had to leave the United States for the very same reason.

Latter-day Saints

Like the Pilgrims and Puritans, they called themselves "saints." Like the early Quakers, they were mostly poor folk. Like those other believers, they were willing to suffer persecution for beliefs that differed from those of the mainstream churches. They were Mormons, members of the Church of Jesus Christ of Latter-day Saints.

Theirs was a new religion, a made-in-America religion, a Bible-based religion founded by Vermont-born Joseph Smith, who had a vision of "two personages [God and Jesus], whose brightness and glory defy all description." Smith said he was led by an angel to find a holy book, the Book of Mormon, engraved on golden tablets. It told the story of an ancient Hebrew tribe that came to America in long-ago times and to whom Jesus had appeared.

Smith, who was raised in Palmyra, New York, founded his religion in 1830 with six followers; within a few years there were thousands of Mormons. That name, *Mormon*, was not one they chose for themselves. Just as the words *Puritan* and *Quaker* had been chosen by others, so, too, with Mormon. The name of their church was too long for most people to bother saying. "Mormons," after their holy book, was an easy label. After a while those who saw themselves as saints learned to accept it.

The Mormons were determined to follow their religion. They formed a tight community, a church-state where they shared their goods, worked hard, and listened to strong leaders. There were those who tried to stop them.

Why would people attack devoted churchgoers? Some people may have been jealous of the success of the Mormons, and some people fear those who seem different. The early Mormons practiced *polygamy* (puh-LIG-uh-mee). Polygamists have more than one wife. Founder Joseph Smith had a whole lot of wives. Polygamy upset many non-Mormons, who thought it morally wrong. (There were more women than men among the early Mormons. Polygamy may have solved

About 5 percent of Mormon men and 12 percent of Mormon women lived in plural families. The Church of Jesus Christ of Latter-day Saints has not sanctioned polygamous marriages since 1890.

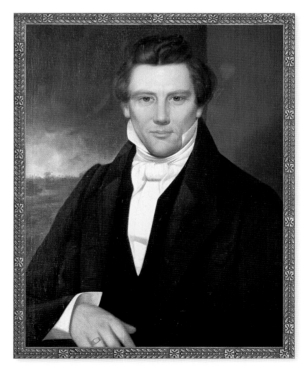

▲ Founder of the Church of Jesus Christ of Latter-day Saints, Joseph Smith

After Joseph Smith's murder, Brigham Young (below) led the Mormons to Utah. ▼

▲ Mormon prophet Joseph Smith was in jail in Carthage, Illinois, when an anti-Mormon mob stormed the place in June 1844. He and his brother, Hyrum, were shot and killed.

that problem.) Mormons tried to convert others to their religion. That made some people very angry, especially those whose children got converted.

The First Amendment to the Constitution forbids religious persecution. That didn't stop some people. Mormons were persecuted. First they moved to Ohio, then to Missouri, and then to Illinois. In Illinois they built a beautiful city—called Nauvoo—with a temple and a university. It was the largest city in Illinois, larger than Chicago. But even in Nauvoo, the Mormons weren't safe from the religious bigots: mobs attacked, destroyed much of the city, and murdered Joseph Smith.

Brigham Young, a Mormon apostle, was campaigning for Smith for president when he heard. He rushed back to Nauvoo and became the new Mormon leader. Young was a strong, inspiring man who had two dozen wives and 58 children.

The next two years were violent. There were more attacks on these religious believers, but now the Mormons fought back with revenge raids. Finally, Young decided to lead his people west, out of the United States, to land held by Mexico. It was land where Mormons could work hard, be productive, and be left alone to follow their beliefs (land only the mountain men and the Indians knew).

▲ Mormon pioneers on the trek to Utah in 1856

In 1845, Young sent a few Mormons west to check out the Great Salt Lake. They liked what they saw. The next winter was shiveringly cold, much colder than usual, and the mighty Mississippi froze into a solid roadway. Brigham Young and some other Mormons crossed the great river on foot and on horseback. They left Nauvoo behind; it was a city of ghostly memories. By the summer of 1847, a long ribbon of Mormon wagon trains was moving across the dusty trail west.

It wasn't easy crossing the treeless plains or climbing into the mountains. Many died doing it. Many Mormons died. But Brigham Young planned well. His may have been the best organized of all the western treks. Certainly it was the largest. Young and his pioneers went ahead to create stopping places, build shelters, plant crops, mark the trail, prepare for the wagon trains.

The land the Mormons chose— in what is now Utah—is known to geographers as the Great Basin: it is a plateau lying between the Wasatch and Sierra Nevada ranges. No other pioneers seemed to want it.

Brigham Young urged poor Europeans to come to America and become Mormons. In 1856, 2,500 of them walked the 1,300 miles from Iowa City to Utah pulling their possessions in handcarts (with no help from mules or oxen). Other Mormons, before and after, came in wagons.

And so they reached the Great Salt Lake and built their religious kingdom and made desert land bloom. When Brigham Young died in 1877, there were 140,000 Mormons living in the Utah territory in 325 towns. They had built railroads, stores, factories, and irrigation projects. Mormon troubles weren't over, but they soon would be. Mormons would give up polygamy, the Utah territory would become a state, and Mormons would become an accepted part of the pluralism—the many-sidedness—that makes our country strong and interesting.

But before that, just as the Mormons were beginning to build their community beside the Great Salt Lake, their settlement became very important. Suddenly a stream of pioneers was heading west. They were people on their way to Oregon and California. Many would have starved and died if Mormons hadn't supplied food, horses, and a place to rest. In 1849, the tide of pioneers turned into a flood. That year 55,000 people followed the Overland Trail, most of them taking the cutoff that led southwest, to California. They were very anxious to get to California. (You'll find one reason for that in the next chapter; the big reason comes later.)

Salt Lake City, headquarters of the Latter-day Saints, in 1850 ▼

Coast-to-Coast Destiny

President James K. Polk wanted California and Oregon, and so did most other Americans. The land was enticing, and there was something that convinced people that it was right to take it. It was an idea called *Manifest Destiny*. Those highfalutin' words were first used by a newspaper reporter. He said it was the Manifest Destiny of the United States to fill the land from coast to coast. Polk believed that America had the right and duty to spread democracy across the continent. Most Americans agreed with him. That phrase, Manifest Destiny, was soon on most people's tongues.

Both Great Britain and the United States claimed Oregon. In 1846, President Polk signed a treaty with England: the Oregon Treaty. The two nations agreed to split the Oregon territory on the 49th parallel. That was the 49th line of latitude, counting up from the equator. England got the land north of the parallel; the United States, the land to the south. (That U.S. land today is Oregon, Washington, Idaho, and parts of Montana and Wyoming. The English land is western Canada.)

California belonged to Mexico. People in the United States didn't know much about the West Coast. Then Richard Henry Dana, who had been to California on a sailing ship, wrote about his adventures

Manifest Destiny

The phrase *Manifest Destiny* was first used by John L. O'Sullivan in an article published in 1845 in the *United States Magazine and Democratic Review*. O'Sullivan said it was "our Manifest Destiny to overspread the continent allotted by Providence for the free development of our yearly multiplying millions." No one wanted to admit that greed might have something to do with the drive to take more land. Manifest Destiny made it sound like a noble thing to do. In this picture a goddess of progress, towing a telegraph wire, shepherds the settlers on their way west. The Indians, bison, and bear have been pushed off the western edge into extinction—which proved to be all too true.

▲ John Gast's *American Progress,* painted in 1872, expressed the spirit of Manifest Destiny that swept the country from the 1840s through the end of the century.

in a book called *Two Years Before the Mast*. It was published in 1840 and was good reading. President Polk and other Americans became excited about California.

Dana had been surprised by the Californians, by their good manners and their fine clothes. They spoke Spanish, they were as elegant as old Spain, and they lived with the ease that seems to come naturally in a sunny climate.

> *Next to the love of dress, I was most struck with the fineness of the voices.… Every common ruffian-looking fellow…appeared to me to be speaking elegant Spanish. It was a pleasure, simply to listen to the sound of the language.… A common bullock-driver, on horseback, delivering a message, seemed to speak like an ambassador at a royal audience.*

The Californians didn't appear to have money, as people did in the East. Instead they used silver or cattle hides. *Certainly never saw… so much silver at one time, as during the week that we were at Monterey*, wrote Dana. *The hides they bring down dried and doubled, in clumsy ox-carts or upon mules' backs.* Sailors called the hides "California bank notes."

But what about the Native Americans? Dana made it clear that they had lost control of their land. How did it happen?

Indians had lived in California for thousands of years, cut off from the rest of the world. Then, after Magellan found a way to sail around South America, explorers and ships made occasional visits. Juan Cabrillo came, and so did Francis Drake. The explorers didn't stay, but they did leave their germs—and those germs killed many of the California natives. (We're not sure of the numbers. Perhaps half the native population died.)

In 1769 (about the time Tom Paine and Patrick Henry were stirring things up on the other side of the continent), the Spanish government sent a few priests and soldiers to California. Spain didn't really seem interested in the place, but it looked as if the Russians might be thinking about moving in, and Spain didn't like that idea.

The priests built Catholic missions. They were agricultural settlements—productive farms built around a church—where Indians were taught about Christianity and forced to do all the hard work of farming and building. The priests believed they were serving God by baptizing and teaching the Native Americans. They planned, they said, to give the missions to the Indians. But that never happened, mostly because the missions became very prosperous. For example, the Mission San Gabriel had 150,000 cattle, 20,000 horses, 40,000 sheep, orchards, a distillery, looms, and more.

Some of the Spanish settlers were convicts sent to California to get them out of Spain or Mexico. (The English did the same thing and sent many of their prisoners to their colonies.)

When Mexico won its independence from Spain in 1821, Mexicans became rulers of California. Spain no longer controlled the missions. The mission land, now quite valuable, was taken by Mexican Californians, who turned most of it into huge cattle ranches. The Native Americans became the workers on those ranches; they were like slaves. "The Indians," Dana wrote, "do all the hard work." But for the rancheros—the owners of the big ranches—life was more than special, it was extraordinary.

▲ On huge cattle ranches (many built on land taken from missions), the cattle weren't bred for beef; until railroad cars were refrigerated, meat could not be sent long distances. The cattle were sold for their tallow, or fat (used to make candles), and for their hides, which were tanned for leather.

The Mission San Carlos Borromeo de Carmelo, in Carmel, California ▼

Historians estimate that there were 300,000 to 1 million Native Americans in California before contact with Europeans, living in 150 groups, each with its own language. By 1849, disease and war with settlers left the Indian population at about 150,000.

Since Mexico was having problems at home (it had 30 presidents in its first 50 years of independence), California was left on its own, which was the way most Spanish-speaking Californians wanted it. There weren't many of them—perhaps 6,000 by 1840. No one knows how many Indians there were, but it was a lot more than that. Of the others—Europeans (including Russians), Americans, and Asians—there were about 400 in all.

One of the most interesting of the Europeans was a Swiss: John Augustus Sutter. He had become a Mexican citizen, acquired a huge land grant, and built a fort-plantation. It was surrounded by a protective adobe wall. Like many feudal towns, Sutter's fort was a little kingdom where crops were grown, clothing made, horses raised, and soldiers trained. Sutter was unusually generous to visitors, to the

What John L. O'Sullivan did in print for manifest destiny, Emanuel Leutze did on canvas with this picture, called *Westward the Course of Empire Takes Its Way*. The 20-foot by 30-foot mural (which hangs in the House of Representatives' wing of the U.S. Capitol) shows rugged-looking mountain men guiding pioneer families on their journey west. ▼

Indians who worked for him, to almost everyone. If you needed a meal, or a bed for the night, or some help or friendly advice—you could count on John Sutter. Many people did. (John Augustus Sutter's name was soon to be known all over the world. You'll find out why in a later chapter.)

Many people began coming overland to California from another country—the United States. Between 1841 and 1848, a few thousand Americans made it over the mountains to the California valleys. They were energetic people. But not everyone was happy to see them. "We find ourselves suddenly threatened by hordes of Yankee immigrants," the Mexican governor wrote. "They are cultivating farms, establishing vineyards, erecting mills, sawing up lumber, building workshops, and doing a thousand things that seem natural to them." Keep in mind that when they arrived in California, those Americans were foreigners in Mexican territory.

Frémont: Explorer, Scientist, Author

John Charles Frémont (FREE-mont) was part explorer and part serious scientist. Courageous, daring, and determined, he mapped large areas of the West and carefully collected scientific specimens. In 1842, Frémont headed west from Kansas City across the Great Plains to Colorado and Wyoming. On his next expedition (1843 to 1844), Frémont went over the Rockies and on to Oregon and California, traversing and mapping much of the far West.

When he returned from his expeditions, Frémont wrote about his adventures, with the help of his wife, Jessie. His books were filled with action and exciting images. The books became best-sellers. Promoters had been advertising Oregon, but hardly anything was known of California. Frémont changed that. He wrote of a romantic land with natural riches and lots of possibilities. And he noted the weakness of the Mexican forces that held the land. Soon many Americans, along with President Polk, wanted California as part of the nation.

John C. Frémont (His last name is French, pronounced fray-MON in France. Americans mostly say FREE-mont.) ▶

Polk's policies are called a second Monroe Doctrine. He wanted Europe's nations to stay away from North America. California's great harbors—especially San Francisco—were tempting. England, Russia, and Spain all wanted to have them.

The land they found was as nature had made it—spectacular. Near the coast, fields of yellow-orange poppies stretched farther than anyone could see. In the mountains, waterfalls dropped a third of a mile and more, and trees grew taller than a 20-story building (although no building had yet been built that high). Prickly pear, primrose, and yucca blossomed in the desert.

As I said, President Polk wanted California. And California, at the time, meant more than today's West Coast state. It meant the land controlled by Mexico that included all or parts of the future states of New Mexico, Arizona, Utah, Nevada, Colorado, and Wyoming, as well as California. President Polk sent a diplomat to Mexico City with an offer to buy that land. The Mexicans were insulted. They said they wouldn't sell and certainly not to the United States, not after what the United States had just done in Texas—which you'll read about soon.

The Lower Yellowstone Falls in Yellowstone National Park, Wyoming ▼

Texas: Tempting and Beautiful

Texas was tempting. All that land…land that seemed made just to grow cotton. That Texas land was part of Mexico and controlled by Spain. It had been so since the 16th century, when Spanish explorers searched for gold and seven fabled cities of Cíbola.

Those seven cities turned out to be imaginary. But the Spanish invaders carried some things with them that were real—although no one then could even imagine them. They were germs; germs that killed most of the Native American population. So, in the early 19th century, the vast land of Texas was almost empty of people. Perhaps 30,000 Indians lived there, and a few thousand Spanish Mexicans. (Thirty thousand may sound like a lot of people, but not in Texas.) The Spaniards had built missions in Texas where priests lived, farmed, and attempted to convert Indians to Christianity. Soldiers lived in *presidios*, which is the Spanish word for forts. The presidios protected the missions. Some Mexicans were ranchers and lived on *haciendas*, which were ranch plantations where cattle and crops were raised. Spanish-speaking cowboys were called *vaqueros*.

The name Texas comes from an Indian word, *texía*, for "friends" or "allies." It was the word a group of Indian tribes used to describe themselves. The Spanish turned it into *téjas* (TAY-huss), and the Anglos (English-speakers) said Texas.

Spanish-speaking cowboys called *vaqueros* lasso a runaway steer. ▼

Spain had hoped that some of its citizens would settle in Texas—as European settlers had settled in the United States—but not many did. There was no gold in Texas, and no political or religious freedom. In the Spanish colonies everyone was expected to be Catholic.

That didn't bother Stephen Austin. In 1821 he led some settlers to Texas from Missouri. The settlers said they would become good Mexican citizens and Catholics. That same year, Mexico rebelled against Spanish rule and became independent. Three years later, in 1824, the Mexicans approved a fine constitution and formed a republic. Unfortunately, there was no tradition of self-government in the Spanish colonies (as there had been in the English colonies).

The people weren't used to running things themselves. That made it easy for strong, ambitious people to take power, and soon a dictator named Antonio López de Santa Anna took over. Santa Anna ignored many of the freedoms the Constitution had promised.

Other people from the United States began settling in Texas. Some of them didn't want to be Mexican citizens. Some of them didn't want to become Catholics. They wanted schools and freedom of religion. They wanted to build towns and to run those towns themselves. Some brought slaves—which was against Mexican law. Some didn't want to share the land with Indians. Some even bragged about killing Indians.

Stephen Austin and his settlers didn't just barge into Texas. Austin's father, Moses, a Connecticut Yankee, had made a colonization agreement with the Spanish government shortly before he died. His son got the agreement renewed, so he thought he had a right to be there. By 1824, 300 settlers had joined him.

Stephen Austin wanted to encourage American settlers in Texas, so he got a law passed that allowed people to bring in slaves. ▶

▲ Texan defenders of the Alamo fight Mexican soldiers within the walls of the fortress. Davy Crockett, with his rifle above his head, died in the siege.

By 1830, there were more English-speaking Americans in Texas than Mexicans. Santa Anna said no more Americans would be allowed to settle in Texas. That didn't stop them. People from the States crossed the border illegally and settled in Mexican territory. They demanded the rights of the Mexican Constitution of 1824. The issues and conflicts were complicated. You can see there would soon be trouble.

Then in December of 1835, some Texas rebels attacked San Antonio.

"We went through the old adobe and picket houses of the Mexicans, using battering rams made of logs ten or twelve feet long.... How the women and children would yell when we knocked holes in the walls through which we passed," wrote one rebel. Other Texans occupied the garrisons of San Patricio and Goliad. The Mexicans were not about to sit back and do nothing. In 1836, Santa Anna marched toward Texas with a big army. He was determined to rout the *anglos* (the English-speaking Americans), some of whom ran back to the United States. But those who stayed gathered in the chapel of an old, walled San Antonio mission named the *Alamo*. They intended to fight. There weren't even 200 of them, but they included Davy Crockett, William Travis, and Jim Bowie.

Crockett had a rifle he called "Old Betsy." He said Old Betsy had killed 105 bears in one season, and maybe that was true. Crockett was a great storyteller. He said it was his storytelling ability, not his speechmaking skills, that got him elected when he decided to go into politics.

The thought of having to make a speech made my knees feel mighty weak, and set my heart to fluttering almost as bad as my first love-scrape. But as good luck would have it, those big candidates spoke nearly all day, and when they quit, the people were worn out with fatigue, which afforded me a good apology for not discussing the government. But I listened mighty close to them and was learning pretty fast about political matters. When they were all done, I got up and told some laughable story and quit. I found I was safe in those parts, and so I went home and I didn't go back again until after the election was over. But to cut this matter short, I was elected, doubling my competitor, and nine votes over.

Davy Crockett, in a frontiersman's buckskins, called his famous rifle "Old Betsy." ▼

Giving a campaign speech may have scared Davy Crockett, but once he got to the U.S. Congress he was fearless. He stood up and spoke out—even when he disagreed with the president, popular Andrew Jackson. When President Jackson sent the Cherokee Indians from their homes in Georgia to the Oklahoma territory, Davy Crockett thought it was wrong and said so. It didn't help the Indians, or Crockett. He lost his seat in Congress. But he kept, he said, "my conscience and my judgment."

Jim Bowie was a fearsome fighter who designed a wicked, razor-sharp knife that is still called by his name. Travis, Crockett, and Bowie and the others in the Alamo held out for 12 days. Supplies and ammunition ran low. "I shall never surrender or retreat... victory or death," Travis declared. (A year before, at Goliad, 330 Americans had surrendered; they were all murdered.) Travis

◄ Sam Houston beat Santa Anna with an army half the size of the Mexican general's.

was not to be victorious. One soldier, a few women and children, and a slave lived to tell the story.

The remaining English-speaking settlers in Texas were furious. On March 2, 1836, four days before the Alamo fell, they decided to fight for independence. They were soon yelling, "Remember the Alamo!"

Their leader was Sam Houston. He had been born in Virginia but, when he was 13 years old, his parents moved to the frontier of Tennessee. At age 15 he was working in a store in Tennessee when he ran away from home. He became a Cherokee Indian—adopted into a tribe—and lived with the Indians for three years. Then he came back

1820

1821 Mexico wins independence from Spain; Stephen Austin begins bringing settlers into Mexican Texas.

1825

1824 Mexico adopts a republican constitution.

1829 Mexico bans slavery.

1830

1830 United States immigrants outnumber Mexicans in Texas; Mexico bans further Anglo American immigration.

1835

1833 Santa Anna becomes president of Mexico and takes on dictatorial powers.

1835 Texas Revolution begins.

1840

1836 Texans declare independence from Mexico; at the Alamo, rebels are defeated by Santa Anna's army; the Texan Army captures Santa Anna at San Jacinto, ending the war.

1845

1845 The U.S. Congress passes a bill authorizing the annexation of the Republic of Texas; Texas becomes the 28th state and a slave state.

1850

The flag of the Republic of Texas, the Lone Star Republic ▶

to the white settlements. These are some of the things he did: taught school, fought in Andrew Jackson's army, studied law, was elected to Congress, and became governor of Tennessee. But when his young wife left him he was in despair. He became an Indian again—this time for four years—and moved to Texas as an Indian trader.

Sam Houston and his followers decided to fight Santa Anna at San Jacinto, which is near the city now called Houston. It was April of 1836; the Texans were outnumbered, but they were smart. They waited until the siesta hour, which is a time after lunch when some Spaniards and Mexicans take a nap. It didn't take long—some say only 15 minutes—and Houston and his men captured Santa Anna and routed the Mexicans. They made Santa Anna sign a treaty that made Texas an independent nation. Sam Houston was elected president of the new nation: the republic of Texas. Texas had its own flag, with one lone star on it.

Houston wanted Texas to become part of the United States. There should have been no problem with that, except that some Texans wanted to have slaves. By this time, the United States was divided: there were slave states and free states, and they were equal in number. If Texas became a state, and a slave state, the South would have more votes in Congress than the North. That would create trouble. President Andrew Jackson had to say no to his old soldier friend Sam Houston. Texas stayed independent.

Finally, in December of 1845, while James K. Polk was president, Congress made Texas a state (the 28th state). Sam Houston was now a Texas senator.

By this time, slavery was becoming a hot issue. The abolitionists were trying to end slavery; the slave owners were trying to convince everyone that slavery was a good thing—they wanted the United States to become a slave nation. When they realized that wasn't going to happen, many Texans and other Southerners began saying that the South should go its own way and that the Southern

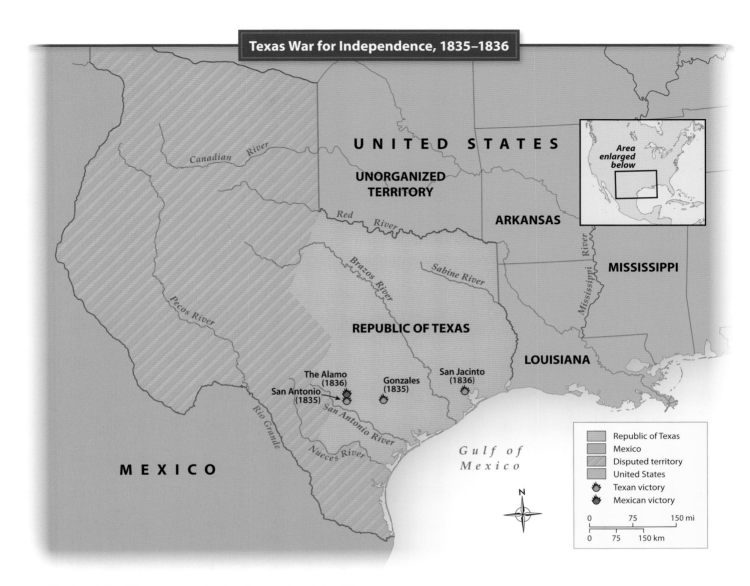

Texas War for Independence, 1835–1836

UNITED STATES

UNORGANIZED TERRITORY

ARKANSAS

MISSISSIPPI

Canadian River

Red River

Pecos River

Brazos River

Sabine River

Mississippi River

REPUBLIC OF TEXAS

LOUISIANA

The Alamo (1836)
San Antonio (1835)
Gonzales (1835)
San Jacinto (1836)

San Antonio River

Rio Grande

Nueces River

MEXICO

Gulf of Mexico

Area enlarged below

Legend:
- Republic of Texas
- Mexico
- Disputed territory
- United States
- Texan victory
- Mexican victory

0   75   150 mi
0   75   150 km

N

▲ The Republic of Texas was smaller than the modern state of Texas.

states should secede (suh-SEED) from the United States and become a separate nation—a nation built on slavery.

Sam Houston disagreed. He had worked hard to make Texas a part of the Union. He hated the idea of secession and he didn't like slavery. It took courage to say what he thought. Especially in 1859, which was when he was elected governor again. But when he refused to take an oath of loyalty to the Confederacy he was forced to resign. That was in 1861. But now it is 1846 and trouble is brewing on the Mexican border.

CHAPTER 29

Fighting Over a Border

The Texans thought their southern border went down to the Rio Grande river. Mexico said, "No, it doesn't." The U.S. said that the Mexicans owed a lot of money to American citizens and it was time to pay up. Things got tense. Both countries sent armies to the Texas border. Both those armies had hotheads.

President James K. Polk had already decided to declare war, when a few Mexicans killed a few Americans. It was May of 1846, and the Mexican War had begun.

The Mexican War began in May 1846. ▼

People in the United States had mixed feelings about the war. President Polk was eager to fight. So were many other people. Thousands rushed to volunteer. Some people thought the United States should take all of Mexico. Slave owners saw Mexico as a place to extend slavery. Some, who thought themselves patriots, said they wanted to spread the American way of life. It was that Manifest Destiny idea.

But not everyone agreed. Some Americans said the United States was acting like a bully, picking on a weak neighbor. It took courage to speak out against the war; it usually does. Frederick Douglass, a leading abolitionist, had courage. Douglass wrote:

> *In our judgment, those who have all along been loudly in favor of… the war, and heralding its bloody triumphs with apparent rapture… have succeeded in robbing Mexico of her territory.… We are not the people to rejoice; we ought rather blush and hang our heads for shame.*

The writer Henry David Thoreau refused to pay his taxes and went to jail. (He didn't want his tax money used to support a war.) Three church groups—Congregational, Quaker, and Unitarian—denounced the war. Walt Whitman, a journalist who would soon become a poet, wrote that "America knows how to crush, as well as how to expand." (He favored peaceful expansion.) From the war front there were soon reports of ransacked towns, drunken soldiers, and senseless killings—on both sides. (Wars are usually like that.) More than 9,000 soldiers deserted the army before the war was over.

Henry Clay, who had been a War Hawk in 1812, wrote, *This is no war of defense, but one of unnecessary and offensive aggression. It is Mexico that is defending her firesides…not we.* A gangly, long-legged, 38-year-old congressman named Abraham Lincoln stood up in Congress

An *abolitionist* works to end slavery.

"I am naturally antislavery," said Abraham Lincoln. "If slavery is not wrong, nothing is wrong." ▼

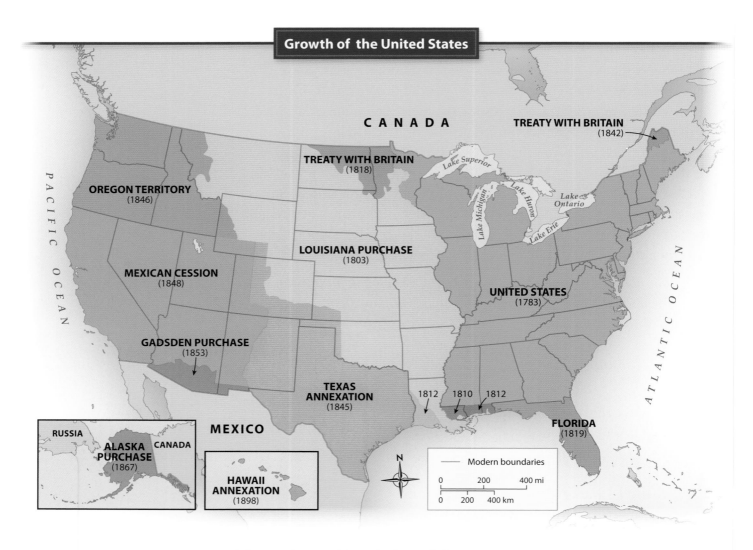

Growth of the United States

CANADA

TREATY WITH BRITAIN
(1842)

TREATY WITH BRITAIN
(1818)

Lake Superior

Lake Michigan *Lake Huron* *Lake Ontario* *Lake Erie*

OREGON TERRITORY
(1846)

MEXICAN CESSION
(1848)

LOUISIANA PURCHASE
(1803)

UNITED STATES
(1783)

GADSDEN PURCHASE
(1853)

TEXAS
ANNEXATION
(1845)

1812   1810   1812

FLORIDA
(1819)

MEXICO

RUSSIA

ALASKA
PURCHASE
(1867)   CANADA

HAWAII
ANNEXATION
(1898)

PACIFIC OCEAN

ATLANTIC OCEAN

N

Modern boundaries

0   200   400 mi
0   200   400 km

▲ By 1848 the United States had extended its territory across the continent
through purchase, annexation, treaty, and war. After the Mexican War, the
United States purchased the southern portions of Arizona and New Mexico
from Mexico and later acquired Alaska and Hawaii.

and attacked President Polk for starting an unnecessary war. *Allow the
president to invade a neighboring nation…whenever he may choose to…and
you allow him to make war at pleasure.* The House of Representatives
passed a resolution condemning Polk.

But in New York, Philadelphia, Indianapolis, and many other
places, the war was very popular. It was a war fought for territory,
not ideals. Many Americans, at the time, seemed to want it that

way. At parades and rallies, citizens cheered the war effort. American soldiers fought all the way to Mexico City, to "the halls of Montezuma." They fought Santa Anna—who was back in power—and they won the war.

Many of the soldiers who fought together in Mexico would soon be fighting against each other. (Some of their names are Robert E. Lee, T. J. "Stonewall" Jackson, Ulysses S. Grant, and George B. McClellan.) None of them realized it then, but the Mexican War was a training school for another war that was soon to come. (Ulysses S. Grant, at the time a young lieutenant, said the Mexican War was "one of the most unjust ever waged by a stronger against a weaker nation.")

General Winfield Scott, who was called "Old Fuss and Feathers" because he always looked splendid in his neat, elegant uniform, became a national hero. So did another general, "Old Rough and Ready" Zachary Taylor, whose uniform wasn't neat at all.

When the war was over, the Texas-Mexico border was set at the Rio Grande river. But the United States got more than that border settlement; under the terms of the Treaty of Guadalupe Hidalgo, signed in 1848, the United States received California—which at the time meant land that stretched from Texas to California and went as far as Wyoming.

▲ Zachary Taylor entered the U.S. Army in 1808, at the age of 24, and served for 39 years.

General Zachary Taylor won one battle after another and became a national hero. Taylor was a Whig. So was another soldier-hero, General Winfield Scott. President Polk, a Democrat, was not pleased with their acclaim. He knew that the last soldier-hero, Andrew Jackson, had been swept into the presidency. (Polk was right to worry; Taylor became president in 1849.)

There's Gold in Them Hills

It wasn't Cíbola, it was California—but it had gold! The gold the Spaniards, the French, and the English had all sought so desperately.

It had been there all along—shiny and pretty—right in California's mountain streams, where a carpenter named James Marshall found it without even looking for it. He was building a mill for John Sutter when, on January 24, 1848, he came across some heavy golden flakes. Right away, he thought he knew what they were, but he took them to his boss to make sure. Sutter tested them, then told Marshall to try to keep them a secret. It was too late for that. The workers at the mill already knew, and Sutter and Marshall did some bragging, too.

James Marshall's discovery of gold near Sutter's Fort led to the California Gold Rush. ▼

Nine days after Marshall's discovery the United States signed the Treaty of Guadalupe Hidalgo. That ended the war with Mexico and gave California to the United States. It took a little longer than that for people in the States and Mexico and the rest of the world to know about California's gold, and a bit of time for them to believe it wasn't a hoax—that it was really true. But that didn't take too long, either. Once they started believing, they just tossed aside whatever they were doing and headed for California.

Farmers left their plows, blacksmiths left their forges, tailors left their needles, sailors left their ships, and doctors left their patients. Where did they all go? Why, to the goldfields, of course.

◄ The first gold nugget found at Sutter's Mill, California, in 1848

▲ Nathaniel Currier made this print in 1849 showing all the possible ways to get to California. What do you think of his suggestions?

There were three ways to get to California from the East. One way was by ship down around Cape Horn at the tip of South America. It was a long trip, and if the ship didn't carry proper provisions, you might have scurvy (the miserable disease that comes from a lack of vitamin C) when you arrived. Still, it may have been the easiest way.

Or you could go by boat to Panama, then overland and upriver to the Pacific Coast, where you waited for another boat to take you north. That was the fastest way to go—if you didn't get robbed or killed in Panama, or catch malaria.

The cheapest way to go, and so the route most people took, was overland. That was difficult—you know that—but it got a little easier each year. At least, it was easier if you had enough sense to get to California before the snows made the Sierra Nevada just about impassable.

A miner on his way to California pauses to exchange a word with a mountain man. ▼

▲ Store owners profited by selling miners food and supplies.

Once you were in California, your cares would be over. Why, you could bend down and pick up gold in the streams. Well, that's what they said back East. You'll be rich in no time at all. Sure.

Guess who got rich? The storekeepers. The people who sold things to all those miners who poured into California. The prospectors (that's what the miners were called) all had to eat. And they needed tents and shovels and shirts and pants. There wasn't much available in California in the way of supplies or food.

So things got mighty expensive. There's an economic law called the *law of supply and demand.* It's a common sense law. Here it is: the less there is of something that everyone wants, the more it will cost (and vice versa).

Pancakes (the miners called them "flapjacks") were everyday food in the mining camps. "We became expert in flapping them over in a frying pan," said miner Lemuel McKeeby. "It wasn't difficult for me to throw them some two or three feet up in the air and land them safely, batterside down, in the pan. I heard some experts in this line who claimed that they could throw them up the chimney, then run around on the outside of the cabin and catch them in the pan!"

In 1848 there were 812 people living in San Francisco. Two years later, San Francisco was a city of 25,000. The mining areas went from no one to thousands. In 1848, 400 settlers arrived in California looking for land. In 1849, when the news of gold was out, 80,000 are said to have arrived looking for gold.

No one was prepared for all those people. So an egg that might have sold for a penny or two in the East sometimes sold for as much as a dollar in California. You can guess what happened to room rents in San Francisco.

Oh, there were a few miners who did strike it rich. But not many.

Many of the forty-niners did find gold, but usually it was gold dust and gold flakes. It often took all they found just to eat.

At first they panned for gold. They washed gravel and sand from the streams. If there was gold it sank to the bottom of the pan, because gold is heavier than sand. Soon most of that surface gold was gone. Mining became much harder.

The prospectors who went to California were called *"forty-niners"* because gold fever hit in 1849.

These forty-niners are panning for gold and hoping to get rich—but only a lucky few did. ▼

Forty-niners young and old had themselves photographed with the miner's tools of trade—some had themselves snapped without ever setting foot in a mine. ▶

▲ Immigrants to California came from many parts of the world.

In 1859, miner John H. Gregory hits pay dirt (gold) in the western part of Kansas territory (today it's Colorado). Newspaper man Horace Greeley is traveling in the area and sends word back east. That does it. By 1860, some 5,000 miners a *week* are pouring into the area. Reaching the ore in the Rockies takes heavy drilling equipment. Most of the miners go home broke. But towns like Boulder, Golden, Carson City, and Colorado Springs are born during the mining fury.

But it was the stories of the lucky miners that filled the newspapers and that kept people coming. They didn't just come from the States—although most did. They came from Mexico, Spain, China, Peru, England; you name a place, and someone was bound to be from there. They all had gold fever—it was contagious.

San Francisco had an assorted population. Sometimes all those different people got along very well. Sometimes they didn't. Sometimes things got rough. No one was in charge in California. The Mexican authorities were out of power and the Americans were just getting organized. (Although, in 1849, Californians did call a convention, write a constitution, elect a governor, and prohibit slavery.)

What about James Marshall and John Sutter? Did they get rich? No. Gold made them both poor. John Sutter was afraid of gold. He knew what gold greed could do to people. It was worse than he imagined. People trampled his property, ate his cattle, and left him ruined. James Marshall never profited from the gold, either; he began to drink and died a sad man.

California wasn't the only place where gold was found. It also turned up in Oregon, Nevada, Wyoming, Montana, and Colorado. Silver, too, in some of those places. Now why hadn't the Spaniards, with all their looking, ever found it? Well, it seems that a few of them may have done so. (This is part of what makes history so interesting. We keep discovering new things about the past.) Archaeologists— those professional diggers—have found the ruins of mines in the Rocky Mountains; they think they were Spanish gold mines. Why didn't anyone know about them? Probably because the Spanish government, back in the 16th and 17th centuries, took one-fifth of the profits from any gold mines for the royal treasury. Now, if you found a gold mine, and you were a Spanish subject, would you tell anyone about it?

The richest mining discovery in U.S. history was the Comstock Lode at Virginia City, Nevada. It was actually discovered by two Irish prospectors, Peter O'Reiley and Pat McLaughlin, but Henry T. P. Comstock came along and kind of bamboozled them into a partnership arrangement. The Comstock Lode had fabulous gold and even more fabulous silver veins. Prospectors poured into the area. They had to live somewhere, so Virginia City sprang up to house the miners. It was boisterous and busy, with prospectors, shopkeepers, peddlers, saloon-keepers, barroom girls, cooks, wagoneers, and others who were just there for the excitement.

Back to California. What did gold do to California? It brought great wealth to a quiet frontier. It brought people and ideas from around the world. It mixed rich and poor. It gave California enough people to become a state—quickly—and that is only part of what it did.

In 1861, Orion Clemens is named secretary of the Territory of Nevada. He takes his younger brother, Samuel Clemens, with him as an assistant. They head for Carson City; there, Sam changes his name to Mark Twain and becomes "smitten with silver fever." Later, Twain writes of his mining experiences in a book called *Roughing It*.

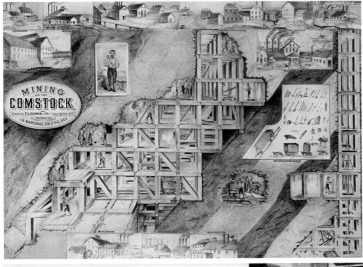

▲ The Comstock Lode at Virginia City, Nevada (shown here in a cutaway view), yielded more than $500 million in silver and gold ore between 1859 and 1879.

Virginia City, Nevada, in about 1860 ▶

The Chinese, the Know-Nothings, and Abraham Lincoln

It was 1849, and the sailors on the Yankee vessels stopping at Canton and Hong Kong had astounding news. They told of gold, mountains of gold, streams filled with gold, all in a place called California. The gold was there for anyone to take, the sailors said. The Chinese needed to hear good news. Wars and rebellions had disrupted the ancient Chinese ways. Many were out of work.

So they took their picks and shovels and headed for California. They didn't intend to stay. They would just reach down and get some of that gold and come home rich. (Many other immigrant groups—the Italians and the Irish, for instance—had the same idea. They would come to America, get rich, and go back to the old country. Some did just that, but most stayed.)

In 1852, more than 20,000 Chinese passed through the San Francisco Customs House on their way to the goldfields. And that was just the beginning. Soon there was a big Chinese population in San Francisco. Chinese miners were working claims in the Sierra Nevadas, Chinese merchants were importing and selling Chinese food and goods, and Chinese opera companies were entertaining theatergoers.

Some of the Chinese miners did find gold. There was plenty of work for the others. There were few women settlers in California and much cooking and laundry to be done. Most American men wouldn't do those traditionally female jobs; Chinese custom held it no disgrace to cook and clean.

At first, the Chinese were treated like the other new Californians. It was an exciting time, and gold was beckoning. But when disappointment set in—most people didn't find gold—someone had to be blamed. So why not blame men who spoke a foreign tongue and wore their hair braided in long pigtails?

▲ A Chinese neighborhood in San Francisco

Soon there were nasty attacks on the Chinese, and discriminatory laws that were another form of attack. Partly this was because of an idea called "nativism." The nativists said only white Anglo-Saxon Protestants were "real" Americans. The nativists wanted to keep most other people from entering the country. And they wanted to keep blacks enslaved. What was really strange was that the nativists didn't even think Native Americans belonged in America! On the West Coast the nativists attacked the Chinese. On the East Coast they attacked the newest European immigrants—especially those from Catholic countries.

The nativists even had their own political party. They called it the American Party. But others called it the "Know-Nothing Party." Don't laugh. The Know-Nothings actually elected six governors.

In 1855, an Illinois lawyer named Abraham Lincoln wrote a letter to a friend saying just what he thought of the Know-Nothing Party. This is what Lincoln wrote:

> As a nation we began by declaring that "all men are created equal." We now practically read it, "all men are created equal, except Negroes." When the Know-Nothings get control, it will read "all men are created equal except Negroes and foreigners and Catholics." When it comes to this, I shall prefer emigrating to some country where they make no pretense of loving liberty.

But Abraham Lincoln didn't have to emigrate; most Americans rejected nativist ideas.

A political cartoon depicts the tension in San Francisco between Chinese immigrants and the mostly Irish members of the Workingmen's Party. ▼

St. Augustine's Catholic Church in Philadelphia, Pennsylvania, was burned during Know-Nothing riots in 1844. ▶

Clipper Ships and Pony Express

In 1850 the 31st star was sewn on the American flag. The star was put there for the new state of California. Do you remember how many states there were in 1789? How many are there now? When did your state become a part of the Union? Do you know when Utah became a state? Or Arizona? Most places in the West were territories for a long time before they became states. California leapfrogged into statehood. That was because so many people moved to California so fast. That created problems, but also opportunities.

Levi Strauss saw an opportunity. He realized miners needed sturdy pants. He bought yards and yards of heavy canvas and turned it into strong pants, with rivets to hold the seams in place. Those pants were called *Levi's*, and still are.

Many of the miners were homesick. They wanted to know what was happening to their loved ones back home in Ohio, or New Hampshire, or Alabama. And the people back home were frantic. Had their fathers and brothers made it to the goldfields? Sometimes a year went by without letters or news. Was Father dead of cholera? Was he rich? Or was he too embarrassed to come home poorer than when he left?

The Bear Flag of the California Republic, first raised in Sonoma in 1846, became the state flag of California. ▼

◀ An ad for Pony Express riders said, "WANTED: Young skinny wirey fellows, not over 18. Must be expert riders willing to risk death daily. Orphans preferred."

The U.S. Post Office in California was not prepared for the thousands and thousands of letters that came in 1849. There weren't enough postal workers, and those doing the job kept quitting to work in the goldfields. No one was around to deliver the mail.

Back East, many people were anxious to get to California. But they wanted a safe, quick means of travel. Americans used their ingenuity to solve those problems.

Soon there were private postal services. (One was called the Pony Express.) Then came telegraph lines; they carried messages with the wizardry of electricity.

Stagecoaches got their name because they traveled in stages, changing horses at each stage (about every 20 miles). ▼

Stagecoaches, changing horses at outposts about every 20 miles, soon whizzed people across the country. (Well, it seemed like whizzing then.)

And clipper ships really did whiz across the seas. Slim, graceful sailing ships with three masts and square sails, they were the largest sailboats that anyone had ever seen.

The classy, designed-in-America clipper ships were the envy of the world. Ships had been taking eight or nine months to make the trip from Boston around Cape Horn to San Francisco. The *Flying Cloud*, one of the largest of the clipper ships, made it around the Horn in 89 days (how many months was that?). Until 1989, no sailing ship ever went faster.

However, if you were really in a hurry to get your mail across the country you could send it by an even speedier route. The fastest mail went by Pony Express. Galloping horses raced from St. Joseph, Missouri, to Sacramento, California, in an incredible 10 days. This is how the Pony Express worked: stations were set up 10 to 15 miles apart, all along the route. Horses were ready at each station. A rider starting in Sacramento rode as fast as he could to the first station. Then he jumped off his tired horse, threw his mailbags onto a fresh one, and headed on. Usually it took two minutes to change horses. About every eight stations, a new rider was ready to take over. Pony Express riders rode through the night, through rain, through blizzards. They had to protect themselves from Indian attack. Some of them, like William "Buffalo Bill" Cody, became famous for their exploits. There were 190 Pony Express stations, 500 horses, and 80 riders.

People who were in a hurry for news, like newspaper editors, sometimes used pigeons. Yes, real birds. They were trained to fly from place to place with small bits of paper taped to their legs. You can understand that a pigeon can't carry a whole lot of news. Samuel F. B. Morse, who was an artist and needed to earn some money, came up with a much better idea. He developed the telegraph. Using electricity, he sent messages on a wire.

In 19th-century America, it was as if an idea volcano had erupted in the United States. Americans came up with all kinds of ideas for useful things. Samuel Morse's telegraph was one of them, although at first most people thought it just an amusing toy.

Samuel F. B. Morse used electrical impulses to transmit dashes and dots in the code he developed. The telegraph revolutionized long-distance communication. ▼

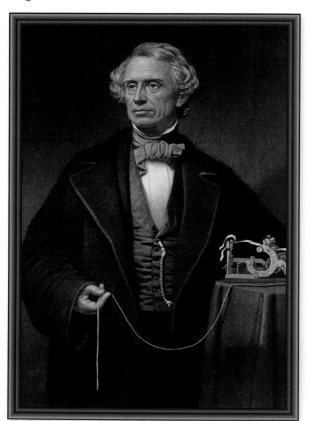

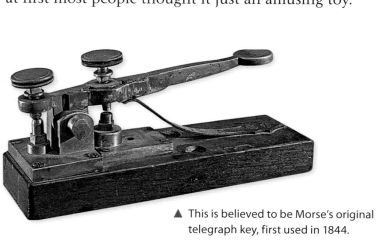

▲ This is believed to be Morse's original telegraph key, first used in 1844.

◀ The Pony Express ran for just 18 months. The completion of transcontinental telegraph wires put the Pony Express out of business.

Morse believed it might be more than a toy. He got interested in the idea on a ship coming home from Europe (where he'd been studying painting). Someone told him about Joseph Henry's work. (Henry was the greatest American scientist after Benjamin Franklin. He did important work in electromagnetism and experimented with a crude telegraph.) Morse wondered if electrical pulses could be sent along a wire in dots and dashes. If so, those dots and dashes could be used as a code to carry messages. Starting with that simple idea, Morse devised the telegraph. It took 12 years to work out the details and get wires strung on poles, but it happened. In 1844 the first message went—by Morse code—from the Supreme Court in Washington to Baltimore. "What hath God wrought?" asked Morse by telegraph. A few seconds later, a message was sent the other way.

So was there any important use for this invention? Well, seconds after Senator Henry Clay was nominated in Baltimore, Maryland, as the Whig candidate for president, people in Washington, D.C., knew about it. Astounding! Newspaper editors and many others began to see that the telegraph was more than a toy. Seventeen years after that first message was sent, the telegraph reached from coast to coast and the Pony Express was out of business.

Soon after Samuel Morse invented Morse code, it was adopted world-wide. In the next quarter century, the continents were linked by under-the-ocean telegraph cables and the world of instant communications was born.

Won the Battle, Lost the War

It was 1826 when Rafael Aquilar, who was a Native American, and *alcalde* (mayor) of the pueblo of Pecos, sent a petition to the New Mexico legislature. The petition was intended to keep Hispanics off Indian lands. New Mexico was a province of the Republic of Mexico. So the Indians were officially Mexican citizens.

The Pecos pueblo sat on a rocky ridge near Santa Fe. With more than 660 rooms surrounding a plaza, the pueblo dated back to the 15th century. In the 1600s Franciscan fathers built a mission at Pecos with a big church, a tannery, and farm buildings. The fathers wanted to replace the Indian way of life. The natives said "no thanks" in an uprising known as the Pueblo Revolt. The Spaniards fled.

After that, the *pecoseños* (residents of the Pecos) tried to go back to their Indian ways. But slowly new settlers came north from Mexico. Some squatted on pueblo land. According to New Mexico law, the Pecos Indians owned the land that surrounded their pueblo. Non-Indians had no rights to those lands, which is what Aquilar said in his petition. The New Mexico legislature agreed and ordered Hispanics off Indian lands.

But it didn't matter. The *pecoseños* were dying from diseases carried by the Hispanics. Apache and Comanche raids were killing them, too. And those who wanted the land were poisoning water holes. Back in 1700 there had been about a thousand *pecoseños*; by 1800 there were fewer than 150. Aquilar won a legal victory, but there were too few Indians to keep Hispanics out. In 1838 the last *pecoseños* gave up and moved across the Rio Grande to Jemez Pueblo.

In California Indians were enslaved to work on ranches and missions. Everyone knew that was wrong. So, when Mexico became a republic, the new leaders said mission lands should be returned to the Indians (while keeping some land for the Christian *padres*). It didn't happen. In 1824, thousands of Indians in Southern California rebelled out of anger and frustration. The Mexicans soon squashed those rebellions. When California became part of the United States in 1849, the Yankee newcomers showed little interest in Indian rights. They wanted land for themselves.

A mounted Comanche war party, as depicted by the American artist George Catlin ▼

Do Girls Have Brains?

In the first years of the 19th century, almost half the boys and girls in the United States never went to school. But a larger percentage of children went to school in the United States than in any European country. (The 1850 census showed that 56 of every 100 white children went to school—but only 2 of every 100 black children did.)

Many children who never went to school still learned to read. In those days, boys and girls often spent more time in church than in school. So some learned to read in Sunday school, and just about everyone read Bible stories or heard them read. Many parents taught their children at home.

Before 1830, there were few free public schools outside New England. New England had a tradition of public schools. Massachusetts set up what may have been the first free public school

An early one-room schoolhouse, where children of all ages studied with one teacher ▼

▲ Winslow Homer painted *The Country School* in 1871.

system in the world; that was way back in 1647. In other places, free schools were mostly for poor children. Wealthy children had private tutors or went to private academies. And, in many communities, parents got together, hired a teacher, and built a schoolhouse.

The public-school idea began to catch on in the 1840s and 1850s as the states started establishing school systems. The Constitution didn't mention education. That wasn't because the Founders thought education unimportant; it was because they expected the states to control schooling. Thomas Jefferson believed the American experiment in government—that new idea called "self-government"—would only work in a country where every citizen was educated. After all, how can you vote and make decisions if you can't read? "If a nation expects to be ignorant and free, in a state of civilization, it expects what never was and never will be," wrote Jefferson in a letter to a friend.

The Second Great Awakening

During the early 19th century, the United States experienced a time of religious revival known as the second Great Awakening. During the first Great Awakening, back in the 18th century, ministers such as Jonathan Edwards had preached frightening sermons about everyone's sinfulness. The preachers of the second Great Awakening were molded by the new, democratic beliefs. They said people and society could be improved: salvation was up to the individual.

Lyman Beecher was one of the influential ministers of the time. He helped make people aware of the problems that came with industry and big cities. Reform movements sprang from religious revivalism. In 1826, Lyman Beecher founded the American Society for the Promotion of Temperance (*temperance* means "no drinking of liquor"). It was one of the first of the social crusades that included abolition, women's rights, workers' rights, school reform, and something new: concern for the poor and handicapped.

Horace Mann of Massachusetts has been called the "Father of American Education." He wanted to improve schools—especially public schools. He thought our democracy depended on good, free, public schools.

As secretary of the Massachusetts Board of Education, he doubled the money Massachusetts spent on schools, organized the first teacher-training schools, doubled teachers' salaries, improved the curriculum, and made sure that every boy and girl in Massachusetts went to school for at least six months every year. Other states turned to Horace Mann for advice, and he gave it.

William H. McGuffey was the most influential of all the educators of his century because of the reading books he compiled. He called them Eclectic Readers—everyone else called them *McGuffey Readers*.

McGuffey thought the elementary grades were the most important school years. "The child," he wrote, "needs more help than the boy, and the boy more than the man; hence, the primary school

▲ Horace Mann, known as the "father of American education"

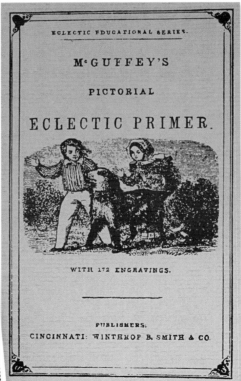

◄ From the mid- to late-19th century, the *McGuffey Readers,* as everyone called them, were used in most American classrooms.

▲ By the 1850s, some schools, like this one (Boston's Emerson School for Girls), were teaching girls serious subjects. As the population grew, women were needed as teachers and so had to be well educated.

the best." He tried to provide the best by including selections in his readers from very good authors. McGuffey's books were very important. For about 50 years, most schoolchildren read them. They gave the nation common stories and common curriculum.

In the 19th century, there were many people who believed that women and blacks weren't meant to learn. There were a few exceptions: in Ohio, Oberlin College accepted women and blacks. A few men's colleges, like Bowdoin, Harvard, and Dartmouth, enrolled black male students. But in 19th-century America, these were the exceptions. Many experts, who were men, claimed that women's brains were smaller than men's and that girls couldn't learn as much as boys. They said black men's brains were even smaller, and as for black women—well, they said it would be silly to attempt to teach them anything. A few of these experts were professors and were so convincing that some 19th-century people of both genders really thought that was the truth.

What about Phillis Wheatley, the black woman who had learned Latin and written poems that were read in faraway England? Or

Webster's Dictionary

Noah Webster, who was born in Connecticut, believed that American children should read American schoolbooks, not the English books they were reading. So he wrote American schoolbooks and an American spelling book. Then he began writing an American dictionary. Webster put everyday words—even some slang words—in his dictionary. That was unusual. It took him 20 years to complete his two-volume *American Dictionary of the English Language*. It was published in 1828. (Do you have a Webster's dictionary in your house or school?)

Before Webster wrote his books, people spelled words any way that made sense to them. As you can imagine, words sometimes got confusing. Webster ended the confusion: he established standard spellings. His speller was soon the best-selling book in America—after the Bible.

Lucy Prince, another poet, born a slave, who at age 67 persuaded a governor's council in Vermont that the town of Guilford needed to protect her family after tearing her fence down? Chief Justice Salmon P. Chase said that Prince "made a better argument than any he had heard from a Vermont lawyer."

"Who is Phillis Wheatley? Who is Lucy Prince?" men asked. Women, such as Phillis Wheatley and Lucy Prince, were not included in the history books of the day. As a result, after the Civil War few people remembered Phillis Wheatley. Few had heard of Lucy Prince.

So, with rare exceptions, colleges would not take women, and there was no way for most women to become doctors, or lawyers, or skilled workers.

If a woman did get a job, she knew that her pay would be about half that of a man doing the same work. Her salary would belong to her husband. Women couldn't vote, so they couldn't change the laws.

A woman married to a bad man was not much better off than a slave. A husband could whip his wife and the law was on his side. A married woman owned nothing. Everything she had—even money from her parents—belonged to her husband. The law made it almost impossible to get a divorce, and when a woman did manage it, many people considered such a thing shameful—although those who divorced were usually desperate. If a wife ran away from her husband, the law said he had rights to the children—even if he was an alcoholic who beat them. If he killed someone in the family, then the law would step in. It was a bit late.

▲ Although Phillis Wheatley's poetry was widely admired by many people, including George Washington, her work was not included in schoolbooks, and so it was not well known by the 1850s.

Mount Holyoke

Mary Lyon wanted to go to college but there were no colleges for women. So Mary Lyon founded one. It was Mount Holyoke College, and it opened in Massachusetts in 1837 with 4 teachers and 116 students. Lyon insisted that it be a democratic school and that the women do their own cooking and cleaning to keep the tuition price low. Because of that, almost anyone who wanted to attend could afford to do so. Most went on to be teachers.

Mount Holyoke, the first women's college in the United States ▶

▲ Angelina and Sarah Grimké

Most people—then and now—are decent. Most 19th-century husbands weren't bad. Most loved their wives and children and treated them well. But even many good men were horrified at the idea of a woman standing up and speaking her mind.

"It's a man's world," they said, and in the 19th century it was.

Some women, however, didn't believe their brains were small. They knew they were as smart as any man; they were determined to use their brains.

Sarah and Angelina Grimké had something to say and they said it to audiences of men and women. The sisters set out on a lecture tour in 1837 to tell what they had seen of slavery.

"What kind of women would speak in front of men?" people asked. "Monster women!" That was what some people said of the Grimké sisters. Ministers said it was wrong for a woman to speak when men were there to hear. Surely the Grimké sisters knew of Adam and Eve, and that Eve should have kept quiet. Were they told of Anne Hutchinson and what happened to her in the Massachusetts Bay Colony?

Those who came to hear the Grimkés saw two women dressed in simple gray Quaker garb. They were Southern women who could no longer live in their slave-owning families and who had come north to tell why.

Women as Equals

The Grimké sisters ran their own school, where they tried to put their ideas about fairness and equality into practice. Sarah Grimké wrote *Letters on the Equality of the Sexes and the Condition of Women*. Here is some of it:

I spent the early part of my life among the butterflies of the fashion world. And of this class of women, I must say, their education is miserably deficient. Their chief business is to attract the notice and win the attention of men. They seldom think men will be allured by intellectual achievements, because they find that where mental superiority exists, a woman is generally shunned.

The general opinion that women are inferior to men also has a tremendous effect on women who work…. A male teacher can command a higher price than a woman even when he teaches the same subjects and is not in any respect superior to the woman. The same is true of every occupation in which both sexes engage.

Men may reject what I say because it wounds their pride but I believe they will find that women as their equal is unquestionably more valuable than women as their inferior both as a moral and intellectual being.

They told of black children being sold away from their families, they told of whippings with lashes, they told of other horrors. And their audiences were astonished, for they did not know of these things. Angelina went before the Massachusetts legislature and presented tens of thousands of antislavery petitions that had been collected by women. She was the first American woman to address a legislative body.

The ministers were angry. It was not because of what the Grimké sisters said, but because women were saying it. A letter was read in every Congregational church in Massachusetts. The letter said that woman "depends on the weakness which God has given her for her protection…but when she assumes the place and tone of man as a public reformer, our care and protection of her seem unnecessary."

▲ Angelina Grimké addressed the Fugitive Slave Law Convention in New York in 1850. The event is shown here in a daguerreotype, an early form of photography.

Some women thought they could stand without support. Half a century earlier, Abigail Adams had been such a woman. Like most women of her time, Adams never went to school. (Remember, she grew up in the 18th century.) She learned to read and write at home. Because she was smart and industrious and kept reading, she soon knew more than most of the school-taught boys.

When Abigail's husband, John, was making laws for a new nation, she wrote to him:

In the new code of laws…I desire you would remember the ladies… [We] will not hold ourselves bound by any laws in which we have no voice or representation.

There were others who believed as she did. But even at Oberlin College, where they were daring enough to educate men and women together, they didn't let women speak out. Only the male students at Oberlin College got to read their graduation essays aloud. If you were a female student you had to let a male professor read your paper for you. Lucy Stone objected. When the other students heard of her protest they agreed with her. But it didn't matter. In 1847, on graduation day, Lucy Stone was not allowed to read her own essay. Some women believed that they needed to change those words *All men are created equal* to *All men and women are created equal.*

Elizabeth Blackwell

Elizabeth Blackwell was the first woman to go to a medical school in the United States. She applied to 29 medical schools before she was accepted, in 1847, at Geneva College (now Hobart College), a small school in upstate New York. Later, Elizabeth found out that the administration had asked the college students to decide whether to admit a woman. The students thought the whole thing was a joke, and so joined in the joke by accepting her.

Here are some entries from Elizabeth Blackwell's medical school journal:

November 15—Today, a second operation at which I was not allowed to be present. This annoys me. I was quite saddened and discouraged by Dr. Webster requesting me to be absent from his demonstrations.... I wrote to him hoping to change things....

November 22—A trying day, and I feel almost worn out, though it was encouraging too, and in some measure a triumph; but 'tis a terrible ordeal! That dissection was just

In the late 1860s, Elizabeth Blackwell, with her sister, Dr. Emily Blackwell, founded the Women's Medical College in New York City to provide medical training for women and health care for the poor. ▼

Elizabeth Blackwell in about 1850 ▶

as much as I could bear. Some of the students blushed, some were hysterical, not one could keep a smile, and some who I am sure would not hurt my feelings for the world if it depended on them, held down their faces and shook.... I sat in grave indifference, though the effort made my heart palpitate most painfully....

November 24—Today the doctor read my note to the class. In this note I told him that I was there as a student with an earnest purpose, and as a student simply I should be regarded; that the study of anatomy was a most serious one, exciting profound reverence, and the suggestion to absent myself from any lectures seemed to me a grave mistake.... I listened joyfully to the very hearty approbation with which it was received by the class, and then entered the amphitheatre and quietly resumed my place.

Seneca Falls and the Rights of Women

Elizabeth Cady read the nation's great Declaration, and it bothered her. *All men are created equal*, it said. But what about all women? Elizabeth's father, Daniel Cady, was a judge; she spent hours in his office listening and learning law. "If only you had been born a boy," he told her. "You could have been a lawyer."

Elizabeth didn't want to be a boy; she was happy being a girl. But she wanted to use her mind—and she did. She decided to learn everything the boys were learning. She asked a scholarly neighbor to teach her Greek. He did, and she learned well. At school she was a top student. But when graduation came and the boys went off to college, Elizabeth couldn't go with them, because she was a girl. She was sent to Emma Willard's seminary, a finishing school for girls. She couldn't be a lawyer, because women weren't allowed to practice law.

Elizabeth was determined to do something with her life; it helped that she married a fine man. He was Henry B. Stanton, a leader of the antislavery movement. When they married, the minister expected her to promise to "obey" her husband. That was a customary part of the marriage ceremony. Elizabeth Cady wouldn't use that word. "I obstinately refused to obey one with whom I supposed I was entering into an equal relation," she wrote. The minister was unhappy, but Henry understood. He was marrying a woman who wouldn't do things that didn't make sense, even if everyone else did them.

Elizabeth Cady Stanton was soon using her intelligence to help women. She and Lucretia Mott and other friends decided to organize a women's rights convention—the first in the nation. It took eight years of planning, but,

Elizabeth Cady Stanton was an early advocate of women's suffrage—the right to vote. ▼

Elizabeth Cady Stanton helped organize the first women's rights convention in the nation, held at Seneca Falls, New York, in 1848. ▶

finally, in July 1848, some 300 people—men and women—met in the Methodist church in Henry Stanton's hometown, Seneca Falls, New York. They wrote a declaration; it is known as the Seneca Falls Declaration, and it says, *We hold these truths to be self-evident: that all men and women are created equal.*

Then, using Jefferson's Declaration of Independence as a guide, the women and men at Seneca Falls went on from there, telling of all the ways they felt women were being wronged. Thomas Jefferson's words accused King George III of tyranny; Elizabeth Stanton's accused "man." One hundred people signed the Seneca Falls Declaration: 32 of them were men.

The newspapers greeted the Seneca Falls Declaration with ridicule. "All the journals from Maine to Texas," Elizabeth Cady Stanton recalled in her autobiography, "seemed to strive with each other to see which could make our movement appear the most ridiculous."

She may have been discouraged, but that didn't stop her. She had started something that would grow and grow. More and more men and women met in conventions and planned how to work for women's rights. They were among many reformers in mid-19th-century America. Most reformers were churchgoers who were fighting for all these things: abolition (to end slavery), temperance (to ban the drinking of alcoholic beverages), and women's and children's rights. (Later, those movements all split apart.)

Amelia Bloomer, who was editor of a temperance newspaper, was one of the reformers. She said women should get out of the long garments that made them trip—or even faint when they were laced too tight at the waist. Bloomer wore long pantaloons (wide trousers) under her short dresses, and tried to talk other women into that fashion. It allowed for freedom of movement, she said. But that was going too far for most 19th-century Americans. People threw stones at the "bloomer girls" and made fun of them. It was a long time before women felt comfortable wearing pants.

One day, in 1851, Amelia Bloomer introduced Elizabeth Cady Stanton to Susan B. Anthony. It was a momentous meeting. Stanton and Anthony formed a team—like Lewis and Clark—that left a big imprint on American history.

They were an uncommon pair; their talents complemented each other. Elizabeth Cady Stanton was chubby and merry, and the mother of a family that kept growing and growing. (She had seven children altogether.) Susan Anthony was slim, reserved, and serious-minded. She never married. When she spoke she made sense.

▲ Elizabeth Cady Stanton and Susan B. Anthony worked together for 50 years on the campaign for women's suffrage.

Dorothea Dix

Dorothea Dix was a lonely child. Her mother was dead, and her father was a traveling preacher. Dorothea was sent from relative to relative to live. Perhaps that was why she had sympathy for those who were troubled—especially the mentally ill. People with mental or emotional problems were being put in privately run, unregulated mental asylums (uh-SY-lums), and they were usually horrible places. In 1843, Dix wrote a *Memorial to the Legislature of Massachusetts* telling of "insane persons confined within this Commonwealth, in cages, closets, cellars, stalls, pens! Chained, naked, beaten with rods, and lashed into obedience." Hardly anyone then concerned themselves with prisons, or poorhouses, or mental asylums. For more than 30 years, Dix traveled about the country, and to other nations, too, visiting asylums and prisons, and writing and speaking about them.

Dorothea Dix devoted her life to improving care for the mentally ill. ▶

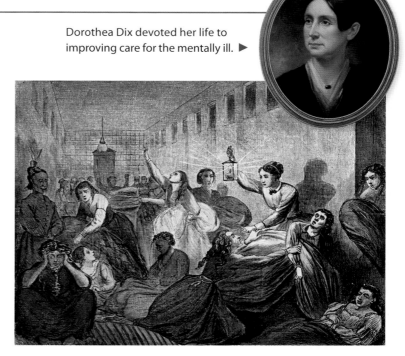

▲ In overcrowded and understaffed mental asylums, like this one in New York City, patients received little or no care.

Susan B. Anthony and Elizabeth Cady Stanton address a meeting of the National Woman Suffrage Association in the 1870s. ▶

In 1853, Anthony attended a teachers' conference in Rochester, New York. She had been a teacher for 15 years, and she asked for permission to speak at the meeting. No woman had done that before. It took the men in charge a half hour to decide. Then they agreed to hear her. This is part of what she said:

> *Do you not see that so long as society says a woman has not brains enough to be a doctor, lawyer or minister, but has plenty to be a teacher, every man of you who chooses to teach…admits…that he has no more brains than a woman?*

Her audience was shocked (and that was what she intended).

Susan B. Anthony was a determined woman, a superb organizer, and the kind of person who never gives up. Together with Elizabeth Cady Stanton, she led the movement that eventually brought the vote to women (although that didn't happen until the 20th century, after both of them were dead).

In the 19th century, many people believed a man represented his whole family when he voted. If women were given the vote, they might disagree with their husbands and vote differently. Would that break up the family? Men and women worried about that. Even Stanton's friend Lucretia Mott wasn't sure that women should vote. She just wanted them to have equal rights. But could they have equal rights if they couldn't vote?

What about women who weren't married? What rights did they have? How could they take part in a democracy? And what about women who did disagree with their husbands? Anthony and Stanton knew that without a vote women were like helpless vines clinging to men.

Working Together

The abolitionists who were working to end slavery often had close ties with those who were working for women's rights. Feminist Susan B. Anthony was a paid agent for the American Anti-Slavery Society, and the abolitionist Frederick Douglass spoke at women's rights meetings.

A Woman Named *Truth*

The man at the women's rights convention in Ohio, in 1851, thought he was telling the truth when he said that women were by nature weak and inferior to men. But a lean, stately woman who heard him didn't agree. She was almost six feet tall and she wore a gray dress with a white shawl; a white turban was wrapped around her head; when she walked it was with the dignity of a queen.

The tall woman was the only black person in the church where the convention was held—and all eyes were upon her. Finally she could bear no more. Her name was Sojourner (SO-jer-ner) Truth, and she stood up and spoke in a voice like rolling thunder. The hall was hushed, and that voice rang out and asked:

> A'n't I a woman? Look at me. Look at my arm. [And she showed powerful muscles.] I have ploughed, and planted, and gathered into barns, and no man could head me! And a'n't I a woman? I could work as much and eat as much as a man—when I could get it—and bear the lash as well! And a'n't I a woman? I have borne thirteen children, and seen them most all sold off to slavery, and when I cried out with my mother's grief, none but Jesus heard me! And a'n't I a woman?

She said more, and said it powerfully. A woman who heard her wrote:

> Amid roars of applause, she returned to her corner, leaving more than one of us with streaming eyes, and hearts beating with gratitude. She had taken us up in her strong arms and carried us safely...turning the whole tide in our favor.

Sojourner Truth had been named Isabella when she was born a slave in New York State. She was treated harshly, as slaves often were. In 1826,

Recalling Sojourner Truth's speech, the chairwoman of the Ohio convention wrote, "I have never... seen anything like the magical influence that...turned the sneers and jeers of an excited crowd into notes of respect and admiration." ▶

the year before New York freed its slaves, she ran away. She was a young mother and she planned to buy her children. But, before she could, her former master sold one of her children—to a buyer in the South. That was against New York law. With the help of a white Quaker family she found a lawyer, went to court, and won the child. That said much for her determination, and also for the fairness of the court. Later, she helped other blacks go to court and fight for their rights.

Isabella's Quaker friends told her, "Before God, all of us are equal." No one had ever said that to her before. She could not read, but they read to her from the Bible. She soon memorized large parts of the Bible. She became deeply religious and had visions of God. She decided to live a godly life and to help others. Isabella chose a new name to celebrate her freedom and her new way of life. It was Sojourner Truth. A *sojourner* is a traveler who stops somewhere for a short time and then continues on. For the next 40 years she traveled and spoke out for truth and justice.

Sojourner Truth worked for women's rights, black rights, prison reform, and temperance. She soon became famous. (Abraham Lincoln invited her to the White House.) She spoke out against injustice wherever she found it.

American Writers

Many 19th-century New Englanders were descendants of 17th-century Puritans. But that old-time religion was now gone. The sermons of the new churches—Congregationalists, Unitarians, Presbyterians—were less stern and more forgiving. The Puritan heritage, however, was there. It taught a love of learning, and it taught honesty and a sense of duty. New England children went to school, worked hard, and learned. In Boston and the nearby towns many children learned Latin and often Greek and Hebrew, too. So on Sunday, when the minister told a joke in Latin, everyone laughed.

Boys and girls who went to school in Boston read many of the great Greek and Latin poets; they knew Homer (whose poems were written down in Greek), they knew Virgil (who wrote in Latin), and they knew the English poets. Then some of them began to realize that something was missing. Where were the great American poets?

George Ticknor taught at Harvard, where the brightest of the New England boys went to college. Ticknor had been everywhere, or so it seemed. He had learned German in Germany, French in France, Spanish in Spain, and Italian in Italy. While he was in all those places he had spoken to the greatest European thinkers and writers. He was

Harvard University in Cambridge, Massachusetts, 1828 ▼

astounded at how much they admired America. A famous English poet, Robert Southey, had even written a poem about King Philip's War. No American poet had written about King Philip.

King Philip's War—between New England settlers and the Wampanoag, Nipmuck, and Narraganset tribes—was fought in 1675 and 1676.

It was time for Americans to write their own stories, said Ticknor. Other Harvard professors said the same thing. They said that to their students, who included Ralph Waldo Emerson, Richard Henry Dana, Henry David Thoreau, and Francis Parkman. Those students did just what their teachers expected—they became great American writers.

Ralph Waldo Emerson lived in Concord. Do you remember Concord? Think hard. It is the town, 30 miles from Boston, where the first shot of the Revolutionary War was fired. Emerson called it "the shot heard round the world."

Louisa May Alcott ▼

In 1850, Concord was a center of American culture. Emerson was known as the "Sage of Concord." (A sage is a wise man.) Henry Thoreau was his neighbor. Nathaniel Hawthorne lived nearby. Hawthorne was a descendant of John Hathorne, who was a judge in the Salem witch trials, which may help explain Nathaniel's haunting stories.

Louisa May Alcott was another neighbor. She, of course, couldn't go to Harvard. Women weren't admitted. She did all right on her own. She had to. Her father, Bronson, who was a teacher and a social reformer, was always doing good things for others, but he never worried about earning a living. His large family was often without money. Louisa Alcott realized she would have to be a breadwinner. When she was 16 she published her first book: a collection of fairy tales. When she wrote *Little Women* she solved the family's financial problems. That novel is based on Louisa's own family.

▲ A scene from *Little Women,* Louisa May Alcott's best-selling novel based on her own family life and experiences as a girl in Massachusetts during the Civil War

▲ American poet Henry Wadsworth Longfellow

Henry Wadsworth Longfellow (a poet who took Professor Ticknor's place when he retired from Harvard in 1835) often came to Concord to visit. Most Americans knew Longfellow's poems. Children read them in school, and (in those days before television) grown-ups read them out loud to each other. They were translated and admired around the world. Longfellow wrote American poems: about an Indian named Hiawatha, about Paul Revere, about a village blacksmith, about the Acadians who were forced by the British to leave their homes.

Francis Parkman, a handsome but almost-blind historian, visited Concord from nearby Boston. He had been to Wyoming and lived with the Sioux.

It was Emerson who drew people to Concord. He was like a team captain who inspires others. Emerson was tall and skinny, with blue eyes and a long nose. He liked to talk and he had interesting things to say. People were attracted to the sage of Concord.

Emerson loved nature; he thought if people learned to understand nature they would understand themselves and many of the secrets of the world. He believed everything has its own place in nature. A fox doesn't try to be a rabbit. The same should be true of people. Find yourself, said Emerson. Do what you can do best. In an essay titled "Self-Reliance," Emerson wrote, "Trust thyself: every heart vibrates to that iron string."

Emerson drew large audiences when he lectured. ▼

▲ Ralph Waldo Emerson

Some people say that of all Ticknor's students, Henry David Thoreau was the best thinker. Thoreau built his own house, a little cabin in the woods on the edge of Walden Pond. He borrowed some tools and chopped down some trees, and the house cost him $28.12. He lived in it for two years—from 1845 to 1847—and wrote a book about his stay there, which he called *Walden*. That little book reads as if it was easy to write. It wasn't. Thoreau wrote and rewrote; he polished his words carefully. He was a craftsman with words. Here are some of Thoreau's well-crafted words from *Walden*:

I should not talk so much about myself if there were anybody else whom I knew as well.

It is never too late to give up our prejudices. No way of thinking or doing, however ancient, can be trusted without proof. What everybody echoes or in silence passes by as true today may turn out to be falsehood tomorrow. Rather than love, than money, than fame, give me truth.

Most people spend their lives working so they may own things. Thoreau wished to own only himself. "No truer American existed than Thoreau," said Emerson.

The tax collector didn't think so. Thoreau thought the government was wrong for allowing slavery and for going to war in Mexico. He protested by not paying a government tax. Thoreau spent a night in jail and would have stayed longer, but a relative paid the tax. Thoreau thought each person can be important if he or she speaks out about injustice. He explained his thoughts in an essay called "Civil Disobedience." That book has inspired people around the world to stand up for freedom and fairness in government. Thoreau believed in nonviolent action. (What does that mean?)

Thoreau loved nature. He looked at the world about him and learned from it. "In Wildness is the preservation of the World," wrote Thoreau. Do you agree?

◀ Henry David Thoreau

WALDEN.

By HENRY D. THOREAU,
AUTHOR OF "A WEEK ON THE CONCORD AND MERRIMACK RIVERS."

I do not propose to write an ode to dejection, but to brag as lustily as chanticleer in the morning, standing on his roost, if only to wake my neighbors up. — Page 92.

BOSTON:
JAMES R. OSGOOD AND COMPANY,
LATE TICKNOR & FIELDS, AND FIELDS, OSGOOD, & CO.
1 8 7 5.

▲ You can visit Concord and see Walden Pond and a reconstruction of Thoreau's cabin as they were when he lived there.

Two great 20th-century leaders, India's Mohandas (Mahatma) Gandhi and America's Martin Luther King, Jr., were inspired by Thoreau's ideas. Thoreau believed in nonviolent protest and in passive resistance. Passive resistance? That sounds like a contradiction (or an oxymoron), but it isn't. It means not fighting back when you are attacked, but not cooperating or running away or backing off, either. That takes real courage.

Melville and Company

Ralph Waldo Emerson and Henry David Thoreau went to Harvard. Herman Melville went to sea. "A whaleship was my Yale College and my Harvard," he wrote.

▲ In Melville's *Moby-Dick*, Captain Ahab vengefully pursues the white whale.

▲ Herman Melville

Herman Melville's first voyage was on a merchant ship to Liverpool, England. Then he went to sea on a whaling ship.

Whaling was important in those days before electric lights. People burned whale oil in the lamps that lit their homes. But whaling was dangerous; many whalers didn't return home to tell of it. Melville was one of the lucky ones.

Melville wrote a book about a huge white whale named Moby-Dick, and about a ship's captain named Ahab who was obsessed with that whale—which means he couldn't get the sea creature out of his mind. That great white whale haunted Ahab; he was determined to capture it. Melville's *Moby-Dick* is the story of that obsession. It is a book of adventure, bravery, cruelty, and daring. It is a great American novel.

But the most popular adventure stories of the 19th century were James Fenimore Cooper's *Leatherstocking Tales*. Their hero, Natty Bumppo, was a lot like Daniel Boone.

Washington Irving wrote about the Hudson River Valley in New York. In *The Legend of Sleepy Hollow*, a superstitious schoolmaster, Ichabod Crane, is pursued by a headless horseman. Another tale tells how Rip van Winkle fell asleep—for 20 years. Can you imagine what it would be

▲ Washington Irving's *The Legend of Sleepy Hollow* featured Ichabod Crane and the Headless Horseman.

like if you fell asleep and woke up 20 years from now? What would happen to your friends in that time? What about the place where you live? King George III was the ruler when Rip fell asleep. Do you know who was in charge when he woke up?

Herman Melville, Washington Irving, and James Fenimore Cooper had something in common: they were New Yorkers. Emerson, Thoreau, Alcott, and Hawthorne were New Englanders. Americans in every region were beginning to write.

Edgar Allan Poe was born in Boston but lived much of his life in the South. He wrote scary stories—very scary stories. Some people think he is the best horror writer of all time. It was only after he died—in 1849, when he was 40—that people began to appreciate his work. If you like good stories, and you don't mind being scared, read "The Tell-Tale Heart." While you're at it,

Cooper's Popularity

James Fenimore Cooper slammed shut the English novel he was reading (Cooper had a temper). "I could write a better book than that!" he told his wife. "Why don't you?" Susan Cooper said. And so began the career of the most popular novelist of his day. Cooper, whose father founded the frontier settlement of Cooperstown, New York (what is Cooperstown famous for today?), was a country gentleman. He soon became a hardworking writer. His tales of frontier heroes and his sea adventures were very successful (though they may seem slow-paced to modern readers). There is a popular movie based on Cooper's novel *Hawkeye*, or *The Last of the Mohicans*.

▲ In Edgar Allan Poe's "The Raven," the mysterious bird repeats the haunting cry, "Nevermore."

try a poem that Poe wrote called "The Raven." It is especially good when read aloud.

But if you want to read poems that sing with exuberance, try some of Walt Whitman's poems. Whitman was a big man, full of energy and good nature, who grew up in Brooklyn, New York, and became a teacher, a newspaper reporter, and an editor. He got fired from his newspaper job because of his antislavery ideas. That gave him time to do what he wanted, and what he wanted was to become a poet. Like Emerson and Thoreau, Whitman thought God could be found in people and in nature.

A long poem Walt Whitman wrote, called "Leaves of Grass," was unlike any poem ever written before. At first no one much bothered to read it—and those who did didn't like it because it doesn't rhyme, as much poetry does. Those who did read it found that it has rhythm and that it is a roaring, rollicking poem all about America, and Whitman, and ordinary things and extraordinary things.

No one knew what to make of Whitman's poem except Ralph Waldo Emerson, who knew, right away, that Whitman was writing with a new kind of voice: an American voice. "Leaves of Grass" was "the most extraordinary piece of wit and wisdom that America has yet contributed," Emerson wrote.

In April 1862, a 31-year-old unmarried woman named Emily Dickinson, living in the college town of Amherst, Massachusetts, wrote a letter to Thomas Wentworth Higginson, editor of the much-respected *Atlantic Monthly*. She asked him if he thought her poetry "breathed."

▲ Tall-tale hero Paul Bunyan was said to be eight feet tall and nearly as strong as his blue ox, Babe.

Tales That Are Whoppers Are Tall

Some Americans were becoming great storytellers. They were developing an American specialty: the tall tale. European stories were often of privileged people: knights, princesses, kings, and queens. American tall tales were exaggerated stories about ordinary people who became heroes because of what they could do, like powerful Paul Bunyan and his blue ox, Babe; or Pecos Bill, a mythical cowboy; or Mike Fink, who was a real frontiersman and boatman, though most of the stories about him are tall tales. At least we think they are.

Higginson didn't know quite what to do with the poems but he recognized a "wholly new" kind of writing. He kept answering Emily's letters and he thanked her for her "beautiful thoughts and words." We might not have had her poetry without him.

At a time when many Americans were adventuring west, Dickinson became a recluse (a stay-at-home) who dressed in white gowns and rarely left her father's big brick house in Amherst, a small village surrounded by farms and fields.

Most 19th-century poetry followed expected rules of meter, rhyme, and punctuation. But neither Whitman nor Dickinson paid attention to those rules. Each wrote with a rhythm and voice unlike any heard before. Eventually their poetry would break teacups in the literary world. Both were going to make people respond to writing that gets inside your head and speaks to your emotions.

But new ideas are never easily accepted. Whitman's poems were not well received; many thought them vulgar. Dickinson wrote about 1,800 poems; during her lifetime eight were published. Today Emily Dickinson and Walt Whitman are thought to be two of America's greatest poets—some say the greatest.

Emily Dickinson's "Letter to the World"

This is my letter to the World
That never wrote to Me—
The simple News that
    Nature told—
With tender Majesty
Her Message is committed
To Hands I cannot see—
For love of Her
    —Sweet—countrymen—
Judge tenderly—of Me.

◄ Most of the 1,800 poems Emily Dickinson wrote were not published until after her death.

From Walt Whitman's "Song of Myself"

I believe a leaf of grass is no less than the journey-work of
    the stars,
And the pismire is equally perfect, and a grain
    of sand, and the egg of the wren,
And the tree-toad is a chef-d'oeuvre
    for the highest.
And the running blackberry would
    adorn the parlors of heaven....
And a mouse is miracle enough to
    stagger sextillions of infidels.
I find I incorporate gneiss, coal, long-threaded
    moss, fruits, grains, esculent roots,
And am stucco'd with quadrupeds and birds
    all over...

A *pismire* is a type of ant.

A *chef-d'oeuvre* (shay-DEV-vrah) is how you say "a work of art" in French.

Gneiss (nice) is a kind of rock.

◄ The poet Walt Whitman described himself as "one of the roughs."

Painter of Birds
and Painter of Indians

His name was John James Audubon. He called himself an "American woodsman," which he was, although, like so many other Americans, he was also an immigrant who never lost his foreign accent.

Audubon was born in Santo Domingo (now Haiti) but grew up in France. His mother died when he was a baby, but his father and stepmother loved him dearly.

His childhood was a happy one. He loved to roam the out-of-doors, and he filled his bedroom with birds' eggs and nests and snakeskins; then he drew pictures of all the things he brought in from the woods. He drew with talent, but no one believed he could earn a living with his drawings. He was expected to go to sea, as his father had. But when he did he got seasick.

In 1803, at age 18, Audubon came to America to escape Napoleon's war. In America, people couldn't help but like young John James Audubon. He was good-natured, charming, and high-spirited. He liked to dance, draw pictures, make music, and go wandering in the woods.

John James Audubon was so popular in England that a friend wrote, "It is Mr. Audubon here and Mr. Audubon there until I am afraid poor Mr. Audubon is in danger of having his head turned." ▼

Then two things happened that changed Audubon's life: he became engaged to Lucy Bakewell, and his parents were no longer able to support him. How would he earn a living? He decided to head out to frontier Kentucky and open a store for settlers who would surely need supplies. He and his business partner climbed aboard a big flatboat and went west on the Ohio River.

Audubon opened his store in Louisville. A year later he returned east, married Lucy, and brought her to Kentucky. Soon they had two sons: Victor and John. But Audubon wasn't very good at shopkeeping. He kept drawing, or going off into the woods to hunt. He wore buckskin clothes and moccasins, carried a tomahawk, and, with his flowing long hair and deep-set eyes, looked like an Indian.

One day a famous bird expert—an ornithologist—came into his store. He was Alexander Wilson and he showed Audubon his drawings of birds. As soon as Audubon saw the drawings, he knew he could do better. Wilson's pictures were of stuffed dead birds. Audubon was drawing birds that were doing things—feeding their young, or building nests. Audubon drew his birds in a real, natural world.

After Audubon saw Wilson's drawings he got serious about his own. Soon it was no longer a hobby; he made it his life's work. He decided he would try to draw all the birds of North America. He was in a good place to do it: vast flocks of birds migrate through the Mississippi Valley. He knew he had to hurry. Hunters were killing many birds, and settlers were cutting down trees and destroying nests; some of the birds would soon be extinct.

Audubon went into the woods and watched the way birds lived and what they ate. Sometimes he caught a bird, put it in a cage, drew it, and then set it free. Sometimes he shot birds and used wires to make them look as if they were alive. He drew birds life-size and he made the size exact.

But people on the frontier didn't need bird drawings. Audubon had to do other things to earn a living. He taught dancing, he taught drawing, and he hunted. Lucy went to work as a teacher. It was discouraging, but he was perfecting his talent as an artist. He was also becoming a scientist. As far as we know, he was the first person to put a band on a bird's leg and then wait to see if it would return in the spring after flying away for the winter. (It did.)

Audubon went to Philadelphia to look for a publisher to print his drawings. But no one in America seemed to have the

▲ Audubon's drawings, like this one of a group of yellow-breasted chat, showed birds doing things such as building nests or feeding their young. He drew the natural world around birds as carefully as he drew the birds themselves.

▲ Wilson's drawings inspired Audubon.

Picture Plates

An engraving is a picture printed from a series of metal plates. The original drawing must first be copied onto the plates. Acid is used to cut the lines of the drawing into the metal. Then colored ink is rubbed on the plate. The ink runs into the cut lines. The rest is wiped away. Paper is pressed against the plate and the ink makes a print. A separate plate is needed for each color ink. The paper is pressed onto the plates, one after the other. Colored drawings, like Audubon's, need many inkings and many plates. A black-and-white engraving needs only one plate.

▲ George Catlin painted Native Americans living in their traditional ways.

skills to do it as carefully as Audubon wished. Lucy had saved some money; she sent it to her husband so he could take his drawings to England. In Liverpool and London, everyone was enchanted with the American woodsman who wore a fur cap and a wolfskin coat. In England people paid to see his drawings. And Audubon found a brilliant engraver in London. It took 11 years to engrave and print *Birds of America*. While that was happening Audubon kept on drawing. He knew that some of the birds and animals he drew might soon disappear from the planet.

George Catlin felt the same way about the people whom he painted. When Catlin's mother was eight she was captured by Iroquois. The little girl, who had been living on a frontier farm, was taken to a longhouse, treated well, and later released. She told her son stories of that adventure, and he never forgot them. When he grew up he became a member of the Pennsylvania Academy of Fine Arts, and, before long, was painting portraits of wealthy folk. But he had a yearning to do more than paint pretty portraits. Maybe it was his mother's stories that made him seek out Indians and sketch and paint them. They were hard to find. Most of the eastern Indians were dead or had been moved west.

In 1830, George Catlin decided to find and paint Indians living in their traditional ways. So he went to St. Louis, which had become the gateway to the West.

Catlin was fascinated by the skills of Comanche horsemen. ▼

The United States of Artists

Charles Willson Peale's portrait of Benjamin Franklin ▶

The Revolutionary War period produced America's first group of fine artists. Most people agreed that the greatest painter of that time was John Singleton Copley of Boston. Copley did portraits of people who seem so real you can almost tell what they're thinking.

Gilbert Stuart, from Rhode Island, was another outstanding portrait painter. You've seen one of his paintings. It is the portrait of George Washington on every dollar bill.

And then there was that extraordinary museum keeper, Charles Willson Peale, who painted 60 portraits of George Washington. He did more than 1,000 other portraits of people, including Martha Washington, Benjamin Franklin, and John Adams. (Remember, there were no cameras. If you wanted to have your picture made, you hired a portrait painter.)

Peale was also a saddlemaker, a watchmaker, a silversmith, and an inventor. And he encouraged young artists, like John James Audubon.

▲ Charles Willson Peale's self-portrait, *The Artist in His Museum*

When he was in Philadelphia, Audubon visited Charles Willson Peale's museum on the second floor of Independence Hall. Peale's museum was said to be the first in the United States. Inside were Indian relics, the skeleton of a mastodon, wax dummies, paintings—anything Peale found interesting. Joshua Johnston, a free black man who lived in the Peale household, was also a skilled portrait artist. Europeans were astounded when they met John Singleton Copley, Charles Willson Peale, and Gilbert Stuart. They seemed marvelous examples of the talent democracy could produce.

◀ John Singleton Copley's *Young Lady with a Bird and Dog*

Bird's Eye View of the Mandan Village, by George Catlin ▶

Then he looked up William Clark—of the Lewis and Clark expedition—and told him what he wanted to do. Clark was 60 and Superintendent of Indian Affairs. Catlin was 34 and eager. They got along splendidly, and, because the young man was sensitive and genuine, Clark taught him what he knew.

In 1832 Catlin took a year-long voyage up the Missouri River. When he returned, he had sketchbooks filled with paintings of the Mandan, Sioux, Blackfoot, and Crow Indians.

At a time when many Americans were ignoring—or attacking— Native Americans, George Catlin was painting them with honesty and affection. About the Indians he came to know, Caitlin said, "I love people who have always made me welcome to the best they had…who are honest without laws…who have no poor house…who never raised a hand against me or stole my property…and oh! how I love a people who don't live for the love of money."

Audubon and Catlin weren't America's only fine artists. In those days, artists were record keepers. There was no other way to have a picture of yourself, or of your home, or of scientific data. So artists, especially portrait artists, were in demand. Philadelphia artist (and friend of Audubon) Thomas Sully was known for his fine manners and graceful portraits; Samuel F. B. Morse, who invented the telegraph, was a portrait artist, too; William Sidney Mount painted Americans in action—farming, dancing, and listening to politicians; and George Caleb Bingham, from Missouri, painted boatmen and trappers and frontier Americans. Hiram Powers, Thomas Cole, Edward Hicks, and Asher B. Durand were other 19th-century American artists.

George Caleb Bingham painted ordinary people on the American frontier, as in *Fur Traders Descending the Missouri.* ▼

PART 3

the ROAD to WAR

History's Paradox

Here comes some difficult history. Put on your thinking cap—you're going to need it. The difficulty has to do with a paradox. A paradox is a contradiction. It may be good and bad at the same time. It is believing one thing and doing something else.

America was born of a dream that this land should be a land of freedom and justice for all.

This is the paradox: America has been both dream and nightmare.

Columbus saw nothing wrong with taking the people he mistakenly named "Indians" and making them slaves. He was doing what many others did, without asking himself if it was right or wrong.

And the Founders—who wrote of liberty and equality in a remarkable declaration and a splendid constitution—gave their consent to slavery, which was the very opposite of liberty and equality.

How come? Were all these people liars? Or dummies?

Of course they weren't. They were trying hard to do the best they could in a world where ideals weren't all that mattered. There were also powerful forces called selfishness, bigotry, hypocrisy, and cruelty.

> *Hypocrisy* is saying one thing when you believe another.

A paradox: many of the signers of the Declaration of Independence, which declared that "all men are created equal," owned slaves. ▼

IN CONGRESS, JULY 4, 1776

The unanimous Declaration of the thirteen united States of America.

▲ By 1850, there were more than 3 million slaves in the United States.

Which brings us to the 19th century in America and that awful paradox: slavery in the land of the free.

The fight to end the paradox, to get rid of the horror of slavery, was to be the most important battle in all our history. It led to war and, finally, to the end of slavery.

There is more to this paradox than you may know. Some blacks, who were free, owned slaves. In 1830, 1,556 free black masters in eight Southern states owned 7,188 slaves. Are you surprised that black people owned slaves? Blacks owned slaves for the same reasons whites did. It made them prosperous. The economic system in the South made it profitable to own slaves. Of course, that didn't make it right.

After 1808 it was against the law to bring Africans into the United States as slaves. In 1820 the penalty for breaking that law became death. Still, between 1820 and 1850, the number of slaves doubled: from a million and a half to more than 3 million. Many of that number were children born in the United States, but many others were new slaves brought in illegally.

The eight Southern states were South Carolina, Georgia, Florida, Alabama, Mississippi, Arkansas, Louisiana, and Texas. Some free blacks in those states owned slaves.

▲ The famous plea on this abolitionist pottery medallion cries, "Am I not a man and a brother?"

A few people—whites and free blacks—were doing everything possible to end the slave trade and to end slavery itself. Some thought the way to end slavery was to return blacks to Africa. Paul Cuffe went to Africa to start a colony for black Americans who wished to return to Africa. James Madison was president of the African Colonization Society; so was Senator Henry Clay. Many well-meaning people joined the colonization movement. They had the idea that black and white people couldn't live together on equal terms, so the only path to peace was separation. What do you think of that idea?

Most blacks who lived in America didn't want to go to Africa. They found they had little in common with Africans. They were Americans, and they wanted to be free and have all the same rights as other Americans. In an article in a Maryland newspaper a black writer said, "Though our bodies differ in color from yours; yet our souls are similar in a desire for freedom. [Difference] in color...can never constitute a [difference] in rights. Reason is shocked at the absurdity! Humanity revolts at the idea!"

In the Declaration of Independence, the Founders told us that we were all created equal and that we all have the right to "life, liberty and the pursuit of happiness." No country before had goals like those. And we had them in writing. Our Founders made fairness a national creed.

In 1808 the United States outlawed the foreign slave trade. That means it became a crime to bring new slaves into the country. (Britain and Spain also made foreign slave trading illegal.) Those who were already slaves could still be bought and sold inside the United States. Be sure that you understand that it was the slave trade—not slavery itself—that was outlawed. After 1808, no more enslaved Africans could be brought into the country legally. But there was still big money to be made by selling slaves, so slavers—those who ran slave ships—kept up an illegal slave trade even though they faced the death penalty if caught.

▲ At a slave auction, husbands could be sold away from wives or mothers from babies.

It doesn't sound very complicated—providing everyone with freedom, equality, and a chance to pursue happiness in a good land—but no nation has ever been completely fair to all its citizens.

Fairness is something you have to keep working at. Each generation has to do its job. In the 19th century, America's black people, along with fair-minded whites, would struggle and fight to end the paradox of slavery in a free nation. They understood that no one is free in a land where some are enslaved.

1 Wench Nam. Eve & Child

If you were a slave, you could be *bought and sold* just as if you were an animal or a piece of furniture. In 1811 Abraham van Vleek bought a collection of goods from Barent van Dupail (who was probably selling because of financial problems). Far and away the most expensive item on the list was a slave named Eve and her child.

1 Faning Mill	$17.25
1 Red Face Cow	$13.25
1 Yearling Calf	4.25
1 Plough	1.6
1 Wench Nam. Eve & Child	156.00
8 Fancy Chairs	9.25
1 Looking Glass. 6 Silver Table Spoons. 6 So. Tea Spoons 10 China saucers. 11 Wo. Cups 1 Tea Pot. Sugar and Milk Cups. 3 Plates Dish and tea Bord	35.1$^{1/2}$
[Total]	236.18^{1/2}$

African Americans

Millions of Africans were torn from their roots and transplanted to America. Like the people who came from Europe and Asia, they were changed by the American land. Soon, very soon, they were different from the brothers and sisters they had left behind. Soon they were no longer Africans. Now they were Americans—African Americans.

An African may have come to the newly discovered land on the first of Columbus's voyages. By 1501, Africans were living in the Caribbean. In 1619 they were living in Jamestown, Virginia, and, a few years later, at Plymouth, Massachusetts.

Africans cleared the woods, tilled the soil, planted tobacco, and harvested cotton. They were farmers, trailblazers, mountain men, cowhands, and pioneers. They were Americans. They panned for gold, dug canals, and helped build railroads. They fought at Concord, Bunker Hill, and Yorktown. A few were free, but most were slaves. Like all Americans, they longed for liberty—for their country and for themselves.

Those who could, spoke out. Elizabeth Freeman was a slave in Massachusetts when the Revolutionary War ended. Everywhere she heard people talking about freedom and equality. She heard of the Declaration of Independence. Why shouldn't she be free, she wondered?

These Africans, captured by slave traders, will soon be transported to America. ▼

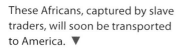

Most African Americans, like these slaves on a cotton plantation, faced lifetimes of hard work without liberty. ▼

Elizabeth Freeman went to a lawyer and asked him to help her. In 1781 her case was heard in a court in Great Barrington, Massachusetts. The jury agreed with Elizabeth Freeman, and she was freed.

In 1783, Nathaniel Jennison beat up Quock Walker. Walker went to court to protest. Jennison told the judge he had every right to beat Walker because Walker was his slave. The judge, William Cushing, chief justice of the Massachusetts Superior Court, didn't agree. He said that:

> *As to the doctrine of slavery and the right…to hold Africans… and sell and treat them as…horses and cattle…whatever [people have believed before]…a different idea has taken place with the people of America, more favorable to the natural rights of mankind…. The idea of slavery is inconsistent with our…constitution.*

Quock Walker was a free man.

Paul Cuffe's father was a free black who had been born a slave. His mother was a Wampanoag Indian. Cuffe went to sea, worked hard, and became the rich owner of a fleet of ships. But, because he was black, he wasn't allowed to vote in Massachusetts. Cuffe refused to pay his taxes. He said, "No taxation without representation." He appealed to the Massachusetts court, reminding the court that blacks and Indians had fought in the Revolutionary War. Cuffe lost his tax case, but the Massachusetts legislature then passed a law giving black people the same rights as whites. Cuffe had won the right to vote.

▲ Elizabeth Freeman, as painted by the daughter of the lawyer who helped her win her freedom

Sold, a Wife

Moses Grandy, suspecting nothing, was standing on the street when his wife passed by, in chains.

> *Mr. Rogerson was with them on his horse, armed with pistols. I said to him, "For God's sake, have you bought my wife?" He said he had; when I asked him what she had done, he said she had done nothing, but that her master wanted money. He drew a pistol out and said that if I went near the wagon on which she was, he would shoot me. I asked for leave to shake hands with her, which he refused, but said I might stand at a distance and talk with her. My heart was so full that I could say very little…. I have never seen or heard from her from that day to this. I loved her as I love my life.*

James Forten served as a powder boy on a ship during the Revolutionary War. After the war, he invented a sail-making device and made a fortune. Forten gave much of his money to help the cause of black freedom. "The spirit of freedom is marching with rapid strides and causing tyrants to tremble," wrote Forten. "May America awake...."

Lemuel Haynes was a soldier in the Continental army. He fought as a minuteman at the Battle of Lexington. After the war, in 1785, he became a minister in the Congregational Church. That was unusual. You see, Haynes's father was a slave, his mother was a white woman, and he was raised by foster parents. But Haynes had a splendid mind and a sense of humor that left people chuckling. When he became pastor of a church in West Rutland, Vermont, the church had 42 members; when he left, 30 years later, there were more than 300. Some of his sermons were printed, and even read in England. In 1804, Middlebury College awarded an honorary degree to Lemuel Haynes. (Colleges give honorary degrees to outstanding people.)

Richard Allen—a bricklayer, a preacher, and a slave—converted his master to the Methodist religion. The master

▲ James Forten

Lemuel Haynes was pastor of a mostly white church. Here (in a scene painted on a tray), he gives one of his famous sermons. ▶

allowed Allen to work extra hours and buy his freedom. One Sunday morning, Allen and his friend Absalom Jones were in a Philadelphia church, on their knees, praying. Some white men rudely grabbed them and said that because Allen and Jones were black, they would have to sit upstairs.

Allen and Jones walked out of the church. Richard Allen founded the African Methodist Episcopal Church and became its first bishop. Then he opened a school for black children in Philadelphia. Allen and Jones founded the Free African Society to fight against slavery. That wasn't all they did. In 1812, when the British burned Washington, Jones and Allen got 2,500 black troops to help protect Philadelphia.

These blacks were not alone—there were whites who cared. There had been since the earliest days of the colonies. In 1700, a Puritan judge, Samuel Sewall of Massachusetts, wrote, "Liberty is in real value next unto life: None ought to part with it themselves, or deprive others of it." The "others" he was talking about were blacks.

John Woolman, a white New Jersey Quaker, wrote in 1763, "I believe...a heavy account lies against us as a civil society for oppressions combated against people who did not injure us." He, too, was talking about blacks and slavery.

So was James Madison when he wrote, "The magnitude of this evil among us is so deeply felt...that no merit could be greater than that of devising a satisfactory remedy for it."

▲ To those who suggested that free blacks should return to Africa, Richard Allen replied, "This land which we have watered with our tears is now our mother country."

Torn Apart

My brothers and sisters were bid off first, and one by one, while my mother, paralyzed with grief, held me by the hand. Then I was offered.... My mother...pushed through the crowd while the bidding for me was going on, to the spot where Riley was standing. She fell at his feet, and clung to his knees, entreating him...to buy her baby [Josiah] as well as herself, and spare to her at least one of her little ones.

This was written by Josiah Henson, a former slave, who escaped to Canada, became a Christian minister, and wrote his autobiography. The auction took place in 1795. Josiah was five. Isaac Riley did not buy Josiah's mother. Instead, he kicked her and left her weeping and childless.

A slave woman begs not to have her family sold away from her. ▶

An escaped slave flees his pursuers. ▶

▲ Some slaves escaped and started new lives.

Thomas Jefferson wrote, "Indeed I tremble for my country when I reflect that God is just." And the Marquis de Lafayette said, "I never would have drawn my sword in the cause of America if I could have conceived that thereby I was helping to found a nation of slaves." President John Quincy Adams called slavery "a cancer gnawing at America."

With all those brilliant people speaking out against slavery, you would think it would be easy to end it. It wasn't. Slaves represented money, and most people don't like to part with their money. Still, a few blacks were becoming free: some were running away, some were earning their freedom, and some were freed by their owners.

A Baptist's Conscience Pricked

From Baptist leader John Mason Peck's journal, entry for January 1, 1842.

Today I attended for a few moments a sale in the [Nashville] marketplace. A negro boy was sold who appeared about 12 years old. He stood by the auctioneer on the market-bench with his hat off, crying and sobbing, his countenance a picture of woe. I know not the circumstances; but it was the first human being I ever saw set up for sale, and it filled me with indescribable emotions. Slavery in Tennessee is certainly not as oppressive, inhuman and depressing as the state of the poorer classes of society in England, Ireland, and many ports of Continental Europe; yet slavery in its best state is a violation of man's nature and of the Christian law of love.

The King and His People

It was a king who was messing things up. The Founders had warned about kings. But they were thinking of those fellows on the English throne. It never occurred to them that tyrannical monarchs might take other forms.

This king was called Cotton. King Cotton sat on his throne for about 60 years: from the time Eli Whitney invented the cotton gin until the terrible war between the states.

Cotton's throne was built of the arms, legs, backs, and hearts of Americans—black Americans—who did all the hard work in the king's empire.

The South that King Cotton ruled was different from the South of the 18th-century tobacco and rice planters. King Cotton's South was a new South, with new lands and new names. It grew fast, very fast, from the frontier lands of the former colonies, to the new states of Mississippi and Louisiana, and on to Texas. Wherever land was cheap and cotton would grow there were men eager to make their fortunes.

> The cotton gin was invented in 1793. The Civil War—also called the War Between the States—began in 1861.

Slaves on a cotton plantation toil under the watchful eye of the plantation overseer. ▼

Andrew Jackson, as you know, became president; John Calhoun was an important senator; and Jefferson Davis was president of the Confederate states—the South—during the Civil War.

Most of the newly rich men—the princes that King Cotton crowned—were frontier boys, born in log cabins. These new plantation owners imitated the style of the Virginia and South Carolina aristocrats but had the energy and ruthlessness of the backwoods. Andrew Jackson was one of them, John C. Calhoun another, and Jefferson Davis yet another.

They were smart, and lucky, too. Each of them bought a little land, worked it, bought a slave or two, worked them, bought more land, and soon had a whole plantation.

There weren't many big plantation owners, but they set the tone for the South. Most of the population was made up of yeoman farmers: people who owned small farms, as Northern farmers did. Most yeomen didn't have slaves, though a few owned a slave or two. In addition, there were poor whites, who had enough to eat and not much more. At the bottom of the ladder were the slaves, who were owned by people who talked of liberty.

The Old South had a tradition of violence: duels were frequent and so were lynchings. In the 20 years from 1840 to 1860, 300 people were lynched by mobs in Southern states. (To *lynch* means to kill without a fair trial.) Most of those lynched were white. There was almost no lynching of slaves—they were worth money.

The word *lynch* came into English about 1830, after John Lynch, a Virginia justice of the peace, set up his own trials and executed people without *due process of law*.

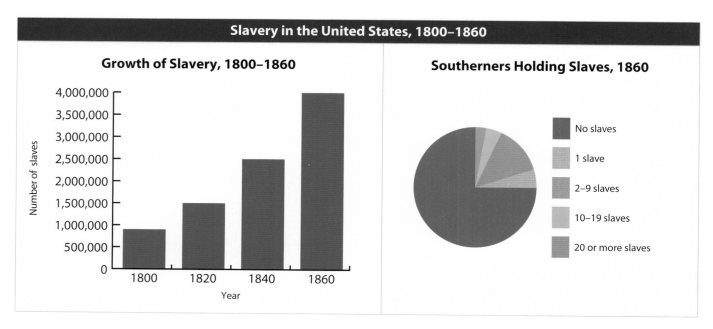

Slavery in the United States, 1800–1860

Growth of Slavery, 1800–1860

Number of slaves / Year

Southerners Holding Slaves, 1860

- No slaves
- 1 slave
- 2–9 slaves
- 10–19 slaves
- 20 or more slaves

If you want to understand about slavery and the conflict between blacks and whites, you will need to do a lot of reading and thinking. Especially if you want to be fair.

You will read tales of kind masters and happy slaves and you will read stories of viciousness, cruelty, and abuse. You will find both truth and exaggeration in most of those stories.

Yes, there was terrible, brutish, inexcusable meanness in slavery. But most slave owners—even if they were cruel—thought of their slaves as valuable property. They might beat them, but they tried not to do them serious harm. They needed to keep their property healthy.

Yes, there were kind slave owners who cared for the people they owned and treated them well. There was genuine affection between blacks and whites. But how would you like to be owned, even by someone nice? And always, behind the sweet-smelling magnolia trees and the white-columned mansions, there were chains, whips, and guns. There would have been no slavery without them.

Remember, in the time of George Washington most Southern whites hadn't liked slavery; they just didn't know how to end a bad system. As time went on, Southerners tried to tell each other that slavery was all right. They said that God had created some people to be slaves. They said black people weren't as smart as white people. Then, to make that true, they passed laws that said it was a crime to teach any black person to read and write. One white woman in Norfolk, Virginia, who taught some free blacks in her home, was arrested and spent a month in jail.

The slaves' battle for liberty is the next act in the drama that began with the Declaration of Independence and those noble words *all men are created equal*.

This ex-slave bears scars from repeated whippings. ▼

The whip was a tool of cruelty. ▶

Abolitionists Want to End Slavery

*A*bolition! Back in 1765 Americans had shouted the word. To *abolish* means to "end or to do away with something." Before the Revolution it was the hated British stamp tax the American colonists wanted to abolish.

Then the word began to be used with a new meaning. It was the slave trade some wanted to abolish, and then slavery itself. In 1773, Ben Franklin wrote in a letter that "a disposition to abolish slavery prevails in North America." That—in plain English—means people in North America want to find a way to end slavery. Two years later Franklin helped found the American Abolition Society.

The official African slave trade did end—when the Constitution said it would—in 1808. But slavery continued. And an illegal slave trade began. The problem was one of finding workers for jobs nobody wanted. No one had anything good to say about slavery—at least not in George Washington's day. But then, slowly, some people's ideas changed.

Partly it was because, during the 1820s and 1830s, some slaves rebelled and killed white people. After that, white Southerners started to be afraid of the slaves. Slavery became even more cruel. New laws were passed that gave slaves almost no rights at all. Some Southerners began finding excuses for slavery. Others began to say it was a fine way of life—for slave and master.

If you read the diaries and letters of white Southerners you will see there were many who knew better. Robert E. Lee, who was to become the South's most famous general in the Civil War, wrote in a letter, "Slavery is a moral evil in any society…more so to the white than to the black." But some people didn't care about morality. The South was having economic problems—and some Southern political leaders began blaming the North for those problems.

Virginia and South Carolina had once been very rich colonies. They had been the envy of all the Americas. Now the Old South was in decline. The tobacco land was worn out. Economic power—money—had moved to the new cotton states and to the new industries in the North.

▲ In the 1820s and 1830s, some slaves rebelled against their owners.

"A Moral Evil"

Moral has to do with understanding the difference between good and evil. A person who is moral acts with goodness in mind. A person who is *immoral* doesn't care about the difference between right and wrong. What did Robert E. Lee mean when he called slavery "a moral evil"? Why was slavery more of a moral evil for whites than for blacks?

Willing Sacrifice

From the beginning of slavery, blacks had fought enslavement. Some had run away to freedom. Some had joined Indian tribes. In 1804, a slave who took part in a rebellion was brought to trial. This is what he told the court:

> I have nothing more to offer than what George Washington would have had to offer had he been taken by the British and put to trial by them. I have adventured my life in endeavoring to obtain the liberty of my countrymen, and am a willing sacrifice to their cause.

Nat Turner, Denmark Vesey, and Gabriel Prosser were slaves who led freedom rebellions, though none was successful. Still, Southern white slaveholders were scared of slave uprisings. They knew that in Santo Domingo (Haiti) a brilliant, self-educated slave named Toussaint L'Ouverture had led a successful rebellion that left 60,000 people dead.

▲ Toussaint L'Ouverture (too-SEHN loo-vair-tyoor) led slaves on the island of Haiti in rebellion against their French colonial masters. Toussaint's triumphs pushed the French to abolish slavery in the colony. Toussaint ruled Haiti for several years until 1802, when Napoleon sent troops, abolished the new constitution, and captured Toussaint. In 1804, France gave up the colony and Haiti declared its independence.

◀ Nat Turner led his fellow slaves in a bloody rebellion that shocked whites in the South.

The Southern leaders didn't seem to understand what was happening. Immigrants and ideas and inventions were changing the North. The South was left out of that excitement. Newcomers didn't want to move south. They knew that as workers they couldn't compete with slaves' jobs. The South became isolated; it didn't grow with the 19th century.

Southerners began to live in a world of olden times. They read stories of the old days and believed those days were better. They wouldn't admit they were trapped in an evil system that got worse and worse each year.

Religious groups got involved. In the North, the Quakers were at the center of the abolitionist movement. But the leaders of some other religions—North and South—defended slavery.

The South became very jealous of political power. So did the North. Each wanted to dominate the nation. Each was afraid of the other. Tempers flared. It got more intense than that old conflict between Federalists and Republicans. But as long as Congress was divided evenly between slave states and free states, there was some stability.

Two Separate Nations?

America in the first half of the 19th century was like two separate nations. The North was becoming a modern, industrial, urban nation, with railroads, canals, steamboats, and factories—as well as farms. Many of the workers in the new factories and mills were immigrants. The South remained an agricultural region. Mostly, immigrants stayed away from the South.

▲ Much of the North had become industrialized and urban by 1850.

◀ The South's economy was based on agriculture, which depended on slave labor.

◀ Quakers meet to discuss their efforts to abolish slavery.

Then, in 1820, Missouri asked to enter the Union as a slave state. Northerners were alarmed. If Missouri became a state, the North would be outvoted in Congress. Northern congressmen were afraid of what might happen next. Suppose Congress voted to allow slavery in all the states! The situation was tense. Finally, a solution was found. Here it is: Maine was carved from Massachusetts and made into a state, a free state. That kept the balance of free and slave states. That action was called the Missouri Compromise. The Missouri Compromise also said that the rest of the Louisiana Purchase territory that was north of Missouri's southern border was to remain free. (Look at the map on page 210. This is complicated but important.) The Missouri Compromise kept some of the anger between North and South under control…for a while.

A Compromise, Not a Solution

The Missouri Compromise maintained a balance between slave states and free states. When Missouri entered the Union as a slave state in 1820, Maine became a free state at the same time, so that there would be an equal number of slave and free states.

James Tallmadge, a New York congressman, proposed a constitutional amendment to ban slavery in Missouri. But the Southern states wouldn't agree to that. So Senator Jesse Thomas of Illinois introduced an amendment to forbid slavery north of 36°30'—except in Missouri.

For about 30 years the Missouri Compromise seemed reasonable; but it only managed to put off the trouble ahead—big trouble.

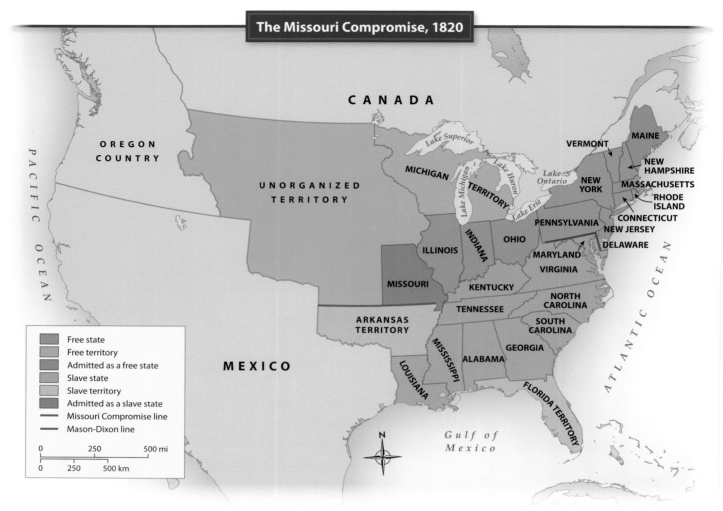

The Missouri Compromise, 1820

CANADA

OREGON
COUNTRY

UNORGANIZED
TERRITORY

MICHIGAN
TERRITORY

MEXICO

ILLINOIS
INDIANA
OHIO
MISSOURI
KENTUCKY
ARKANSAS
TERRITORY
TENNESSEE
MISSISSIPPI
ALABAMA
LOUISIANA

VERMONT
MAINE
NEW
HAMPSHIRE
NEW
YORK
MASSACHUSETTS
RHODE
ISLAND
CONNECTICUT
PENNSYLVANIA
NEW JERSEY
DELAWARE
MARYLAND
VIRGINIA
NORTH
CAROLINA
SOUTH
CAROLINA
GEORGIA
FLORIDA TERRITORY

Lake Superior
Lake Michigan
Lake Huron
Lake Ontario
Lake Erie

PACIFIC OCEAN
ATLANTIC OCEAN
Gulf of
Mexico

Legend:
- Free state
- Free territory
- Admitted as a free state
- Slave state
- Slave territory
- Admitted as a slave state
- Missouri Compromise line
- Mason-Dixon line

0 250 500 mi
0 250 500 km

▲ The Missouri Compromise divided lands that could become slave states from lands that could become free states.

Meanwhile, in the first years of the 19th century, most European countries abolished—ended—slavery. Those countries began to criticize the United States for allowing it. Some people in the North—who for a long time hadn't seemed to care about it—started speaking out against slavery. By 1840 there were said to be about 2,000 abolitionist societies in the North. While some Northerners and Southerners talked of gradually freeing the slaves and even paying the slave owners, the abolitionists wanted to do away with slavery at once.

Don't think this was a case of good Northerners and bad Southerners. Many white Southerners hated slavery and treated blacks decently. And many white Northerners didn't seem to know about the Golden Rule ("Do unto others..."). Northern blacks were rarely

Abolitionist groups spread their message in publications like this 1840 almanac. ▼

▲ Elijah Lovejoy, an Illinois printer, kept publishing about the wrongs of slavery even when his printing press was destroyed. After he was murdered, his brother Owen carried on his fight.

given the rights of citizens: in most places they weren't allowed to vote or serve on juries. In the North, blacks often held the worst jobs, and black children were usually not allowed in white schools.

Many white Northerners hated the abolitionists. Some Northern industries depended on Southern business. Because of that, some Northerners didn't want to upset the South. Other Northerners were just afraid of change. (And what the abolitionists were demanding was a major change in the United States.) Unfortunately, there are always people who fear new ideas. In the North, abolitionist presses were burned and destroyed and one abolitionist was actually murdered.

Slave States and Free States

These were the 12 free states in 1820 at the time of the Missouri Compromise: Connecticut, Illinois, Indiana, Maine, Massachusetts, New Hampshire, New Jersey, New York, Ohio, Pennsylvania, Rhode Island, and Vermont. And these were the 12 slave states: Alabama, Delaware, Georgia, Kentucky, Louisiana, Maryland, Mississippi, Missouri, North Carolina, South Carolina, Tennessee, and Virginia. According to the 1820 census, 5.1 million Americans lived in the free states and territories; 4.4 million lived in the Southern slave states.

In the South, the abolitionists were really hated. When Northerners talked about abolishing slavery it made white Southerners furious. They didn't think it was the Yankees' business, and they didn't want to hear criticism of their beloved South. They didn't want to be told they were doing something immoral. Many white Southerners believed their liberty and property were being threatened by outsiders. They didn't worry about black liberty or property.

You can see this was an argument that was heating up. The abolitionists wrote and printed newspapers and books. Former slaves began to speak out and tell their stories. The abolitionists got angrier and angrier. Some abolitionists were so outraged by slavery they suggested that New England secede from the Union. That means they wanted to separate themselves from the other states. They wanted to form their own country. Some people in the South began saying the same thing. They wanted to secede and form their own country. These people were serious. No good would come of this.

"I Will Be Heard!"

On January 1, 1831, a white Massachusetts man, William Lloyd Garrison, began publishing *The Liberator*. It soon became the leading abolitionist newspaper.

In the first issue of *The Liberator,* Garrison wrote these famous words:

I do not wish to think, or speak, or write with moderation. No! No! Tell a man whose house is on fire, to give a moderate alarm…but urge me not to use moderation in a cause like the present. I am in earnest—I will not equivocate—I will not excuse—I will not retreat a single inch—AND I WILL BE HEARD.

▲ An 1831 abolitionist banner

The masthead from Garrison's *The Liberator* ▶

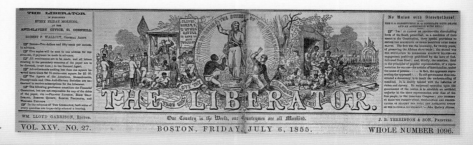

Frederick Douglass

What was it like to be a slave? Most white Americans—especially those in the North—didn't know. And then, in 1841, a tall, handsome man, a runaway slave whose name was Frederick Douglass, spoke up at an abolitionist meeting on Nantucket Island, near Boston. "I felt strongly moved to speak," Douglass wrote later. But he hesitated; his legs shook. "The truth was, I felt myself a slave, and the idea of speaking to white people weighed me down."

Yet he found the courage to speak out. When he did, eloquent words poured from his mouth. Frederick Douglass just told his own story: how he had lived and what he had seen. That was enough to send chills down the backs of his listeners.

Douglass soon became famous. He traveled from Nantucket Island to Indiana as a speaker for the Massachusetts Anti-Slavery Society. Northerners wanted to hear this man who spoke so well and told of his life as a slave. When he started an abolitionist newspaper, whites and blacks subscribed. Then he wrote a book and called it

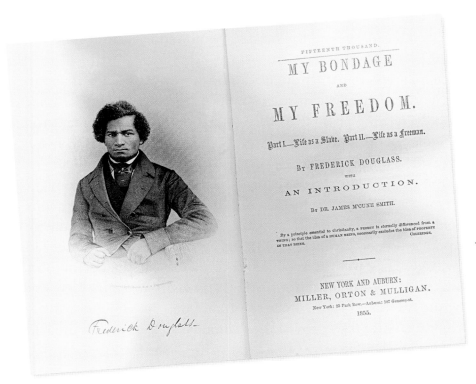

◀ By telling his life story, Frederick Douglass helped people see the evils of slavery. This is the title page of *My Bondage and My Freedom*, an autobiographical account he wrote after his *Narrative of the Life of Frederick Douglass*.

When Mrs. Sophia was forbidden to teach young Frederick Douglass to read, he realized that the aim was to keep blacks ignorant. "From that moment," he later wrote, "I understood the pathway from slavery to freedom."

Narrative of the Life of Frederick Douglass, an American Slave. Here is some of his story:

I never saw my mother...more than four or five times in my life.... She made her journeys to see me in the night, travelling the whole distance on foot [12 miles], after the performance of her day's work. She was a field hand, and a whipping is the penalty of not being in the field at sunrise.... I do not recollect of ever seeing my mother by the light of day. She was with me in the night. She would lie down with me, and get me to sleep, but long before I waked she was gone.... She died when I was about seven years old.... I was not allowed to be present during her illness, at her death, or burial.

Young Frederick was sent to Baltimore to be a companion to a little white boy. For a slave, that was a lucky break. That chance, he said, "opened the gateway to all my subsequent prosperity." His new mistress, Mrs. Sophia, was young and kindly. She began to teach the eager boy to read—until her husband saw her doing it and ordered her to stop. Reading, said the master, "would forever unfit him to be a slave."

The man was right. Through reading, a slave might learn about liberty and equality. The mistress stopped teaching Frederick. In fact, she did everything possible to keep books and magazines away from him. She began to turn mean. "Slavery proved as injurious to her as it did to me," Douglass wrote.

But it was too late. Frederick had been bitten by the learning bug. Now he became determined to learn to read and to write, too. He had to be clever to do it. He was often sent on errands where he met poor white boys. They were hungry for food; he was hungry for knowledge. They went to school and could read; he had extra food. He was soon trading bread for reading lessons. Sometimes he teased his white friends. "I can write better than you," he said, knowing he couldn't. After they proved they could write their letters, he had something he could copy.

From an 1831 North Carolina law: "Be it enacted by the General Assembly.... That any free person, who shall hereafter teach, or attempt to teach, any slave within the State to read or write...shall be liable to indictment in any court of record in this State." (To be *indicted* (in-DYTE-uhd) is to be charged with a criminal offense.)

Then he was sent away. The Baltimore people had just rented him. His owner took him back and sent him to a new master. This one was cruel, very cruel. Now he was beaten with a whip until he was bloody and scarred. He was not given enough to eat. He was sent into the fields to work long, long hours. He saw all the terrible things that happen when one person has complete power over another. "But for the hope of being free," Douglass wrote later, "I have no doubt but that I should have killed myself."

What happened to him next is all put down in his book—and it is exciting. But he didn't tell how he escaped to freedom. If he had, the slave catchers would have known how to capture others who might use the same route. He did tell the names of all the slave owners who had used and abused him. He told where they lived and all about them. That took great courage. He was still a runaway, and he knew slave catchers might come after him.

Frederick Douglass kept telling people this simple truth: *Justice to the Negro is safety to the nation.* (What do you think he meant by "safety to the nation"? Was he hinting at a slave uprising? Or did he think democracy might be at risk in a slave nation?) It was too bad more people didn't listen to him and ask themselves questions.

These are the words of Frederick Douglass:

People in general will say they like colored men as well as any other, but in their proper place. They assign us that place; they don't let us do it ourselves nor will they allow us a voice in the decision. They will not allow that we have a head to think, and a heart to feel and a soul to aspire.… That's the way we are liked. You degrade us, and then ask why we are degraded—you shut our mouths and then ask why we don't speak—you close your colleges and seminaries against us, and then ask why we don't know more.

"You have seen how a man was made a slave," wrote Douglass. "You shall see how a slave was made a man." ▶

▲ Frederick Douglass in his later years, in his office in Washington, D.C.

The country would pay an awful price for its injustice and bigotry.

He also said, "You may rely upon me as one who will never desert the cause of the poor, no matter whether black or white." And he never did. He fought for human rights for all. In his later years he fought to get the vote for blacks and for women; he spoke out against the mistreatment of Chinese immigrants and American Indians; he worked for better schools for all.

Always he had the courage to stand up for his beliefs—well, not always; once it took all his strength to sit for those beliefs. He was in a railroad car and was asked to leave because he was black. He wouldn't budge. A group of white men tried to make him go. Douglass held on while they pulled the railroad seat out of the floor of the car. It was astounding how far hatred was taking some people.

Frederick Douglass became an adviser to President Abraham Lincoln, and a giant figure of American history. Do you think anyone knows, or cares, what happened to the bullies who threw him and the seat from the train?

For Captive Millions

Some Americans didn't think much about the Declaration of Independence or the ideals of the Founders, but slaves and free blacks understood just how precious freedom was. In 1837, James Forten, Jr., spoke at the Ladies' Anti-Slavery Society:

> *My friends, do you ask why I thus speak? It is because I love America; it is my native land; because I feel as one should feel who sees destruction, like a corroding cancer, eating into the very heart of his country, and would make one struggle to save her; —because I love the stars and stripes, emblems of our National Flag—and long to see the day when not a slave shall be found resting under its shadow; when it shall play with the winds pure and unstained by the blood of "captive millions."*

A Triumvirate Is Three People

If you could pick a time in all of history to sit in the galleries of Congress and listen, you would do well to consider the first half of the 19th century. It was an age of oratory. The House and Senate echoed with eloquence. But among the silver-tongued speech makers, three were outstanding. Each of these three brilliant men wanted to be president. Even Patrick Henry might have met his match in a debate with any of them. Their names were Henry Clay, John C. Calhoun, and Daniel Webster.

They say that when New England's Daniel Webster spoke, even his enemies came to marvel. He was a heroic figure of a man, sturdy, with dark hair and flashing eyes. But it was his deep, strong voice that most people remembered.

Being a Yankee, Daniel Webster supported the interests of the Massachusetts factory owners, bankers, and ship owners. He hated slavery and used strong words to attack it. He loved the Union and did everything he could to protect it. He wanted to be president.

So did Henry Clay, who was called "the great compromiser." Some say that if Clay had been president there would have been no Civil War. Perhaps. He certainly tried to get the job. He ran for president five times and was well qualified for the position. He was a senator when he was 29 (even though the Constitution says you must be 30); after that he became speaker of the House of Representatives, secretary of state under John Quincy Adams, and a senator again.

Triumvirate comes from the Latin words *trium* (which means "of three") and *vir* ("man"). There were times in ancient Rome when government control was divided among three men so that no one person would be too powerful.

Daniel Webster said, "We may be tossed upon an ocean where we can see no land…. But there is a chart and compass for us to study…. That chart is the Constitution." ▼

Henry Clay said, "The Constitution of the United States was made not merely for the generation that then existed, but for posterity—unlimited, undefined, endless, perpetual posterity." ▶

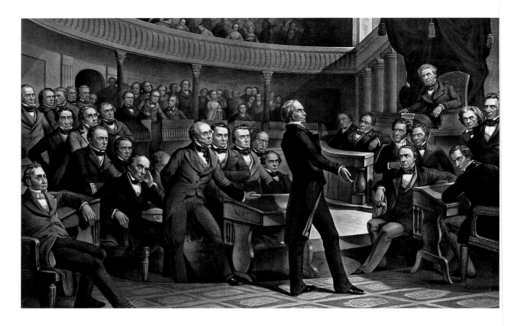

When Henry Clay spoke, people listened. Here, he urges the U.S. Senate to adopt the Compromise of 1850 to avert a civil war. ▶

Clay was born in Virginia but moved to Kentucky, which was frontier country. In Congress he was known as "Harry of the West."

What a speaker he was! His speeches were said to be "magnetic." It was his intelligence that scared his enemies. They knew they could not control him as they could some of the weaker men who became president. Clay spoke out against slavery, and yet he had slaves himself. Like Daniel Webster, Clay loved the Union and would do everything he could to save it.

Andrew Jackson was head of the Democratic Party. (It had evolved from Thomas Jefferson's old Democratic-Republican Party.) But the people who couldn't stand Jackson (and there were quite a few of them) needed a party to express their ideas. Henry Clay was their leader. He founded the Whig Party. It was named for the English political party that had opposed the king. Clay accused Jackson of acting like a king.

Jackson's enemies called him King Andrew; they said he trampled on the Constitution and did whatever he wanted. ▶

John Calhoun was another man who wanted to be president. Calhoun, from South Carolina, had gone to college and law school in New England. Still, he was no friend of Daniel Webster's friends. Calhoun was serious, and he had a serious mission. He needed to explain slavery and make people believe, as he did, that slavery was necessary and even good. He thought what he was doing was right. Calhoun loved the Union, but he loved the Southern way of life even more.

And he was afraid that way of life was in danger. Once, the South had been more powerful than the North. By 1820, that was changing. If the western territories joined the Union as free states—if they voted with the North—then they might vote to end slavery. It would be the end of the South that Calhoun knew and loved. Calhoun wanted the new states to become slave states.

Calhoun fought the tariffs the North wanted. A tariff is a tax or duty on goods brought from a foreign nation. If foreign goods are taxed, they become more expensive than untaxed goods made at home. High tariffs helped the Northern industries that were just beginning to grow. Tariffs hurt the Southerners who sold cotton in Europe and bought manufactured goods there. Calhoun said if a state believed a law was unconstitutional, it didn't have to obey that law. He said the Southern states should not collect tariffs. John Calhoun was Andrew Jackson's vice president, but Jackson was furious when he heard Calhoun's ideas on not collecting tariffs, and he didn't agree with Calhoun's hard stand on slavery.

There were powerful differences in America, and the Senate was just the place to argue them. The small Senate chamber had a high, domed ceiling that reflected even a hushed voice. The 48 senators sat at desks in semicircular rows, each row higher than the one in front of it. The senators had no clerks, or assistants, or offices (as they do today), so all their work was done at their Senate desks. Because of that, the Senate was often a noisy place. But when one of the great orators spoke, the room became still and the balcony quickly filled with spectators.

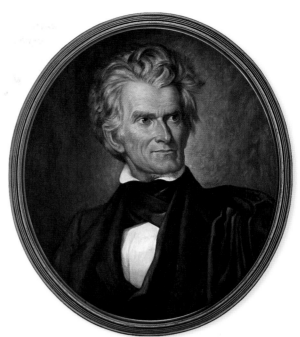

▲ "There never has yet existed a wealthy and civilized society in which one portion of the community did not…live on the labor of the other," said John Calhoun.

Despite their differing ideas, Webster, Clay, and Calhoun respected each other. Calhoun said of Henry Clay, "He is a bad man, an imposter, a creator of wicked schemes. I wouldn't speak to him, but, by God, I love him."

▲ Sam Houston lost his Senate seat in Texas after he spoke out against slavery.

▲ John Quincy Adams wrote, "My life has been… marked by great and signal successes which I neither aimed at nor anticipated."

Do you think you might have liked being there just to listen? Besides Clay, Calhoun, and Webster, there was the senator from Texas, Sam Houston, who spoke boldly for what he thought was right—and, though he lived with slavery, he didn't think it right. He didn't agree with John Calhoun and said so. Texas was a slave state, and what Houston said was not popular in Texas. He lost his seat in the Senate, as he knew he would.

And there was Senator William Seward of New York, the man who bought Alaska for the nation. (That would happen in 1867.) Seward was an uncompromising enemy of slavery. The Constitution allowed slavery. Seward said, "There is a higher law." What did he mean?

But the Senate wasn't the only place where you could hear eloquent speakers. John Quincy Adams was in the House of Representatives. That's right, JQA was in Congress—elected to the House after Andrew Jackson beat him in his second try for the presidency.

The people of Plymouth, Massachusetts, asked him to serve, and Adams said he would if he could vote his conscience and not worry about what they thought. That was a typical John Quincy Adams request; the people of Plymouth weren't surprised a bit and were proud to send him to Washington.

"Do you find it hard serving in Congress after being president?" he was asked.

He didn't find it hard at all. Liked it better than anything he had done before. For John Quincy, serving the public was reward enough. "Old Man Eloquent" was what they called him in Congress, and, because he always made sense, people stopped whatever they were doing to listen when he spoke. In Congress he was a leader in the fight against slavery. And it was in Congress, in 1848, that he had a stroke and died—which may have been the way he wanted to go.

But it was a debate in the Senate, in 1830, that I want you to hear. Some people say it was the greatest debate ever heard in the Senate. Some people say it was the greatest in U.S. history. Now you can decide for yourself.

The Great Debate

Let's take seats in the Senate gallery. From here we can look over the railing and see what is going on below. It is 1830, and Vice President John Calhoun is presiding. (The vice president leads the Senate but cannot give speeches or vote—unless there is a tie.) South Carolina's popular 38-year-old senator, Robert Young Hayne, is speaking. Hayne is slim, good-looking, and well respected. But some say that it is Calhoun who is really talking today. Because the vice president cannot speak in the Senate, they say that Hayne is just mouthing Calhoun's words. That isn't fair. Hayne is also a brilliant man, and a fine speaker. Yet there is no question that Hayne looks up to Calhoun. Calhoun will nod and smile at him as he speaks.

Hayne is urging the West to unite with the South and oppose the North and its tariff. Together the South and West can dominate the nation, he says. Senator Hayne talks of "states' rights." It is that old argument of Patrick Henry's. Hayne believes the country was formed by and for the states—not the people in general. He fears a strong federal government; he wants each state to keep final power for itself. His arguments are clear and brilliant. Can anyone answer him?

Daniel Webster rises. His is a speech no one will forget. He will talk for two days, trying to defend the Union against the Southern congressmen who now say that their liberty is more important than the Union. They are beginning to talk openly of secession. That means leaving the Union and forming a separate new nation in the South.

> A big argument in Congress was over states' rights versus federal power. Which should be stronger? Some people are still arguing about that.

◀ "The inherent right in the people to reform their government I do not deny," said Daniel Webster. "And they have another right, and that is to resist unconstitutional laws without overturning the government."

Picture a big man dressed in a blue coat with brass buttons, a cream-colored vest, and a white tie. He uses his voice like a musician playing an organ. Sometimes the voice thunders and fills the hushed hall; sometimes the voice is soft and sweet and people must concentrate so they won't miss a word. There isn't an empty seat in the Senate. So many congressmen have come to listen that the House of Representatives cannot conduct its normal business.

What is this government of ours, Webster asks? Does it belong to the state legislatures, or to the people? And he answers his own question:

> *The Constitution is not the creature of the State government. It is, sir, the people's Constitution, the people's government, made for the people, made by the people, and answerable to the people. The people of the United States have declared that this Constitution shall be supreme law.*

The states have powers, he tells his hushed listeners, and he describes the powers the Constitution gives the states. He tells of the checks and balances and limits on power. He is giving his audience a lecture on constitutional law. The Constitution is the great law of the land, he says. Who shall decide if a law is constitutional? For Webster there is only one answer: it cannot be the states; it must be the Supreme Court.

"My Country 'Tis of Thee"
Samuel F. Smith is asked to write a hymn for a children's choir. He writes out words about our country and fits them to a tune in a German songbook. It is 1832, and Smith calls his hymn "My Country 'Tis of Thee." Later, he discovers he has chosen a melody that is also sung with the words "God Save the King"—which is the British national anthem.

The song "My Country 'Tis of Thee" is also known as "America." ▶

But it is secession that really worries him. The great orator uses patriotic phrases to fight that idea. Webster's speech will become so famous that children in school will be required to memorize long parts of it. *When my eyes shall be turned to behold for the last time the sun in heaven, may I not see him shining on the broken and dishonored fragments of a once glorious Union,* he pleads. He warns of civil feuds and the shedding of brothers' blood. How can his listeners know that he is predicting the future? Then he speaks of an idea of John Calhoun's—Liberty first and Union afterwards—and calls it folly. Finally, he ends with these ringing words: *Liberty and Union, now and forever, one and inseparable!*

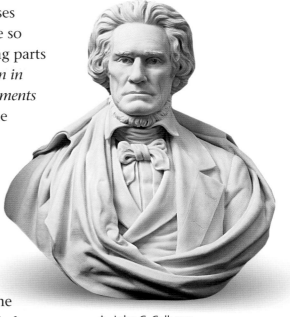

▲ John C. Calhoun

The western senators are won over. Daniel Webster has crushed the Southern hope that the West and the South can band together. But Webster has not crushed John Calhoun.

Calhoun understands that if the South is to keep slavery, all the nation must approve of it. He must make the nation approve, or help form a separate Southern nation. Calhoun will develop a philosophy that makes slavery sound noble. Earlier Southern leaders, men like Jefferson and Madison, talked of slavery as an evil they were unable to control. Calhoun will call it a "positive good." Other Southern leaders will say it is God-inspired. Many people will believe them.

President Andrew Jackson is not one of them. He is a strange mixture of fighter, democrat, and practical politician. He is a slave owner, but he never suggests that slavery is good. Yet he doesn't say that slavery is bad, either. He doesn't provide much leadership on this issue that is so important to the United States and its peoples.

But Jackson does put the nation ahead of his home region. When South Carolina refuses to collect the tariff, Jackson threatens to send an army to his native state. "I will hang John Calhoun," he fumes. He doesn't really mean that, but he and his vice president are now bitter enemies.

Soon after his debate with Daniel Webster, Robert Hayne gives up his seat in the Senate to become governor of South Carolina. As soon as that happens, John Calhoun resigns as vice president. If he can't be president, Calhoun would rather be a senator. He knows the nation's future is being decided on the floor of Congress. Calhoun is appointed to replace Hayne. For the next 20 years John Calhoun will speak for himself in the Senate. He will have much to say.

Mutiny on the Amistad

▲ A scene from a movie based on the *Amistad* mutiny

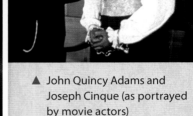

▲ John Quincy Adams and Joseph Cinque (as portrayed by movie actors)

In 1839—years after Britain had outlawed the foreign slave trade—Sengbe Pieh was working near his village in Sierra Leone, a British colony in Africa. Four strange men stepped out of the bush and surrounded him. At gunpoint, the men marched Sengbe Pieh and other Sierra Leoneans to the coast. Pieh never got to say good-bye to his wife and three children.

He and the other captives were chained and thrown inside a ship—an illegal slave trading ship. One in every three of them died on the trip to Cuba, a Spanish colony at the time. In Cuba, Sengbe Pieh and the others who survived the trip were given European names and false identity papers saying they were Spanish-speaking slaves not born in Africa. Such slaves could still be sold. Sengbe Pieh became Joseph Cinque (SIN-kay).

In Havana, the Cuban capital, Joseph Cinque was sold into slavery. He and others were dragged on board a Spanish ship, a small schooner called the *Amistad*. They were headed for an island port. The captain and crew knew they were breaking the law but they weren't worried. They had done this before.

Cinque was terrified. Using sign language, he asked the cook what was going to happen to them. The cook—in a cruel joke—ran his finger across his throat and pointed to barrels of beef. Cinque thought he was to be turned into meat.

Then he found a big iron nail. Quietly Cinque used the nail to pick the lock on the chain that circled his neck. That night he freed the others. They looked for weapons and found boxes of sugarcane knives with fierce blades two feet long.

The mutiny began at 4 a.m. Fifteen minutes later it was over. The captain was dead, and so was the cook. Two sailors had jumped overboard and others were Cinque's prisoners.

Now, how to get back to Africa? Cinque didn't know how to sail. So he ordered the sailors to head for Africa. But they tricked Cinque. The *Amistad* was soon captured in the waters near Connecticut.

"Send the blacks back to Cuba," said those who approved of slavery.

"Set them free," said those who didn't.

This matter would have to be decided in the courts. In Connecticut a judge said the Africans had been captured illegally. The laws prohibiting the slave trade had been broken, he said, and the captives should be freed.

The case was appealed all the way to the U.S. Supreme Court. Abolitionists who were trying to help Cinque and the other Africans were worried because five of the nine Supreme Court justices were Southerners. The abolitionists asked an old man to help them. He agreed and said he would take no money for doing it. His name was John Quincy Adams.

In 1841, Adams stood before the Supreme Court and talked for eight hours. One of the justices said it was an "extraordinary" argument. It all came down to one thing, said the former president, and that could be found in the Declaration of Independence.

I know of no other law that reaches the case of my clients, but the law of Nature and of Nature's God on which our fathers placed our own national existence.

The Supreme Court agreed. Cinque and his companions were free.

Webster Defends the Union

The year is 1850. The century's three most eminent senators—Henry Clay, John C. Calhoun, and Daniel Webster—are old men. All will soon be dead. But they will not go quietly. They are about to play their last scene in the national drama, and it will be a knockout performance. The country is being pulled apart—everyone can see that. Each time a new state enters the Union, the balance in Congress between North and South is threatened. Now California wants to become a state. California's constitution prohibits slavery. If California enters the Union, free states will outnumber slave states. Suppose the free states pass a law outlawing slavery?

John Calhoun, from South Carolina, cannot imagine the South without slavery. Calhoun calls slavery a "positive good." He says slavery is good for slaves and masters. He really seems to believe that. He is trying to unite the South. Calhoun says that if a state thinks a law is unconstitutional, then the state has the right to "nullify," or not obey, that law. He even says each state has the right to secede—to leave the Union—if it wishes. Some Southerners are beginning to talk of secession.

▲ From left to right, John C. Calhoun, Daniel Webster, and Henry Clay

But other Southerners don't agree with Calhoun's states' rights argument. They don't like the idea of secession, even though they like slavery. They are Unionists. They believe in the United States.

Some white Southerners hate slavery. Virginia's Robert E. Lee has made that clear in letters to his family—but he has not spoken out in public. Kentucky's Cassius Marcellus Clay has. He is Henry Clay's cousin, and he has freed his slaves and taken abuse and even gunfire for his beliefs. Slavery is ruining the South, says Cassius Clay. He says the slaves should be freed gradually and the slave owners paid for their financial loss. It is not a bad idea, but most abolitionists won't even consider it.

Calhoun won't consider it either; he will have nothing but a slave-based society. He is a powerful thinker who has convinced most white Southerners with his arguments.

But he hasn't convinced Henry Clay. Clay, another Kentuckian, has been working on a compromise. As soon as people hear he is to speak, they pack the Senate chamber. Clay is 73 years old and white-haired, but still a commanding figure. He is wearing a black suit and a stiff white collar that touches his ears. Clay has a bad cough, but that does not keep him from speaking clearly and eloquently.

Jackson's Proclamation

The argument about the nature of states' rights was not new in 1850. Twenty years earlier, the South Carolina legislature had declared a federal tax law null and void in South Carolina and threatened to leave the Union if the federal government tried to enforce the law. Andrew Jackson, president at the time, was outraged. He issued a Proclamation to the People of South Carolina explaining his view of the Constitution and states' rights. In part, he said:

> I consider, then, the power to annul a law of the United States, assumed by one State, incompatible with the existence of the Union, contradicted expressly by the letter of the Constitution, unauthorized by its spirit, inconsistent with every principle on which it was founded, and destructive of the great object for which it was formed....
>
> To say that any State may at pleasure secede from the Union is to say that the United States are not a nation, because it would be a solecism to contend that any part of a nation might dissolve its connection with the other parts, to their injury or ruin, without committing any offense. Secession, like any other revolutionary act, may be morally justified by the extremity of oppression; but to call it a constitutional right is confounding the meaning of terms, and can only be done through gross error....

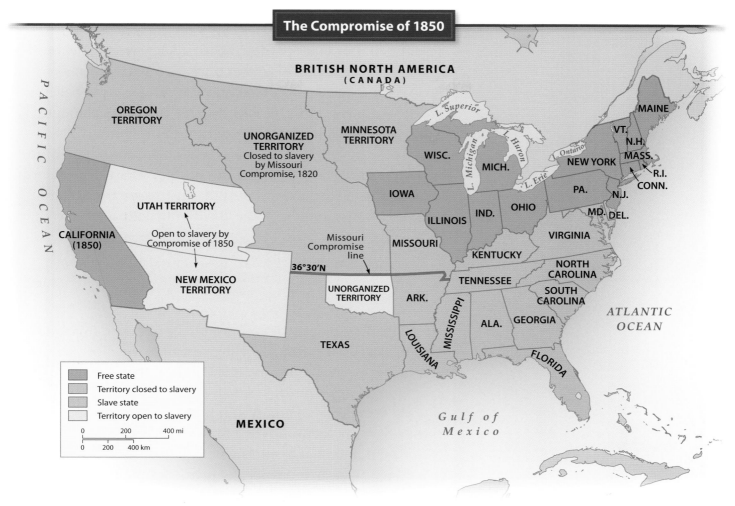

The Compromise of 1850

BRITISH NORTH AMERICA (CANADA)

OREGON TERRITORY

UNORGANIZED TERRITORY
Closed to slavery by Missouri Compromise, 1820

MINNESOTA TERRITORY

WISC.

MICH.

L. Superior

L. Michigan

L. Huron

L. Ontario

L. Erie

MAINE

VT.

N.H.

MASS.

NEW YORK

R.I.

CONN.

PA.

N.J.

IOWA

UTAH TERRITORY

CALIFORNIA (1850)

Open to slavery by Compromise of 1850

NEW MEXICO TERRITORY

ILLINOIS

IND.

OHIO

MD. DEL.

MISSOURI

Missouri Compromise line

36°30′N

UNORGANIZED TERRITORY

ARK.

VIRGINIA

KENTUCKY

TENNESSEE

NORTH CAROLINA

SOUTH CAROLINA

ATLANTIC OCEAN

TEXAS

LOUISIANA

MISSISSIPPI

ALA.

GEORGIA

FLORIDA

MEXICO

Gulf of Mexico

PACIFIC OCEAN

Legend:
- Free state
- Territory closed to slavery
- Slave state
- Territory open to slavery

0   200   400 mi
0   200   400 km

▲ The Compromise of 1850 temporarily defused the confrontation between the slave states of the South and the free states of the North.

He pleads for tolerance and understanding. Then he introduces his compromise.

(Today it is known as the Compromise of 1850.) This is what it says:

1. California is to be admitted to the Union as a free state.

2. New Mexico and Utah will become territories. (No mention is made of slavery; it is assumed the territories will decide that for themselves.)

3. A fugitive slave law will be enforced. (That means runaway slaves who make it to free states must be returned to their owners.)

4. Slaves may no longer be bought and sold in the nation's capital.

Slavery, however, will still be legal in the District of Columbia.

▲ Daniel Webster: "I speak today for the preservation of the Union."

John Calhoun is too sick to attend the session, but he learns all the details of Clay's speech. A few weeks later he comes to the Senate to answer Clay. He is wrapped in a great cloak and needs help to reach his seat. His face is so pale that he looks like a ghost. His dark eyes are feverish. Calhoun is too ill to speak; his speech must be read for him.

Clay thought he had given Calhoun what he wanted: a fugitive slave law. But Calhoun is still not satisfied. The North must stop talking about slavery, it must "cease the agitation on the slave question." If the abolitionists are not silenced,

let the States…agree to separate.… If you are unwilling we should part in peace, tell us so, and we shall know what to do.

A month later, John C. Calhoun is dead.

The debate over the compromise is not over. It is now Daniel Webster's turn. He will give one of the most famous speeches in Senate history. It is Webster's last Senate oration. Perhaps he knows that. Certainly everyone else does. There isn't an empty seat in the Senate chamber. "I wish to speak today, not as a Massachusetts man, nor as a Northern man, but as an American," says the mighty Daniel Webster. "I speak today for the preservation of the Union. Hear me for my cause." Webster has always been Clay's

Party Time

It was the middle of the century, and the two big parties, the Whigs and the Democrats, were split inside themselves over slavery and the growing conflict between North and South. The Free Soil Party—which stood against the idea of bringing slavery to the western territories—just couldn't seem to find a strong presidential candidate. And the men who got elected—Millard Fillmore (Whig) and then Franklin Pierce (Democrat)—were, at best, mediocre. A new party was certainly needed. So, in 1854, some political leaders met in Ripon, Wisconsin. The Republican Party developed out of that meeting. That same year, the Republicans won 100 seats in Congress. The party was against slavery in the American West— but not for the moral reasons that led the abolitionists. At first the party's main appeal was to free white workingmen who didn't want to compete with slave labor. Six years after its founding, the Republicans put a president in the White House. His name was Abraham Lincoln.

opponent—now he is agreeing with Henry Clay! People gasp. But Webster will do almost anything to save the Union.

I hear with distress, and anguish the word "secession," especially when it falls from the lips of those who are eminently patriotic, and known to the country, and known all over the world, for their political services. Secession! Peaceable secession! Sir, your eyes and mine are never destined to see that miracle.… There can be no such thing as a peaceable secession. Peaceable secession is an utter impossibility. Is the great Constitution under which we live, covering this whole country; is it to be thawed and melted away by secession, as the snows on the mountain melt under the influence of a vernal sun— disappear almost unobserved and run off? No, sir! No, sir! I will not state what might produce the disruption of the Union; but, sir, I see it as plainly as I see the sun in heaven. What that disruption must produce…such a war as I will not describe.

To avoid that war, Webster will agree to a compromise. He believes in the Union and the American system:

We have a great, popular, constitutional government, guarded by law and by judicature, and defended by the affections of the whole people.

When Webster finishes his oration some people weep. Is it because they know the Union is falling apart? Or is it because their hero, the "Godlike Daniel," has agreed to a fugitive slave law?

Webster knows that if the South secedes now, the North will not be able to stop it. There will be two nations—one slave, one free—and perhaps wars between them. His speech does what it was meant to do. It holds the Union together. Congress votes to accept Henry Clay's compromise. The real problem is that no one knows how to end slavery and still hold North and South together.

The Kansas-Nebraska Act ended the Missouri Compromise and allowed the people in the territories to choose whether to permit or ban slavery. ▼

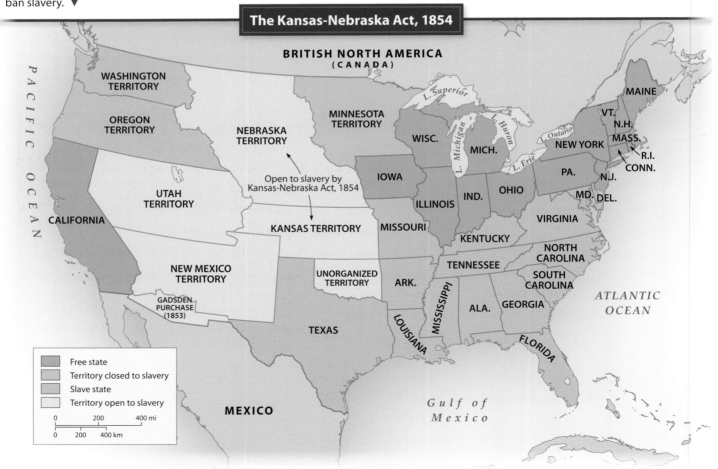

The Kansas-Nebraska Act, 1854

BRITISH NORTH AMERICA
(CANADA)

WASHINGTON TERRITORY

OREGON TERRITORY

MINNESOTA TERRITORY

NEBRASKA TERRITORY

L. Superior

WISC.

MICH.

MAINE

VT.
N.H.
MASS.

NEW YORK

R.I.
CONN.

Open to slavery by Kansas-Nebraska Act, 1854

IOWA

PA.

N.J.

UTAH TERRITORY

ILLINOIS

IND.

OHIO

MD. DEL.

CALIFORNIA

KANSAS TERRITORY

MISSOURI

VIRGINIA

KENTUCKY

NEW MEXICO TERRITORY

UNORGANIZED TERRITORY

ARK.

TENNESSEE

NORTH CAROLINA

SOUTH CAROLINA

GADSDEN PURCHASE (1853)

MISSISSIPPI

ALA.

GEORGIA

ATLANTIC OCEAN

TEXAS

LOUISIANA

FLORIDA

MEXICO

Gulf of Mexico

PACIFIC OCEAN

L. Michigan

L. Huron

Ontario

L. Erie

Free state
Territory closed to slavery
Slave state
Territory open to slavery

0   200   400 mi
0   200   400 km

The Kansas-Nebraska Act

The South was convinced that the North wanted to squash it—economically and politically. The answer to their problem was more land and power. Where could they find it? By controlling the western territories and making them slave territories.

Senator Stephen A. Douglas of Illinois had his eye on some of those western lands. He had made his fortune in land speculation and in that new enterprise, railroads. He knew a transcontinental railroad would someday stretch from coast to coast. He wanted it to follow a route from Chicago to San Francisco, which would make his own Chicago property even more valuable. But Southern

◀ Stephen Douglas was committed to "popular sovereignty" as a way of deciding the slavery issue in the territories.

congressmen, such as Jefferson Davis, wanted the transcontinental railroad to take a southern route, through New Mexico and Arizona.

Senator Douglas introduced a bill in the Senate to organize lands left from the Louisiana Purchase as the Nebraska Territory. (Most of this land was guaranteed to the Indians, but Indian treaties had been broken before.) Settlers (and land speculators) would be allowed to buy this land. Once there were settlers, the railroad trains would follow. And as soon as there were enough people living there, the territory would turn into states. According to the terms of the Missouri Compromise, they would be free states. (Remember, the Missouri Compromise, passed back in 1820, said that there was to be no slavery in the Louisiana Territory north of latitude 36°30', except in Missouri.)

If Stephen Douglas really wanted his railroad, then Southerners said he would have to write a new bill that did away with the Missouri Compromise and opened the territory to slavery. So Douglas introduced a new bill known as the Kansas-Nebraska Act. This act divided the territory into two regions, Kansas and Nebraska (the regions were much bigger than today's states with those names). The Missouri Compromise was repealed: the ban on slavery was ended. Douglas called for *popular sovereignty*, which means letting the people decide. The residents of the territories were to decide for themselves about whether to allow slavery.

Northerners responded to the Kansas-Nebraska Act with a torrent of fiery speeches, editorials, and sermons. But that didn't stop the act from getting passed. In the South there was a feeling of triumph. An Illinois politician, Abraham Lincoln, had this to say in a speech he gave about the Kansas-Nebraska Act:

The spirit of [17]76 and the spirit of Nebraska, are utter antagonisms.... We began declaring that all men are created equal; but now from that beginning we have run down to the other declaration, that for some men to enslave others is a "sacred right of self-government." These principles cannot stand together....

Now that popular sovereignty had been declared, Kansans could vote for slavery or against it. Slave owners and abolitionists rushed into Kansas. Each group was determined to win the region. Supporters of slavery rigged the elections and so won the first round. Soon, things got so bad that the Free Soilers—the antislavery settlers—held their own elections. So, in 1856, Kansas had two governments—one for slavery and one against.

A posse of some 800 proslavery raiders headed for the free town of Lawrence, Kansas, dragging five cannons with them. They destroyed the place. When a fierce-eyed, fanatical abolitionist named John Brown learned what had happened in Lawrence, he told his followers, "We must fight fire with fire" and "strike terror in the hearts of the proslavery people." Brown and seven of his followers kidnapped five proslavery settlers. Then they murdered them with swords. Kansas was now called "Bleeding Kansas." It was proslavery versus no-slavery, and it was the first act of a drama that was about to unfold.

The Kansas-Nebraska Act of 1854, says historian James McPherson, "may have been the most important single event pushing the nation toward civil war."

"I am naturally antislavery," said Abraham Lincoln. "If slavery is not wrong, nothing is wrong." ▶

Violence broke out between slave owners and abolitionists in Kansas. ▼

A Dreadful Decision

It is March 4, 1857. James Buchanan has been elected president and the Supreme Court is considering a very important case—a case that deals with slavery. Buchanan knows—though it is improper that he does—what the court's decision will be. So he stands before the nation on this inaugural day and says that slavery is a question that "belongs to the Supreme Court of the United States, before whom it is now pending, and will, it is understood, be speedily and finally settled."

The slavery issue finally settled—how wonderful that would be! The case, *Dred Scott v. Sandford*, deals with a slave living in Missouri, a slave state. That slave, Dred Scott, lived for several years in Wisconsin, a free territory. Does his residence in the Wisconsin territory (now Minnesota) make him a free man? There is legal precedent in Missouri saying it does—other blacks have been freed after living in a free state.

> In law, a *precedent* is a legal decision or procedure that serves as a rule for future similar cases.

Scott sues his owner, Irene Emerson, for his freedom and also that of his wife. It seems a clear case, but the legal papers are filed incorrectly and the case is set aside—for three years. Meanwhile, Scott and his wife have been hired out. Their salaries are held by the sheriff. Do they go free and get their earnings? Or does Irene Emerson keep them and the money they've earned? She is getting married and has other things on her mind; she hands her affairs to her brother, John Sanford (the court misspelled the name of the case).

Because Sanford is a New Yorker, the case goes to a federal court and then to the Supreme Court. (Mrs. Emerson's new husband is an abolitionist.

Chief Justice Roger Taney listens to an argument in the Dred Scott case. ▶

A matter in *litigation* is part of ongoing legal proceedings in a court.

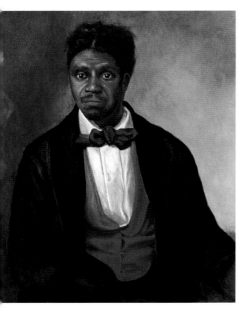

▲ After his case was over, Dred Scott was freed and got a job as a porter.

He doesn't know about this. When he learns what has happened he tries to free Scott, but he can't while the matter is in litigation.)

Seventy-nine-year-old Roger Taney (pronounced TAH-nee) is chief justice, appointed by Andrew Jackson to replace the renowned John Marshall. Taney is well respected. So is the court. Two days after Buchanan's inauguration, the Supreme Court issues its decision. All nine justices write opinions—so different are their views. This is what Chief Justice Taney has to say in his majority opinion in the case of *Dred Scott v. Sandford:*

> *The question before us is, whether Negroes compose a portion of the American people and are constituent members of this sovereignty. We think they are not. On the contrary, they are a subordinate and inferior class of beings, who have been subjugated by the dominant race. They can therefore claim none of the rights and privileges which the Constitution provides for citizens of the United States.*

It couldn't have been stated more clearly: slaves are property and the Fifth Amendment protects property. The Missouri Compromise, prohibiting slavery in the territories, is unconstitutional. So, according to Taney and a majority of justices, Wisconsin was not free territory when Dred Scott lived there (even though no one had realized it). Furthermore, says the court, blacks have no right to citizenship. Even free blacks have "no rights which the white man is bound to respect...."

In Springfield, Illinois, Abraham Lincoln says, "We think the decision is erroneous." He also says that slavery is "an unqualified evil to the Negro, the white man, and the State." President James Buchanan thought this decision would settle the slavery question! What it settles is the question of war. It makes war almost certain.

Today, the Supreme Court's decision in the Dred Scott case is usually considered the worst decision in the court's history.

On March 7, 1857, the *New York Daily Times* headline read, "DECISION IN THE DRED SCOTT CASE; the [Northwest] Ordinance of 1787 and the Missouri Compromise Declared Unconstitutional." The same front page gave the menu at President Buchanan's inaugural party. Truffles, venison, mutton, boar's head, and pheasant were served.

Fleeing to Freedom

Ellen Craft was 22, slim, sweet-natured, and shy. She was very intelligent, but she couldn't read or write. She had curiosity, but she had never been far from home. Ellen had white skin, but she was a slave. She would soon be the best-known black woman of her day. Are you confused? Ellen was both white and black. She was biracial (by-RAY-shul). Read on and you will understand.

Ellen was the daughter of James Smith, one of Georgia's wealthiest plantation owners. Smith had a wife and children. Smith had a wife and children. Do you think I made a mistake and wrote the same sentence twice? That was no mistake. Smith had two families. His legal wife was white and mistress of the plantation. The other woman, whom he never married legally, was black and a slave.

Ellen's mother was the slave. Ellen's father treated Ellen and his other slave children like slaves. When Ellen was 11 she was given as a wedding present to her white half-sister. That means she was sent away from the mother who loved her. You can imagine how she felt—she was still a young girl and she was lonely and unhappy. Her half-sister would never admit they were related. Ellen was now a house servant. She learned to be a skilled seamstress; she also learned to be a good listener. She heard the white people talk about the troubles between North and South. She heard

▲ Ellen Craft—her mother was an African American slave, and her father was a white plantation owner.

Born to Shame

From Elizabeth Cady Stanton's speech to the American Anti-Slavery Society, published in the abolitionist paper *The Liberator,* May 18, 1860:

To you, white man, the world throws wide her gates; the way is clear to wealth, to fame, to glory, to renown; the high places of independence and honor and trust are yours; all your efforts are praised and encouraged; all your successes are welcomed with loud hurrahs and cheers; but the black man and the woman are born to shame. The badge of degradation is the skin and the sex.… For while the man is born to do whatever he can, for the woman and the negro there is no such privilege.

Women's suffrage champion Elizabeth Cady Stanton also worked to end slavery. ▶

▲ Ellen and William Craft made
their freedom journey in
December 1848 with Ellen
disguised as a young white
man. When they were buying
steamship tickets in Macon,
Georgia, the steamer's officer
looked suspiciously at William
and said, "Boy, do you belong to
that gentleman?"

that there were people in the North, called abolitionists, who wanted
to free the slaves. She decided that she would run away to the North.

Then Ellen fell in love with William Craft, who was a slave and
a carpenter. He fell in love with Ellen. William had money saved
because his owner allowed him to earn extra money and keep it for
himself. They made plans to run away together. They knew that if
they were caught they would be beaten, separated, and perhaps sold.
It took courage to do what they planned to do.

It was Ellen's idea. She pretended to be a man, a young, sickly
white man. She pretended to be journeying to Philadelphia for medical
treatment. William was her slave. Because she had listened carefully to
her owner's conversations, she knew all about Philadelphia's doctors.
But neither Ellen nor William Craft knew how to read a map, or buy
tickets for a journey, or sign a name on a hotel register. How could they
travel north? How could they carry out their scheme?

Ellen put her arm in a sling. She said it was injured. That
explained why she couldn't write. She put a big bandage around her
cheeks to hide her smooth face. No one would wonder why she didn't
have whiskers. William bought her a man's suit; he also bought her
high-heeled boots to make her seem taller.

Now Ellen had to forget her shyness. She had to act like a slave
owner and order William around. She had to buy tickets. She did it.
"A ticket for William Johnson and slave," she said in a strong voice.
She was William Johnson. Because whites and blacks could not
sit together, they rode in separate cars. Ellen was frightened. Then
something fearful happened. The man who sat next to her was a
white man she knew. Would he recognize her in spite of the man's
suit she wore? She pretended to be very sick, groaning answers to his
questions. He moved away.

Ellen and William Craft—who were now William Johnson and
slave—traveled by train and boat. They stayed in a fine hotel; William
Johnson ate in the hotel's dining room. They had more than one
close call, but they made it—to Philadelphia and freedom.

When they reached Philadelphia, they found free blacks who sent
them to the home of an abolitionist family. But when Ellen saw the
people she refused to enter their house. They were white. Ellen didn't
know that white people could be nice. She didn't believe that white
people would help her. She thought it was all a trick. But she began

to find that skin color has nothing to do with kindness or meanness. Those white people became her friends.

Ellen and William Craft were soon famous. People wanted to hear their story. They moved to Boston, which was a center of abolitionism. They made speeches. Articles were written about them. They would have preferred a quiet life, but they understood the need to tell their story to help others who were still enslaved.

When slave catchers came from Georgia just to capture the Crafts, a friend helped Ellen and William flee to England. In England they learned to read and write. They taught sewing and carpentry. Then some English merchants sent William to Africa to sell their goods. But in Africa the king of Dahomey took his goods and gave him chained slaves in return. Craft would have nothing to do with slavery. He freed the slaves. That was the end of that job.

Ellen and William were homesick. They longed for their own country. Finally the time came (after the Civil War) when it was safe for them to go home. They spent the rest of their lives in the South, teaching and helping others.

When William Johnson and slave walked down that long, winding American road toward freedom and justice, they didn't realize they would be speaking out for all those left behind. They learned that it would take hard work to make the words of the Declaration of Independence mean what they said. Ellen and William Craft were willing to do their part.

▲ Frederick Douglass became an adviser to President Lincoln.

Common Destiny

Frederick Douglass, the great abolitionist, had also been a slave and had run away to freedom. In 1851 he said this to white people:

Have we not a right here? For 300 years or more, we have had a foothold on this continent. We have grown up with you. We leveled your forests. Our hands removed the stumps from your fields and raised the first crops and brought the first produce to your tables. We have fought for this country.… I consider it settled that the black and white people of America ought to share common destiny. The white and black must fall or flourish together. We have been with you, are still with you, and mean to be with you to the end. We shall neither die out nor be driven out. But we shall go with you and stand either as a testimony against you or as evidence in your favor throughout all your generations.

Over the River and Underground

John Price was a slave in Kentucky. We don't know much about him—what he thought about or what he was like—but we do know he must have hated being a slave. He was willing to risk his life to run away.

He got a chance to do it one cold winter. It was so cold that the wide Ohio River froze over. Price and two friends—a woman named Dinah and a man named Frank—decided to cross the river. In the dark of night they took two of their master's horses and headed out onto the slick ice. When they got to the Ohio side of the river there was no way to get onto the land. The river's banks were too steep and the horses kept slipping. Soon the three runaways feared they might freeze to death. Then, as morning came, they saw where a road cut through the hilly bank. They had made it to a free state.

But that didn't mean they were free. According to the Fugitive Slave Law, anyone who found them in Ohio was obliged to return them to their owner. If you broke the law you could go to jail, or be fined, or both.

▲ A slave escapes across a river on horseback.

Under the Fugitive Slave Law, escaped slaves discovered in free states had to be returned to their owners in the South. ▶

John, Dinah, and Frank were lucky: the first person they met was a Quaker man who would not obey the Fugitive Slave Law. He was willing to risk a jail sentence. He fed them and gave them a place to rest.

The fugitives were heading for Canada, where slavery had been abolished. Before they went on they let their horses go, sending them back toward Kentucky, where their owner found them. Then Dinah started out; she thought it safer to go by herself. No one knows what happened to her. John and Frank went next. The Quaker man sent them all traveling on the Underground Railroad.

You may have heard of that railroad. Well, it wasn't a real railroad, and it wasn't underground. Still, the name made sense. The Underground Railroad was a secret way of travel, with conductors and stations and passengers. The passengers were blacks escaping from slavery. The conductors—who were black and white—helped them along the way. The stations were places where people could be trusted to feed and house and help the runaways. Some of those places were houses with special hidden rooms and some were barns; some were even riverboats.

Henry Brown had himself packed in a box and mailed to abolitionists in Philadelphia. For the rest of his life, he was known as "Box" Brown. ▼

A fugitive slave, always wary of pursuers, makes his way north. ▼

▲ Slave owners sometimes used hunting dogs to track escaped slaves.

▲ Escaping slaves traveled at night, following the North Star when it was visible. Even in bad weather they kept moving to stay ahead of slave hunters.

The fugitives traveled at night, following the North Star. Sometimes the nights were cloudy and there were no stars to follow. Sometimes hunting dogs were sent to track them down. Usually the passengers traveled through places they had never been before. Often they were hungry. Always they were scared. But the idea of freedom gave them the courage they needed. As they went they whispered the locations of the railroad's stations to one another.

John Price made it to northern Ohio and then he stopped. He didn't think he needed to go farther. He was in Oberlin, which was known as an abolitionist town. It was built around a small college, called Oberlin College, where blacks and whites, men and women, all went to school together. There wasn't another college in the country like that.

Oberlin was different because of the people who founded it. They were mostly Quakers and Presbyterians who thought slavery wrong and against the will of their God. They were people of strong beliefs; most were studying to be ministers. They went out from the college and preached against slavery.

John Price found work as a laborer. He was a pleasant, well-liked man. One day a boy of 13, Shakespeare Boynton, told Price he knew someone who had a job for him. Shakespeare was not telling the truth. He had been paid to lie to John Price. He took the money and led Price into a trap. He led him to some men who were slave catchers. They had been sent from Kentucky just to catch Price.

John Price was handcuffed and put in a wagon. His captors headed to a nearby town. On the way, their horse and wagon passed two Oberlin men. When Price saw them he shouted out, "Help, help!"

Those men rushed to Oberlin and told others what they had seen. People were outraged. Never had anyone been kidnapped from Oberlin! Blacks and whites hitched their horses to their wagons and galloped off.

In the meantime, Price was in a hotel with his captors waiting for the next train south. Soon the street in front of the hotel was filled with angry people from Oberlin. They recaptured Price and put him on a train for Canada. It was September of 1858, and he was not heard of again.

But that isn't the end of his story. The men who freed him had broken the Fugitive Slave Law. They were in trouble. There was a crowd of them: a doctor, a carpenter, a cabinetmaker, a printer, an undertaker, a schoolteacher, a brick maker, a lawyer, a grocer, a harness maker, some students, three fugitive slaves living in Oberlin, and some farmers.

They had defied the government and its laws. President James Buchanan wasn't going to let them get away with that. The rescue in Oberlin was talked about throughout the country. Those who believed in slavery saw it as a test case. Would the government

Most slaves were Christians, and, like the abolitionists, they found a message of fairness and brotherhood in their religion. Southern slaveholders read passages in Christian scripture that told them that slaves should obey their masters. Slaves read the Bible's stories of freedom. Each group found what it wanted in the same Bible.

A station on the Underground Railroad—from 1830 to 1860, about 40,000 fugitives passed through Ohio alone. ▼

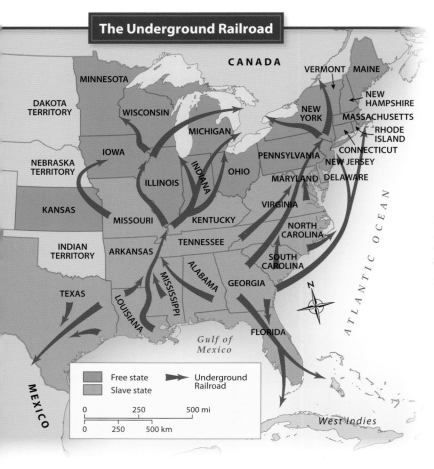

The Underground Railroad

CANADA

MINNESOTA

DAKOTA TERRITORY

WISCONSIN

MICHIGAN

VERMONT MAINE

NEW HAMPSHIRE

NEW YORK

MASSACHUSETTS

RHODE ISLAND

CONNECTICUT

IOWA

PENNSYLVANIA

NEW JERSEY

NEBRASKA TERRITORY

INDIANA

OHIO

ILLINOIS

MARYLAND DELAWARE

KANSAS

VIRGINIA

MISSOURI

KENTUCKY

NORTH CAROLINA

INDIAN TERRITORY

ARKANSAS

TENNESSEE

SOUTH CAROLINA

ALABAMA

GEORGIA

TEXAS

MISSISSIPPI

LOUISIANA

ATLANTIC OCEAN

FLORIDA

Gulf of Mexico

MEXICO

West Indies

| Free state | Underground Railroad |
| Slave state | |

0   250   500 mi

0   250   500 km

▲ Thousands of slaves escaped to freedom following secret routes to the North, Canada, Mexico, or the Caribbean.

enforce the Fugitive Slave Law, they asked? The people who were against slavery also saw it as a test case. Would the government send the leading citizens of a community to jail for helping someone to become free?

The trial was big news. I won't go into all the details—it would take too much space—but all the accused men were kept in jail while waiting for their trials. The jailer, who liked them, tried to make them as comfortable as possible. Still, there were rats and roaches in the jail, and, of course, they couldn't go home when they wanted to. But friends were allowed to visit, including all the children in the Sunday-school class that one prisoner taught.

Finally it was time for their cases to come before the court. Simeon Bushnell, a 29-year-old Oberlin printer who was married and father of a baby, was first to be tried. Bushnell, a quiet-natured working man with no spare money, was short and stocky, with a beard and dark eyes. He was known to be a conductor on the Underground Railroad. Bushnell was found guilty, given a prison sentence, and fined.

The next person to be tried was a 40-year-old schoolteacher named Charles Langston. Langston, a Virginian, was part black, part white, and part Indian. He had devoted much of his life to fighting slavery. Langston was an officer in the Ohio Anti-Slavery Society and an agent for the Sons of Temperance (people who were against drinking). Charles Langston spoke before the court. This is some of what he said:

My father was a revolutionary soldier…he served under Lafayette, and fought through the whole war; and…he always told me that he fought for my freedom as much as for his own…. [He taught me] that the fundamental doctrine of this government was that all men have a right to life and liberty.

Langston asked the judge what he would do if his wife, or child, or brother were taken into slavery. Would the judge resist the laws? Langston believed he would.

We have a common humanity. You would do so; your manhood would require it; and no matter what the laws might be, you would honor yourself for doing it; your friends would honor you for doing it; and every good and honest man would say, you have done right!

The courtroom rang with applause.

It didn't matter. Langston was convicted, sentenced, and fined.

Now it just happened that the citizens of Oberlin were not the only ones who had broken the law. The slave catchers had not taken John Price legally. Slaves couldn't just be kidnapped. The slave catchers had to show the proper papers. That hadn't been done. The Oberlin lawyers got busy. They had the slave catchers arrested.

The slave catchers were terrified of going to jail. They knew the jailers would not be nice to them. They agreed to drop their case if the Oberlin people did the same thing. So, finally, it was all over. Except, of course, it wasn't at all. The issue of slavery hadn't been solved. The conflict was just beginning.

Elizabeth Jennings, a 24-year-old schoolteacher, was in a hurry to play the organ in church. The trolley conductor told her to wait for a car for colored people. Jennings stayed in her seat until it was pulled away. She sued, and won the first legal decision allowing all New Yorkers an equal right to public transportation. This was in 1854.

Abolitionists throughout the North spoke out against the Fugitive Slave Law. ▼

Harriet, Also Known As Moses

Harriet Tubman's faith was strong. She said, "I always told God, 'I'm going to hold steady on you, and you've got to see me through.'"

Harriet Tubman, also known as Moses, was born a slave.

There was none of the spirit of an enslaved person in Harriet Tubman. She was a fighter: tough, brave, and brilliant. She was tiny—just five feet tall—but stronger than most men. She could lift great weights, withstand cold and heat, chop down big trees, and go without food when necessary. She had been trained, in childhood, to take abuse. That was part of what it meant to be a slave. She put that training to good use.

Harriet never knew for sure when she was born; few people recorded slaves' birthdays. But it was in Maryland, on what is known as the Eastern Shore, in about 1820. (The Eastern Shore is the peninsula that looks a bit like a fist, with a finger pointing to Norfolk, Virginia, and its wrist near Wilmington, Delaware.)

Her owner considered her a problem child. He sent her off to work when she was six. He got the wages, she did the work. She was sent to dust and sweep and tend a baby. But she didn't know how to dust or sweep. She had grown up in a slave cabin with a dirt floor and no furniture—just old blankets to sleep on. The woman she worked for didn't think about that. When Harriet didn't dust well she beat her. Hard. When the baby cried, Harriet was supposed to rock her and make her stop crying. Sometimes little Harriet fell asleep. Her mistress beat her. Hard.

Harriet ran away. But she didn't know where to go, so she hid in a pigpen. Living with pigs may have been easier than living with cruel humans, but she didn't have anything to eat except the potato peelings the pigs ate. Soon she was starving and had to go back. This time her mistress beat her so hard she carried scars for the rest of her life. Now Harriet was too sick to work at all, so she was sent back home. Her mother and father nursed her back to health. The master sent her out to work again—this time to a house where the woman was a weaver and the man a hunter. They were just as cruel as the first people. Harriet was supposed to help with the weaving, but she hated the work and was no good at it. She was sent to check the hunter's traps. She had to wade through cold water. One day she said she was too sick to go. The hunter didn't believe her. Harriet had the measles and bronchitis. After going in the cold water she almost died. She was sent back home again. Again her parents cared for her, but her throat had been damaged. After that she always had a low, husky voice.

She was happy to be back home with her parents and her 10 brothers and sisters. The slave owner could see that she was no good to hire out, so he sent her to work in the fields. Even though she was still very young and very small, she did hard work and she liked being outdoors. Of course, slaves couldn't go to school, so no one taught Harriet to read and write, but she learned to listen and to remember, and she soon had an unusual memory. She listened to the blacks who whispered about freedom. She learned that a few slaves were freed by their masters. She learned that others ran away north, and found freedom. She learned that if a slave tried to escape and was caught, he would be whipped, branded, and sold. He would be sold south, far south, to cotton plantations where life was even harder for blacks than it was in Maryland and there was little chance of escape.

Some blacks were sold south just because the master needed money (and all lived in fear of that). Two of Harriet's sisters were sold, and her parents grieved as parents grieve for dead children.

Harriet learned that some people—black and white—helped escaping blacks. They were part of the Underground Railroad. As you know, it wasn't a real railroad, although Harriet thought it was when she first heard of it. The Underground Railroad was a way to get north. It was a series of places where blacks would find help. The places—houses, barns, and boats—were called stations. People who traveled the route were called passengers. People who led them were conductors.

There was one of two things I had a right to, liberty, or death; if I could not have one, I would have the other; for no man should take me alive; I should fight for my liberty as long as my strength lasted, and when the time came for me to go, the Lord would let them take me.

—Harriet Tubman

American Quaker and abolitionist Levi Coffin used his home in Cincinnati as a station on the Underground Railroad. ▼

▲ Conductors help passengers to a station on the Underground Railroad. Despite what this painting suggests, most slaves ran away alone because it was simpler and safer.

But most of what Harriet heard from the whispering was guesses. No one who escaped ever came back. No one really knew what happened to them. Harriet would be different: she would escape and she would come back. That was in the future; she still had some growing up to do.

One day Harriet was in a store. An overseer was there. Suddenly he yelled at a slave who was running. Then he yelled at Harriet to stop the slave. Harriet didn't move. The overseer threw a lead weight at the running slave. The weight hit Harriet, right in her forehead. She passed out. For months she lay unconscious. Everyone thought she would die. For the rest of her life she had fainting spells and times when she would just fall asleep and no one could wake her.

Her master decided to sell her, but no one would buy a slave who was always falling asleep. (And Harriet made sure she fell asleep whenever a buyer was around.) She was sent to work with her father, who was one of the most trusted slaves on the plantation. He never told a lie. He was in charge of a woodcutting operation. Harriet soon learned to cut trees as easily as the strongest of men.

Her father taught her the ways of the woods. He taught her to walk softly, as the Native Americans did. He showed her the plants she could eat and the ones that were poisonous.

Then she met a white woman who said she could help her. Harriet guessed that the woman was part of the Underground Railroad. She guessed right.

I can't tell the whole story of Harriet Tubman. It takes a book to do that. I will tell you that after she escaped north, to freedom, she didn't feel free without her family and friends. So she went back and got them. She got all of her brothers and sisters and her parents—except for the two sisters who were sold south. It took many trips; it wasn't easy.

She didn't stop with just her family. She became the most famous conductor on the Underground Railroad She is said to have led 300 blacks to freedom.

She made Northerners think differently about slavery. Southerners, like Senator John Calhoun, were saying that slavery was a good thing. They said slaves were well treated and loved their masters and mistresses. But people who are well treated don't risk everything— sometimes even their lives—to run away. The blacks who escaped on the Underground Railroad told of children being taken from their parents, they showed scars from whippings, and they told of abuses that made many Northerners change their minds about slavery.

Try to imagine that you are going north on the Underground Railroad. You'll travel at night, the darker the better, so you can escape the slave catchers. Follow the North Star and you'll be

Escaping slaves often tried to keep dogs from picking up their scent by walking through creeks and streams. ▼

◄ Harriet Tubman leads a group of slaves north. She is said to have led 300 blacks to freedom.

▲ Harriet Tubman with a group of slaves who have reached safety and freedom

going in the right direction. Keep off the roads as much as possible—the woods are safer. If wild animals and snakes bother you, too bad: no screaming or loud talking allowed. If you hear dogs you'd better make for a river, even if it's freezing cold. Dogs can't follow your scent in the water. If you see strangers you'll have to think and act quickly.

Harriet Tubman was a quick thinker. Once, she and some slaves were about to board a train heading north. She saw some slave catchers. So, quickly, she had everyone get on a train going south. No one suspected slaves heading south.

She was daring and ingenious and soon there was a huge reward for her capture. Often she wore disguises: sometimes she dressed as a man, sometimes she pretended to be a very old woman. Once she saw her old master coming toward her. She knew he would recognize her. She was carrying some live chickens. So she let them go and chased after them. The man laughed and yelled, "Go get them, Granny." He had no idea that Granny was Harriet Tubman, the most wanted runaway slave in the nation.

Harriet never stopped fighting for what she thought was right, never for a minute. When the Civil War began she was asked to help the Union army. She did.

She went to South Carolina, where again she helped blacks escape; she also went behind the lines as a scout and spy. She went to Virginia and worked as a nurse in an army hospital at Fortress Monroe. She was never paid for her work but lived by her wits, buying and selling vegetables, baking pies, and brewing root beer in order to eat.

After the war she moved to Auburn, New York, married a war veteran, cared for her parents, and opened a home for elderly blacks. She was often asked to speak of her experiences, and she did. She spoke out for equal rights for women. Though she had never been lucky enough to go to school, she knew the importance of learning. She worked to get schools for the newly freed blacks. The queen of England, Queen Victoria, heard of Harriet Tubman and wrote a letter inviting her to England for a visit. Harriet didn't have the money to go.

Maybe it didn't matter. She became more famous than most of the people who curtsied to the queen. Few people in American history had the courage and determination of Harriet Tubman. Now do you know why she was called Moses?

Breaking the Law—A Discussion of Ethics

Today we think of the people who ran the Underground Railroad as heroes. But they were lawbreakers. The law said that runaway slaves were to be returned to their owners. If you believe in a government of laws—and most Americans do—then breaking a law is a very serious thing to do.

In the 19th century, people in the North and South who hated slavery were faced with some hard questions. Yes, there were people in the South who hated slavery. Some of them taught slaves to read. They broke the law. Some helped slaves escape. They broke the law.

I have an answer to this dilemma of the evil law, but before I tell you my thoughts, come up with answers of your own. You are entitled to your own opinion.

Okay, here is my opinion:

Government under law is the only reasonable form of government in our complex world. So it is important that citizens respect the law. However, laws are made by human beings, and sometimes people make mistakes. Sometimes laws are unjust. The best way to handle an unjust law is to work to get it changed. Write your senator or representative in Congress. Even better, if you are old enough, get elected to Congress.

But suppose the unjust law doesn't get changed. Then, sometimes, for some people, the best course is to break the law.

That's a big decision. Lawbreakers must be prepared to pay a price. They must be prepared to go to jail. The writer Henry David Thoreau was willing to go to jail for his beliefs. Some of the abolitionists went to jail for helping slaves. That is one of the reasons they were heroic.

Read the Declaration of Independence again, and you will see how the men who founded this nation felt about resistance to evil laws.

The problem of the unjust law will be around as long as there are people and governments. One hundred years after the Civil War, a Christian minister named Martin Luther King, Jr., wrote a letter from jail in Birmingham, Alabama. The laws in Alabama said that blacks could not sit in "white" restaurants or sit where they wished on public buses.

King thought those laws unjust; he broke them and went to jail. In jail he wrote, "An individual who breaks a law that conscience tells him is unjust, and willingly accepts the penalty by staying in jail…is in reality expressing the highest regard for the law." Do you agree? Or disagree? Why?

This group of abolitionists, known as the Oberlin Rescuers, broke the law when they helped to rescue the fugitive slave John Price. ▼

Harriet and Uncle Tom

Harriet Beecher grew up in Connecticut in a houseful of children: seven boys and four girls. Her father, Lyman Beecher, was a Congregational minister known throughout New England for his fine sermons. The Congregationalists were descendants of the Puritans: serious and moral in their religion. All Lyman Beecher's boys became ministers. One of them, Henry Ward Beecher, was said to be the greatest preacher of his day. Thousands of people packed his church when he spoke. Another son, Edward, was a college president.

Catharine and Isabella, two Beecher daughters, were pioneers in the fight for women's rights.

Harriet was the smallest of Lyman and Roxana Beecher's children. She never grew to be more than five feet tall. But size has nothing to do with ability: she was the sister everyone depended upon. She had a way of getting things done. She became the most famous Beecher of all. In fact, Harriet Beecher, who married Calvin Stowe and then was Harriet Beecher Stowe, was the most famous American woman of her day. And all because of a book she wrote, a book that changed history.

▲ Harriet Beecher Stowe, American author and abolitionist

The Reverend Lyman Beecher (front row, center) with 9 of his 11 children. Harriet is on the far right, with Henry behind her; Isabella is at far left, with Catharine next to her. ▶

◄ Harriet Beecher Stowe wrote at home with her children running in and out. Her stories and articles for magazines helped support her large family.

When Harriet was 13, her sister Catharine, who was 24, opened a school for girls. Harriet went as a student, but then she began teaching as well. She discovered what every teacher knows: teaching is a good way to learn. Harriet was also beginning to write and to care about words. Then Lyman Beecher moved to Cincinnati, Ohio, where he became head of a college to train ministers. He wanted his family with him, so Catharine and Harriet became Midwesterners.

In New England, slavery had seemed far away. Now it was close by. Ohio was a free state: there was no slavery there. But Kentucky, just across the Ohio River, was a slave state. Harriet stood on the banks of the river and watched boats filled with slaves in chains who

At the age of 12, Harriet read her favorite book, Sir Walter Scott's *Ivanhoe*, seven times in *one* month.

Anguish means "sadness and pain."

were being shipped south to be sold at slave markets. One day she saw a baby pulled from its chained mother's arms. She saw a look of anguish on the mother's face. She never forgot that look.

Once, Harriet was invited to Kentucky to visit a friend who lived on a plantation and owned slaves. The friend and her family were kind people, and she saw slavery at its best. But when Harriet and her friend rode horses to a neighboring plantation, they saw a cruel overseer abusing blacks. Harriet remembered the kindness and the cruelty, for she was becoming a writer and so she observed and remembered.

She wrote stories and essays and poems. Then, when she married Calvin Stowe and had babies, there never seemed to be enough money. Calvin was a teacher in her father's college, and not paid a high salary. So Harriet wrote stories to earn money.

Calvin got a job teaching at Bowdoin College in Maine. By this time Harriet had learned a lot about slavery, and it made her very angry. Her brother Edward's wife said to her, "If I could write as you do I would write something to make this whole nation feel what an accursed thing slavery is." And that was just what Harriet Beecher Stowe did. She wrote *Uncle Tom's Cabin*.

It was the most important American book written in the 19th century. It may be the most influential book ever written in America. Its chapters were first printed in a newspaper. Within a week of its publication as a book (in 1852), 10,000 copies had been sold—and *Uncle Tom's Cabin* was just getting started. Before the Civil War even began, 2 million copies were bought in the United States, and it was translated into many languages and sold around the world.

It is a very exciting book. Some critics say it is not great literature, but you can judge that for yourself. *Uncle Tom's Cabin* is good reading and not difficult, except that it is full of dialect, the everyday talk of blacks in

Uncle Tom's Cabin changed people's ideas about slavery. It is perhaps the most influential book ever written in America. ▼

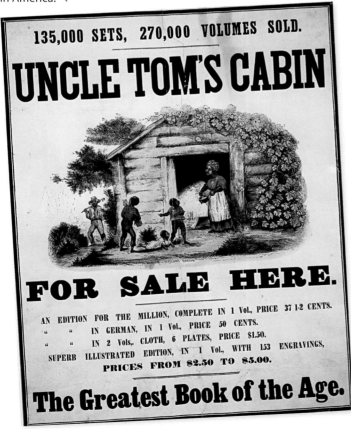

135,000 SETS, 270,000 VOLUMES SOLD.

UNCLE TOM'S CABIN

FOR SALE HERE.

AN EDITION FOR THE MILLION, COMPLETE IN 1 Vol., PRICE 37 1-2 CENTS.
" " IN GERMAN, IN 1 Vol., PRICE 50 CENTS.
" " IN 2 Vols., CLOTH, 6 PLATES, PRICE $1.50.
SUPERB ILLUSTRATED EDITION, IN 1 Vol., WITH 153 ENGRAVINGS,
PRICES FROM $2.50 TO $5.00.

The Greatest Book of the Age.

Simon Legree, the villain of *Uncle Tom's Cabin,* threatens Tom, saying, "Down, you dog!" Today, someone who is a cruel or heartless taskmaster may be called a "Simon Legree."

the old South. If you can handle the dialect you will like the book—a lot. Anyone who reads *Uncle Tom's Cabin* and doesn't cry at the end has a hard heart. It was the first American novel to make real people of blacks, and it made people care. Harriet Beecher Stowe tried to be fair when she wrote the book. She made the horrible overseer, Simon Legree, a Northerner. Legree is the villain in the story. Uncle Tom, a saintly black man, is strong and heroic, the finest person in the book. Two black men who beat him are evil. Some white plantation owners are good people. Harriet was trying to show that color has nothing to do with whether a person is good or bad. What she showed very well was that the system of slavery was evil and that even good people did evil things when they were part of that system.

Uncle Tom's Cabin changed people's ideas about slavery. It made people in the North angry. It made them willing to fight a war to end slavery. In much of the South it was against the law to buy or sell the book. When President Abraham Lincoln met Harriet Beecher Stowe during the Civil War he said to her, "So this is the little lady who wrote the book that made this great war."

Calling someone an "Uncle Tom" today is an insult. It means a black person who behaves humbly or submissively toward white people. The Uncle Tom in Harriet Beecher Stowe's book is a heroic figure.

In Maryland, Samuel Green, a free black, was sentenced to 10 years in prison for having copies of *Uncle Tom's Cabin* and some other antislavery works.

CHAPTER 50

John Brown's Body

By 1856 there was civil war in Kansas. Those who believed in slavery were shooting those who did not. It was called "Bloody Kansas," and the nation should have taken warning.

In May of 1856, a tall, fierce-eyed, Bible-quoting white man led a group that brutally murdered five proslavery Kansans. The tall man was named John Brown, and while some people thought him half mad, others called him a saint. Like Nat Turner (the man who had started a slave rebellion in Virginia), Brown burned with religious fire. He believed he was acting for God.

In March of 1857, the Dred Scott case was decided by the Supreme Court. Dred Scott was a slave; his owner took him into a free state. Scott claimed that made him free. The Supreme Court said it didn't. The court didn't stop with that. It ruled that Scott was not even a legal person; it ruled that he was property and must be returned to slavery.

This mural depicting John Brown and the clash of Bleeding Kansas is in the Kansas State House. ▼

▲ Harpers Ferry is located where the Shenandoah and Potomac rivers meet. This view is from the Potomac side.

In Springfield, Illinois, Abraham Lincoln said, "We think the decision is erroneous." Lincoln also said that slavery was "an unqualified evil to the negro, the white man, and the State."

Meanwhile, John Brown had left Kansas and grown a bushy white beard. It was a disguise; he intended to start a revolution. He expected slaves to rise up and join him. One dark, rainy night in 1859, he and 21 followers put rifles over their shoulders, covered the rifles with long gray scarves, and quietly marched into Harpers Ferry in Virginia. Brown had picked that pretty little town as the perfect place to start his slave uprising. It was at a strategic spot: a gap in the mountains where two rivers, the Potomac and the Shenandoah, come together. He planned a guerrilla war, and the mountain setting seemed right. Besides, a railroad ran through the town. Even more important, Harpers Ferry was the site of a government arsenal and armory. Guns were made and stored there.

Only one guard stood on duty when Brown and his small army marched into town; the guard thought the men were playing some kind

Erroneous (uh-RO-nee-us) means "mistaken" or "wrong."

Harpers Ferry was in Virginia in 1859. It was soon to be in a new state: West Virginia.

of joke. When he saw rifles pointed in his direction, he knew differently. He was soon a prisoner, and John Brown and his followers controlled the armory. Then a train came by.

Disciplined soldiers might have acted calmly, but Brown's men panicked and killed an innocent railroad worker (who happened to be black, and free). After that, they let the railroad cars go on their way. That was foolish. The people on the train took news of the uprising to Washington and Baltimore.

Meanwhile, some of Brown's fighting abolitionists were knocking down Colonel Lewis W. Washington's front door. Colonel Washington, who lived near Harpers Ferry, was George Washington's great-great-nephew. He owned a sword that the king of Prussia had given the first president. John Brown wanted that sword. General Washington had fought for American freedom; John Brown believed he was doing the same thing. The colonel, the sword, and some townspeople were hauled off to the armory and held hostage.

Maybe Brown was insane, or maybe he wanted to die for his cause, because, although he had planned the raid for months, he brought no food with him and he kept all his plans a great secret. The slaves he said would rise up and join him never came. No one knows if they would have come if they'd known what was happening. They didn't learn about John Brown until too late.

It was white Virginians who responded with astonishing speed. Church bells in all the neighboring communities rang the alarm and men on horseback spread the word. Soon, very soon, the town was filled with militia and armed farmers.

Marines and soldiers captured John Brown at Harpers Ferry. ▶

Some of them began to drink, and the atmosphere got ugly. Shots rang out. People were killed. One was the kindly mayor of Harpers Ferry. Two of Brown's men were gunned down when they came out of the armory carrying a white flag.

Then the U.S. Army and the U.S. Marines arrived. They charged into the engine house, where Brown made his last stand, and soon it was all over. Brown was captured—by an army officer named Robert E. Lee—and given a trial that all the nation followed.

John Brown lay in the courtroom on a cot. He said his wounds—sword cuts around the head—made it necessary for him to lie down. Some 500 spectators crammed into the small country courtroom. Peanut shells littered the floors and fingerprints marked the dirty white walls. Outside, on the streets of Charlestown (10 miles from Harpers Ferry), several thousand people stood around hoping to see something of the now-famous man.

Brown pleaded not guilty to treason and murder. His captors did not realize the fiery abolitionist had the skills of a brilliant actor. They gave him an audience that included people all over the country, and other nations, too. Newspaper reporters wrote of his every word and action. John Brown put on a performance few forgot. Often he lied, but he knew how to make people believe in him, and there was truth in the cause he argued. His words inflamed the North:

> *I deny everything but…a design on my part to free slaves.… Had I interfered in the manner which I admit…in behalf of the rich, the powerful, the intelligent, the so-called great…every man in this court would have deemed it an act worthy of reward rather than punishment.*

This Question Is Still to Be Settled

While in prison, John Brown told his captors:

> *I want you to understand, gentlemen…that I respect the rights of the poorest and weakest of colored people, oppressed by the slave system, just as much as I do those of the most wealthy and powerful. That is the idea that has moved me, and that alone.*

And then he issued this warning:

> *I wish to say furthermore, that you had better—all you people at the South—prepare yourselves for a settlement of that question that must come up for settlement sooner than you are prepared for it.… You may dispose of me very easily; I am nearly disposed of now; but this question is still to be settled—this negro question I mean—the end of that is not yet.*

▲ One of many legends that sprang up after John Brown's death said that he kissed a slave child on his way to execution.

The abolitionists were outraged by the trial. They said it wasn't fair. Brown became their martyr hero.

Southerners were outraged, too. They were terrified at the idea of a slave uprising. They thought John Brown was a dangerous villain and they wanted him convicted—quickly. They got their wish.

Brown sat on his black walnut coffin in a furniture wagon, and rode to his death. It was a misty Virginia morning, and he looked up at the Blue Ridge Mountains and said, "This is beautiful country. I never had the pleasure of really seeing it before." Then he got down from his coffin, holding his head high—like a proud, beaked, white-tufted eagle—and mounted the steps of the gallows. A square of soldiers surrounded him. (One militiaman was a Richmond actor named John Wilkes Booth—remember that name.)

Brown handed his jailer a slip of paper. It said: *I John Brown am now quite certain that the crimes of this guilty land will never be purged away, but with blood.* He was right.

John Brown stuck his head in a noose made of South Carolina cotton. His ghost would soon haunt both North and South.

Northern soldiers would sing a rousing song about him and Southerners would hate him. Only a few people were able to talk of John Brown with any sense at all.

One of them was Abraham Lincoln. He said, "Old John Brown has been executed for treason against a State. We cannot object, even though he agreed with us in thinking slavery wrong. That cannot excuse violence, bloodshed, and treason."

That winter, Lincoln, who was campaigning for president, said:

One-sixth of the population of the United States are slaves, looked upon as property, as nothing but property. The cash value of these slaves, at a moderate estimate, is two billion dollars. This amount of property value has a vast influence on the minds of its owners, very naturally. The same amount of property would have an equal influence upon us if owned in the North. Human nature is the same—people at the South are the same as those at the North, barring the difference in circumstances.

And so it came to that. Slaves represented money, and few people will give up their wealth without a fight.

Abraham Lincoln

Abraham Lincoln's brother Jacob Lincoln fought with George Washington during the Revolutionary War. Abraham was a captain in the Virginia Militia.

Now don't get confused. This Abraham Lincoln of 1776 did not become president. It was his grandson who did. Grandfather Abraham never even knew his grandson. You see, he was killed by an Indian bullet. That was after he moved to Kentucky. He went there because his good friend Daniel Boone told him of the fine land in Kentucky. But it was Indian land, and the Native Americans would not give it up easily. If the English-speaking settlers were to have it they would have to fight for it.

Abraham's son, Thomas, who was only eight, saw his father killed. When Thomas grew up he told his son, young Abraham, stories of his grandfather and Daniel Boone and Indians.

They were poor folk, those Lincolns. They didn't have much except stories and hope. That was enough to keep them on the move, seeking good land and good fortune. It never seemed to happen.

Thomas did have good luck with the two women he chose to marry. Nancy Hanks, who was first, was shy and quiet and loved God and the Bible. Her son, Abraham, was born on a cold Sunday

◀ The baby who was born in this Kentucky log cabin in 1809 became the first U.S. president to be born outside the original 13 states.

▲ Abraham was a tall, strong boy and very good at splitting wood.

in February of 1809 in a cabin made of logs with a floor of hard-packed dirt. The cabin had one small window, a fireplace, and a door that swung on hinges made of animal hide. It was no different from the slave cabins on many Virginia plantations.

As Abraham grew, he heard stories told aloud. From his mother he heard of Adam and Eve and Noah and of others in the Bible. From his father, who was a carpenter and a farmer and a good storyteller, he heard tales of the mountain folks.

Abe had a sister, Sarah, who was older by two years. Sometimes they went to school. It was called a "blab" school. There were different ages in the log cabin, which was just one room with a door and no window. Everyone said his or her own lessons—out loud—all at the same time, so the noise was like one big blab.

The Lincolns were members of the South Fork Baptist Church in Kentucky. Kentucky was a slave state, but some of the Baptists hated slavery and thought it was wrong. The Lincolns felt that way. Other members of the church approved of slavery. The fights between those who were for slavery and those who were against got so bad that finally the church had to close its doors.

Soon after that, Nancy and Thomas, their two children, and Abe's cousin Dennis Hanks all moved across the river to the free state of Indiana. Indiana's constitution said, *All men are born equally free and independent,* and *the holding of any part of the human creation in slavery…tyranny.* Land in Indiana was two dollars an acre.

Thomas went first. He hacked a trail through the deep woods and claimed land that looked good to him near Little Pigeon Creek. Then he took some logs and built a three-sided shed. The family spent its first winter in that hut with a blazing fire on the fourth side to frighten off wolves and mountain lions and to keep them warm. Even for a pioneer family, it was a primitive way to live. There were blizzards and soaking rains, and when the wind whipped at the fire the smoke drove them from the hut.

Later, Abraham wrote, "We reached our new home about the time the state came into the Union. It was a wild region, with many bears and other wild animals still in the woods. There I grew up."

Hunting was easy. Besides the woodland animals—raccoons, squirrels, opossums, deer, bears, wildcats—flocks of ducks, geese, and wild parakeets flew overhead and passenger pigeons were so thick

Tyranny is the unjust or cruel use of power.

they made the sky dark. Young Abe took his father's rifle, aimed through a chink in their new log cabin, and shot a wild turkey. He found he didn't like killing animals and never shot anything larger than that turkey.

When Abe was nine his mother died of the milk sickness, an illness that poisoned cattle first and then people who drank milk from infected cows. After the death of their mother, Abraham and his sister ached with loneliness, and they turned to each other and became especially good friends.

A man on the frontier with a family needs a woman, and so, within a year, Thomas Lincoln married Sarah Bush Johnston, who had three children of her own.

Sarah was a fine, industrious woman who came into the wilderness and tried to make something of the Lincoln clan and did a good job of it. She got Thomas to put a floor in the log cabin and to make good beds and other improvements. She took Dennis, Abe, and Sarah to the spring and soaped and scrubbed. Then she mended their old garments and made new clothes for them. She did more than that. She gave them love and encouraged them to learn. Abraham didn't need much encouraging. More than anything else he seemed to love to read. But books were scarce in Indiana—so he read the same ones over and over. He read Aesop's *Fables, Robinson Crusoe*, the *Arabian Nights*, the family Bible, and anything else he could find.

The young Lincoln read everything he could find despite the scarcity of books and the expense of candles on the frontier. ▼

He borrowed *The Life of George Washington* and put it in bed beside him. One night snow came through the chinks in the roof and wet the book through. At first Abraham didn't know what to do, but his father had taught him always to be honest. So he went to Josiah Crawford, the man who owned the book, told him what had happened, did some work for him, and got the book as a gift.

All that book reading seemed strange to his neighbors, who couldn't read and didn't see the sense of it. One neighbor said, "[Abe Lincoln] worked for me.... [He] was always reading and thinking. I used to get mad at him.... I say Abe was awful lazy. He would laugh and talk and crack jokes and tell stories all the time.... Lincoln said to me one day that his father taught him to work but never learned him to love it."

He was a friendly boy who loved playing jokes, told good stories, and sometimes climbed on a tree stump and pretended to be a preacher or an orator. As he grew tall (by the time he was 17 he was six feet four) he also grew strong, and soon was stronger than anyone about. One day three men were getting poles ready to lift and move a chicken house. Abe picked up the chicken house all by himself. Another time a big bully claimed he could beat up anyone around. He met his match when Lincoln trounced him.

As he grew, he learned to use an ax and to split rails for fences. He was faster than anyone he knew. He worked with his father, cutting timber, sawing lumber, and making things. Sometimes he earned money as a butcher. He built a boat and ferried passengers across a river, until he was arrested for not having a license. That taught him something about the law. For a while he clerked in a store; then he got a job rafting a load of goods down the Ohio and Mississippi rivers to New Orleans. New Orleans was a metropolis of 44,000 people. He was 20, and it was the first time he'd seen a city.

Lincoln is sometimes called the "rail splitter," one of many jobs he held as a young man. ▼

Abraham's parents moved again and he helped them move; this time it was to Illinois. But he didn't stay with them. He was 22. His beloved sister, Sarah, had died; he needed to get away, to be on his own. So, with the promise of a job, he walked to the frontier town of New Salem. It had 25 families and was the same size as another Illinois town: Chicago.

He had been trained to do hard physical work—to build, to plow, to plant. He was good at those things, but he didn't like them. It was books and the world of the mind that kept tugging at him. There were opportunities for learning in New Salem, and he found them. He became a shopkeeper, a postmaster, a scholar, a surveyor, a law student, and a political candidate.

Not all the lessons were easy. Abraham was a partner in a store, and while his partner drank most of the profits he sat over a book and ignored the business. When it failed he was left with what he called "the national debt." It took years to pay off; he did it.

He was a friend of the Clary boys, who were rough and wild—hooligans, some called them. But Lincoln would not drink, or cuss, or gamble, even though they did.

Soon tales were told of Lincoln's honesty. One day he discovered that he had overcharged a customer by a few pennies; after he closed the store he hiked six miles to return the change.

He walked to the house of the schoolmaster, Mentor Graham (who was well named), and said he wanted to learn grammar. Graham was a born teacher and knew a good student when he found one. They went from grammar to arithmetic to literature to history.

Then the country boy joined the debating society and surprised those who thought he could only joke and tell stories. When he gave a speech it was well crafted and made sense.

▲ Abraham Lincoln worked as a traveling lawyer in the 1850s.

After the store failed he had no job, so he enlisted in the Army and went off to fight Indians in the Black Hawk War—but he said the only fighting he did was against wild onions and mosquitoes.

During Andrew Jackson's presidency Lincoln was named postmaster of New Salem, even though he supported Henry Clay, who was Jackson's rival. He said New Salem was so small no one bothered about his politics. He put letters in his hat and delivered them. There were no stamps. The person who got the letter paid. It was six cents a sheet if delivered within 30 miles. The cost got higher for greater distances.

What the tall young man really wanted to do was study law. In those days there were few law schools. To be a lawyer you studied the law and then passed a test. Abe got some law books and read them, and talked to lawyers and read the books some more. He became a lawyer, a good one. The law would make him wealthy.

His friends urged him to run for public office and he did that, too. The first time he lost, but learned. The next time he got more votes than any other candidate.

In the Illinois General Assembly he spoke only when he had something to say, and that was noted. When the assembly voted 77 to 6 in support of slavery, the young representative was one of the 6. He said, "The institution of slavery is founded on both injustice and bad policy."

Someday he would have much to say on that subject, but first he had more learning to do. He never stopped learning, not as long as he lived.

Mr. President Lincoln

▲ Although Lincoln had been born in a slave state, he believed slavery was wrong.

He was smart, no question of that, and honest, and ambitious. Still, he was a rough country boy. How in the world did he get to be president?

Well, it did take some luck, and some hard work, and a lot of public speaking. But mostly it was the nation that was lucky. Because he was the right man for the job—and perhaps people sensed that.

He was against slavery, but he didn't think he could end that terrible practice. He said he just wanted to stop slavery from spreading into the western territories. Abraham Lincoln was different from most of those who opposed slavery. He was without malice (which means spitefulness). He didn't hate the slave owners. Human nature being what it is, he said, Southern whites were doing what Northern whites would do if they were in their place.

That, however, didn't excuse slavery. Lincoln understood, and said, that "slavery is founded in the selfishness of man's nature— opposition to it, in his love of justice." He knew that those opposing forces, selfishness and love of justice, are found in all people.

Luck came when he ran for the Senate against Stephen A. Douglas. Douglas, who was more than a foot shorter than Lincoln, was called the "little giant." He was a very important man. His suits were made by the best tailors; his friends were influential people. The Illinois Central Railroad lent him a private railroad car so he could campaign in style.

As he toured the state of Illinois giving speeches, people paid attention. And they couldn't ignore his opponent, Abe Lincoln, the

Huge numbers of people came to hear Stephen Douglas debate Abraham Lincoln. In Freeport there was a crowd of 15,000. When Lincoln lost the Senate race, he said he felt like "the boy who stubbed his toe; I am too big to cry and too badly hurt to laugh." ▶

candidate of the new Republican Party. Lincoln, dressed in a rumpled suit (showing wrists and ankles), sometimes rode in the same train, but always in an ordinary car and in an ordinary seat. At train stops, Lincoln found Douglas and they debated.

Douglas talked about *popular sovereignty*, the right of the people to govern themselves. (He said that meant the right of the voters to decide if they wanted to have slaves.)

Lincoln said Douglas was hiding from the real issue, which was slavery itself. "The doctrine of self-government is right, absolutely and eternally right," said Lincoln, but that was not the point. "When the white man governs himself, that is self-government; but when he governs himself and also governs another man, that is more than self-government; that is despotism."

Wherever they spoke crowds came; thousands of people poured into small prairie towns. Perhaps they sensed that history was being made.

They were called the Lincoln-Douglas debates—those railroad-stop speeches—and no political contest in American history has ever been as impressive.

Douglas was brilliant; he could have bested almost anyone else, but in Lincoln he met his match. Besides, his cause wouldn't hold up against Lincoln's cold, clear logic. It was 1858, and the South was no longer satisfied with keeping slavery in the Southern states. Nor were Southerners really happy with the idea of "popular sovereignty." The Southern extremists—and they were now in control—wanted a slave nation.

They had demanded that Congress pass a fugitive slave law. Such a law was passed, as part of the Compromise of 1850. The law said Northerners had to return runaway slaves to their owners. It made helping an escaped slave a crime. And that made Northerners angry. Now they could not say that slavery involved

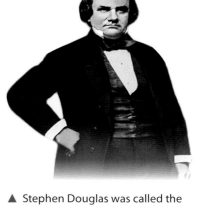

▲ Stephen Douglas was called the "little giant."

Despotism is tyranny, the taking away of freedom, or absolute power over others.

▲ Mary Todd Lincoln

Mary Todd

Abraham Lincoln moved to Springfield (which was Illinois's capital and the place to be for an ambitious young man). There he met a pretty, plump, vivacious young woman who had come from Lexington, Kentucky, to live with her married sister. She was Mary Todd, and they fell in love and married. He told her then, and later, too, that she was the only woman he ever really loved. They soon had four boys, and, as a Chicago man said, "Mrs. Lincoln often entertained numbers of friends at dinner and somewhat larger numbers at evening parties. Her table was famed for the excellence of its rare Kentucky dishes." But some people thought Mary Todd Lincoln acted uppity.

only Southerners. Now they were involved. Some Northerners were willing to break the law rather than return blacks to slavery. Some Northerners—the abolitionists—wanted laws that would end slavery.

Some abolitionists wrote harsh things about the slave owners and the Southern way of life. White Southerners said to the abolitionists, "Mind your own business." Many hated the abolitionists.

Some white Northerners hated the abolitionists, too. They were afraid the abolitionists were stirring up trouble. And, of course, they were. But most Northerners didn't want to face the whole slavery problem; they just wanted it to stay in the South, away from them.

Lincoln made them see the moral issue. He put it in sensible words; he had none of the anger of the abolitionists. He could see both sides. He had been born in a slave state and his wife was a Southerner, but he believed slavery wrong and said so.

He said black people are "entitled to all the natural rights enumerated in the Declaration of Independence, the right to life, liberty and the pursuit of happiness." And he said:

*"A house divided against itself cannot stand." I believe this
government cannot endure permanently half slave and half
free. I do not expect the Union to be dissolved—I do not expect
the house to fall—but I do expect it will cease to be divided.
It will become all one thing, or all the other.*

And:

*Let us have faith that right makes might, and in that faith let us,
to the end, dare to do our duty as we understand it.*

Lincoln was heading home on a wet, rainy night when he heard the news that he had lost the election to the Senate. He slipped on the path, got his balance, and said, "It was a slip, not a fall."

Lincoln was no quitter; he would try again.

Stephen Douglas became the senator from Illinois. But the tall, gangling country lawyer was now well known; the Lincoln-Douglas debates had been read across the nation. Two years later, when both men ran for the presidency, people were ready for Lincoln's words. In 1860, Abraham Lincoln was elected president of the United States.

Before he even had a chance to take office, seven Southern states seceded from the Union. More would follow.

PART 4

CIVIL WAR AND RECONSTRUCTION

Americans Fighting Americans

It was the worst war in American history. It was called the Civil War, or the War Between the States, and sometimes brother fought brother and father fought son. More than 620,000 Americans died. Cities were destroyed, farms burned, homes leveled, and, on one bloody day at a place called Antietam, more men were killed than on any other day in all our history. The total deaths were almost as many as in all of our other wars combined. If the same percentage of today's population were killed it would mean 5 million deaths.

It was the South against the North and, although the North won, neither side came out ahead. The South, which had once been

In the Civil War, the Battle of Antietam was the single bloodiest battle in American history. ▼

Secession, 1860–1861

CANADA

WASHINGTON
TERRITORY

OREGON

MINNESOTA

MAINE

DAKOTA
TERRITORY

VERMONT NEW
HAMPSHIRE

WISCONSIN

MICHIGAN

NEW YORK MASSACHUSETTS

NEVADA
TERRITORY

NEBRASKA
TERRITORY

IOWA

PENNSYLVANIA

RHODE
ISLAND

CONNECTICUT

NEW JERSEY

UTAH
TERRITORY

ILLINOIS

INDIANA

OHIO

DELAWARE

CALIFORNIA

COLORADO
TERRITORY

KANSAS

MISSOURI

WEST
VIRGINIA

VIRGINIA

MARYLAND

KENTUCKY

West Virginia
seceded from
Virginia and
was admitted
into the Union
in 1863.

NEW MEXICO
TERRITORY

INDIAN
TERRITORY

ARKANSAS

TENNESSEE

NORTH
CAROLINA

SOUTH
CAROLINA

TEXAS

LOUISIANA

MISSISSIPPI

ALABAMA

GEORGIA

FLORIDA

MEXICO

N

Union
Confederacy
Border state

0   250   500 mi
0   250   500 km

▲ By 1861, 11 states had seceded from the Union and formed the
Confederate States of America.

prosperous, was in ruins. The North was left with huge war debts.
And both North and South had the graves of fathers, sons, and
husbands to weep over.

What was it all about? Why were Americans fighting
Americans?

When the war began, people on both sides claimed they weren't
fighting over slavery. But they were fooling themselves. Before the
end of the war it was clear: slavery was the main issue. Most white
Southerners wanted to keep slavery because they thought their way
of life depended on it. Most Northerners thought slavery wrong and
that, as Abraham Lincoln said, the nation could not exist half slave
and half free.

▲ Although some people
on both sides did not
acknowledge it at first, the
main issue of the Civil War
was slavery.

White Southerners were willing to fight to keep slavery because their way of life depended on it. This photograph was taken in Virginia in 1862. ▶

You think slavery is right and ought to be extended, while we think it is wrong and ought to be restricted. That I suppose is the rub. It is certainly the only difference between us.

—Abraham Lincoln

There were other issues, too: the Southerners, who were also called "Rebels," believed in "states' rights." They thought any state should have the right to pull out of the United States (they usually called it "the Union"). They said it was tyranny to hold states in the Union against their wishes. They said they were doing the same thing that George Washington and John Adams and the other revolutionaries had done against King George—fighting for their freedom. But it was white freedom they were fighting for. They didn't want to consider the fact that they were tyrannizing black people.

What they did was form their own nation. Eleven Southern states seceded from the Union. They created the Confederate States of America and elected a president and a congress. They said all they wished was to go peacefully from the Union.

The North wouldn't let them do it. Revolution is only right, said President Abraham Lincoln, "for a morally justified cause." But the South had no just cause. So, said Lincoln, secession was "simply a wicked exercise of physical power."

This was an important issue they were deciding. The American nation was still considered an experiment. Would a people's government survive? Lincoln said Americans needed to prove "that popular government is not an absurdity." Then he added,

"We must settle this question now, whether in a free government the minority have the right to break up the government whenever they choose."

The Northerners, who were also called "Yankees," or "Federals," were willing to fight for the American form of government—for the Constitution, for the Union. They said that when the states joined the Union they agreed to uphold the Constitution and they couldn't just pull out anytime they wanted. If that were allowed, soon there would be no Union at all.

▲ A portrait of a young Confederate soldier

▲ A portrait of a young Union soldier

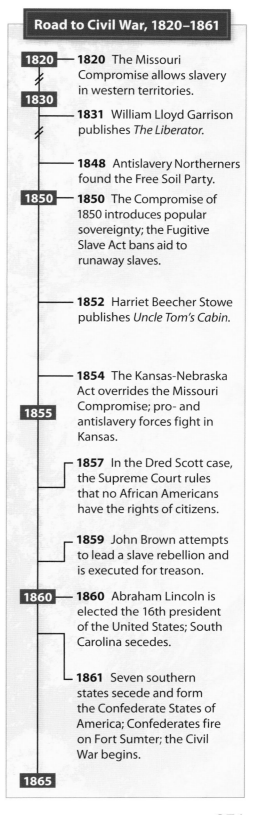

Road to Civil War, 1820–1861

1820 — **1820** The Missouri Compromise allows slavery in western territories.

1830

1831 William Lloyd Garrison publishes *The Liberator*.

1848 Antislavery Northerners found the Free Soil Party.

1850 — **1850** The Compromise of 1850 introduces popular sovereignty; the Fugitive Slave Act bans aid to runaway slaves.

1852 Harriet Beecher Stowe publishes *Uncle Tom's Cabin*.

1854 The Kansas-Nebraska Act overrides the Missouri Compromise; pro- and antislavery forces fight in Kansas.

1855

1857 In the Dred Scott case, the Supreme Court rules that no African Americans have the rights of citizens.

1859 John Brown attempts to lead a slave rebellion and is executed for treason.

1860 — **1860** Abraham Lincoln is elected the 16th president of the United States; South Carolina secedes.

1861 Seven southern states secede and form the Confederate States of America; Confederates fire on Fort Sumter; the Civil War begins.

1865

Lincoln's Problems

South Carolina led the way. It was the first state to secede. Mississippi, one of the richest states in the nation (with more millionaires in the town of Natchez, per capita, than anywhere else in the country), followed eagerly. So did Florida, Alabama, Georgia, Louisiana, and Texas.

The other slave states hesitated until President Lincoln called for volunteers to fight in the South. That decided it for four more states: Virginia, Arkansas, North Carolina, and Tennessee. They would not fight their sister states.

When Virginia joined the Rebels the Confederate government was invited to make its headquarters in Richmond. That turned out to be a mistake for Virginia, because much of the war was fought on her land. But in 1861, no one knew what was ahead. War preparations made Richmond an exciting place: there were jobs to be done and political power to be distributed. Richmond's population increased by one-third. The city was an industrial hub.

> *Per capita* is Latin and means "by the head." Considering the number of people in Natchez, the city had a larger percentage of millionaires than anywhere in the country.

South Carolina seceded in December 1860. ▼

CHARLESTON
MERCURY
EXTRA:

Passed unanimously at 1.15 o'clock, P.M., December 20th, 1860.

AN ORDINANCE

To dissolve the Union between the State of South Carolina and other States united with her the compact entitled "The Constitution of the United States of America."

THE

UNION
IS
DISSOLVED!

High Street in Richmond, Virginia, during the Civil War ▼

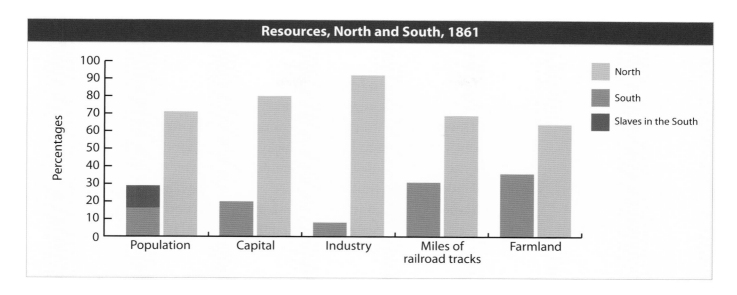

Resources, North and South, 1861

Percentages

| North |
| South |
| Slaves in the South |

Population · Capital · Industry · Miles of railroad tracks · Farmland

Its iron foundry began pouring out weapons. Workers, soldiers, and white citizens all seemed committed to what they called a "glorious cause." The war preparations had a kind of dreamlike, romantic quality. It was as if the plans were for a game—not the real thing.

Few people talked about the side of war that is serious and deadly. What they talked of was heroism and glory. Plays were performed in the city's theaters and fancy-dress balls held in its handsome homes. Confederate President Jefferson Davis (you'll read more about him soon) and his family moved into an elegant, high-ceilinged mansion (to be called the White House of the Confederacy). The columned Virginia capitol (the building Thomas Jefferson designed) was now the Confederate capitol. Most white Virginians were optimistic and determined. Most black Virginians were in no position to act for themselves.

Actually, not all of Virginia seceded. The people over the mountains, to the west, didn't agree with the plantation owners and the others of eastern Virginia. They were small farmers, and loyal to the Union—so they seceded from Virginia, formed West Virginia, and became the 35th state.

There were four other slave states (besides those that had seceded), and they were undecided. Should they join the Confederate cause? Or stay in the United States? Those slave states were Maryland, Kentucky, Missouri, and Delaware. They were border states—touching North and South. All had influential citizens who wanted to join the

South Carolina had a larger proportion of blacks than any other state. More than half (57 percent) of its people were black.

Confederacy. What do you think might have happened if they had left the Union? Maryland enclosed Washington, D.C., on three sides. Virginia was on the fourth side.

Could the capital have been saved with Maryland as an enemy? How about Kentucky? Control of Kentucky meant control of the important Ohio River. You can move armies and supplies down a river. Abraham Lincoln said he had to have Kentucky and Maryland and the other border states. He didn't think he could win the war without them.

In addition to vital land, those border states had factories, large populations (to turn into soldiers), and mules and horses. But holding the border states created a problem for Lincoln. If he freed the slaves, the border states might leave the Union.

Meanwhile, the abolitionists were screaming for him to free the slaves. They were calling Lincoln all sorts of nasty names. Lincoln said that if he freed the slaves, lost the war, and destroyed the Union, he wouldn't help the slaves or anybody else.

Besides, he knew many white Northerners were racists. That was unfortunate (and heartless), but it was 19th-century reality. Lincoln was a practical man and a politician. He couldn't move too fast. He knew the people had to be behind him. There seemed to be two Lincolns. One was the private man who had personal opinions and hated slavery. The other was the president who felt he must reflect the will of the people. And the people had not yet fully decided to abolish slavery. (Harriet Beecher Stowe's book was helping push them in that direction.)

Richmond had a large population of free blacks. The war put them in a strange position. Most worked for Confederates but hoped for the South's defeat. As for the slaves, when they could, many ran away to Yankee army camps. Some remained loyal to the whites they knew. Others waited— to see what would happen.

A recently freed slave presents himself to be enrolled in the Union army. ▶

In his first inaugural address (the speech he gave when he became president), Lincoln said slavery would be left alone in the slave states. "I have no purpose, directly or indirectly, to interfere with the institution of slavery in the states where it exists," he said. His goal was to preserve the Union. "We are not enemies but friends. We must not be enemies," he said.

President Lincoln understood that slavery was a leftover from another age. He believed slavery was doomed. Decent people could not tolerate it much longer. To a Philadelphia audience he offered hope that "the weights would be lifted from the shoulders of all men, and that all should have an equal chance." But he would not start a war to end slavery. "The government will not use force unless force is used against it," he said. He knew if there was war, and if the South won, there would be two American nations and continuing battles between them: over runaways and western lands and power. And he knew that the South had a good chance of winning a civil war.

When we look at things today, it seems as if the North should have had an easy time winning. After all, the North had many advantages: more men, more industry, more food. But rebellions are always fought by underdogs. People in power don't try to change things. The outcome of war is often surprising. Our revolution taught us that. And the South was far more powerful than the colonies had been when they fought England.

Like the colonies, the Confederacy wasn't trying to conquer anyone. Its leaders said they just wanted to leave the United States. But that wasn't quite true. They wanted some of those western lands. They wanted to create a slave nation and they wanted it to grow. And they wanted slaves who ran away to free lands returned. But they didn't talk much about that. They just talked about states' rights.

The North had a tough job to do. It had to conquer 11 Southern states and then hold them. That would be difficult.

Many Southerners were skilled fighters. They were mostly farmers, used to shooting guns, riding horses, and being out of doors. Many Northern soldiers were city boys who had never shot a gun or sat a horse. Besides, most of the Rebels believed they were fighting for their

▲ Abraham Lincoln takes the presidential oath during his first inauguration in 1861.

land; they were told the Yankees were nasty people who wanted to rule them. Lincoln knew they wouldn't give up easily.

But Lincoln would not let the Confederacy bully him. The Union had forts on the southern coast. One of those, Fort Sumter, was in the harbor at Charleston, South Carolina. That was where the war began. Here is how it started.

On December 20, 1860, at a state convention, South Carolina voted to secede from—to leave—the Union. It demanded that Fort Sumter be turned over to its new government. U.S. troops were to leave the fort. President Lincoln wouldn't agree to that. Fort Sumter belonged to all the people of the United States, not just to South Carolina, he said. The Carolinians were determined to have the fort. They threatened to starve the men stationed there. Lincoln sent food and supplies. The Rebels fired on the supply ship. Then they fired on the fort—and destroyed it. That was how the war began. It was April 1861.

In the North there were some who urged Lincoln to let the South go. "The Union doesn't need the South," they said. "Who cares about slaves?" they added.

Lincoln didn't agree. But he knew this would be no easy contest. He needed strength and courage to win this war.

April 12, 1861—the Civil War begins as Federal soldiers return fire on Confederate forces firing on Fort Sumter. ▶

The War Begins

Most people, North and South, thought the war would last a few months. The Southerners liked the idea of soldiering. It seemed adventurous and heroic. Many Southern leaders were graduates of the military academy at West Point. Besides, they were sure the Yankees were all cowards. Just wait until they met on the battlefield; they'd scare the wits out of those Yankees. Or so they boasted to their wives and girlfriends as they marched off in their handsome gray uniforms.

The Northern men were just as confident. One big battle, they said, and the war would be over. They knew the North had many advantages: more men, more industry, more money. But that wasn't what made them confident. They were sure the Southern soldiers were lazy. Why, without their slaves they wouldn't be able to do a thing. They'd run for the hills at the first shots, or so the Northerners boasted to their wives and girlfriends as they marched off in their handsome blue uniforms.

Soldiers practice firing artillery at the U.S. Military Academy at West Point. ▼

It didn't quite turn out the way they expected. Men on both sides were brave, very brave, and willing to die for their beliefs. A generation of men would die. But no one realized that in the summer of 1861.

The war began when Southern guns fired on U.S. troops stationed at a small island fort in the harbor at Charleston, South Carolina. That fort—Fort Sumter—was a U.S. government fort, and those shots announced that South Carolina was serious about leaving the United States. The Southerners meant to capture the fort, and they did. A few South Carolinians were dismayed, but many came to the Charleston waterfront in party clothes and cheered when the cannons blasted. They were rebels—eager to battle what had been their own government—and they were excited by what they were doing. Some of the young men who applauded the firing were afraid the war would be over before they got a chance to fight. One political leader said he would use his handkerchief to wipe up all the Southern blood that would be spilled—and people believed him.

The first big battle was fought at a place called Manassas, not far from the city of Washington. It was fought near a muddy stream known as Bull Run. So some people call it the battle of Bull Run, and others the battle of Manassas.

Manassas was a logical place to have a battle. It was a railroad junction: the place where two railroad lines met. This would be the first

Confederate forces fire on Fort Sumter in Charleston, South Carolina. ▶

▲ The first major battle of the Civil War took place at Bull Run, near Manassas, Virginia.

war in which modern transportation was used. Again and again, the railroads would make a difference. They would help decide this battle of Manassas.

The Northern generals thought they would take Manassas and then march south, to the Confederate capital at Richmond, Virginia.

When that July day began, in 1861, war seemed a bit like a show. And hundreds of Washingtonians didn't want to miss that show. (After all, they couldn't watch it on TV.) They decided to go to Manassas with their picnic baskets, settle down near Bull Run stream, and watch the fighting. They came on horseback and by carriage and wagon and they spread out in the fields and listened to the guns and watched a smoky haze form above the noisy cannons.

But they didn't see what they expected. It wasn't a picture-book battle; it was real, and disorderly. There were untrained beginners out there—soldiers and officers—who didn't know what they were doing.

The officers were trying to fight war as Napoleon had, for Napoleon was considered the military genius of the age. But Napoleon had a trained army able to follow complicated military orders. And guns had changed since Napoleon's day—they were now more deadly and accurate. It took time for the officers to realize the old tactics needed to be thrown out. Besides, American soldiers weren't like Europeans.

▲ Confederate troops resist a Federal charge at Bull Run.

Confederate general T. J. Jackson (soon to be known as Stonewall Jackson) surveys the battle at Bull Run. ▶

The American soldier was an independent kind of fellow; he didn't take orders well. But he could fight like fury, as everyone soon found out.

Both sides fought all day. They fought hard, and even though there was much confusion, there was also much bravery. One of the bravest of the fighters was a Confederate general, Thomas J. Jackson. "There is Jackson standing like a stone wall," shouted a Southern officer when he saw Jackson and his men holding firm against the enemy. Jackson would, from that moment, always be known as Stonewall Jackson.

The battle raged, over meadows and wooded hills and on the steep banks of Bull Run Creek. It was a hot, very hot, humid summer day. Most of the men wore heavy wool uniforms, as was customary then. Those uniforms were anything but "uniform." Some were official Southern gray or Northern blue. But many men wore the uniforms of their state militias (some southern militias had blue uniforms). Some men had borrowed old Revolutionary War uniforms. Some wore fancy wide pants and colorful sashes copied from French Zouave soldiers. Some just wore their regular clothes. It was confusing, and more than a few soldiers were killed by bullets shot from their own side.

By afternoon everyone was exhausted, bodies littered the ground, the earth was bloody and beginning to smell, and neither side seemed to be winning. Then fresh Southern troops arrived by train. That made the difference. It gave new energy to the Rebels. General Jackson—Stonewall—told them to "yell like furies." They did. They attacked with bloodcurdling shouts; they called it the "rebel yell." And that was too much for the Yankees. They dropped their guns and fled. Some couldn't run fast enough.

The South won that battle of Bull Run. The Northern soldiers, who had planned to fight on to Richmond, now went the other way, back to Washington. They hadn't expected to do that. The citizens who had come to watch the battle hadn't expected it either.

Troops and civilians were together on the road back to Washington when a stray shell exploded and upset a wagon. That blocked a bridge and wounded soldiers, cavalry, frightened troops, and families in their carriages were all stuck. Someone shouted that the Southern cavalry was attacking. (It wasn't really.)

That was like yelling "Fire!" in a crowded theater. It started a panic—a shoving, pushing, screaming panic.

It didn't take long for people to realize that war is no picnic. Although, even then, no one dreamed that the war would be as long, hard, and bloody as it turned out to be.

> *They plunged through Bull Run wherever they came to it, regardless of fords or bridges, and there many drowned.… We found…along the road, parasols and dainty shawls lost in their flight by the fair, fair ones who had seats in most of the carriages.*
> —Lt. Col. W. W. Blackford,
> 1st Cavalry, Virginia

Defeated, the Federal army retreats to Washington, D.C. ▼

President Jefferson Davis

Jefferson Davis became president of the Confederate States of America. Like Abe Lincoln, Jeff Davis was born in a log cabin in Kentucky.

Soon after Jefferson's birth, his family moved—first to Louisiana, and then again to Mississippi. In Mississippi they found what they were looking for: prosperity. They grew cotton and became rich.

Joseph, the oldest son, became the richest planter in the state. He was a lawyer, and he owned the finest library in Mississippi. He helped raise his young brother Jefferson and saw that he went to the best schools and to the Military Academy at West Point. He would see that Jefferson had his own plantation and slaves.

Jefferson grew up, became a soldier, fought Indians in the Black Hawk War, and fell in love with the daughter of "Old Rough and Ready," General Zachary Taylor. Knox Taylor loved him, too. Old Zack didn't want the brash soldier boy for a son-in-law. So they eloped—Jeff and Knox—and got married. Then both caught a malarial fever, and Knox died.

Jefferson was sick for a long time; when he recovered he was different. He looked different: hollow-eyed and gaunt. He was now serious and studious. He went to his brother's library and became one of the most learned men in the South. He tended his plantation and was a model slave owner, allowing his slaves their own system of justice, with their own court to punish those who did wrong.

And he fell in love again, this time with fair Varina Howell, who made him a good wife. She was 18, he was 36, and the year they married Davis was elected to Congress.

Mississippi's governor appointed Davis to the U.S. Senate. Historian Shelby Foote has said that he "was perhaps the best informed, probably the best educated, and certainly the most intellectual man in the Senate." In the Senate, Davis followed the path of South Carolina's Senator John C. Calhoun and argued for Southern power, for the extension of slavery into the Western territories, for the right of a state to secede. Those were the issues that would cause the South to leave the Union. When the Confederate nation looked for a president, it could find no one more qualified than Jefferson Davis.

▲ Jefferson and Varina Davis

Choosing Sides

It was more than a war that split the nation. It was a war that split families, too.

Yes, brothers really fought brothers. Major Clifton Prentiss—Union army—and his younger brother, William—Confederate army—both fought and died in the same battle at Petersburg, Virginia.

Four of Abraham Lincoln's brothers-in-law fought for the Confederacy; three died for it. Three grandsons of Henry Clay fought for the Union, four for the Confederacy. In one battle, Confederate cavalry general J. E. B. Stuart was chased by Union cavalry general Phillip St. George Cooke, who was Stuart's father-in-law. (General Stuart said General Cooke would regret being a Union man "but once, and that will be continuously.") Senator John Crittenden's two sons became generals: one for the South, one for the North.

Most men went to war for their region. But some believed in the cause of the other part of the nation and fought for those beliefs.

Admiral David G. Farragut was a naval commander (a great one) on the side of the North, though he was from Alabama. Robert E. Lee's cousin, Samuel P. Lee, commanded the Union

◀ Admiral David Farragut came from the South, but he fought for the North. He led a Union naval fleet to victory in the Battle of Mobile Bay in 1864.

▲ Confederate fortifications at Yorktown, Virginia

naval forces on the James River. Generals Winfield Scott and George H. Thomas, both Virginians, fought for the Union.

Choosing sides was not easy. Two army officers were stationed at a small western outpost named Los Angeles when war was declared. They were outstanding men. Both were natural leaders: strong, kind, and courageous. They were best friends. One, Captain Winfield Scott Hancock, stayed in the Union army. The other, Captain Lewis Armistead, became a Confederate. When they parted, Armistead looked at Hancock and said, "You'll never know what this is costing me, but goodbye, goodbye."

They were to meet again, two years later, at a ferocious battle near a little Pennsylvania town named Gettysburg. What happened? Well, keep reading and you'll find out.

Did they hate each other, Northerners and Southerners? Often they thought they did, but when they got to know each other it wasn't so. There were too many stories of friendliness for the hatred to be real. It wasn't unusual for Northern soldiers to camp in trenches facing Southern soldiers while both sides waited for orders to fight— and that could take weeks or months. At first they yelled at each other, then they talked; occasionally they even sang together.

Once some Yankee soldiers were invited to a dance by some Rebels. The Yankees went and had a good time until an officer found out, came for them, and made sure they never did that again.

Sometimes they traded things, or exchanged letters. Then, when the orders came, they would settle down to killing each other. After all, that's what war is about.

But they did have beliefs, and most of them knew in their hearts that they were fighting for things they believed in. Yes, they knew it had something to do with slavery, and where they lived, and states' rights versus national unity, but there was something more than that. They were fighting, on each side, for a way of life. The Southern way of life was different from the Northern way.

The North was becoming urban. There were cities and factories and all the problems and opportunities that come with industry and change.

In the South, life was pastoral, conservative, and orderly. It was where the old European class society had taken root in the New World. The South offered great opportunity and ease for a small number of white people. For many other white people living was comfortable and secure. But for poor whites and blacks it wasn't comfortable at all.

Life in the antebellum South was not fair. Everyone is not created equal, or given an equal chance, in a slave society.

> *Pastoral* means "rural, having to do with country life."

Changing Times

Yankee society was changing its economic base. It was going from an agricultural society to an industrial one. It was the way of the future—but that was hard to see. These were changing times. The South, and its agricultural plantations, had once led the nation. The South had been home to great leaders, and great wealth. Now the North was surging ahead.

Actually, there were two Souths. The Old South of the East Coast states was in trouble. The soil on its plantations was worn out. So were its ideas. Slavery had become inefficient there. The New South, to the west, was filled with cotton plantations that were harvesting riches for a small group of white families—at the expense of black laborers.

▲ The South's economy was based on agriculture.

Only about one-fourth of the 1.55 million white families in the South actually owned slaves. Of the slave owners, just one in seven had more than 10 slaves. Most Southerners were small farmers without slaves. Some were mountain folk who hardly knew any black people. The big plantation owners—who had hundreds of slaves—were very few in number. But they dominated the South and controlled the legislatures.

The leaders of the Old South blamed Northerners for all their troubles. They couldn't believe that their ideas needed changing. The leaders of the New South were terrified that they might lose their slaves, who were the key to their wealth.

To be a fair society, the South needed industry, railroads, roads, and schools. It needed to give opportunity to all. Some Southerners understood that; most did not. The people of the South followed the wrong-thinking leaders.

Some Southerners (and Northerners, too) believed Africans were "savages" and they were "civilizing" them. They believed the white race was superior. That was a racist idea—although they didn't understand that—and it would lead to evil action wherever it was expressed. It was that same racism that made the settlers treat Indians so cruelly.

In a slave society some men and women are treated like prisoners, even though they have committed no crime. In some Southern states, such as South Carolina, more than half the population was black. Blacks were the prisoners. They did the hard work in the South so that life could be easy for others.

The North was fighting for democracy. Democracy is rarely orderly, but it attempts to be fair. Northern factory workers and farm laborers were not rich; sometimes their lives were very difficult, but they were free and better off than workers almost anywhere else in the world.

Virginia's senator James M. Mason understood the differences between North and South. He said, "I look upon it [the Civil War] then, sir, as a war of…one form of society against another form of society."

So if someone asks you if the war made a difference, you can say yes. It not only ended slavery and preserved the Union, it settled that democratic question. After the Civil War, the United States was committed by constitutional amendments to democracy—to fairness—to equality of opportunity.

Did that mean that everyone was now treated fairly? No, it didn't. It is easier to change laws than it is to change ideas and habits. The fight for real equality of opportunity continued. It continues today. But the goal of fairness was established in the law. The flaw in the Constitution that allowed slavery was amended. No one could ever again argue that slavery was a positive good. Now it was clear: tyranny and persecution and bigotry were forbidden by the Constitution. They were un-American.

The issue of slavery was settled once and for all by the Civil War. ▶

The Soldiers

Their median age was 24. That means that half of the Civil War soldiers were younger than 24, and half were older. Many were 18 or 19. Some were even younger. Eleven-year-old Johnny Clem was a drummer boy in a Michigan regiment. When a Confederate colonel tried to take him prisoner, Johnny picked up a musket and killed the colonel. He was made a sergeant.

The Union rules said a soldier was supposed to be at least 18 years old. But boys who were eager to fight found a way around that. They wrote the number 18 on a piece of paper and put it in their shoe. Then, when asked, they could say, "I'm over 18."

Young men weren't the only ones anxious to fight for their beliefs. Iowa had a famous "Graybeard Regiment." Everyone in it was over 45. "So old were these men, and so young their state," wrote historian Bruce Catton, "that not a man in the regiment could claim Iowa as his birthplace. There had been no Iowa when these Iowans were born."

At first there were so many volunteers that neither army could handle them all. Later, when the volunteers wrote home about the battles and the deaths and the conditions, fewer came willingly, so the governments paid cash rewards for volunteers and finally both sides had to draft men. (Which means they had to force them to sign up.)

Some people called it "a rich man's war and a poor man's fight."

That was because, if you were rich enough, you didn't have to be in the army. Confederates who owned 20 or more slaves could be excused, although many fought anyway. And Northerners who could afford the cost were allowed to pay someone to fight for them. Many did.

Most soldiers were farmers, because it was a country of farmers. Some were small-town boys; most had never been far from home. Soldiering sounded like an adventurous thing to do, and for a while it was a bit like boys' camp. One Illinois recruit wrote in a letter home, "It is fun to lie around,

◀ Johnny Clem was a drummer boy in the Union army.

▲ At the start of the war, many volunteers, like these Confederate soldiers, enlisted eagerly. "We were all afraid it would be over and we not in the fight," said 21-year-old Sam Watkins, whose family owned no slaves.

face unwashed, hair uncombed, shirt unbuttoned and everything un-everythinged."

For the soldier boys there were new friends and uniforms and parades and drills—but that soon changed. Then, often, there were long marches, long, boring encampments, homesickness, bad food, hunger, and disease. For every man who died in battle, two died of sickness. (Few people then understood about germs and the importance of good food and cleanliness, or how to deal with epidemics.)

Many of the new soldiers—especially town-bred Northerners—didn't know how to handle the rifles they were given. Some were thrown into battle without training—they had to learn under fire. Many of their officers were volunteers, too, and knew no more than the men they led.

Northern armies were well fed and well supplied; Southerners often went hungry. Both sides usually had guns enough, although they were not always the best available. An inventive Yankee named Christian Sharps spent six years developing a breech-loading rifle. It was a single-shot weapon but much better than most guns in use. Abraham Lincoln examined a Sharps rifle, loaded and shot it, and thought it a "wonderful gun." Some new weapons could be fired more than once without reloading. The Spencer seven-shot was the best of the repeating rifles. Richard Gatling devised a machine gun that fired 250 rounds a minute from six revolving barrels. Before the end of the war, several thousand Union soldiers were using new weapons.

But most soldiers used rifled muskets that were loaded from the shooting end (the muzzle). A rifled musket has a barrel with grooves inside that make the bullet spin and go farther and with more accuracy than bullets shot from a plain barrel. Very skilled soldiers could get off three shots a minute.

A *breech-loading* gun is loaded at the bottom of the barrel, near the trigger, as most rifles are today.

▲ Civil War rifles

The new rifled guns were much better than the muskets used in the Revolutionary War or in the Mexican War. During the Revolution, most of the fighting was eyeball to eyeball, and many deaths were from bayonet wounds. That wasn't true in the Civil War. Rifled guns could kill a man a half mile away. There were new bullets, too, and they were killers, and cannons—artillery—that were much more powerful and accurate than those used in Mexico. Much of the fighting, however, was still done in the old way. Most of the generals had gone to West Point and learned battle strategy by studying the old battles. The old lessons didn't work with new weapons, and that was part of the reason for the incredibly high numbers of battlefield deaths.

Picture two sides fighting: on one side are the attackers, on the other the defenders. The defenders line their men up in two rows. The front row is kneeling, guns in position. Behind them men stand ready to shoot over their heads.

Here come the attackers. Shoulder to shoulder they charge in great waves of men. They march to the beat of a drummer boy. The beat tells the men when to stop to fire and reload.

Civil War battlefields—such as these at the Battle of Corinth, Mississippi—could become so thick with smoke that soldiers couldn't see the enemy. ▼

Union general Daniel Butterfield didn't like the bugle call that was played to tell soldiers to turn their lights out. So he scribbled some musical notes on the back of an envelope and gave them to his bugler. It was 1862, and the tune was called "Taps." It was soon being played by both armies.

To that picture of attackers and defenders you need to add some soldiers on horseback with swords flashing. And something else: noise. The explosions of cannons and muskets, and the din of men yelling and horses snorting. You can add something else again. Smoke. Lots of smoke. Smokeless powder hadn't been developed, so the battlefield was soon so thick with smoke—especially from cannons—that no one could see what was going on. It isn't surprising that many men were killed by shots from their own side.

How does the battle turn out? Usually the attackers get mowed down. (When the defenders dig trenches and protect themselves—which happened for the first time in the Civil War—the defenders are clearly in the best position.)

It is easy for us, today, to understand that. It wasn't so easy for the generals back in the 19th century. In the old days of muskets, before the Civil War, when bullets weren't as deadly, or guns as accurate, the attackers usually had the advantage. They could charge across an open battlefield and overwhelm the defenders with bayonets and swords. It took time for the Civil War generals to adjust to the new weapons and technology.

Besides, armies of volunteer civilians fighting for a cause just don't fight the same way as professional soldiers. They fight harder. The generals had to learn that, too.

And they had to learn the importance of new transportation and communication methods. With railroads, armies could be moved with astonishing speed. With the telegraph, you could instantly find out what was going on hundreds of miles away.

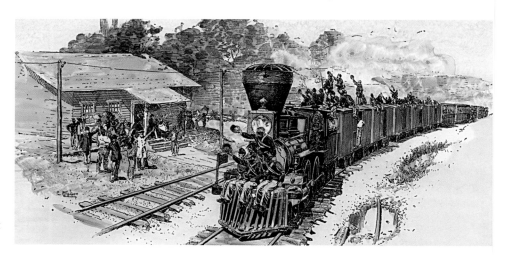

Railroads made it possible to transport troops quickly. ▶

During the Civil War, for the first time in America, war took to the air: hot-air balloons went aloft carrying spies in floating baskets who peered down over enemy lines. The balloons were tethered—that means they were tied to the ground with long ropes. One balloon broke its tether and floated away with a general aboard; luckily for him, the wind shifted and brought him back to his own lines. Balloons weren't the only Civil War novelty: a submarine sank an enemy ship—and got sunk itself in the process.

When war began, battles were still expected to be controlled fights between armies. Remember how civilians brought picnic baskets to see the battle at Bull Run? They expected a by-the-rules, orderly skirmish. But in this war all the rules changed. It has been called the first modern war. Cities and farms were burned and civilian populations terrorized. It was total war, and it got out of control.

A Union army observation balloon ▼

The *H. L. Hunley,* a submarine used by the Confederacy during the Civil War ▼

The Union Generals

General Winfield Scott was in charge of the Union army. He was an old man and in terrible physical shape. He even had to be helped onto his horse. But there was nothing wrong with his mind—it was as sharp as ever.

General Scott looked at the situation when the war began and he figured it would take at least two or three years to win a war against the South. He came up with a plan. To begin, he thought the North should blockade Southern ports. That means Northern ships would patrol the Southern coast and keep ships from entering or leaving. That wouldn't be easy, and a few ships would probably slip through the blockade, but if the South could be kept from trading with Europe it would be in trouble. The Confederacy was an agricultural nation. It didn't manufacture much of anything. If the South was to fight a war, it would need cash to buy goods—especially weapons. To get cash it needed to sell its cotton in Europe. A blockade that closed Southern ports would really hurt the Confederacy.

Cotton Is King

Many Southerners believed cotton was going to determine the outcome of this war. Without cotton, English cotton mills would be in big trouble, they said. England had to enter the war on the side of the South, they added. Here are South Carolina senator M. B. Hammond's words (and they were widely believed):

What would happen if no cotton were furnished for three years? England would topple head-long and carry the whole civilized world with her, save the South.... No, you dare not make war on cotton. No power on earth dare make war upon it. Cotton is king!

▲ Bales of cotton are unloaded from riverboats on the levee at the important port of New Orleans. To finance the war, the South needed to sell cotton to Europe.

General Scott also thought the North had to control the Mississippi River. That would cut off Louisiana, Texas, and Arkansas from the rest of the Confederacy. It would close more ports and keep that cotton from being exported.

As to the actual fighting, the Union could send armies from the east and armies from the west to squeeze the Confederacy.

And that is pretty much what happened during the Civil War. But it didn't take two or three years, it took four years: from April of 1861 to April of 1865.

Guess what happened when people heard of Winfield Scott's plan. They laughed. The war lasting two or three years? Why, that was the nonsense of an old man. This was a war that would be over in a few months, everyone knew that. A plan to squeeze the enemy? That was just plain silly.

They called Winfield's plan the "Anaconda Plan"—because an anaconda is a snake that squeezes its prey—and it caused so much dismay that President Lincoln was forced to look for a new general. He found a man who was handsome and intelligent and popular with his troops. He was a graduate of the U.S. Military Academy at West Point and a former railroad superintendent. His name was George Brinton McClellan.

McClellan was an excellent organizer. That's an important ability when you are in charge of large numbers of people. A general has to feed, house, and equip his armies. He has to be able to move them long distances. He has to inspire them. He has to train them. McClellan was good at all those things. There was just one problem. It was a big problem for a general. He didn't like to fight. He kept hesitating, and making excuses, and pulling back. Once Lincoln ordered McClellan to advance immediately. "It was 19 days before he put a man over the river, 9 days longer before he got his army across, and then he stopped again," said Lincoln, who fired him.

Abraham Lincoln meets with General George B. McClellan. ▼

▲ Lincoln's general Ulysses S. Grant (above, at the battle of Cold Harbor) once said, "I don't know whether I am like other men or not, but when I have nothing to do, I get blue and depressed."

Lincoln tried Generals McClellan, Frémont, Burnside, Halleck, Hooker, Pope, Meade, and some others. Not one of them fought the way Lincoln thought they should. Every time the North lost a battle—and it lost quite a few—Lincoln got blamed, even though the generals weren't doing what the president was asking.

There just didn't seem to be a leader he could trust. Then he looked out west and found a general who was winning battles. A general who trapped a whole Confederate army and took all the soldiers prisoners of war. That general, who was good at fighting, was named Ulysses S. Grant. (He even had initials to match his country.) Lincoln called him "the quietest little fellow you ever saw."

Grant had been to West Point, where he was nicknamed "Uncle Sam" because of those initials. His Army friends called him Sam Grant. At West Point Sam Grant was a fair student but too small to excel at any sport but riding. He fought in the Mexican War, then left the Army, and wasn't much of a success in civilian life. He was poor, really poor, when he inherited a slave. He could have sold the slave for $1,000, but he didn't do it. He gave the man his freedom.

It didn't look as if Grant would amount to anything, until the Civil War came along, and it made him famous (famous enough to one day be president). He was the kind of general who didn't worry much about military theories. He just outkilled or outlasted his enemy. General Grant and his friend, red-bearded General William Tecumseh Sherman (whom we will get to later), were just the kind of generals Lincoln had been looking for.

The Confederate Generals

Southern boys liked to play soldier. When they grew up many of them went to military academies. Because of that soldiering tradition, the South had good generals—lots of good generals. To begin, there was James Longstreet. "Old Pete" was what his men called him. He was a big man, with bones that stood out like those of an old hunting dog. Longstreet was cold-eyed and looked like what he was—a fighter. He usually wore old clothes, dirty boots, and a black hat. While a battle raged, you might see him whittling on a stick. He knew how to act calm. But no one ever questioned his bravery. When he was needed, he was in the front line, leading charges.

Then there was J. E. B. "Jeb" Stuart, who wore elbow-length white gloves, a red-lined cape, gold spurs, and an ostrich feather in his hat. He wanted to look like an English cavalier, and he did. Stuart was one of the most daring cavalry leaders the world has known.

And there was George Pickett, another man who dressed like a dandy, wore his hair long and curled, and put a feather in his broad-brimmed hat. Pickett was at the bottom of his West Point class. It didn't matter; he did well enough on the battlefield. Besides, everyone liked George Pickett. You couldn't help liking him—he was easygoing, good-natured, and friendly. He didn't drink or gamble, because he had promised his girlfriend, Sallie, that he wouldn't, and he stuck to his word. More than anything, Pickett wanted a chance to fight and show how brave he was. He would have that chance.

The greatest Southern generals were Thomas J. "Stonewall" Jackson and Robert E. Lee.

Jackson was an orphan child who grew into a strange, brooding man. Like Grant and Lee, and most of the other generals on both sides of this conflict, Jackson went to West Point and fought in the Mexican War. He was a teacher at the Virginia Military Institute when this war began. He wasn't popular. He was strict and had no sense of humor. The boys called him "Tom Fool" behind his back.

Generals Longstreet (standing) and Pickett (on horseback) confer during the Battle of Gettysburg. ▼

▲ General Stonewall Jackson meets for the last time with General Robert E. Lee.

It was different when he took command. His troops were in awe of him. Although, sometimes, it was hard to understand why. Jackson kept apart from his fellow officers and was stern with his soldiers. But he was a winner, and soon everyone knew it. He was intelligent, and daring, and—perhaps because he had a strong religious faith—nothing scared him.

Stonewall Jackson kept doing things that couldn't be done. He marched his men farther and faster than armies could march, beat forces much larger than his, and won battles that were said to be unwinnable.

Once he captured 400 Federal railroad cars. He threw most of them into a river, but some he had hitched to horses and pulled to Southern railroad tracks.

▲ Rose O'Neal Greenhow and her daughter

Secret Service

When the Union army headed south from Washington—on its way to Manassas for that first battle of Bull Run—Confederate general P. G. T. Beauregard knew the Yankees were coming. A spy—Rose O'Neal Greenhow—had sent the information in a coded note hidden in the hair of a pretty Southern girl. Greenhow, a prominent Washington society lady and Stephen A. Douglas's aunt, had an ear for gossip. And she believed in the Southern cause. She sent important information to the Rebels until, in 1862, she was caught, convicted of spying, and banished from the capital. That didn't stop Rose Greenhow. Two years later she was on a ship smuggling gold from England to the Confederacy. But the ship was wrecked; the society belle went to the bottom of the sea. Both sides used spies during the war—when they could find them and trust them.

If you'd seen Jackson, you wouldn't have been impressed. He was awkward and rumpled. But he was an unflinching fighter who saw the hand of God in everything he did—and much of what he did seemed miraculous. In Virginia's Shenandoah Valley, he marched a small army over 400 miles (in just over a month), kept a large Federal army off balance, seized needed supplies, inflicted heavy casualties, and inspired legends and a feeling of invincibility in his troops.

Robert E. Lee was different. He did look as a general should look: handsome, gray-haired, and dignified. He sat erect and unruffled on his beautiful horse, Traveller, and commanded as a general should command: with fairness, audacity, and courage. Men were awed by him, and rushed into battle and died for him. If ever there was a born leader, it was General Robert E. Lee.

His wife was a granddaughter of Martha Washington. His father was "Light Horse Harry" Lee, a Virginia planter and Revolutionary War cavalry hero. Robert E. Lee loved America and he loved people

Robert E. Lee and his generals ▼

of the North as well as those of the South. He didn't like slavery, and he freed his slaves before the war ended. He didn't think much of states' rights, either. So it wasn't easy for him to join the Confederate cause. In a letter to his son, Lee wrote:

> *Secession is nothing but revolution. The framers of our Constitution never exhausted so much labour, wisdom and forbearance in its formation, and surrounded it with so many guards and securities, if it was intended to be broken by any member of the Confederacy at will.... Still, a Union that can only be maintained by swords and bayonets, and in which strife and civil war are to take the place of brotherly love and kindness, has no charm for me. If the Union is dissolved, the government disrupted, I shall return to my native state and share the miseries of my people. Save in her defense, I will draw my sword no more.*

Robert E. Lee said, "I cannot raise my hand against my birthplace, my home, my children." ▼

General Lee surveys the terrain near Fredericksburg, Virginia. ▼

When the war began, Lee was thought to be the outstanding officer in the U.S. Army. President Lincoln offered him command of the whole Union army. It was hard to turn that job down. His wife said he stayed up all night walking back and forth, trying to decide what to do. He had been a loyal officer in the U.S. Army. Still, when he had to make a choice, he chose Virginia. It is difficult for us to understand today, but many, like Lee, were above all devoted to their home states.

Some say Lee was the finest general America has produced. Perhaps—although the men who fought for him died in terrible numbers. He took bold chances and when they worked, as they often did, he seemed touched by genius.

Few generals have ever inspired people as General Lee did. Few people convey the integrity and intelligence and decency that Lee did. On the battlefield he was cool and daring, but it was in defeat that he showed the best of himself. When the war was over he refused to be bitter, or angry, or anything but noble. He was a symbol to the South of all that was good in themselves and to all Americans he became a heroic figure.

> *I have fought against the people of the North because I believed they were seeking to wrest from the South its dearest rights. But I have never cherished toward them bitter or vindictive feelings, and I have never seen the day when I did not pray for them.*
>
> —Robert E. Lee

President Davis's Problems

President Jefferson Davis had superb generals. What he didn't have enough of was food, clothing, weapons, and ships. Slavery had kept the South agricultural while much of the world was turning industrial. Poor planning had made the region dependent on just a few crops. Southern land was used mostly for growing cotton, tobacco, rice, or sugar. During the war, meat, vegetables, and grains were in short supply. The Confederacy's railroads weren't as good as those in the North.

Poor transportation made it difficult to get food to where it was needed. Poor management made things worse than they had to be.

President Davis and the Confederate leaders were sure England would provide supplies. After all, England had always bought Southern cotton and tobacco, and Southerners had always bought manufactured goods from England. And England needed cotton for her cotton mills.

But English warehouses were filled with cotton. There was a surplus on hand. And, when the Union navy blockaded Southern ports, the British navy didn't like the idea of interfering with a blockade.

The world was changing, and England, too. Slavery was now recognized as evil. Great Britain had abolished slavery in 1772, but it was Harriet Beecher Stowe's book that made the British understand that slaves were real people. A million and a half copies of *Uncle Tom's Cabin* were sold in England in one year. It was astonishing: everywhere people were weeping over Uncle Tom and Eliza. Even the queen wept, or so it was said. Some British politicians wanted to help the South, but most of England's people had become ardent abolitionists.

McClellan's Campaign and the War at Sea

After that big battle at Manassas (Bull Run) the North got serious. General George B. McClellan took charge. He organized an army of 100,000 men—more than had ever been commanded by one man in the history of the Western Hemisphere.

By spring of 1862, that army was ready to fight. McClellan made plans to capture Richmond, the capital of the Confederacy, and one of the few industrial cities in the South. Guns and steel and even uniforms were made there. If Richmond fell, the Confederacy might collapse and the war would be over.

McClellan was great at planning and organizing but very slow and cautious when it came to action. He sent most of his army by boat to the Virginia Peninsula, the land between the York and James rivers. Then the army just sat there while he organized and organized. That gave the Confederate army time to get ready.

The machinery of war—artillery and cannonballs—waiting for action. The Union armies often had nearly as many men guarding supplies as fighting at the front; even so, they lost huge quantities of arms to Confederate raiders. ▼

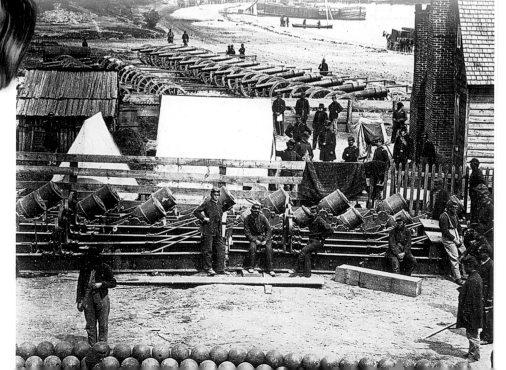

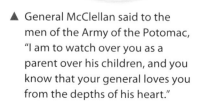

▲ General McClellan said to the men of the Army of the Potomac, "I am to watch over you as a parent over his children, and you know that your general loves you from the depths of his heart."

◀ The Union army defeated the Confederate Army of Tennessee at the Battle of Nashville.

Heavy rains in the spring of 1862 caused more delay. Finally, McClellan's Union soldiers marched slowly and cautiously to the outskirts of Richmond. McClellan believed the Confederate army was much larger than the Union army. (The opposite was true.) He hesitated. The Confederates took advantage of McClellan's indecision. Robert E. Lee attacked. For seven days the two armies battled fiercely. Both sides fought bravely. Both suffered terrible losses. In the end, there was no clear winner. McClellan ordered his army to retreat. The Yankees had lost the chance to capture Richmond and end the war.

The next two years brought many bloody encounters and much frustration—and not just on battlefields in the East. Terrible battles were fought in Tennessee and Mississippi and Louisiana and Missouri. In the West the Union forces often seemed to be ahead, in the East it was the Confederacy—but mostly it was a draw. Both armies began to have a problem with soldiers deserting. And, as long as there was no clear victory, Presidents Lincoln and Davis were mocked and blamed by their own citizens.

From the start of the war—after the first shells were fired at Fort Sumter—Lincoln had ordered the Union navy to blockade Southern

The South Loses a Hero

In May of 1863, there was a clash at dusty Chancellorsville, Virginia, a crossroads edging an area so dense with trees that it was called the Wilderness. (Another battle would be fought there a year later.) Lee was outnumbered and yet he won the fight. But it wasn't worth the cost. Stonewall Jackson was wounded by one of his own men in the smoke and confusion of battle. After Jackson's left arm was amputated he seemed to be getting better; then he got pneumonia, which often happened after battlefield injuries. In Richmond, 20,000 hushed, tearful people lined the streets as four white horses pulled his coffin in a solemn military cortège.

▲ General Stonewall Jackson

ports. That was a tough order. The U.S. Navy had only 90 ships, and that included ships on the Atlantic Coast, the Gulf of Mexico, the Mississippi, and on other inland rivers.

The Confederacy had no navy at all. Both sides got busy. Northern shipyards worked at top speed. By the time the war ended, the North had about 700 ships in service. The Confederates knew they could never match the Yankees when it came to numbers of ships, so they secretly ordered fast cruisers from English shipyards. (England was neutral and not supposed to help one side or the other. The shipbuilders pretended the ships were going to Italy.) The sleek, agile cruisers were designed to be able to attack Northern cargo ships. The most famous Confederate cruiser, the *Alabama*, captured 62 Yankee merchant ships in two years before it was finally sunk.

In 1862, Admiral David Farragut commanded a fleet of 17 Union ships sent to blockade the mouth of the Mississippi River. He set out to capture New Orleans, the South's largest city and busiest port. To get to the city, Admiral Farragut had to pass two heavily armed Confederate forts.

▲ A Union ship prepares to fire on a blockade runner.

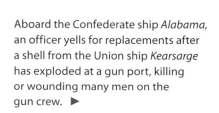

Aboard the Confederate ship *Alabama*, an officer yells for replacements after a shell from the Union ship *Kearsarge* has exploded at a gun port, killing or wounding many men on the gun crew. ▶

▲ Admiral David Farragut's fleet of 17 Union ships captured New Orleans in April 1862.

In addition, a chain of hulks (old ships) was laid across the Mississippi to keep Yankee ships out. "Nothing afloat could pass the forts," said a citizen of New Orleans.

Farragut's fleet headed up the river. The Confederates opened fire. One ship was hit 42 times. Farragut's flagship was set ablaze. "The passing of the forts…was one of the most awful sights and events I ever saw…. [It] seemed as if all the artillery of heaven were playing upon the earth," said Farragut. That didn't stop him. His sailors put out the fires and got the ships moving.

They did what they intended. They captured New Orleans. A few months later Farragut sailed his ships up the river to Vicksburg, through more Confederate fire. That gave the North control of most of the Mississippi. (By July 1863, the Union had the whole river.)

Ruler of the President's Navy

When David Glasgow Farragut was a boy he was adopted by David Porter (who was a naval hero in the War of 1812). He wanted to be like his adopted father, so he went to sea and was a midshipman by the time he was 9 years old. At 13 he was in command of a captured British ship. Farragut was 58 when the Civil War began; he volunteered to fight for the Union cause. That was surprising, because he was a Southerner from Alabama, but Farragut believed in the United States. Abraham Lincoln said he was his best appointment of the war.

Farragut stands lashed to the upper mast of his flagship the USS *Hartford* during the Battle of Mobile Bay. ▶

Iron Ships: "A New Era in Warfare"

At the time of the Civil War, almost all ships were made of wood. Wooden ships were fast and easy to float; they were also fragile and flammable. Throw a match on one and—whoosh! A ship with a layer of iron all over it, however, would be difficult to set on fire. An iron ship could also be a powerful weapon: imagine it ramming a wooden boat. A few ironclad ships had been experimented with in Europe—but none had been tested in battle.

A Union vessel named *Merrimack* had sunk near Norfolk, Virginia. The Confederates raised the ship out of the water, cut down her burned top, and covered her with slanting metal plates. That produced a weird-looking boat that looked like a floating roof. On each side of the roof were holes for five powerful guns. A center chimney let out steam from the engines. The *Merrimack* was big and clumsy and moved very slowly, but that metal coat made it strong and fierce-looking. Now that she had a new form she needed a new name. The Confederates called her the *Virginia*.

It had taken months to get the *Virginia* ready, but, finally, on March 8, 1862, she slid into the water for what everyone thought was a trial run. Everyone but the men in charge. They intended to fight that day, and fight they did. Before the day was over two big Union frigates were destroyed and dozens of men were dead. Three Union ships came hurrying to the rescue—they would have been destroyed, too, but their captains soon realized what was going on and turned around and fled. Shells that hit the *Virginia* bounced harmlessly off her sides.

▲ A painting of the famous battle between the *Monitor* and the *Merrimack* (the *Virginia*). The two ironclads survived the battle. Later that year, the *Monitor* sank in a storm off Cape Hatteras, N.C. (It was found in 1973 lying in 220 feet of water.)

When news of the battle reached Washington, people were frantic. Lincoln's cabinet was meeting and the secretary of war, Edwin M. Stanton, said the *Virginia* could sink every vessel in the North, steam up the Potomac River to Washington, and "destroy the Capitol and public buildings." (That wasn't true; fear sometimes makes people think hysterically.)

But there was something that even Secretary Stanton did not know. Long before the launching, spies had informed the navy department that the *Virginia* was being built. So the U.S. Navy decided to secretly build its own ironclad vessel. That ship, the *Monitor*, was on its way to meet the *Virginia* at Hampton Roads (the Virginia waterway where three rivers come together, meet the Chesapeake Bay, and flow into the ocean).

The *Monitor* looked like a surfboard carrying a round, flat-topped box. Inside the box, which revolved, were two powerful guns. Could a two-gun ship face a ten-gunner? (The *Virginia's* guns were stationary—five to a side.) Well, the *Monitor* was smaller than the *Virginia* but faster and easier to maneuver.

It was Sunday, March 9, 1862, when they met. The shores of Hampton Roads were lined with people. No battle like this had ever been fought before. If the *Monitor* lost, the Union-held Fortress Monroe, on the Hampton side, could be starved into surrender.

For four hours they battled. The *Virginia's* guns kept firing, but the *Monitor* was an impossible target—it was small and agile, and never stayed where it was expected. It didn't matter; neither ship was able to sink the other. Cannonballs bounced off their sides. The battle was a draw, although both sides claimed victory. Actually, it was iron ships that won; that battle finished wooden warships.

Charles Francis Adams, who was U.S. minister to England (and John Quincy Adams's son), wrote from England that the battle of the *Monitor* and the *Merrimack* "dates the commencement of a new era in warfare."

Civil War ironclads had metal-skinned hulls, were propelled by steam-powered engines, and fired explosive shells. ▼

Emancipation Means Freedom

Lincoln needed a victory because he wanted to do something important. He wanted to make an announcement, he wanted to change the purpose of the war, and he didn't want to do it as the leader of a discouraged, defeated army.

Then finally it came. It wasn't the kind of victory Lincoln had hoped for. Too many men had been killed—more than ever before. But the Northern army had stopped General Lee's army at Antietam Creek, and that would have to do.

The battle of Antietam is sometimes called the battle of Sharpsburg, because Antietam Creek is near the little town of Sharpsburg, Maryland. McClellan had some unexpected luck just before the battle at Sharpsburg. One of his men found three cigars wrapped in some paper. The cigars probably dropped from the pocket of a Confederate officer. The paper showed Robert E. Lee's battle plans. "Here is a paper," boasted McClellan to an old West Point friend, "with which if I cannot whip Bobbie Lee, I will be willing to go home." McClellan now knew

Both sides suffered heavy losses at Antietam. ▶

exactly where all of Lee's forces would be. Even with that help, he didn't whip Robert E. Lee on September 17, 1862—the bloodiest day of the war—but he did stop him.

Both sides suffered terrible losses at Antietam Creek, but when it was over things were worse for the Confederates. They were hungry and exhausted, they had few supplies, and they were in easy reach of the Yankee army. Another attack by the North and they might have been finished. But two days after the battle, McClellan watched the Rebels retreat. He let them cross the Potomac River, back to Virginia.

Lincoln took a train to Sharpsburg and urged McClellan to go after Lee. McClellan had two divisions of fresh soldiers. "I came back thinking he would move at once," said Lincoln. "I...ordered him to advance." McClellan sat for 19 days; then he moved slowly. He let the Confederate army get away. Lincoln was enraged. He believed he had lost a chance to end the war. He wasn't the only one. Northern soldier Elisha Rhodes wrote a letter home saying, "Oh, why did we not attack them and drive them into the river? I do not understand these things. But then I am only a boy."

(Soon after Antietam Lincoln did send McClellan home; McClellan did not go willingly. He said, "They have made a great mistake. Alas for my poor country!")

Still, Antietam was a victory for the North, and an important one. Robert E. Lee had been on his way to the northern state of Pennsylvania. He had intended to cut important railroad lines

▲ General Lee on his famous horse, Traveller

Angel of the Battlefield

Clara Barton was a clerk in the Patent Office in Washington when war broke out. She was a tiny woman, but full of energy, and she used it visiting homesick troops from her native Massachusetts. She brought soap and lemons and homemade food. But when she saw the suffering of the soldiers after the battle of Bull Run, she knew she could do more.

So she organized an agency to get supplies for wounded soldiers. But that wasn't enough for Clara Barton; she decided to go where there was fighting.

At the battle of Antietam, she arrived with a wagonload of bandages, anesthetics, and oil lanterns. Then she set to work in a field hospital: bandaging, feeding, and consoling the wounded. When shells began exploding close by, most of the male nurses ran for cover. Barton stayed and held the operating table steady for a surgeon who called her "the true heroine of the age, the angel of the battlefield." After the war was over, Clara Barton founded the American Red Cross.

▲ When the war was over, Clara Barton led a search for missing soldiers.

▲ Hat, gloves, and boots worn by a Confederate soldier

In this painting titled *The Hour of Emancipation,* slaves hear about their newly declared freedom. ▼

in Harrisburg, Pennsylvania. He had hoped to find shoes and supplies for his army in the North. Now a discouraged Confederate army was back in Virginia. Lincoln could make the announcement he had planned for several months.

Lincoln now changed the war from a fight to save the Union into something much greater. He changed it into a battle for human freedom, a battle to end slavery. He did that with a document called an *Emancipation Proclamation.* It said all the slaves in the Rebel states were free. I'm going to repeat that: *all the slaves in the Rebel states were free.*

It was about time, said the abolitionists. It was the right time, said Lincoln.

He read the proclamation in September of 1862; it became official on January 1, 1863. It didn't free slaves in the North. (There were few slaves there.) It didn't free slaves in the border states. (The president didn't have the power to do that. It could only be done

by a constitutional amendment, or by the state legislatures.) It freed slaves in the Confederate states. (Where Lincoln had no power. Do you think Southern slave owners would be likely to free their slaves because their enemy said they should do so?)

Today, when you think about that, it doesn't sound as if Lincoln really did much. People in 1862 knew differently. They knew what he had done was very important. When he signed that document it meant there would be no going back. When the war was over there would be no chance of compromise on slavery. Slavery was dead in the South. And, if it was dead there, it would soon die in the border states.

People's ideas had changed. And Lincoln's ideas, too. He had never liked slavery—in fact he hated it—but he thought it more important to save the Union than to end slavery. He had come to realize that was impossible. Slavery was like a worm in a good apple—it was making the whole apple rotten. It was no longer enough just to save the Union. Who wants to fight for a nation with a rotten core? The nation could not allow an evil practice and believe in itself. It could not speak of liberty and equality and be cruel and hateful to a large group of its own people.

And so the Civil War became a revolution. Not a revolution as the Southern leaders saw it. They still thought they were fighting

The war in America has resolved itself into a war between freedom and slavery.

—London Gazette

On the first day of January, in the year of our Lord one thousand eight hundred and sixty three, all persons held as slaves within any State, or designated part of a State, whereof shall then be in rebellion against the United States, shall be then, thenceforth, and forever free.

—Abraham Lincoln

We shout for joy that we live to record this righteous decree....."free forever"...oh, ye millions of free and loyal men who have earnestly sought to free your bleeding country from the dreadful ravages of revolution and anarchy, lift up now your voices with joy and thanksgiving for with freedom to the slave will come peace and safety to your country.

—Frederick Douglass

A statue of a slave breaking his bonds ▶

for independence. What those leaders wanted was independence to oppress other people.

No, this was a revolution in men's and women's ideas. They had been led by the logic of Thomas Jefferson's Declaration of Independence. Was this a nation that really believed that all people have the right to "life, liberty and the pursuit of happiness"? And that all "are created equal"? Or were those just empty words that applied only to special people? If blacks could be enslaved, then what about Northern factory workers, or war prisoners, or any group of people?

The war was making people think. It was making them question ideas they had never really considered. Are some people actually better than others just because their skin is a different color? Perhaps green-eyed people are the best, or short people. Could curly hair be superior to straight hair? And what about baldies? Maybe they would make good slaves.

One thing everyone knew: this war, begun with such gaiety, had become a national nightmare. It was not a game. The corpses of American boys were being shoveled into the earth—hundreds of thousands of them. And so people asked themselves: *What is this war really about?*

At Antietam alone, 23,000 Americans lost their lives. ▼

It was clear in the South. Southerners were fighting to preserve their way of life. It was a way of life that was often elegant and attractive, but it was based on a mean, despicable practice—slavery. If the South was fighting to preserve slavery, then the North must be fighting to end it. And so it was.

But it took Abraham Lincoln and most Northerners some time to figure that out. Perhaps that was because there was much racial prejudice in the North, and that had to be overcome.

Voices were speaking out against that racial hatred; finally people began listening to them. One of the voices belonged to a man who spoke clearly and said the North must "lift the war into the dignity of a war for progress and civilization."

The man's name was Frederick Douglass, and he had been a slave and had whip marks on his back to prove it. Douglass had learned to read and write—against great odds—and was one of the most eloquent writers and speakers of his time.

He knew it was folly to fight just to save the Union. Douglass wrote:

To fight against slaveholders, without fighting against slavery, is but a half-hearted business, and paralyzes the hands engaged in it. Fire must be met with water.... War for the destruction of liberty must be met with war for the destruction of slavery.

And thus the Civil War became a war to make the United States what it had meant to be from its beginnings: a fair nation. A great nation. A nation that fulfilled the best ideas of its founders. A nation that would set equality of opportunity as a goal. A nation that could promise "life, liberty and the pursuit of happiness" and mean it for all its peoples.

Usually the president signed government bills with a simple *A. Lincoln.* But when he signed the Emancipation Proclamation, Abraham Lincoln wrote his name in full. "Gentlemen," he said to the cabinet officers standing near him, "I never, in my life, felt more certain that I was doing right than in signing this paper."

▲ Abraham Lincoln's signature

Willie and Tad

As the war progressed, Abraham Lincoln got sadder and sadder. But there was something that could always cheer him up—the antics of his two younger sons, Willie and Tad (a nickname for Thomas). They were merry boys, often mischievous, who turned the White House into a playground. Sometimes, in the middle of an important meeting, one or the other would come into Lincoln's office, climb in his lap, give him a hug, and then disappear.

Tad was a boy who loved to have fun. Willie was quieter. He wrote poetry and liked to read. Those who knew him said he was the boy who was most like his father.

There was an older son, Robert, who was at Harvard as a student. A fourth son, Eddie, had died at age four when they lived in Springfield, Illinois. The Lincolns never got over that loss; perhaps that was why they seemed to love their boys with such abandon.

One night the president and his wife, Mary Todd Lincoln, prepared to host an elegant dinner party at the White House. Then the boys got sick. There was talk of canceling the party, but the invitations had been sent and the doctors didn't seem worried.

Tad got better, but Willie's fever wouldn't go away. He got weaker and weaker. All night long the president and his wife took turns going upstairs and sitting with Willie and putting wet towels on his head. Although they didn't know it, Willie had typhoid fever. When he died, the president and his wife suffered a war death of their own. It was almost more than they could bear.

▲ Tad was a boy who loved to have fun. He found schoolwork hard and did not learn to read until he was 12.

◄ When 12-year-old Willie died, a friend of the family wrote of Lincoln, "I never saw a man so bowed down with grief."

Determined Soldiers

What would you think if you learned that a large group of strong men who wanted to fight for the Union were turned down? Would you think that was dumb? You're right. It was worse than dumb—it was idiotic. But racial prejudice is always like that—it is always stupid.

Prejudice turns up in all times and places, but in the 19th century it was a sickness that infected much of the nation—North as well as South.

If the South had been without prejudice there would have been no war; if the North had been without prejudice the war might have been much shorter. There were large numbers of blacks who wanted to fight in the war. Because of racial prejudice, the Union army wouldn't have them—at least not at first.

Now this may sound ridiculous to you, but many people actually believed that blacks couldn't fight. That is what they believed and said. Many whites had forgotten—or never knew—that blacks had been explorers and mountain men and early settlers. African Americans fought in the Revolutionary War and the War of 1812. Of course they wanted to fight in this war. But neither side would have them as soldiers—not the North or the South.

In the South slaves helped the war effort; they had no choice. They raised crops and did farmwork so that white men were free to be soldiers. Slaves worked in Southern factories. (Yes, the South did have ironworks and factories—just not as many as the North had.) Rebel armies used slaves to build and cook and do other necessary work. The Confederacy could not have fought long without slaves.

Abraham F. Brown of the 54th Massachusetts Volunteer Infantry Regiment ▶

▲ After the Emancipation Proclamation, many black men fought for the Union, including these soldiers at Camp William Penn, Pennsylvania.

When they could, African Americans ran away to Yankee army camps. At first the Union officers didn't know what to do with them. A few sent the slaves back to slave masters, but most let them stay. The Union officers called the blacks *contrabands*. Contraband of war is property seized from the enemy—especially property that can help the war effort. Soon the contrabands were doing useful work for the Northern armies.

But what they really wanted to do was to fight.

They wanted to fight because they cared about America as much as anyone else. They wanted to fight because they knew that fighting men would never be thought of as slaves again.

They wanted to fight because they knew—long before most white people—that this was a war about slavery.

Finally it became possible. A month after Lincoln read the Emancipation Proclamation, a group of black contrabands fought as soldiers in Missouri. Ten died, the first black combat victims of the war. Soon there were legions of black soldiers. They fought well. The assistant secretary of war visited General Grant's army and said that *the bravery of the blacks completely revolutionized the sentiment of the army.... I heard prominent officers who formerly in private had sneered at the idea of negroes fighting express themselves after that as heartily in favor of it.*

Massachusetts organized a regiment of black soldiers (called the 54th Massachusetts) under the command of a young (white) Bostonian, Colonel Robert Gould Shaw. The men of the 54th Massachusetts led a bayonet attack on Fort Wagner—a massive fort of wood and earth that stood on an island at the entry to Charleston Harbor. The Confederates, protected by the thick walls of the fort, shot cannons and naval guns at the charging men. Almost half of them were wounded, captured, or killed. After that,

Members of the 54th Massachusetts clash with Confederate soldiers at Fort Wagner. ▼

▲ African American soldiers fought with bravery and honor, and many, like this wounded soldier, made great sacrifices for their country.

no one asked if blacks could fight. "Prejudice is down," wrote a man who was there.

Everyone knew it took special courage for blacks to fight and for white officers to fight with them. They realized that, if they were captured, they would not be treated like the other soldiers.

Confederate officials had announced that any captured white Northern officers who led black troops would be put to death as criminals. Captured black soldiers knew they would be sold into slavery, if they weren't murdered. Nonetheless, they kept volunteering. Before the war was over, more than 180,000 black soldiers fought with the Union army. Lincoln said they made victory possible.

In 1864 a newspaper reporter wrote about black troops marching in New York City. He said:

> *Had any man predicted it last year he would have been thought a fool.... Eight months ago the African race in this City were literally hunted down like wild beasts [in the New York race riots]. They fled for their lives....*

How astonishingly has all this been changed. The same men...now march in solid platoons, with shouldered muskets, slung knapsacks, and buckled cartridge boxes down through our gayest avenues... to the pealing strains of martial music and are everywhere saluted with waving handkerchiefs, with descending flowers.

The *New York Times* reporter said that the marching soldiers were a sign of the "marvelous times"; he also said there was a "revolution [of] the public mind." What did he mean by that? And what did Abraham Lincoln mean when he said, "In giving freedom to the slave, we assure freedom to the free"?

◄ Sergeant William Carney was the first African American to be awarded the Congressional Medal of Honor.

Marching Soldiers: On to Gettysburg

I can tell you something for sure: you wouldn't want an army marching through your front yard! Picture tens of thousands of soldiers on the march. Where do they sleep? What do they eat? How do they stay warm and dry?

The first thing Civil War soldiers did when they made a new camp was cut down trees and fences. Sometimes they built huts for shelter. Even when they slept in tents, they often cut wood supports to make the tents stronger and more comfortable. Sometimes they pushed people out of their houses and used the houses. To keep warm they burned logs, furniture, books, or whatever they could find.

The army quartermaster supplied them with flour, coffee, bacon, and a heavy cracker called "hardtack." But most soldiers wanted fresh meat and vegetables. So they took food from the farms they passed; they trampled fields where they marched.

As the war went on, the generals began to realize that anything they could do to weaken the enemy would help win the war. If they made life difficult for

▲ Sometimes women and families followed the armies and did laundry, mending, and other tasks.

Union army troops, camped at Cumberland Landing on the Pamunkey River during the Peninsular Campaign, wait for marching orders. ▼

The war affected civilians as well as soldiers. This family's house has suffered damage from a recent battle. ▶

ordinary people in their homes, those people might stop supporting the war. So the armies began destroying barns and crops on purpose. It was a strategy called "total war," and it brought grief to the civilian population.

Mostly it was the South that suffered, because most of the war was fought on Southern land. Much of it in Robert E. Lee's beloved Virginia. The South was being ruined. Lee wanted the North to suffer. He knew there were strong peace movements in the North. If his soldiers won some Northern territory, if they beat the Yankees on their own home ground, he thought the North would soon beg for peace.

He might have been right. It was an enormous gamble, but Lee's daring had made him successful in the past. He decided to go for it. He decided to march his army north.

Remember, General Lee had marched north before and had been stopped at Sharpsburg, Maryland—by Antietam Creek. That was in September of 1862. But Antietam was really a draw. The Confederates had been stopped, but not beaten. After Antietam,

Lee had two spectacular victories in Virginia: one at Fredericksburg, the other at Chancellorsville. Now, in the early summer of 1863, the Confederates were confident. The South seemed to be winning the war. Robert E. Lee decided to take the war north: he headed for Pennsylvania.

The U.S. Army went after them. This time the army was commanded by thin, tough, hot-tempered George G. Meade. He didn't seem to be afraid of Robert E. Lee, which was unusual for a Union general.

The two armies met in a quiet college town named Gettysburg, where roads come together like the spokes of a wheel. The town lies in a gentle valley with hills and ridges and knolls about. In 1863, Gettysburg was 12 blocks long, six blocks wide, and had 2,400 inhabitants.

It was postcard-pretty land: green and peaceful. In July 1863, it became the scene of one of the worst battles in American history.

No one planned to fight in Gettysburg. But when a Rebel officer saw an advertisement for a shoe store it made him head for that Pennsylvania town. He was searching for shoes for his soldiers when he ran into Union cavalry. That started things.

In the early summer of 1863, General Robert E. Lee—here shown with many of his officers—was encouraged by recent Confederate victories and ready to take the war north. ▼

▲ A Massachusetts soldier said of Pickett's charge, "Foot to foot, body to body, and man to man they struggled and pushed and strived and killed. The mass of wounded and heaps of dead entangled...hatless, coatless, drowned in sweat, black with powder, red with blood."

Actually there weren't any shoes—or much of anything—left in Gettysburg. When the townsfolk heard that soldiers were in the area they took their cattle and sheep and store goods and got them out of town. Gates Fahnestock's dad and uncles owned the biggest store in Gettysburg. The store was called Fahnestock Brothers. The Fahnestocks rented a railroad car, filled it three times, and sent almost everything in the store off to Philadelphia for safekeeping.

Gates, who was 10, was more interested in soldiers than in store matters. He climbed up on the roof of his house to watch the Rebel soldiers march into town. They came shouting and firing guns into the air, but Gates couldn't help noticing that many of them were barefoot and in rags.

Like almost everyone else in Gettysburg, Gates didn't cheer those Southerners. He wanted the Union to win. So when General John Buford's U.S. cavalry rode into town, he did cheer. Then a bullet whistled over the roof and he hightailed it inside.

Eighteen-year-old Daniel Skelly was perched in a tree on a nearby ridge. He and a group of men and boys wanted to see some action. But when "shot and shell began to fly over our heads, there was a general stampede towards town." It was July 1, 1863, and the fireworks were about to begin.

Neither army had all its soldiers in place—many were marching toward Gettysburg—but that didn't stop these armies. They were eager to fight. They wanted to finish this war; it had gone on too long. The soldiers who marched into Gettysburg singing were soon fighting like savages. First one side seemed to be winning, then the other. By afternoon the Union army was exhausted.

Rebels had pushed the Union forces through the town. When they stormed into Gates Fahnestock's house they captured eight Union soldiers; one was hiding in the potato bin. They asked Gates to get some hay. He did, and they piled it up in front of his house and made comfortable beds for themselves.

The Rebels won the first day's battle, but fresh soldiers were pouring into the area. General Buford sent a message to General Meade. "Get soldiers here at once. This is a good location for a fight."

Buford's horsemen had discovered that Gettysburg sits on a series of ridges with a shallow valley in between. Whoever held the high ground would have a big advantage. The Yankees had fewer troops than the Rebels, but Buford and his men were on Cemetery Ridge, south of the village. It was a good place to be. Any attack by the Confederates would have to come uphill.

The Confederates had a problem. Their dashing, show-off cavalry star, J. E. B. Stuart had gone off in the wrong direction. No one knew where he and his men were. Cavalry are the eyes of the army. The Southern army was blind. The Confederates had no idea of the topography of the area. Still, they were confident. After the big win at Chancellorsville it was hard to imagine that Union soldiers could beat them.

▲ Major General J. E. B. Stuart, whom Robert E. Lee called "the eyes and ears of my army"

Confederate general J. E. B. Stuart ▶

The night of July 1 was warm and clear and the sky was full of stars. Union soldiers slept in the cemetery and prayed they would see another night.

Confederates were saying the same prayers in their camp on Seminary Ridge, another high area. A religious school—a Lutheran seminary—was located on that ridge. The two ridges, about a mile apart, were separated by woods, open farmland, and peach orchards.

July 2 came, and the fighting began early and was even more murderous than on the 1st—and that was bad enough. That the day was blazing hot didn't make a difference. Men fought and died with a frenzy that is still hard to believe. A Northern regiment—the 1st Minnesota—had 262 men when the day began; 42 survived. By nightfall the land was cluttered with the bodies of men and horses. When that terrible second day ended each side thought itself ahead, although the deaths made both sides losers.

And then July 3 dawned, and the battle that some say decided the war (although it would be a while before that was understood). Let's watch what happens. General Lee now has fewer men than General Meade. That doesn't scare Lee; he has been outnumbered before. At Chancellorsville he fought and beat an army twice the size of his.

The Confederates have a bold plan. They begin by blasting the Union line with a cannonade fiercer than anything tried before: two hours of nonstop artillery fire. "The very earth shook beneath our feet," wrote a soldier, "and the hills and rocks seemed to reel like drunken men." Gates Fahnestock and his family huddle in their cellar. The noise and the shaking of the house are like an earthquake that doesn't stop.

Confederate major general George E. Pickett has arrived in Gettysburg with fresh troops. Pickett is known to be courageous. His soldiers are ready to reinforce the Rebel line and Pickett is eager to fight. He will lead the most famous military charge in all of American history.

But General Longstreet doesn't like it a bit. He is Robert E. Lee's most trusted aide. Theirs is an unusual friendship. Longstreet is big, rumpled, tough-talking, and sometimes crude. He says what he thinks. Lee is a courtly gentleman, always polite, always in control.

This painting by the American artist Winslow Homer depicts a drummer and a bugler in a Civil War camp. (Homer had been hired by a popular magazine to cover the war.) ▼

◀ Confederate soldiers charge up Cemetery Hill at the Battle of Gettysburg.

▲ This is the sword carried by Confederate general Lewis A. Armistead during Pickett's Charge at Gettysburg.

Lee has planned a great military charge across three-fourths of a mile of open fields. Longstreet argues against it. He wants to pull out of Gettysburg. He believes in defensive fighting. But Longstreet loses the argument. Defensive fighting isn't heroic to most soldiers. The Confederate army prepares to advance toward Cemetery Hill.

Suddenly it is quiet. The shelling has stopped. Line after line of gray-uniformed men march out of the woods. The bright sun reflects on silver bayonets and red flags. George Pickett, riding a white horse, "his jaunty cap raked well over his right ear, and his long auburn locks…hanging almost to his shoulder," shouts his orders. Then, elbow to elbow, like a grand parade, 15,000 awesome fighters step forward in an incredible, orderly, moving rectangle almost a mile wide and half a mile deep.

Lee has gambled everything on this old-fashioned military charge. It is like something from the Middle Ages—from the days of knighthood. The charge is glorious, and daring. If it works, who knows? The heart may go out of the Yankees.

▲ The 72nd Pennsylvania Infantry Regiment advances during the Battle of Gettysburg.

▲ Perched in a tree, a Union army sharpshooter takes aim during the Battle of Gettysburg.

Winfield Scott Hancock is in command of the Yankees crouched behind a low stone wall on Cemetery Ridge. For two hours Rebel shells have been exploding over their heads: the noise, the July heat, the smoke, and the tension of waiting for battle have been almost more than the men can bear. Luckily for them, the cannons are aimed poorly, and much of the shot has gone too high and fallen behind the lines. It has hit ambulances, and men eating in the grass, and men in tents. But it has not done the harm intended. The Confederates don't know this. They march on cheerfully. Later, Confederate captain W. W. Wood will remember, "We believed the battle was practically over, and we had nothing to do but march unopposed to Cemetery [Hill] and occupy it."

On that hill, the Union soldiers are having a hard time staying calm, especially now, as the massed Rebel army advances. It is a sight these men will never forget.

"It was," said a U.S. colonel, "the most beautiful thing I ever saw."

Hancock gives the order for the Union artillery to fire. The cannons fire more than cannonballs. The new firepower includes cans that explode and send off a hail of metal that murders the oncoming soldiers. Bravely they close ranks and keep coming.

The commander says, "Let them come up close before you fire, and then aim low and steadily."

Imagine: You are there. Your gun is resting on the stone wall. You're a sharpshooter, and you are using a rifled musket that is accurate at half a mile, but even if you were a bad shot it would be hard to miss this target.

The Confederates, a tight mass of men in light gray uniforms, are caught in deadly fire. The Yankees are shooting at them from different angles all along Cemetery Ridge. This is a massacre. Some Rebels run away, but most keep coming, stepping over the bodies of those who have fallen before them.

A few make it to the stone wall. One who does—an officer—puts his hat on the tip of his sword, holds the sword high—and charges.

General Lee and exhausted Confederate soldiers depart from the blood-soaked fields of Gettysburg. ▼

He leaps the low stone wall and is followed by 200 soldiers. They don't get far. The brave officer is Confederate general Lewis Armistead, General Hancock's old friend. Armistead is hit. A Union officer rushes to his side, awed by the valiant Confederate. Armistead asks the officer to give General Hancock his watch; he sends Mrs. Hancock his Bible. They are his last wishes. Hancock, too, has been wounded, but he will recover.

The charge is over. The men around you sing "John Brown's Body" and the "Battle Hymn of the Republic." You cheer the victory, and then you weep for your dead friends.

In the Rebel camp, General Lee, great leader that he is, blames no one but himself. He has used a straight down-the-center frontal attack. That strategy is out of date. The generals—on both sides—don't seem to understand that. It will be tried again.

After the Battle

Union losses at Gettysburg are 23,000, one-fourth of their army. The Confederates have lost (killed, wounded, or missing) 28,000 men: that's one-third of their army. There is no more talk of invading the North. Lee needs to get his tired men home. It has begun to rain—hard—and the Potomac River, which they must cross, is flooding. Wagons carrying the 5,000 wounded men stretch for 17 miles. Many will die before they reach home. Many who rode north now walk south; thousands of horses have been killed.

Lincoln sees a chance to finish Lee's army. Lee is trapped; his men are exhausted. The president expects action, but once again Lincoln has a general who is cautious. Besides, Union general George Meade is facing a general known as the "Gray Fox." Lee, the fox, sends a soldier into the Northern camp. The soldier pretends to be a Rebel deserter;

The photographer Matthew Brady captured many compelling images of the Civil War, including this 1863 photograph of a sick Union soldier and his comrade. ▼

◀ Both soldiers and civilians suffered when General Grant starved and bombed Vicksburg during a 48-day siege.

he tells the Yankees the Confederates are ready to fight. Meade hesitates, and the Confederate army makes it back to Virginia. "We had them within our grasp," moans Lincoln. The war will continue.

Still, when news of the victory at Gettysburg arrives in Washington on the Fourth of July, the city celebrates. In a few days people will learn that on this same July Fourth, General U. S. Grant has won a major victory in Mississippi.

In Mississippi, Grant moved his army where no one thought an army could be moved. He left his supply base (no general is supposed to do that); he decided to take a risk. He believed he could feed his men with food from the farms in the Mississippi countryside. He was right. Grant's army laid siege to Vicksburg. The navy blockaded the river entry to the city. Vicksburg's citizens were trapped. They couldn't leave, and no one could help them.

Then Union cannons began shelling the city. The siege lasted 48 days. Before it was over, those in Vicksburg were eating rats—and anything else they could find. Grant starved and bombed them into surrender. The 30,000 Confederate soldiers in the city surrendered, too.

Union forces now control Vicksburg, and that means they control the Mississippi River. Abe Lincoln can say of the river, "The father of waters flows unvexed to the sea." (What does he mean by that?)

Those two victories—Gettysburg and Vicksburg—reverse the war. Gettysburg shows that Robert E. Lee is beatable. Of Vicksburg, Grant later says, "The fate of the Confederacy was sealed when Vicksburg fell." For the South, those defeats mean that England will no longer consider sending support.

But the Confederates are stubborn. As the South becomes desperate, Southern soldiers fight harder than ever.

A Union officer watches over Confederate prisoners. ▼

Speeches at Gettysburg

Weeks after the battle at Gettysburg, bodies still lie on the ground unburied. The citizens of the little town of Gettysburg are overwhelmed by the tragedy around them. In addition to the dead, some 16,000 wounded soldiers have turned every house, barn, and building into a hospital.

Tourists and sightseers and grieving families are now pouring into Gettysburg. Some come to help. Eighteen states agree to share the costs of a national cemetery to be established on Cemetery Hill. The dead soldiers—all Yankees—will finally rest in peace.

A ceremony is planned for November 19 to honor them. Edward Everett is to be the main speaker. He is a fine choice. Everett has been president of Harvard, a senator, secretary of state, and ambassador to Britain. He is thought to be the greatest orator of the day; all are sure he will say the right things.

A few weeks before the occasion someone thinks to invite the president. No one expects him to accept the invitation. But he does. He is asked to make "a few appropriate remarks." It is not intended that he say much—it is Edward Everett people will come to hear.

◀ A nurse attends to the injured after the Battle of Gettysburg.

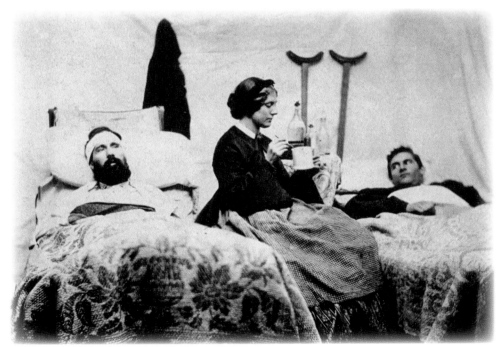

It takes six hours by train from Washington to the Pennsylvania town of Gettysburg. Lincoln doesn't want to miss this occasion; he comes a day early and then settles in his room to work on his speech. It is already written, but he revises and rewrites—as is his way. (You can see the speech in Lincoln's handwriting in the Library of Congress in Washington, D.C.)

He will use this opportunity to try to explain the meaning of the war. Many Northerners are crying out for peace. They no longer care about the Union or the slaves. In New York, recently, there were riots when calls came for more soldiers. (When the draft was announced in New York City, many people protested. Blacks were attacked because the rioters saw them as the reason for the war—and for the draft, too.)

Lincoln knows the nation can have peace any time it wants. But that would end the United States. It would end the Founders' dream: the dream that people can govern themselves; the dream that people are "created equal" with inalienable rights to "life, liberty, and the pursuit of happiness." Lincoln believes this terrible war has a purpose. He believes it must give a new birth to the dream.

Thousands of men and women have gathered at Gettysburg. They include famous citizens, veterans, cabinet members, and ordinary people. All march together to the battlefield. A band plays and the marchers form a parade. Abraham Lincoln rides a brown horse. Someone has chosen poorly. The horse is tiny, and Lincoln's

There was no official photographer at the Gettysburg Address. A local man took some pictures, and Lincoln is just about visible here. His speech was over so fast that the slow cameras of the time wouldn't have managed it anyway. ▶

legs almost touch the ground. Along the way a mother hands her daughter to the president. He puts the little girl in front of him and she rides, too. Someday she will tell her children and grandchildren how she rode with the president at Gettysburg.

The distinguished guests climb onto a wooden platform and wait for Edward Everett before the ceremonies can begin. Everett is getting ready in a special tent set aside for his use.

He talks for almost two hours, without notes, in a voice deep and rich. Later, no one seems to remember what he said, but they knew he said it well. There are prayers and other speeches, and the 15,000 listeners who sit or stand in the afternoon sun are hot and tired when the president finally rises, puts on his steel-rimmed glasses, and reads his few remarks. His is a country voice, and it sounds dull after the polished tones of orator Everett. A snicker runs through the crowd. The speech takes two minutes. When the president finishes there is not a sound—not a clap, not a cheer. People seem to have expected more.

The speech was a failure; so Lincoln tells his friends, and so he believes. But he is wrong. The presidency has changed Lincoln. He has grown in greatness. He has learned to use words as a poet uses them—with great care and precision. He had been an able country lawyer with a good mind and a taste for jokes. Now he is much more than that. The deaths and the burdens of war are making him noble, and thoughtful, and understanding, and sad.

Most of those who listen that day at Gettysburg do not know they are hearing one of the greatest speeches ever written, but all know their president is speaking from his heart. A few understand that this is no ordinary speech. Edward Everett says, "Mr. President, I should be glad if I could flatter myself that I came as near to the central idea of the occasion in two hours, as you did in two minutes."

This is what the president said on November 19, 1863; this is how he explained the meaning of the war:

▲ One reason Lincoln worked hard on his speeches was that he did not speak well extemporaneously. In his election campaign he made off-the-cuff speeches that gave him political trouble.

Lincoln's Gettysburg Address is engraved in stone at the Lincoln Memorial in Washington, D.C. ▶

A score is 20 years. Lincoln wanted to remind Americans of the number of years since 1776. He wanted to remind them of the Founding Fathers and their purposes. He could have said the number (what is it?), but *four score and seven* has a solemn, majestic sound. He liked the music of those words.

Four score and seven years ago our fathers brought forth on this continent, a new nation, conceived in Liberty, and dedicated to the proposition that all men are created equal.

Now we are engaged in a great civil war, testing whether that nation, or any nation so conceived and so dedicated, can long endure. We are met on a great battlefield of that war. We have come to dedicate a portion of that field, as a final resting place for those who here gave their lives that that nation might live. It is altogether fitting and proper that we should do this.

But, in a larger sense, we can not dedicate—we can not consecrate—we can not hallow this ground. The brave men, living and dead, who struggled here, have consecrated it, far above our poor power to add or detract. The world will little note, nor long remember, what we say here, but it can never forget what they did here. It is for us the living, rather, to be dedicated here to the unfinished work which they who fought here have thus far so nobly advanced. It is rather for us to be here dedicated to the great task remaining before us—that from these honored dead we take increased devotion to that cause for which they gave the last full measure of devotion—that we here highly resolve that these dead shall not have died in vain—that this nation, under God, shall have a new birth of freedom—and that government of the people, by the people, for the people, shall not perish from the earth.

If you can only remember one thing from this book, make it the Gettysburg Address. Read it aloud. Then read it again. And again. You'll be surprised; it won't be long before you know it by heart.

More Battles—Will It Ever End?

Abraham Lincoln asked Ulysses S. Grant to take charge of all the Union armies. And, finally, the president found the general he'd been looking for.

Lincoln had noticed that nothing seemed to scare Grant. But then nothing seemed to scare Robert E. Lee, either. Those two warriors—Grant and Lee—were now pitted against each other. Lee was an aristocrat: dignified—and tough. Grant was an everyday kind of fellow: soft-spoken—and tough.

Both were devoted family men, and decent, and their followers respected that.

Grant was anxious to fight it out with Lee and end the war. Both he and Lee knew that the longer the fighting continued the more likely it was that Northern people would get tired of supporting

Ulysses S. Grant said, "The art of war is simple enough. Find out where your enemy is. Get at him as soon as you can. Strike at him as hard as you can and as often as you can, and keep moving on." ▼

▲ Union and Confederate cavalry clash at the Battle of the Wilderness. The North wasn't defeated, but it had so many killed or wounded (18,000) that it didn't win, either.

the war and give up. The Southern strategy was to wear the North out; the Northern was to end things as quickly as possible.

Grant led a huge army south from Washington—he was heading for Richmond. He had almost 120,000 men. Lee had a little more than half that number.

Grant attacked and attacked and attacked. One dreadful battle, called the Battle of the Wilderness, was fought in thick woods. It was horrible. The trees caught on fire, and no one could see through the trees and smoke. Tens of thousands of men were killed or wounded or burned in that blind inferno.

Neither general was a quitter, nor was either the kind of leader who conserved men. The death lists became gruesomely long. The Confederates won the battles—they lost fewer men than the Yankees—but the losses hurt them more: they had fewer men to lose. And Grant kept pushing on, getting closer and closer to Richmond.

Grant soon learned what every other Union general knew—you couldn't attack Robert E. Lee and win. Grant had to trap the Confederate army if he was to be victorious. He made plans to lay a siege (as he had at Vicksburg).

If you check a map you'll see that Petersburg and Richmond are not far apart. Petersburg was the supply center for Lee's army. Five railroad lines came into Petersburg, and so did several major roads. Two rivers—the James and the Appomattox—meet at nearby City Point. Petersburg was a key. Without food from there, Richmond (the Confederate capital) would starve.

Grant decided to besiege Petersburg. But first he had to get there, and that wouldn't be easy. Petersburg is on the southwest side of the broad James River. Grant and his army were northeast of the James. Lee's army was in between (in and around Richmond) and not about to stand aside and let 100,000 men march by.

It is hard to believe what happened—but it was something amazing. Grant and his army disappeared. For three days the Confederate army couldn't find them. The Northern army was marching south—quickly and quietly. The Confederate army lost track of them, and that gave the U.S. Army engineers just enough time. They put pontoons in the river. Picture rowboat-like pontoons, one next to another, stretched across the water. Then imagine wooden planks connecting the pontoons, and a road laid on those planks. Now see in your mind an army marching across that bridge. An army that stretches back 50 miles!

▲ Union soldiers in the trenches at Petersburg.

◀ Pontoon bridges helped the Union win the war. U.S. Army engineers built this pontoon bridge over the Appomattox River in Virginia in preparation for the siege of Petersburg that began in June 1864.

Major Battles of the Civil War

DAKOTA TERRITORY

IOWA

MICHIGAN

NEW YORK

PENNSYLVANIA

Gettysburg (1863)

NEW JERSEY

ILLINOIS   INDIANA   OHIO

Antietam (1862)

Bull Run (1861, 1862)

MARYLAND   DELAWARE

KANSAS

MISSOURI

Chancellorsville (1863)

Washington, D.C.

WEST VIRGINIA

Fredericksburg (1862)

Wilderness (1864)

Seven Days (1862)

KENTUCKY

Richmond

Monitor and *Merrimac* (1862)

INDIAN TERRITORY

Petersburg (1862–1865)

VIRGINIA

Fort Donelson (1862)

Nashville (1864)

NORTH CAROLINA

Raleigh

Franklin (1864)

TENNESSEE

Memphis

Shiloh (1862)

ARKANSAS

Chattanooga (1863)

Chickamauga (1863)

Wilmington

Atlanta (1864)

SOUTH CAROLINA

MISSISSIPPI

Vicksburg (1863)

Jackson

ALABAMA

Charleston

Fort Sumter (1861)

Fort Wagner (1863)

TEXAS

Savannah

ATLANTIC OCEAN

LOUISIANA

Mobile

Pensacola

GEORGIA

Jacksonville

New Orleans (1862)

FLORIDA

Gulf of Mexico

	Legend
	Union
	Confederacy
	Border state
	Union victory
	Confederate victory
	Union blockade
	Sherman's March to the Sea

0   100   200 mi

0   100   200 km

▲ Of the 10 Civil War battles with the highest number of casualties, five were fought in Virginia.

The bridge was 10 feet wide and almost half a mile long (from one side of the river to the other). When men, wagons, horses, and artillery marched on it, the bridge went up and down and up and down. The James River has a swift-moving current, so the bridge also swayed from side to side. It took two days to get the whole army across the river. Then the pontoon bridge was broken up and towed away. The U.S. Army could now march up the west side of the James to City Point. Grant was ready to begin his siege of Petersburg and Richmond. It went on for 10 long, dreary months. Ten months with some fighting and shelling, but mostly it was waiting time: boring, nerve-racking, and tense.

Imagine that you live in Petersburg and the siege is on. You are hungry—very hungry. Some citizens have siege parties to keep up their spirits. At one party the only refreshment is water from the muddy James River.

Now imagine that you have a brother or father fighting in the war. Or maybe you are a soldier—a starving Confederate stuck in Petersburg all through a long, hot summer and then a cold, gloomy winter. Try being a Yankee soldier. You're not hungry, but you are weary of living in a tent, being far from your family, and never knowing when a shell may head your way.

A fair number of Rebels just sneak off from the camps. Many are mountain boys who never cared about slavery; they are tired of this war. They run away from the army; they desert. The penalty for desertion is death. So the deserters have a problem. They can't go home. They can't get caught. Bands of them roam the South, living as outlaws. They have to steal to live. They make life difficult for the Southern people.

By 1864, Southerners didn't need extra troubles; they were having a hard enough time. All of the fighting was now in the South. It was destroying the country. The armies were gathering food from the farms. When they couldn't use the food themselves they sometimes burned it so the other side wouldn't get it.

Then General William Tecumseh Sherman marched the U.S. Army of the West from Tennessee, through Georgia, and on to the Carolinas. That army's march is one of the most famous—and terrible—in military history.

Before the war, red-bearded General Sherman had been head of a military academy in Louisiana. He was asked to be a Confederate officer. But, although he had many Southern friends, he believed in the Union.

Sherman's men called him "Uncle Billy." Uncle Billy was about to squeeze the South as a coiled anaconda snake squeezes its prey. Like Grant at Vicksburg, Sherman broke the rules he had learned when he was a cadet at West Point. When he marched east he left his supply lines, and an army is never supposed to do that. Sherman gambled that he could find enough food in the agriculturally rich South. He

General Sherman's army marched on Atlanta in two huge columns several miles apart. They cut down forests to build corduroy roads and pulled up railroad tracks to make sure the Confederates couldn't use them again. ▼

▲ Sherman's Union troops march toward Atlanta, leaving a trail of destruction in their wake.

was right. But the Yankees didn't have it easy. They fought a Rebel army much of the way.

Before long the Northern soldiers were out of control. They, too, were tired of the war and they blamed the Southerners for it. So they stole and burned and destroyed the country as they went south. Sherman's army cut a path 40 miles wide. Nothing much was left on that path but empty fields, burned barns and homes, and slaughtered livestock.

Sherman believed army battles alone would not win the war. He believed in "total war." He thought that the Southern people who were supporting the war needed to be hurt. He believed that the Southern ability to make war—its food and arms production—must be destroyed. His army did a lot of destroying. It was cruel, because many innocent people were hurt. Sherman may have been right. He probably shortened the war. But he left bitterness and hatred and anguish. Those who still thought of war as a patriotic venture with rules of decency would never forgive him.

Meanwhile, up North, no one knew exactly where he was or what he was doing. General Sherman seemed to be lost somewhere in

Georgia. There were rumors that he was losing battles. People in the North were sick of the war. In every town people were mourning their lost sons. They blamed the president.

They could do something about him. Lincoln was running for reelection. General George McClellan was running against him. McClellan said he would end the war quickly. Everyone was tired of the war. Many no longer cared about the Union. Some didn't care about slavery. It looked as if Lincoln would lose. He was sure of it. "I am going to be beaten," he said, "and unless some great change takes place, badly beaten." He might have been right, but a great change did take place. General Sherman won an astonishing victory. He captured the city of Atlanta.

▲ After capturing Atlanta, Sherman ordered the destruction of all the city's war resources, including these railroad tracks.

The Second Inaugural

Abraham Lincoln won reelection. By a big margin. The American people were beginning to appreciate the tall man who was their president. They were beginning to understand his greatness: to understand that he was kind, compassionate, and humble. And also to understand that he was strong and determined.

Four years earlier, when he was first elected, he had hoped to prevent war. He had been willing to do almost anything to keep the country from splitting apart. He had even been willing to allow slavery to continue in the South. Now he felt differently. The war had been ghastly, much worse than anyone had ever imagined it could be;

Crowds gathered for Lincoln's second inauguration. When he heard the election results, Lincoln said, "I give thanks to the Almighty for this evidence of the people's resolution to stand by free government and the rights of humanity." ▶

▲ Sherman's army left a path of destruction 40 miles wide through Georgia. It also left a legacy of bitterness and hatred.

but now he saw a purpose in that war. Slavery would be ended. It might not have happened without the war. He thought it was all part of God's mysterious way, and that was what he said in his second inaugural address, the speech he gave after being reelected president.

The war was winding down. Sherman was devastating the Deep South; Grant was laying siege to Petersburg; troops were threatening Richmond. Lincoln knew the South could not hold out much longer. But what would become of the nation when the war was over? How should the defeated South be treated? Were they enemy? Or were they brothers and sisters who had behaved badly?

Suppose you have a terrible fight with a friend. Suppose that friend really hurts you. What would you do when the fight is over? Hate the friend? Or shake hands and say, "Let's forget it"?

Sometimes it isn't easy to forgive a former enemy. People in the North were hurt. Many wanted to punish the South. Lincoln thought the war had been punishment enough. He wanted to welcome Southerners back into the United States—as long as they agreed to play by the rules of the Constitution and the Emancipation Proclamation.

▲ Charleston, South Carolina, and other cities of the South lay in ruins at the end of the war.

Rebuilding the country was going to be difficult. Rebuilding the South would be especially difficult. He was worried about that. That process of rebuilding was being called "Reconstruction." Lincoln wanted Reconstruction to be carried out in a friendly, helpful way. Slavery had been wrong, terribly wrong, but now it was done with. In his second inaugural address he said it was not a just God's purpose to have men "wringing their bread from the sweat of other men's faces."

Wringing their bread from the sweat of other men's faces. Lincoln was talking to those who approved of slavery when he used that phrase. (What did he mean?)

He was talking to those who hated the slave owners when he used a thought from the Bible and said: *Let us judge not that we be not judged.* (What does that mean?)

In that famous second inaugural address, Abraham Lincoln told the American people—North and South—that he wanted them to be kind and generous toward each other. He used these eloquent words:

> ...Both [North and South] read the same Bible, and pray to the same God; and each invokes His aid against the other. It may seem strange that any men should dare to ask a just God's assistance in wringing their bread from the sweat of other men's faces; but let us judge not that we be not judged. The prayers of both could not be answered; that of neither has been answered fully.... With malice toward none, with charity for all; with firmness in the right, as God gives us to see the right, let us strive on to finish the work we are in; to bind up the nation's wounds; to care for him who shall have borne the battle, and for his widow, and his orphan—to do all which may achieve and cherish a just, and lasting peace, among ourselves, and with all nations.

Charles Francis Adams, Jr., who was John Adams's great-grandson, said of the president's reelection speech: "That rail-splitting lawyer is one of the wonders of the day.... Not a prince or minister in all Europe could have risen to such an equality with the occasion."

The Fall of Richmond

On April 1, 1865, Union troops won a battle at Five Forks, a strategic spot near Petersburg, Virginia, where roads came together near a railroad line. The next day, Robert E. Lee told Jefferson Davis to leave Richmond; then Lee and his army left Petersburg.

Confederate troops decided to set fire to supplies in Richmond. They didn't want to leave anything for the Yankees. The flames soon spread. Food that might have fed hungry Richmonders was destroyed. People's homes were lost in the flames. Documents and records that went back to the founding of Jamestown were among the things burned.

When news of the fall of Richmond reached Washington, the citizens went wild with excitement. Cannons boomed, banners flew, people hugged and kissed and cried with happiness. After four years of worry and gloom, finally the Confederate capital was captured.

On April 4, Lincoln went to Richmond. As he walked through the streets of Richmond, he was surrounded by the city's former slaves. Once, when he stopped to rest, an old black man with tears running down his cheeks came up to the tall man, took off his hat, bowed, and said, "May the good Lord bless you, President Lincoln." The president took off his hat and silently bowed back.

But the war wasn't won yet. Lincoln knew that. General Grant knew that, too. He knew he would have to capture or defeat Lee's army before it could end. That tired, shoeless army was now racing west. The soldiers were hungry, and their horses were half-starved. Grant sent part of his army ahead; he was laying a trap. He wanted to surround Lee's army so there would be no way out. And finally he did that, at a place called Appomattox Court House.

As Lincoln walked through the streets of Richmond, he was surrounded by the city's former slaves. One old woman said, "I know I am free, for I have seen Father Abraham." ▼

▲ As Richmond burned, citizens bundled what they could into carriages and scrambled behind the troops across the James River to safety.

Mr. McLean's Parlor

Wilmer McLean didn't like to be hassled. So when he retired from business he bought a comfortable farm with pleasant fields, woods, and a stream. He planned to live there quietly with his family. McLean's farm was in Virginia, not far from Washington. It was near an important railroad junction. The stream that crossed the farm was called *Bull Run*.

Do you think you know what happened on his farm? Well, you don't know all of it. Let's go back in time—to 1861. In April, you remember, the war began when Confederates in Charleston, South Carolina, fired their cannons at Fort Sumter. We are now in July of 1861. As yet there have been no big battles.

The two armies—North and South—are gathered near Manassas Junction. The Confederates are using Wilmer McLean's farm as a meeting place. One day some Southern officers are about to have lunch with the McLeans when the Union artillery zooms a cannonball at the house. It goes straight through the roof and lands in a kettle of stew. The shell explodes, so does the kettle, and stew is spattered all over the room!

The ruins of the Manassas Junction railroad station after the First Battle of Bull Run ▼

That is just the beginning of farmer McLean's troubles. Because of its railroad lines, Manassas is a strategic spot. Neither army wants the other to control it. After the battle of Bull Run, soldiers stay around, and, a year later, another battle is fought there. Wilmer McLean has had enough. He decides to move someplace very quiet. He wants to be as far from the war as possible. So he moves to a tiny, out-of-the-way village called Appomattox Court House.

Maybe Wilmer McLean had magnets in his blood: he seemed to attract historic occasions. In 1865 the two armies—North and South— found themselves at Appomattox Court House. A Confederate officer was looking for a place to have an important meeting. Wilmer

McLean showed him an empty building. It wouldn't do. So McLean took him to his comfortable redbrick house. That turned out to be just fine. It was in Wilmer McLean's front parlor that Robert E. Lee officially surrendered to Ulysses S. Grant. In later years McLean is supposed to have said, "The war began in my dining room and ended in my parlor."

On April 9, 1865, Robert E. Lee—proud, erect, and wearing his handsomest uniform—walked into Wilmer McLean's parlor. Strapped to his side was a gorgeous, shining sword with a handle shaped like a lion's head. The sword was decorated with carvings and held in a fine leather scabbard.

First battle of Bull Run (also called First Manassas): July 21, 1861. Second battle of Bull Run (also called Second Manassas): August 29 to 30, 1862.

Robert E. Lee surrenders to Ulysses S. Grant in Wilmer McLean's parlor in the village of Appomattox Court House ▼

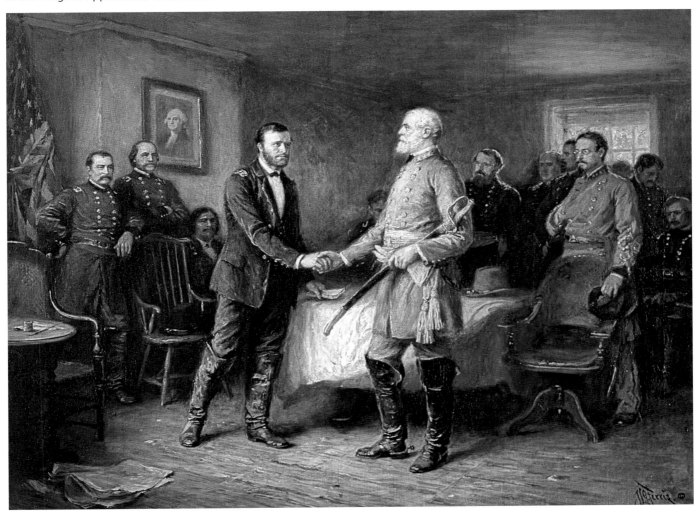

General Grant and his aides couldn't help looking at the beautiful sword. They all knew that, according to the rules of war, the defeated general must give his sword to the winner.

General Lee knew that, too. But he was not the kind of person who would bring an old sword to give away. He had brought his most precious sword. He had worn his best uniform. He held his head high. He knew he had fought as hard as he could. He had lost the war—fair and square—but he had not lost pride in himself and his men. Robert E. Lee's dignity and courage would be an example to his men when they returned to their homes. They didn't need to apologize for themselves; they had fought as well as men can fight.

General Grant understood that. Later, he described his feelings on that day:

> I felt…sad at the downfall of a foe who had fought so long and so valiantly, and had suffered so much for a cause, though that cause was, I believe, one of the worst for which a people ever fought.

But what should Grant do with Lee's sword? Keep it as a treasure to give to his children and grandchildren? Turn it over to the country to put in a museum?

Ulysses S. Grant didn't do either of those things. He wrote out the official surrender terms. They were kinder than anyone had expected. The Southern soldiers could go home, and—as long as they gave their promise not to fight against the country again—they would not be prosecuted for treason. They must surrender their guns but could take their horses. General Grant inserted a phrase in the document: the surrender did not include "the side arms of the officers." No one in the room said anything about it, but they knew: Lee's sword would stay strapped to his side.

But there is something more important than a sword to remember about that ceremony in McLean's parlor. There were important words said there, and General Grant didn't say them; nor did General Lee. They came after the signing of the papers, when there were handshakes all around. General Lee was introduced to General Grant's staff. One of Grant's aides was copper-skinned Lieutenant Colonel Ely Parker. Lee looked at him for a moment and said, "I am glad to see one real American here." Parker—a Seneca Iroquois—replied firmly, "We are all Americans."

Robert E. Lee—brave and heroic as he was—still didn't seem to understand why so many men and women had been willing to fight and sacrifice and die in this terrible war. *We are all Americans*. It was in those words.

Ely Parker knew we aren't all the same. Our skins are different colors, our religions are different, our abilities are different, our backgrounds may be different. So what is it that makes us the same? What is it that makes us *all Americans*?

An idea. We share an idea. That's what makes us alike. Other nations didn't begin with ideas; most began with barons and kings.

We started with a declaration that said *all men are created equal*. That new and powerful idea excited people all over the world. But our Constitution had not guaranteed that equality. This Civil War—terrible as it was—caused the Constitution to be changed for the better. Three constitutional amendments—the 13th, 14th, and 15th—would soon be passed (you'll soon learn more about them). They would make sure that *we are all Americans*. They would give the nation a *new birth of freedom*.

We Are All Americans

Ely Parker's real name was Donehogawa, and he was Keeper of the Western Door of the Long House of the Iroquois. As a boy, Donehogawa decided that he wanted to be successful in the world of white men and women. So he chose a white man's name for himself and studied law. But when it came time to be admitted to the bar and become a lawyer, he was told that only white males were acceptable. Parker/Donehogawa was not the kind of person who gave up. He decided to try another profession. He went to college, became an engineer, and helped supervise the building of the Erie Canal. His work took him to Galena, Illinois, where he became friends with a clerk in a harness shop who was without prejudice. The clerk was named Ulysses S. Grant. When Grant became General Grant and needed an engineer he turned to his friend Ely Parker.

After the war, Parker/Donehogawa was a brigadier general; he became commissioner of Indian affairs for the government. He tried his best to help his people. U.S. citizens were pushing west and taking the Indian lands. No one—not even Ely Parker—could stop them. Parker resigned as Indian affairs commissioner and became wealthy as a Wall Street investor.

▲ Donehogawa, who took the name Ely Samuel Parker, became an engineer, a general, and a commissioner of Indian affairs.

A Play at Ford's Theatre

Abraham Lincoln was in a good mood. A recent vacation and the exciting events of the past week had given him back his energy and optimism. It was April 14, 1865—and he was meeting with his cabinet. General Grant, now a great war hero, was a guest at the meeting. The two men enjoyed being together, and, since the war was just about over, they could joke a bit and relax.

The president told Grant and the cabinet members of a dream he had the previous night. He was on a boat heading for a distant, misty shore. It was not such an unusual dream, but what was unusual was that he had had that same dream before. Each time he dreamed of the boat and the misty shore he learned big war news. So now he was sure the nation would hear something important before the day was over. Perhaps, he said, General Sherman had captured the last remaining Confederate army.

The cabinet members were in a good mood, too. They laughed about the dream and went on to serious matters. It was

This photograph of Lincoln was taken just four days before he was assassinated. ▼

Reconstruction they talked about. *Reconstruction* was the name Lincoln used for the process of bringing North and South together into a united nation. There was much to be decided. How would the South be brought back into the Union? That was the important problem facing the nation. What should be done to help the newly freed men and women become useful citizens? They needed schooling, they needed land to farm, they needed jobs. How were the defeated white Southern leaders to be treated? After four years of terrible war many Northerners were in no mood to forgive them.

Some wanted the Southern leaders hanged. There was much talk but no decisions. Lincoln listened. He would announce his plans soon, he said.

The war had changed the president. He was not the same man he had been four years earlier. Everyone could see that. Lincoln had suffered terribly: his son had died, he had seen a generation of young Americans die. He had a spiritual quality now—some people called it a kind of saintliness. Whatever it was, he seemed to have found peace within himself.

He had always believed that blacks should be treated like whites. It was the only fair thing. And he was a fair-minded man. Before the war he had had suspicions that the races were different. That maybe blacks did not have the same needs, desires, and abilities as whites. That was before he got to know some black leaders. Before he listened to black soldiers. Before a black woman became his wife's friend, and his. Now he knew differently. He planned to use that knowledge to make the country wiser, and better.

He knew that while the cabinet was meeting, an American flag was being raised at Fort Sumter in the harbor at Charleston, South Carolina. The flag was the very one that had been lowered exactly five Aprils earlier. It was bullet-torn. Shots fired at that flag at Fort Sumter had begun the war. Now there would be cheers for the flag and there would be words of peace spoken. The nation's best-known abolitionist, William Lloyd Garrison, was in Charleston. So was the Reverend Henry Ward Beecher, who was Harriet Beecher Stowe's brother and the country's most famous preacher. Northerners were going south again—and not as soldiers. Some had already opened schools for the newly freed men, women, and children. Doctors and nurses were helping the sick and wounded.

In Washington, at the cabinet session, someone handed General Grant a note. It was from his wife. The note said they were to go to Philadelphia to be with their sons. President Lincoln was disappointed. He had looked forward to spending the evening with the general. The Grants had been invited, along with the Lincolns, to a play at Ford's Theatre, the popular Washington playhouse located between the White House and the Capitol. Lincoln enjoyed going to the theater, although this was said to be a silly play. When he heard Grant was not going, the president told an aide he didn't want to go, either. But he knew Mrs. Lincoln was looking forward to an evening out, and he didn't want to disappoint her.

▲ A poster advertising the performance that Lincoln attended on April 14, 1865

John Wilkes Booth fires at Abraham Lincoln in the Presidential Box at Ford's Theatre. ▶

So they went, with some other guests, and sat in the flag-covered Presidential Box. The box was a small, separate balcony that hung over the stage. It was a good place to see the play, and, even though the audience couldn't quite see Lincoln behind the curtains and flags, they saw him enter and they stood while the orchestra played "Hail to the Chief." The play was funny, and Abraham Lincoln enjoyed laughing, so he must have relaxed in the comfortable chair the managers had put in the box especially for him.

Then something happened. It was as if the play shifted to the president's box. No one could believe what they saw and heard. Perhaps it was all part of the act. That was what some of the people in the audience thought. There was a sound like a small thunder boom and some smoke. Then a wild-acting man climbed up out of the president's box, leaped onto the stage, said something in Latin, and was gone. A woman screamed and a voice cried out, *The president has been shot.* And everyone knew that this was no act. It was real.

Abraham Lincoln died the next day in the place he was carried to—a small house across the street from the theater. It was April 15, 1865.

That very same day Andrew Johnson was sworn in as president. A month and a half earlier, on the day of Lincoln's second

What the assassin is believed to have said is *Sic semper tyrannis*—"thus ever to tyrants"—which means "This is the way tyrants are treated." It is Virginia's state motto.

inauguration, when Johnson was named vice president, he had embarrassed everyone by being drunk.

Never was a murder more terrible for a nation. In ancient Rome, Caesar was cruelly killed and the flow of history changed. This was worse. A 26-year-old actor had shot a great and good president just when he was most needed.

John Wilkes Booth—the assassin—had not fought in the war and was plagued with feelings of cowardice. He wanted to feel important. He called Lincoln a tyrant. He was sure people in the South would cheer his act and think him a hero. They didn't. Confederate general George Pickett said, "The South has lost her best friend and protector in this her direst hour of need."

John Wilkes Booth was hunted and trapped in a Virginia tobacco barn. The barn was set on fire. When Booth wouldn't come out, he was shot.

Southerners hadn't wanted Lincoln assassinated. He was their president, too. In Norfolk, Virginia, on the day of Lincoln's funeral, a long procession of people marched through the streets while a military band played sad music. Many of the marchers were former Confederate soldiers.

Though the war was over, peace was yet to be won. Still, the war had accomplished much. The United States had withstood the terrible fire of civil war. Lincoln had seen that war as a test of free, democratic government. Could people rule themselves? Could they put down a rebellion from within the country? Well, they had. The Union had held. Its citizens had been willing to die to save it. They had shown the strength of the American vision.

What seemed to be remarkable was that when the war was over, it really was over. There was no more fighting. In other lands, rebel forces often took to the hills, became guerrilla fighters, and carried on for years. Some Confederates had said they would go into the hills and fight on, "like rabbits and partridges." But General Lee told them to go home, plant crops, and be good citizens—and they did.

Something else was remarkable. Lincoln had said, "This nation under God shall have a new birth of freedom." And it would happen. But it would be more than a century before the wounds of war were fully healed.

The Whole World Bowed in Grief

A few hours after her husband's death, Mary Todd Lincoln asked Elizabeth Keckley to come and be with her. Keckley, born a slave, was a successful Washington seamstress, a friend of Mary Lincoln, and an almost daily visitor to the White House. Here, Keckley writes of that time:

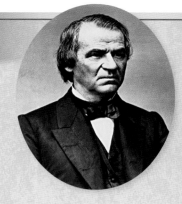

Andrew Johnson became the 17th president of the United States when he was sworn in on the day Lincoln died. ▶

> When [Mrs. Lincoln] became a little quiet, I asked and received permission to go into the Guests' Room, where the body of the President lay in state. When I crossed the threshold of the room, I could not help recalling the day on which I had seen little Willie lying in his coffin where the body of his father now lay. I remembered how the President had wept over the pale beautiful face of his gifted boy, and now the President himself was dead. The last time I saw him he spoke kindly to me, but alas! the lips would never move again. The light had faded from his eyes, and when the light went out the soul went with it!
>
> What a noble soul was his—noble in all the noble attributes of God. Never did I enter the solemn chamber of death with such palpitating heart and trembling footsteps as I entered it that day. No common mortal had died. The Moses of my people had fallen in his hour of triumph.... When I entered the room, the members of the Cabinet and many distinguished people were grouped around the body of their fallen chief. They made room for me, and, approaching the body, I lifted the white cloth from the white face of the man that I had worshipped as an idol.... There lurked the sweetness and gentleness of childhood, and the stately grandeur of godlike intellect. I gazed long at the face, and turned away with tears in my eyes and a choking sensation in my throat. Ah! never was a man so widely mourned before. The whole world bowed their heads in grief when Abraham Lincoln died.

The funeral train carrying the slain president to his resting place in Springfield, Illinois, took a 1,700-mile route and stopped in several cities along the way, including Philadelphia, shown here. Hundreds of thousands of Americans turned out to pay their respects. ▶

Reconstruction Means Rebuilding

The Civil War was over, and all across the land mothers and fathers buried their sons, wept, and tried to forgive the enemy now that they were pledging allegiance to the same flag. Most people seemed to understand that the country had to be made whole again. Its wounds needed to be bandaged.

President Lincoln had been determined to use kindness in bringing the South back into the Union. Actually, Lincoln said the South had never left the Union. Some Southern people had rebelled—that was what had happened, Lincoln said. It was like a family fight. They were still part of the family. Lincoln wanted to make it as easy as possible for the nation to reunite. Others felt differently.

Some Northerners were very angry. After all, it was the South that had started the war. It had been more terrible than anyone could have imagined. How should the North treat its former enemy? Should it be punished? Some thought the Rebel leaders should be hanged.

Did you ever lose a fight? Were you embarrassed and angry? White Southerners were angry, confused, hurt, and miserable.

You can understand that. Their lovely, elegant, aristocratic South was in ruins. Their sons were dead. Everything they had fought for seemed gone. (*Gone with the wind*, said one Southern woman in a famous book.)

A visitor to Charleston, South Carolina, wrote of "vacant houses, of widowed women, of rotting wharves, of deserted warehouses, of weed-wild gardens, of miles of grass-grown streets." Most of the South's cities were in the same shape. And the countryside? "We had no cattle, hogs, sheep, or horses or anything else," a Virginian wrote. "The barns were all burned, chimneys standing without

▲ A woman in mourning dress holds a framed photograph of a loved one lost in the war.

Women dressed in mourning clothes survey the ruins of the once-beautiful city of Richmond, Virginia. ▼

▲ This wounded Union soldier was one of tens of thousands of men on both sides who lost limbs during the war.

These former slaves were now free. But without land, without law and order, without civil rights backed by guarantees, what did "freedom" mean? ▶

houses and houses standing without roofs, or doors, or windows." Across the South everything seemed collapsed and disordered. There was no government, no courts, no post offices, no sheriffs, no police. Guerrilla bands looted at will.

A generation of white Southern men was dead. Those who came home brought wounds with them. In 1866, the year after war's end, Mississippi spent one-fifth of its revenues on artificial arms and legs for returning veterans.

Southern whites had to blame someone for their misery, and people don't like to blame themselves, so the former Rebels blamed Northerners. They said everything that went wrong after the war was the Northerners' fault. And as for the Civil War itself, all they had tried to do, they said, was form their own nation. How could they forgive the North for stopping them?

What of the four million black Southerners who were now freedmen and freedwomen? What were they to do now? For many, freedom meant going somewhere—anywhere. But where were they to go? What were they to do? Should they be paid for all their years of past work? There were rumors that each former slave would get 40 free acres of land and a mule to work it. Would that happen?

Most of the ex-slaves couldn't read or write. They wanted to learn. Who would their teachers be? Many had no idea what freedom really meant. Some thought it meant they would never have to work again.

Someone needed to do some organizing. Someone needed to maintain law and order. Help was needed.

The time in the South after the Civil War, when people attempted to reorganize and remake the region—without slavery—is called "Reconstruction."

How did it go? With a whole lot of confusion. It was the most promising, despairing, noble, awful, idealistic, reactionary, hopeful, hopeless time in all of American history. It didn't end up very well.

Immigrants Are Changing Things

It wasn't just war and Reconstruction that were happening in the 1860s. People were pouring into the country. They were emigrating from Ireland, China, Scandinavia, England, Greece, and other nations, and they were bringing new ideas and new skills. After the Civil War—in spite of the 620,000 war deaths—there were more people in the country than when the war began.

Many of those people settled in the North, but others headed west. In one western region there were so many people from Germany that the Native Americans began speaking German. Some areas had Swedish speakers, some had Russians, others had Danes. Some of the territories became as *polyglot* ("many-tongued") as New York City.

> *Reactionary* means "in favor of a return to a former or less advanced stage in politics or economics," or "extremely conservative."

◄ Many European immigrants headed west in the 1860s.

Who Was Andrew Johnson?

It was an actor's bullet that gave the country a new president. Now everyone was asking what kind of a man he was. People didn't know quite what to expect of President Andrew Johnson.

He was almost exactly the same age as Abraham Lincoln, and, like Lincoln, Johnson had been a poor boy who'd made his own way in life. Johnson had once been a tailor, but when he got up at a political meeting and began speaking, he found he had a talent. He could captivate and hold an audience.

Andy Johnson didn't have much education, but he was smart and he soon became prosperous. His wife helped smooth his rough edges and taught him some book learning, too. He was a Democrat and a slave owner.

In his home state, Tennessee, he became governor, congressman, and senator. (Back in 1852, when Andrew Johnson ran for governor, the Know-Nothing Party was whipping up anti-Catholic feeling in Tennessee, where most people were Baptists or Methodists. Johnson would have none of that. He said American Catholics were American citizens—and he won the election.)

Johnson was in the Senate when the Southern states, including Tennessee, seceded. He stuck with the Union. When Union forces captured Tennessee, President Lincoln made him military governor. He held that post during the war. He was often in danger. But Andrew Johnson was courageous. He was a good man for the job. Even though Johnson was a Democrat, and Lincoln a Republican, Abraham Lincoln asked Andrew Johnson to be vice president. Now the awful war was over. It was time for healing. Most people were encouraged.

Johnson seemed the perfect person to bring South and North together again. After all, Johnson was a Southerner who had had the courage to stay with the Union. Both Democrats and Republicans supported him. Perhaps it was all for the best.

But those who knew Johnson weren't so sure. Yes, he had courage, no doubt about that. But he was also stubborn. Mulishly stubborn. He didn't ask for advice or listen when it was given. Lincoln asked questions, listened, and changed his mind when he thought it needed changing. He knew how to compromise. Andrew Johnson was uncompromising. He was like a wall: rigid. You know how walls act. They don't bend, but, with enough force, you can break them.

Well, the wall was about to be charged.

"I love my country," Andrew Johnson said. "Every public act of my life testifies that is so." ▼

Presidential Reconstruction

During the first two years of Reconstruction, President Andrew Johnson was in control. That time is called "presidential Reconstruction."

In the beginning, things seemed to go well.

Congress had created a Freedmen's Bureau even before the war ended. It was to help the newly freed blacks. They needed food, clothing, and shelter. Some Northerners went south to help. Many of them were teachers.

The Freedmen's Bureau began opening schools. Slaves had been starved for learning. In the years of the Confederacy, every Southern state except Tennessee had laws making it a crime to teach slaves to read and write. Now, as free people, they were thirsty for knowledge. In Mississippi, when a Freedmen's Bureau agent told a group of 3,000 they were to have schools, he reported that "their joy knew no bounds. They fairly jumped and shouted in gladness." When schools

◀ Former slaves of all ages were eager for education.

Some freedmen's schools, such as the Hampton Normal and Agricultural Institute at Hampton, Virginia, emphasized "industrial training" in, for example, sewing, printing, and agricultural trades. ▶

opened, parents often sat in classrooms with children. As soon as they could read and write, the new learners taught others.

Many of their teachers were white missionaries sent by Northern churches. Others, like Mary Peake (who founded the first school for blacks in Hampton, Virginia), were educated Northern blacks.

But it's hard to learn if you're hungry, and many Southerners were hungry. Their farms were in terrible shape. The wheat crop failed in 1865. It didn't do much better the next year.

Legal Eagles

William Henry Johnson, who had been a slave in Richmond, Virginia, escaped to Massachusetts during the Civil War and got a job as a janitor in a law office. He became interested in reading law books and soon was a regular law student in Francis Porter's office. In 1865, Johnson was admitted to the Massachusetts bar (which means he received a license from the state to practice law). Johnson was a leader in the temperance movement and, in 1880, was elected to the Common Council in New Bedford, Massachusetts.

When lawyer Edward Garrison Walker was elected to the Massachusetts legislature in 1866, he became the first black legislator in the nation. Walker was a skilled criminal lawyer who had won some important murder cases. As a state legislator, he was a pioneer in the women's suffrage movement.

In 1869, George Lewis Ruffin became the first black to graduate from Harvard Law School. He was a barber when he began to study law. Ruffin "distinguished himself by completing the three-year course in one year." He was elected to the Massachusetts legislature, and, later, he was named a judge.

The Freedmen's Bureau kept most people from starving. Clothing was distributed. In some places more of its help went to whites than blacks. There was nothing wrong with that. Anyone who needed help was meant to have it.

In addition to providing food to former slaves and impoverished whites, the Freedmen's Bureau distributed clothing and other necessities. Here, children recently freed from slavery move from rags to decent clothing.

And people helped each other. A former house slave found a job and, each week, brought five dollars to his old mistress. Many white Southerners helped the freedmen and freedwomen.

Northern soldiers kept order. A citizen of Lynchburg, Virginia, said, "A more gentlemanly and humane set of officers, and I may add, of soldiers, never occupied an enemy's country." But not everyone agreed. Just looking at those blue uniforms upset many Southerners. And some whites still couldn't accept the idea of a society where people were equal.

Thousands of Southerners left the country for Mexico and South America. Some Confederates went to Brazil, where there was still slavery (although abolition soon came to that nation, too). General Lee was not pleased to see Southerners leave the United States. "Virginia has need of all her sons and can ill afford to spare you," he wrote one of them. To others he said, "Abandon all these local animosities and make your sons Americans." (*Animosity* is hatred or ill feeling.)

Most Americans put the war behind them. Northerners and Southerners were soon visiting each other again. Young Southern men went north to enroll in the military academies at West Point and Annapolis. And some North-South romances blossomed (although Jefferson Davis wouldn't let his daughter marry a Yankee).

It seemed like it took a long time for freedom to come. Everything just kept on like it was. We heard that lots of slaves was getting land and some mules to set up for theirselves. I never knowed any what got land or mules nor nothing.

—Millie Freeman, former slave

Thomas Nast's 1868 cartoon depicts Democrats as the oppressors of the black race. A black Union soldier, carrying the American flag and a ballot box, is trampled by men representing immigrants, the Ku Klux Klan, and northern capitalists.

A few Southerners attempted a new kind of cooperation between the races; their experiments in racial harmony wouldn't be tried again for a hundred years. But, mostly, white people in the South still didn't understand. They were willing to be good United States citizens, except—and it was a big exception—except when it came to treating their black fellow citizens fairly. And, once again, they turned to short-sighted leaders.

Right after the war (in 1865 and 1866) most of the same old Southern leaders were in charge, and every Southern state passed laws that discriminated against blacks. The laws were called "black codes." They made blacks practically slaves again. The codes gave whites almost unlimited power. No Southern state would establish public schools for blacks.

Race riots erupted in Memphis and New Orleans. Hot-headed whites were attacking blacks. They blamed the former slaves for the war. That was irrational, but violence rarely makes sense. What happened was gruesome. General Philip Sheridan called the New Orleans riot a massacre (he was there). Thirty-four blacks and three whites (who stood with them) were killed. More than 100 people were injured.

The deadly race riot at Memphis, Tennessee, in May 1866 ▶

Some whites put masks over their faces and burned black churches and schools; they terrorized and killed blacks. These were grown-ups, members of a newly formed hate organization, the Ku Klux Klan, and they didn't have the courage to show their faces.

The state governments did not bring them to justice.

When the Southern states sent representatives to Congress, they sent Confederate warriors and politicians. Alexander Stephens, vice president of the Confederacy, was sent to Congress. Northerners were outraged. After many wars, defeated leaders are tried and sometimes even executed. Northerners thought they had been generous. Many of the Southern officers had trained in the U.S. Army before the war. That means they had pledged allegiance to the United States. They broke that pledge when they became Rebels. Technically they were traitors. Yet the North had not asked for revenge. General Grant had paroled the Rebel soldiers and officers. But should they be rewarded and made congressmen?

And what of those other things? "Black codes" that bound black workers to labor contracts and gave them no legal rights? That sounded like slavery. Race riots? Murders? That wasn't American justice. "Why did we fight a war?" people in the North asked.

President Johnson urged the Southern states to protect the freedmen and freedwomen's rights. But he didn't do anything to see that they were protected. There was something else disturbing. He was being nasty to Southerners who had supported the Union (as he had). He seemed to be taking sides at a time when he should have tried to be president of all the people.

What was going on?

Something very important. The war had been fought over issues that would determine what our nation was to stand for. Those issues had not been settled. What were they?

▲ Masked Ku Klux Klan members terrorized black people, sometimes pretending to be ghosts of Confederate soldiers.

There had been four years of warfare over slavery and states' rights and it still wasn't over. Now the fight had switched from the battlefields to the halls of Congress.

Slavery and States' Rights

The 13th Amendment was ratified on December 6, 1865. That did it. It ended slavery. The Emancipation Proclamation was now the law of the land.

But some thinking people were already asking themselves, "Is being free of slavery enough?" If you are free and can't vote, are you really free? If you are free but laws say you can't quit your job or leave your plantation—as the black codes said—then are you really free?

Those thinking people started talking about the whole meaning of America. The United States was still an experiment. It was still the only people's government around. Those thinkers went right back to the Declaration of Independence.

> *We hold these truths to be self-evident, that all men are created equal, that they are endowed by their Creator with certain unalienable Rights, that among these are Life, Liberty and the pursuit of Happiness.*

Unalienable rights. That means rights that belong to each of us—not to the government. No government has any right meddling with our rights to life, liberty and the pursuit of happiness, says the Declaration.

Before 1865, the Southern states had pretended that blacks didn't have those same rights. They had pretended that blacks were different. They had acted as if unalienable rights were only for whites.

Unalienable, inalienable—which is correct? Both: Jefferson used *unalienable; inalienable* is usually used today.

Amendment 13

Section 1. Neither slavery nor involuntary servitude, except as a punishment for crime whereof the party shall have been duly convicted, shall exist within the United States, or any place subject to their jurisdiction.
Section 2. Congress shall have power to enforce this article by appropriate legislation.

The emancipation of Southern slaves is celebrated in this illustration by Thomas Nast. ▶

The war had been fought to end slavery. Slavery was ended. But the black codes were there to do the same old thing: to keep blacks from their unalienable rights.

A group of leaders in Congress said, "Hold on." And then they said, "Stop." They wrote laws to protect the civil rights of blacks. Those congressional leaders were a small but powerful group within the Republican Party. They were called Radical Republicans. In 1866 the Radical Republicans got Congress to pass a Civil Rights Act. It was designed to nullify the black codes.

President Johnson vetoed the Civil Rights Act. Johnson was a former slave owner. Although he no longer believed in slavery, he did not believe in equality. Johnson also thought it was up to the states, not the central government, to protect individual rights. (That was the *states' rights* argument.)

Congress passed the civil rights law over the president's veto. (Study the Constitution to find out how that is possible.) It was the first time in American history that an important piece of legislation was passed over a president's veto. As you know, Andrew Johnson was stubborn. But so were the Radical Republicans. The battle between them now grew fierce.

▲ In the foreground, former slave Henry Garnet speaks with newspaper editor Horace Greeley after the passage of the 1866 Civil Rights Act.

Radical means "extreme." It means going as far as you can go with an idea or a change.

Nullify means "to negate or make into nothing."

A *veto* is a *no* vote. The president's veto usually means that a law will not be passed.

Justice for All?

Five years after war's end, black boys and girls were attending 4,000 new schools in the South. At least nine black colleges had opened (including Fisk and Howard universities and Hampton and Tuskegee institutes). Black churches were being built in every city and hamlet. Ten years after war's end, Congress passed a civil rights bill prohibiting discrimination in hotels, theaters, and amusement parks. It sought "equal and exact justice to all, of whatever…race, color or persuasions, religious or political." But, in 1883, the Supreme Court ruled that the civil rights law was unconstitutional. (In the 20th century the Court would see things differently.)

Black students learn to make and repair wheels in the wheelwright shop at the Tuskegee Institute in Alabama. ▶

Indeed, it was war between President Andrew Johnson and the Radical Republicans. Once the Republicans realized they could pass laws over Johnson's veto, they took control of Reconstruction.

The next thing the Radicals did was to write the 14th Amendment. It is a long but *very important* amendment. Here is a key part of it:

> *No State shall deprive any person of life, liberty, or property, without due process of law; nor deny to any person within its jurisdiction the equal protection of the laws.*

That amendment says no state can take away any person's rights. We are all entitled to the safeguards provided by the Constitution— even against a state!

Back in 1787, the Constitution makers had worried about protecting citizens from abuses by Congress, or the president, or the federal government—but not from abuses by their states. Each state was expected to protect its own citizens. But suppose they didn't? This amendment was saying that the U.S. government would protect all its citizens, even against the states. The U.S. government was to be superior to any state.

Whew! This was a powerful amendment. The South had fought for states' rights. Many Southerners thought each state should be free to make its own decisions. If a state wanted an aristocratic society with layers of privilege and unfairness—well, if that was what the majority of its people really wanted, why shouldn't they have it?

Free at Last...

When black men, women, and children learned they were free, there was singing and shouting "an' carryin' on." Charlotte Brown, who lived in Wood's Crossing, Virginia, remembered that. Then, she said, a few days later, on Sunday morning, "we was all sitting roun' restin' and tryin' to think what freedom meant an' everybody was quiet and peaceful." They knew freedom meant being able to move wherever they wanted, to find work wherever they could, to choose new names, to plant their own gardens, to search for family members, to practice their own religion, and to go to school and learn.

"We belong to ourselves," they shouted out, and after years of slavery, that was enough for some. But others realized that freedom was more than that. Sometimes they were surprised to find that freedom means choices and responsibilities. Just what is freedom? What does it mean to you?

Making Amends

When the Constitution was written back in 1787, it had a terrible flaw. (What was that terrible flaw?) After the Civil War three amendments to the Constitution—the 13th, 14th, and 15th—were passed. They corrected the flaw and did something else, too. The amendments added more of the spirit of the Declaration of Independence to the Constitution.

The 13th Amendment, adopted in 1865, prohibited slavery. (It went further than Lincoln's Emancipation Proclamation; it made emancipation the law of the whole land.)

The 14th Amendment, adopted in 1868, gave equal protection of the law to ALL Americans.

The 15th Amendment, passed in 1870, said that all citizens have the right to vote. Are women citizens? This amendment didn't say yes and it didn't say no, which was too bad. It would take another amendment to make that clear.

▲ This illustration celebrates the passage of the 15th Amendment, which guaranteed all citizens the right to vote. Surrounding the central image of a celebratory parade in Baltimore are pictures of blacks running for political office, owning land, and worshipping freely. Also pictured are Frederick Douglass, Abraham Lincoln, and John Brown.

The Constitution makers had thought about that. They said majorities are sometimes tyrannical. They worried about the rights of minorities. The Bill of Rights was to protect minorities even from majority will.

Were we to stick with the goals of the Founders? Were we to respect the inalienable rights of all citizens?

Should we be a nation with a constitution that guarantees fairness to all? If so, then if people vote for unfair state laws, those laws need to be made unconstitutional. And that is just what the 14th Amendment does.

It was a big step. Andrew Johnson didn't like it a bit. It took power from the states. It gave power to the Supreme Court. Johnson didn't like the 14th Amendment and he hated the man who was the force behind it. (You'll read about him soon.)

Congressional Reconstruction

Congress decided to send soldiers south to guarantee freedom to the former slaves. That happened in 1867. The soldiers stayed for about 10 years. That period is called "congressional Reconstruction." (You may also hear it called "military Reconstruction.") During that time, many Northerners went south. They went to teach, to help with aid programs, to help the state governments get going again, and sometimes to make money for themselves.

Most Southerners hated carpetbaggers, as this cartoon shows, and thought they wanted only to profit from the South's problems. ▼

All those Yankees were known as "carpetbaggers." In those days a traveling bag was sometimes made of carpet material. Some Southerners said the carpetbaggers were people who threw a few things in a suitcase and came South only to make money for themselves. Mostly, that was a myth.

Many Southerners found it hard to put up with Northerners in their midst, especially Yankees who were telling them how to behave. Most white Southerners who had been Confederates hated the carpetbaggers. The carpetbaggers reminded them of the war and their losses.

Some Northerners did take advantage of the South. Often they were businessmen who didn't even bother to visit the region. Northern lumbermen looked greedily at Southern forests. In 1876 they got Congress to sell Southern land cheaply. One congressman took 110,000 acres of Louisiana land for himself. A Michigan firm got 700,000 acres of pine land. Another Northern firm bought more than a million acres at 45 cents an acre. What they did has been called the most reckless destruction of forest land in history.

Southerners who cooperated with the North were called "scalawags." Some scalawags wanted power and influence. But some, like James Longstreet (the man General Lee affectionately called "my old war horse"), just wanted to forget the war and do business in a united nation.

But most of the Northerners who went south went to help. They wanted to see blacks treated fairly. Many had great courage. Many worked in the Freedmen's Bureau. For five years that bureau set up schools, distributed food, and helped the newly freed citizens with their problems.

Congress passed a Reconstruction Act. Naturally, President Johnson vetoed it. Enough votes were gathered in Congress to get the act passed over his veto. The act said that to become part of the Union again, each Southern state had to write a new constitution that was true to the U.S. Constitution. The act also said that all males over 21 could vote, except for convicted criminals and those who had participated "in the rebellion." That meant that former Confederate soldiers could not vote, but black men could. As you might guess, that made some whites angry and bitter.

Northern soldiers made sure that black men were able to vote. It was amazing. Men who had been slaves a few years earlier were lining up at the polls. Many were illiterate (they couldn't read or write), but about one-fifth of the South's white population was illiterate, too. Being illiterate doesn't mean being stupid. The new voters did exactly what James Madison expected them to do. They voted for what they believed to be their own interests.

▲ After the war, black men gained the right to vote, which gave blacks real power. Then (until well into the 20th century) they lost the vote and their power.

John Willis Menard of Louisiana (just right of center) was the first black elected to the House of Representatives. ▼

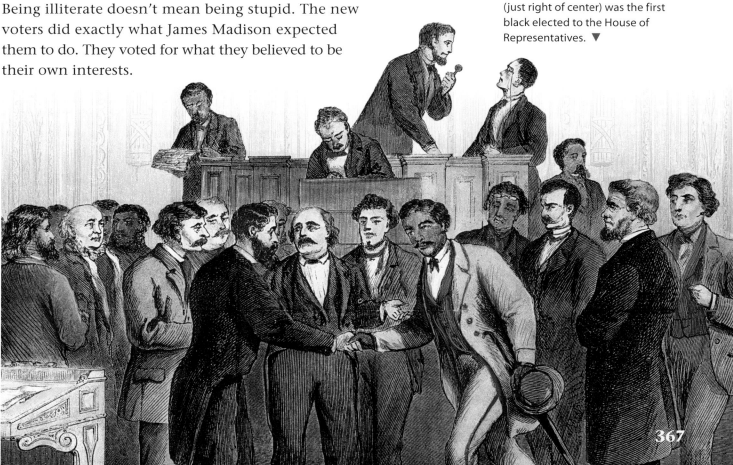

Madison had thought that made sense. In a large democratic nation, he said, all the special interests need to be heard. They would balance each other. Before the war only the interests of the planters had been represented. Now many blacks were being elected to office. And some poor whites, too.

Mississippians Blanche K. Bruce and Hiram R. Revels became U.S. senators. Both were college men. Revels took Jefferson Davis's old seat in the Senate. The day he was sworn in, the Senate galleries were packed, and everyone stood as he walked down the aisle. Some observers burst into cheers to see a black as a senator. "Never since the birth of the republic," said an editorial in the *Philadelphia Press*, "has such an audience been assembled under one single roof. It embraced the greatest and the least American citizens." That was an exaggeration, but those who were there knew it was a historic moment.

Sixteen blacks served in the U.S. Congress during Reconstruction; more than 600 were elected to state legislatures and hundreds more held local offices like sheriff or justice of the peace. Blacks and whites served together on juries, on school boards, and on city councils. They ensured fairness in ways that had not been done before (and would not be done again until the second half of the 20th century).

▲ This lithograph issued by Currier and Ives in 1872 portrays (from left to right) Senator Hiram Revels of Mississippi and Representatives Benjamin Turner of Alabama, Robert DeLarge of South Carolina, Josiah Walls of Florida, Jefferson Long of Georgia, and Joseph Rainey and Robert B. Elliott of South Carolina.

Bruce, a wealthy farmer and landowner, had attended Oberlin College. In the Senate he worked for equal rights for all. Few people, then, worried about rights for Indians and Asians. But Bruce did. He was an eloquent, dignified senator who worked to help the growing railroads and to improve navigation on the Mississippi River. At a time when there was much corruption in government and business, Blanche Bruce was known for his integrity.

Still, it was difficult for some white people to accept what was happening. Blacks in Congress! Blacks in the state legislatures! Some whites really believed the racist myths. They didn't believe blacks could think as well as whites. They didn't believe women could think as well as men. In the North most white men wouldn't take a chance (and there weren't many black voters), so only a few blacks were elected in Northern states. And no women were elected at all—north or south—because women still couldn't vote.

Reconstruction Legislatures

Charleston, South Carolina, January 14, 1868—the members of the state legislature are about to write a new constitution.

Most of South Carolina's citizens are black. Now that they can vote they have elected black lawmakers to their legislature.

Seventy-six black men and 48 white men are gathered. Outside, a noisy crowd surges through the streets. Most are former slaves, and they are full of hope. Charleston's white aristocrats worry. Will the assembly demand revenge for the years of slavery?

At this convention is Robert Brown Elliott, age 25, who has studied at Eton (a famous school in England), is fluent in French and Spanish, and is trained in the law. Soon, Robert Elliott will go to Washington and enter the House of Representatives as a congressman from South Carolina, where he will work to get civil rights laws passed.

Also at the January 1868 meeting is Francis Louis Cardozo, the son of a Jewish economist and a free black woman. Cardozo, who graduated with honors from the University of Glasgow, in Scotland, is a brilliant administrator who will save millions of dollars for South Carolina when he exposes corrupt businessmen who are taking advantage of the state.

Robert Smalls, also the son of a Jewish father and a black mother, is at the meeting in Charleston. A few years ago he stunned both North and South when, all by himself, he sailed a Confederate steamer through the guns of Charleston Harbor and handed it over to the U.S. Navy.

And there stands six-foot-two-inch William Beverly Nash, a former slave, who has taught himself to read and quotes Shakespeare with ease.

Some say this legislative session is the beginning of "America's Second Revolution," an attempt at a genuine interracial society. Poor whites are represented here, and former slaves, and wealthy white men who are accustomed to rule. The legislature will soon move to South Carolina's capital, Columbia, and will continue with state business.

All across the South, Reconstruction legislatures are at work. The lawmakers ask themselves: Should they take land from the Confederates who rebelled against their nation? Should they give it to the slaves who have worked the land and made others rich? Can they divide the land and be fair? How do you give opportunity and justice to all?

These Reconstruction legislatures will vote for free public schools; almost none have existed in the South before. They will vote for roads. They will not demand revenge on the white aristocracy. They will do as well as most legislatures and far better than the U.S. Congress, which, at the time, is shockingly corrupt. But they will topple. So-called "redeemer" governments—controlled by former Confederates—will take their place.

Robert B. Elliott addresses the House of Representatives in 1874 about the Civil Rights Bill. ▶

Thaddeus Stevens, Radical

This chapter is about President Andrew Johnson's enemy.

When he was a boy Thaddeus Stevens had three big problems: he was very poor, his father was an alcoholic who deserted the family, and he was handicapped. Thaddeus had a deformed leg and foot—a clubfoot—that made him limp badly. The leg made him self-conscious, and some boys and girls made fun of him. That didn't help.

But Thad had some things going for him: he had an amazing mind and he was fiercely honest. He was handsome, too. He could have been a model for a Greek sculptor. His face had strong, regular features and deep-set hazel eyes. His curly hair was the color of chestnuts.

Thaddeus Stevens grew up in Vermont, where people say what they think and don't waste words. When he was 24, in September 1816, he moved to a pretty little Pennsylvania town. You've heard of it. It was called Gettysburg.

He was soon the best lawyer in Gettysburg. And then the best in Pennsylvania. The richest, too. He owned an iron foundry (which was destroyed by Robert E. Lee's troops at the battle of Gettysburg). In addition, he was a shrewd investor: he took his money and put it in other businesses and made more money. His Gettysburg neighbors thought well of him; they sent him to Congress and kept him there for many years.

White Southerners would soon call him the vilest of all Yankees. Blacks would see him as a hero and rank him close to the angels. Those who knew him best either admired or hated him—you couldn't have halfway feelings about Thad Stevens.

He didn't try to make himself liked. He went around with a frowning, stern look on his face. He thought most people were selfish and many were evil. He never married. An illness left him bald in his thirties, so he wore a dark wig. The wig didn't fit well.

In those days most people went to church every Sunday. Not Thaddeus Stevens, though he had been raised a Baptist. People whispered about him, because he wouldn't do as others

"Who is the United States?" asked Stevens. "Not the judiciary, not the president, but the sovereign power of the people." ▼

did, but when he heard that two young men wanted to study to be ministers, and didn't have the money for tuition, he quietly paid for their schooling.

Once he was riding his horse home when he saw a crowd in front of a farm. He stopped and learned that a widow's farm was being auctioned. The widow had no money to pay her bills. So he bought the farm, gave it back to the widow, got on his horse, and quickly rode off.

Stevens did what he wanted, said what he wanted, and didn't seem to care a bit what others thought. He was unwaveringly honest and couldn't be bribed or tempted—everyone agreed about that.

In 1838 (which was way before the Civil War) he refused to sign the Pennsylvania Constitution—because it gave the vote only to white men. People called him an abolitionist—a name that was no help to a politician in that antebellum time. Stevens didn't answer his critics and kept working to end slavery. When fugitive slaves needed help, he was their lawyer and never charged a fee. He worked hard for free schools, and some wealthy people hated him for that because it raised their taxes and because they believed ordinary people should be kept ignorant.

> *Antebellum* is Latin and means "before *(ante)* the war *(bellum)*." In America, it always means the time before the Civil War.

If Thaddeus Stevens believed in something, he was willing to fight for it no matter how unpopular that made him. And what he really believed in were those words of Thomas Jefferson's: *all men are created equal.* His Yankee mind told him that all men meant *all* men—not all white men. So, starting in the 1830s, he began battling for abolition, and then emancipation, and then equal rights. He never stopped fighting, and he never kept quiet.

He wrote civil rights laws. He was the chief author of the 14th Amendment. He laid the foundations for the 15th Amendment (which gave the vote to black males).

Ahead of Its Time?

Thaddeus Stevens intended that the 14th Amendment be a weapon against bigotry and injustice. But for almost a century it was ignored or abused. Perhaps if Stevens had been more forgiving, his ideas might have had a better chance in his lifetime. Or maybe he was just ahead of his time. In the second half of the 20th century the kind of civil rights laws Thaddeus Stevens wanted were finally passed and implemented. The 14th Amendment made them possible. Today, the majority of people agree that, aside from the Bill of Rights, the 14th is the most important of all the amendments.

▲ A joint House and Senate Reconstruction Committee writes the 14th Amendment.

THE VETO.

The Freedmen's Bureau bill of 1866 was intended to make the bureau stronger and to help former slaves if they were discriminated against. In this cartoon, Andrew Johnson vetoes the bill and sends the bureau tumbling, spilling helpless blacks out of its drawers.

Abraham Lincoln was a moderate, a man who believed in compromise. He thought people, at heart, were good. Lincoln had planned a kindly, forgiving Reconstruction. Stevens had no faith in moderation—or in most people. He thought strong laws were needed to make people behave properly.

"We are building a nation," said Stevens, who understood that his ideas would help change a collection of states into a centralized nation.

He believed that the Southern states should not be admitted back into the Union until blacks were given the vote, given land, and given guarantees of equality under the law. Those were radical demands.

Thaddeus Stevens was a leader of the Radical Republicans. The radicals became very powerful while Andrew Johnson was president. Johnson hated the radicals. But his hatred helped his political enemies.

President Johnson threw away his popularity. It was that stubborn, narrow-minded streak of his; it made him a poor leader. He didn't listen. He didn't try to represent the whole country. He didn't know how to compromise. He seemed to stand against most Northerners, all blacks, and the moderate Southern Unionists. He went on a speaking tour and said wild and nasty things about Congress. Often, he didn't act dignified or presidential. Some people were ashamed of their president.

But Andrew Johnson did have sincere beliefs. He was convinced that it was not the responsibility of the nation to help the newly freed men and women get fair and equal treatment before the law. He thought that was the states' job.

Stevens knew the states had not done that and would not. None of them—North or South.

Thaddeus Stevens detested President Johnson. Their beliefs collided. Johnson called Stevens a traitor and said he should be hanged. Stevens said the president should be impeached.

The Constitution includes a process—called "impeachment"—that allows us to bring to trial federal officials accused of *Treason, Bribery, or other high Crimes and Misdemeanors*. (Look up those words to be sure you know what they mean.) Impeachment is a way to get rid of officials who take advantage of high office and break the law. (It is a process borrowed from the English system of government.)

Thaddeus Stevens said it was "a moral necessity" to impeach President Johnson. Stevens wasn't the only one who wanted the impeachment. Many of this nation's citizens (except those in the South) seemed to want it.

It was 1868. Would the president be impeached? If so, would he then be convicted of high crimes and misdemeanors and thrown out of the White House?

The nation held its breath, waiting to find out.

In 1867, Congress passed a bill called the Tenure of Office Act. It was another attempt by Congress to challenge the authority of President Andrew Johnson. The bill prevented the president from firing his own cabinet members.

How to Impeach

The writers of the Constitution hadn't made it easy to remove a president (or any other high official) from office. This is the process as written in the Constitution (Article I, Section 2):

The House of Representatives shall…have the sole power of impeachment.

That means that if a majority of the House of Representatives votes to impeach a president he will be impeached (charged with misconduct). Then the Constitution (Article I, Section 3) says:

The Senate shall have the sole Power to try all impeachments. When sitting for that Purpose, they shall be on Oath or Affirmation. When the President of the United States is tried, the Chief Justice shall preside and no Person shall be convicted without the Concurrence of two thirds of the Members present.

Thaddeus Stevens calls for the impeachment of President Andrew Johnson. ▶

Impeaching a President

The debate in the House of Representatives lasted more than two months. Then the House voted. It voted to impeach. After that, it was time for the members of the Senate to try Andrew Johnson. Remember, two-thirds of the Senate needs to vote for conviction in order to remove a president from office. All the senators but one said in advance how they would vote. And two-thirds of the senators—minus one—said they planned to vote against Johnson. The fate of the president would be decided by one vote. That vote belonged to a newly elected senator: quiet, mild-mannered Edmund G. Ross of Kansas.

Ross, a former newspaperman, had been a major in the Union army. He hated slavery and he didn't like President Johnson. He had voted with the Radical Republicans on every issue. Kansas was a Radical Republican state, so Senator Ross knew most of the people he represented couldn't stand President Johnson, either. But the young senator said he wasn't going to make up his mind until he heard the evidence.

The day of the trial came, and the chief justice of the Supreme Court administered an oath to each senator, "to do impartial justice."

The United States Senate served as a court of impeachment for the trial of President Andrew Johnson in 1868. ▼

◀ According to one reporter, the impeachment trial of President Johnson was marked by "the clapping of hands, the waving of handkerchiefs, [and] the tumult of excited approbation."

Picture the scene: a president is on trial. A thousand tickets are printed for admission to the Senate galleries; people do everything possible to get them. One Washington woman wakes a congressman at midnight and won't leave his house until he promises her a ticket. Reporters cover the impeachment as if it were a murder trial. All over the country, day after day, newspaper headlines scream the details.

Edmund Ross gets a telegram from Kansas.

KANSAS HAS HEARD THE EVIDENCE AND DEMANDS THE CONVICTION OF THE PRESIDENT.

It is signed D. R. ANTHONY AND 1,000 OTHERS. Ross answers the telegram:

TO D. R. ANTHONY AND 1,000 OTHERS:...I HAVE TAKEN AN OATH TO DO IMPARTIAL JUSTICE ACCORDING TO THE CONSTITUTION AND LAWS, AND TRUST THAT I SHALL HAVE THE COURAGE TO VOTE ACCORDING TO THE DICTATES OF MY JUDGMENT AND FOR THE HIGHEST GOOD OF THE COUNTRY.

Later, Ross described the scene on the day of the vote:

The galleries were packed. Tickets of admission were at an enormous premium. The House had adjourned and all of its members were in the Senate chamber. Every chair on the Senate floor was filled with a Senator, a Cabinet Officer, a member of the President's counsel or a member of the House.

The vote begins. *Guilty. Not guilty.* Senator James W. Grimes of Iowa, paralyzed from a stroke, has been carried into the Capitol

A ticket of admission to the U.S. Senate galleries for the impeachment trial of President Johnson ▼

▲ A cartoon depicts "President 'Andy' Johnson's Joy upon his Acquittal from Impeachment."

on a stretcher. He votes *not guilty*. Thaddeus Stevens, now an old man, and ailing, is carried in on a chair. He is said to look like "cold marble."

He votes *guilty*. Every senator is present. The chief justice reminds "citizens and strangers in the galleries that absolute silence and perfect order are required."

And then, the moment everyone is waiting for. The chief justice says, "Mr. Senator Ross, how say you? Is the respondent Andrew Johnson guilty or not guilty of a high misdemeanor as charged in this Article?"

Ross remembered it this way:

Not a foot moved, not the rustle of a garment, not a whisper was heard.... Hope and fear seemed blended in every face. The Senators in their seats leaned over their desks, many with hand to ear.... It was a tremendous responsibility.... I almost literally looked down into my open grave. Friendships, position, fortune, everything that makes life desirable to an ambitious man were about to be swept away by the breath of my mouth, perhaps forever.

Softly, Edmund Ross says, "Not guilty."
The president is saved.

D. R. Anthony writes to Edmund Ross, *Kansas repudiates you as she does all perjurers and skunks*. Others accuse him of taking bribes. He hasn't.

What he has done is to show tremendous courage. Ross did what he believed was right; he didn't let other people bully him. Later generations will call him a hero, but most people in his time don't understand. Ross is never elected to political office again.

When Thaddeus Stevens hears the vote he says, "The country is going to the devil." Stevens was wrong.

Johnson's mulishness was a disaster for the nation—no question of that. He encouraged racial bigotry. He was a poor leader. He slowed the process of achieving "justice for all." But there were two issues involved, and getting them separated was complicated.

Impeaching a president is a big step. The Constitution says it is to be done for "high crimes and misdemeanors." Johnson was not guilty of that. So it was his ideas that were really on trial. Those ideas were awful—but ideas aren't meant to be impeached or tried. The Founders meant for voters to vote bad ideas out of office.

Most Americans came to believe that the impeachment and trial were mistakes that had threatened the constitutional balance of power. They blamed Stevens and forgot his accomplishments. The 14th and 15th amendments would not have been achieved without him.

Stevens lived for only a few weeks after the trial ended. He spent those weeks writing laws and working on a plan for free schools for the District of Columbia. When he died, his body lay in state in the Capitol. Thousands walked past his casket. Only Abraham Lincoln had received more tribute. He was buried in a cemetery where blacks and whites rest side by side. The words chiseled on his tombstone are his own. They didn't surprise anyone who knew him:

I repose in this quiet and secluded spot,
Not from any natural preference for solitude
But, finding other Cemeteries limited as to Race by Charter Rules,
I have chosen this that I might illustrate in my death
The Principles which I advocated
Through a long life.

In Andrew Johnson's impeachment trial, the committee representing the House of Representatives included Thaddeus Stevens (front row, second from left). ▼

A Failed Revolution

Successful revolutions are rare.

During the Reconstruction period black lawmakers voted for schools, roads, and railroads. Schools, roads, and railroads are especially helpful to the average person. However, you need to levy taxes to pay for them, and taxes cost big landowners more than they cost the average person. Do you see a problem here? The landowners were not happy at all about some of the new laws.

Besides, there was another problem at the bottom of all this. If blacks could be congressmen and responsible citizens, then the whole idea of black inferiority didn't make sense. So slavery must really have been wrong. Many white Southerners still couldn't accept that idea. They had been through a ghastly war. They had lost their loved ones. If slavery was wrong, their sons and fathers had died for nothing. How could they believe that? White Southerners were not monsters; they were not angels; they were human beings. They needed help understanding what had happened to them and to their beloved South.

Abraham Lincoln, who might have led them wisely, was gone, killed by an assassin's bullet. The former Confederates hated the Radical Republicans—and, as you know, Andrew Johnson was the wrong man as president. So was the next president. This may come as a surprise to you, but Ulysses S. Grant—General Grant, the hero of the Union, the powerful warrior who had once been compared to the Greek hero Ulysses—was now sometimes called "Useless" S. Grant. Being a great general had made him a popular hero and gotten him elected president, but it had not prepared him for political life.

▲ Grant struggles under the burden of the country's problems. A newspaper editor wrote, "It is a political position and he knows nothing of politics."

Most Americans loved President Grant. And there were good reasons for that. He was a fine man, honest and honorable. But he was too trusting. Grant trusted the men around him; unfortunately, they turned out to be untrustworthy. They stole from the nation. They took millions and millions of dollars in public lands and resources. Ulysses Grant, and the American people, were their victims. The Grant years were years of terrible corruption.

The world was changing. The United States was going from agrarian nation to industrial giant. But no one quite understood what was ahead, and at first almost no controls were put on the new businesses. Many Americans were soon making useful goods and providing important services; but others took advantage, sold empty promises, and ran with unearned profits.

That economic chaos made many Americans forget about civil rights. By the time Grant left the presidency, in 1877, the North's citizens were tired of hearing about the need for a just society in the South. They had their own problems, and when they thought about it, they realized their society wasn't perfect, either. Maybe they should leave the South alone. When hate groups began blaming immigrants and blacks for the nation's problems, many listened. Then, when Rutherford B. Hayes promised to pull the federal troops out of the South if he became president, he got elected. And he kept his promise.

The old guard in the South began to take power again. And they didn't worry about sharing it. They didn't worry about justice for all. They passed laws that made voters pay *a poll tax:* that meant most blacks couldn't vote. They made it impossible for blacks to get a decent education or to buy land. They would not allow blacks to have fair trials. Soon many Southern blacks were not much better off than they had been when they were slaves. Some were worse off. It was clear: Reconstruction was failing.

All of that still wasn't enough for some white racists. So they joined terrorist organizations like the Ku Klux Klan and lynched and intimidated blacks who wanted to vote. To *lynch* means to "execute without due process of the law, especially by hanging." In simpler words: lynching is murder, usually murder by a mob.

▲ This illustration, titled *One Vote Less,* depicts how black voters were suppressed by violence and terror.

Poll is an old word for "head." So a poll tax is a tax you pay just because you're a person. Most blacks couldn't afford to pay the tax, and if you didn't pay the tax you weren't allowed to vote.

The good people didn't stop the bad actors. Most of the Northerners who had tried to help in the South got discouraged and left. Some of them were lynched. The Southern whites who tried to be fair were ridiculed—or lynched. Slowly, a policy of separation of races was instituted—it was called "segregation." Blacks were not allowed to sit on the same seats that whites used. They were not allowed in the same restaurants. They had to sit in the back of horse-drawn public streetcars. They could not go to school with whites. State and local laws were passed that made all those unfair things possible. No one did anything about them. The Supreme Court didn't seem to care—sometimes it sided with the racists. Whites and blacks who tried to fight for equal rights were forlorn. There was no leader big enough to reach people's hearts.

When President Rutherford B. Hayes did what he had promised—he pulled the soldiers out of the South—congressional Reconstruction was just about finished. In Arkansas, men with guns made black lawmakers leave the state. In most Southern states blacks were prevented from voting.

An Appeal for Justice

The following petition was made to the U.S. Congress on March 25, 1871:

We the colored citizens of Frankfort and vicinity…in this state of Kentucky…would respectfully state that life, liberty, and property are unprotected among the colored race of this state. Organized bands of desperate and lawless men, mainly composed of soldiers of the late Rebel armies, armed, disciplined, and disguised, and bound by oath and secret obligations, have by force, terror, and violence subverted all civil society among the colored people.… We believe you are not familiar with…the Ku Klux Klan's riding nightly over the country, going from county to county, and… spreading terror wherever they go by robbing, whipping, ravishing, and killing our people without provocation.… Our people are driven from their homes in great numbers.… We would state that we have been law-abiding citizens, pay our tax, and, in many parts of the state, our people have been driven from the polls—refused the right to vote. Many have been slaughtered while attempting to vote; we ask how long is this state of things to last. We appeal to you…to enact some laws that will protect us and that will enable us to exercise the rights of citizens.

Members of the Ku Klux Klan often rode at night, hiding their identities behind white robes and hoods. ▼

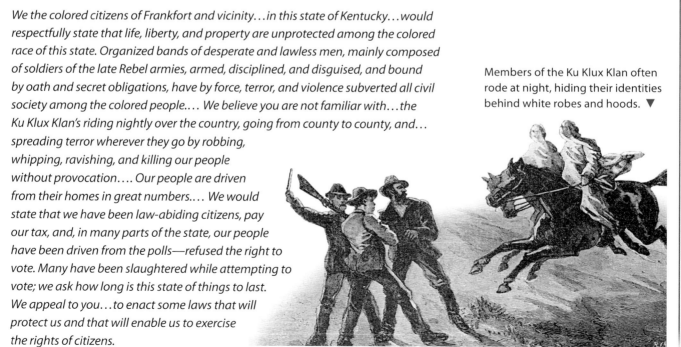

Sharecropping

In the South, a new form of farming had developed after the war. It was called "sharecropping." A landowner supplied land, tools, and seed to a landless farmer, who then gave the owner one-third or one-half of all he grew. At first it seemed a fair system, but it rarely turned out that way. After sharecroppers had paid the landowner they usually had almost nothing left for themselves.

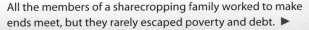
All the members of a sharecropping family worked to make ends meet, but they rarely escaped poverty and debt. ▶

In one Southern state after another, lawmakers opposed to Reconstruction took charge. By 1877, as one historian has put it, Reconstruction had breathed its "final gasp."

Reconstruction wasn't totally over in 1877, but it was close to it. To make things worse, a Northerner, a fool named Jim Crow (a clown character who believed in separating the races), had come south.

That policy of white supremacy didn't help either the black or the white South. It did just the opposite. Industry and new ideas abounded in the North and West. But until fairness began

No Redeeming Features

The Republican Party was the party of Reconstruction. The Democratic Party (in the South) was determined to bring back as much of the old South as possible. Conservative Democrats called themselves "redeemers." The Redeemer Democrats had no interest in working with blacks. They were not concerned with black needs, and they certainly didn't want blacks to hold office. Nor did the Democrats approve of the idea of an active government trying to improve conditions for all people. The Republicans wanted the state governments to support railroads and businesses and to improve schools and welfare institutions (orphanages, prisons, etc.). The Redeemer Democrats laughed at those ideas (they all cost money). The Democrats wanted to lower taxes. They redeemed one state after another, driving the Republicans from power. (Remember, this was the 19th century; the parties are very different today.)

▲ Cotton on the wharf in
New Orleans in 1884

to return (after World War II) immigrants and most big industries stayed away from much of the South. Southern industry consisted of foundries, carpentry shops, and small manufacturing plants. Tobacco and cotton were still the major crops. Wages were low. The South became the poorest section of the nation. Southern students ranked at the bottom of the national charts. (This is where studying history helps you understand some things. Poor leadership cost the South prosperity. It limited opportunities for all its citizens.)

But don't be too hard on the South. A fair-minded interracial society didn't exist anywhere in the world in the 19th century. Not in the North, not in the West, not in Europe, not in Asia, not in Africa, not anywhere. In the United States a first step had been taken. That first step had been in the South during Reconstruction. And that time had also produced those three remarkable amendments: the 13th, 14th, and 15th.

In Virginia, a few blacks continued to be elected to state office until 1901, when Virginia held a convention to write another state constitution. The new constitution took the vote from most blacks and most poor whites. Now Reconstruction was really dead and done with. It had failed in its goal: to make the South into a just society where people of all races could live in harmony.

In the second half of the 20th century a black minister would help heal the old wounds and begin real reconstruction in America. And then, finally, America would have its first black governor. He would be elected in Virginia.

Appendix:
Some Primary Sources

James Monroe, The Monroe Doctrine (1823)

The Monroe Doctrine declared that the United States opposed the establishment of new European colonies and nondemocratic governments in the Western Hemisphere. President James Monroe proclaimed this principle in 1823, at a time when the United States was concerned about Russian and European activity in the Americas. British leaders suggested that the United States and Britain issue a joint statement against European intervention in Latin America, but Secretary of State John Quincy Adams recommended that President Monroe issue a unilateral statement. The president did. President Monroe announced that the United States would not interfere in European affairs and regarded the Western Hemisphere closed to future European colonization. He pledged that the United States would regard any European attempt "to extend their system to any portion of this hemisphere as dangerous to our peace and safety." During the early 20th century, the Monroe Doctrine was often used to justify American intervention in Central America and the Caribbean. During the Cold War, it was used to justify U.S. support for anti-Communist governments in Latin America and opposition to unfriendly governments in Cuba, Guatemala, Nicaragua, and elsewhere.

amicable: friendly

acceded: agreed

manifesting: demonstrating

solicitude: care

cultivate: nurture, grow

At the proposal of the Russian imperial government, made through the minister of the Emperor residing here, full power and instructions have been transmitted to the Minister of the United States at St. Petersburg, to arrange, by amicable negotiation, the respective rights and interests of the two nations on the northwest coast of this continent. A similar proposal has been made by his Imperial Majesty to the government of Great Britain, which has likewise been acceded to. The government of the United States has been desirous, by this friendly proceeding, of manifesting the great value which they have invariably attached to the friendship of the emperor, and their solicitude to cultivate the best understanding with his government. In the discussions to which this interest has given rise, and in the arrangements by which they may terminate, the occasion has been judged proper for asserting, as a principle in which the rights and interests of the United States are involved, that the American continents, by the free and independent condition which they have assumed and maintain, are henceforth not to be considered as subjects for future colonization by any European powers.

It was stated at the commencement of the last session, that a great effort was then making in Spain and Portugal, to improve the condition of the people of those countries; and that it appeared to be conducted with extraordinary moderation. It need scarcely be remarked, that the result has been, so far, very different from what was then anticipated. Of events in that quarter of the globe, with which we have so much intercourse, and from which we derive our origin, we have always been anxious and interested spectators. The citizens of the United States cherish sentiments the most friendly, in favor of the liberty and happiness of their fellow men on that side of the Atlantic. In the wars of the European powers, in matters relating to themselves, we have never taken any part, nor does it comport with our policy so to do. It is only when our rights are invaded, or seriously menaced, that we resent injuries, or make preparation for our defense. With the movements in this hemisphere, we are, of necessity, more immediately connected, and by causes which must be obvious to all enlightened and impartial observers. The political system of the allied powers is essentially different, in this respect, from that of America. This difference proceeds from that which exists in their respective governments. And to the defence of our own, which has been achieved by the loss of so much blood and treasure, and matured by the wisdom of their most enlightened citizens, and under which we have enjoyed unexampled felicity, this whole nation is devoted. We owe it, therefore, to candor, and to the amicable relations existing between the United States and those powers, to declare, that we should consider any attempt on their part to extend their system to any portion of this hemisphere, as dangerous to our peace and safety. With the existing

colonization: made subservient to a foreign or distant land

commencement: beginning

derive: gain

comport: agree

hemisphere: half of the globe

impartial: not favoring one side or another

felicity: happiness

candor: honesty

colonies or dependencies of any European power, we have not interfered, and shall not interfere. But, with the governments who have declared their independence and maintained it, and whose independence we have, on great consideration, and on just principles, acknowledged, we could not view any interposition for the purpose of oppressing them, or controlling, in any other manner, their destiny, by any European power, in any other light than as the manifestation of an unfriendly disposition towards the United States. In the war between these new governments and Spain, we declared our neutrality at the time of their recognition, and to this we have adhered, and shall continue to adhere, provided no change shall occur, which, in the judgment of the competent authorities of this government, shall make a corresponding change, on the part of the United States, indispensable to their security.

The late events in Spain and Portugal, shew that Europe is still unsettled. Of this important fact, no stronger proof can be adduced than that the allied powers should have thought it proper, on any principle satisfactory to themselves, to have interposed, by force, in the internal concerns of Spain. To what extent such interposition may be carried, on the same principle, is a question, in which all independent powers, whose governments differ from theirs, are interested; even those most remote, and surely none more so than the United States. Our policy, in regard to Europe, which was adopted at an early stage of the wars which have so long agitated that quarter of the globe, nevertheless remains the same, which is, not to interfere in the internal concerns of any of its powers; to consider the government de facto as the legitimate government for us; to cultivate friendly relations with it, and to preserve those relations by a frank, firm, and manly policy, meeting, in all instances, the just claims of every power; submitting to injuries from none. But, in regard to those continents, circumstances are eminently and conspicuously different.

interposition: getting involved with the affairs of another

oppressing: holding down or back

manifestation: sign

disposition: attitude

neutrality: lack of special favorites

adhered: stuck

competent: appropriate

shew: show

adduced: shown

interposed: interfered

agitated: stirred up

de facto: in reality, but not by law

eminently: importantly

conspicuously: clearly

It is impossible that the allied powers should extend their political system to any portion of either continent, without endangering our peace and happiness; nor can any one believe that our Southern Brethren, if left to themselves, would adopt it of their own accord. It is equally impossible, therefore, that we should behold such interposition, in any form, with indifference. If we look to the comparative strength and resources of Spain and those new governments, and their distance from each other, it must be obvious that she can never subdue them. It is still the true policy of the United States, to leave the parties to themselves, in the hope that other powers will pursue the same course.

subdue: beat

From "Memorial and Protest of the Cherokee Nation" (1836)

As late as the 1820s, the Creeks, Choctaws, Chickasaws, and Cherokees occupied much of the land that would become the South's Cotton Kingdom. After Andrew Jackson became president, Congress adopted the Indian Removal Act of 1830, providing funds to acquire tribal lands and relocate the tribes living there to Oklahoma and Arkansas. By 1840, almost all of these tribes had been moved west of the Mississippi River.

The Cherokees had little interest in moving west. In 1791, they had signed a treaty that recognized Cherokee territory in Georgia as independent. An 1832 Supreme Court decision, *Worcester v. Georgia*, ruled that "The Cherokee Nation is a distinct community occupying its own territory in which the laws of Georgia have no right to enter without the consent of the Cherokees." In 1835, however, President Jackson persuaded a minority of Cherokees to sign a treaty giving up their homelands in western Georgia for new Western lands. The tribe's leaders submitted the following "Memorial and Protest of the Cherokee Nation" to Congress in 1836. It showed that President Jackson had obtained the 1835 treaty by fraud. Nevertheless, the army evicted the Cherokees from their land in 1838. Thousands of Cherokees died from malnutrition, disease, and physical hardship as they followed the Trail of Tears westward.

We are aware that some persons suppose it will be for our advantage to remove beyond the Mississippi. We think otherwise. Our people universally think otherwise. Thinking that it would be fatal to their interests, they have almost to a man sent their memorial to Congress, deprecating the necessity of a removal.... It is incredible that Georgia should ever have enacted the oppressive laws to which reference is here made, unless she had supposed that something extremely terrific in its character was necessary in order to make the Cherokees willing to remove. We are not willing to remove; and if we could be brought to this extremity, it would be not by argument, nor because our judgment was satisfied, not because our condition will be improved; but only because we cannot endure to be deprived of our national and individual rights and subjected to a process of intolerable oppression.

We wish to remain on the land of our fathers. We have a perfect and original right to remain without interruption or molestation. The treaties with us, and laws of the United States made in pursuance of treaties, guaranty our residence and our privileges, and secure us against intruders. Our only request is, that these treaties may be fulfilled, and these laws executed.

But if we are compelled to leave our country, we see nothing but ruin before us. The country west of the Arkansas territory is unknown to us. From what we can learn of it, we have no prepossessions in its favor. All the inviting parts of it, as we believe, are preoccupied by various Indian nations, to which it has been assigned. They would regard us as intruders.... The far greater part of that region is, beyond all controversy, badly supplied with wood and water; and no Indian tribe can live as agriculturists without these articles. All our neighbors...would speak a language totally different from ours, and practice different customs. The original possessors of that region are now wandering savages lurking for prey in the neighborhood.... Were the country to which we are urged much better than it is represented to be,...still it is not the land of our birth, nor of our affections. It contains neither the scenes of our childhood, nor the graves of our fathers....

deprecating: protesting against

oppressive: unjust in the application of power

prepossessions: preliminary opinions

agriculturalists: farmers

We have been called a poor, ignorant, and degraded people. We certainly are not rich; nor have we ever boasted of our knowledge, or our moral or intellectual elevation. But there is not a man within our limits so ignorant as not to know that he has a right to live on the land of his fathers, in the possession of his immemorial privileges, and that this right has been acknowledged by the United States; nor is there a man so degraded as not to feel a keen sense of injury, on being deprived of his right and driven into exile....

From Sojourner Truth, "A'n't I a Woman": Address to the Women's Rights Convention, Akron, Ohio (1851)

As a slave in New York's Hudson River Valley, Sojourner Truth was known simply as Isabella. But a decade and a half after escaping bondage, she adopted a new name. As Sojourner Truth, she became a legend in the struggle to abolish slavery and achieve equal rights for women. In a speech delivered at a women's rights convention in Akron, Ohio, in 1851, she demanded recognition that hard labor made enslaved and working women the equals of men. "I have plowed and reaped and husked and chopped and mowed," she said. "Can any man do more than that?" At her death in 1883, Sojourner Truth was rightly remembered as one of America's most eloquent opponents of discrimination in all forms.

Sojourner Truth never learned to write, and so our knowledge of what she said is based on the recollections of people who attended her speeches. The most dramatic account of her 1851 speech was by Frances Dana Gage, an abolitionist who presided over the convention. Published 12 years after the event, Gage's recollections almost certainly contain some inaccuracies. Earlier accounts do not indicate that Truth had to face down a hostile audience that was afraid of mixing the causes of women's rights and antislavery. Nor do these earlier descriptions have her repeat the famous words, "Ain't I a woman?" It is unlikely that the Northern-born Truth spoke in the dialect that Gage and other whites used to record the language of African Americans during the 19th century. Nevertheless, Gage's memorable account of the speech certainly gives us a sense of Sojourner Truth's power as an orator.

Well, children, where there is so much racket there must be something out o'kilter. I think that 'twixt the Negroes of the South and the women of the North all a-talking about rights, the white men will be in a fix pretty soon.

But what's all this here talking about? That man over there says that women need to be helped into carriages, and lifted over ditches, and to have the best place everywhere. Nobody ever helps me into carriages, or over mud puddles or gives me any best place (*and raising herself to her full height and her voice to a pitch like rolling thunder, she asked*), and a'n't I a woman? Look at me! Look at my arm! (*And she bared her right arm to the shoulder, showing her tremendous muscular power.*) I have plowed, and planted, and gathered into barns, and no man could head me— and a'n't I a woman? I could work as much and eat as much as a man (when I could get it), and bear the lash as well—and a'n't I a woman? I have borne thirteen children and seen them almost all sold off into slavery, and when I cried out with a mother's grief, none but Jesus heard—and a'n't I a woman? Then they talk about this thing in the head—what's this they call it? (*"Intellect,"* *whispered someone near.*) That's it honey. What's that got to do with woman's rights or Negroes' rights? If my cup won't hold but a pint and yours holds a quart, wouldn't you be mean not to let me have my little half-measure full? (*And she pointed her significant finger and sent a keen glance at the minister who had made the argument. The cheering was long and loud.*)

Then that little man in black there, he says women can't have as much rights as man, 'cause Christ wasn't a woman. Where did your Christ come from? (*Rolling thunder could not have stilled that crowd as did those deep, wonderful tones, as she stood there with outstretched arms and eye of fire. Raising her voice still louder, she repeated,*) Where did your Christ come from? From God and a woman. Man had nothing to do with him. (*Oh! what a rebuke she gave the little man.*)

(Turning again to another objector, she took up the defense of mother Eve. I cannot follower [sic] her through it all. It was pointed, and witty, and solemn, eliciting at almost every sentence deafening applause; and she ended [sic] by asserting that) If the first woman God ever made was strong enough to turn the world upside down, all alone, these together *(and she glanced her eye over us)*, ought to be able to turn it back and get it right side up again; and now they are asking to do it, the men better let them. *(Long-continued cheering.)*

'Bliged to you for hearing on me, and now old Sojourner hasn't got anything more to say.

eliciting: drawing out

From the Declaration of Sentiments (1848)

Seneca Falls, New York, is the birthplace of the women's rights movement in the United States. On July 19, 1848, the first convention dedicated to equal treatment of women opened in this fast-growing village of 4,000. Some 300 people, including 40 men, attended the meeting at the redbrick Wesleyan Methodist Chapel.

After a series of brief speeches by other delegates, Elizabeth Cady Stanton read a bold statement of purpose. Modeled on the Declaration of Independence, this Declaration of Sentiments stated, "We hold these truths to be self-evident, that all men and women are created equal." It listed a series of injuries that men had inflicted on women. It concluded by accusing men of "endeavoring to destroy" a woman's "confidence in her own powers, to lessen her self-respect, and to make her willing to lead a dependent and abject life."

The convention then voted on a series of resolutions. One by one the resolutions were approved, until the convention reached the ninth, demanding the vote for women. Opponents considered this demand impractical, but a speech by the abolitionist Frederick Douglass persuaded many delegates that rights could not be restricted by gender. When the meeting was over, exactly 100 people—68 women and 32 men—signed the Declaration of Sentiments. Only two women who signed the document lived long enough to see women gain the right to vote in 1920.

hitherto: so far

inalienable: unable to be separated from

prudence: common sense

transient: changing

usurpations: acts of theft

evinces: shows

despotism: unchecked power

elective franchise: vote

When, in the course of human events, it becomes necessary for one portion of the family of man to assume among the people of the earth a position different from that which they have hitherto occupied, but one to which the laws of nature and of nature's God entitle them, a decent respect to the opinions of mankind requires that they should declare the causes that impel them to such a course.

We hold these truths to be self-evident: that all men and women are created equal; that they are endowed by their Creator with certain inalienable rights; that among these are life, liberty, and the pursuit of happiness; that to secure these rights governments are instituted, deriving their just powers from the consent of the governed. Whenever any form of government becomes destructive of these ends, it is the right of those who suffer from it to refuse allegiance to it, and to insist upon the institution of a new government, laying its foundation on such principles, and organizing its powers in such form, as to them shall seem most likely to effect their safety and happiness. Prudence, indeed, will dictate that governments long established should not be changed for light and transient causes; and accordingly all experience hath shown that mankind are more disposed to suffer, while evils are sufferable, than to right themselves by abolishing the forms to which they were accustomed. But when a long train of abuses and usurpations, pursuing invariably the same object, evinces a design to reduce them under absolute despotism, it is their duty to throw off such government, and to provide new guards for their future security. Such has been the patient sufferance of the women under this government, and such is now the necessity which constrains them to demand the equal station to which they are entitled.

The history of mankind is a history of repeated injuries and usurpations on the part of man toward woman, having in direct object the establishment of an absolute tyranny over her. To prove this, let facts be submitted to a candid world.

He has never permitted her to exercise her inalienable right to the elective franchise.

He has compelled her to submit to laws, in the formation of which she had no voice....

Having deprived her of this first right of a citizen, the elective franchise, thereby leaving her without representation in the halls of legislation, he has oppressed her on all sides.

He has made her, if married, in the eye of the law, civilly dead.

He has taken from her all right in property, even to the wages she earns....

He has monopolized nearly all the profitable employments, and from those she is permitted to follow, she receives but a scanty remuneration. He closes against her all the avenues to wealth and distinction which he considers most honorable to himself. As a teacher of theology, medicine, or law, she is not known.

monopolized: taken control of

scanty: very little

remuneration: pay, compensation

He has denied her the facilities for obtaining a thorough education, all colleges being closed against her....

He has endeavored, in every way that he could, to destroy her confidence in her own powers, to lessen her self-respect, and to make her willing to lead a dependent and abject life.

abject: without dignity or liberty

Now, in view of this entire disfranchisement of one-half the people of this country, their social and religious degradation—in view of the unjust laws above mentioned, and because women do feel themselves aggrieved, oppressed, and fraudulently deprived of their most sacred rights, we insist that they have immediate admission to all the rights and privileges which belong to them as citizens of the United States.

degradation: humiliation

aggrieved: pained

oppressed: held down or back

In entering upon the great work before us, we anticipate no small amount of misconception, misrepresentation, and ridicule; but we shall use every instrumentality within our power to effect our object. We shall employ agents, circulate tracts, petition the State and National legislatures, and endeavor to enlist the pulpit and the press in our behalf. We hope this Convention will be followed by a series of Conventions embracing every part of the country.

instrumentality: method

tracts: pamphlets

Abraham Lincoln, The Gettysburg Address (1863)

The Battle of Gettysburg, fought on July 3, 1863, was the bloodiest battle of the Civil War. It resulted in 50,000 casualties, including 8,000 deaths. In November 1863, with the war still raging, President Lincoln went to Gettysburg to dedicate a military cemetery. He hoped to use the occasion to restate the nation's ideals and to define the aims of the war. Although Lincoln said nothing specifically about slavery or the Emancipation Proclamation, he explained in just 272 words that the "honored dead" had fought for certain fundamental democratic principles, especially the idea of human equality.

Instead of recounting the details of the battle, Lincoln said that the Battle of Gettysburg was a test of constitutional government. And he emphasized a rededication to the ideals of the Declaration of Independence.

four score and seven: 87; a score is 20 years

Four score and seven years ago our fathers brought forth, on this continent, a new nation, conceived in Liberty, and dedicated to the proposition that all men are created equal.

Now we are engaged in a great civil war, testing whether that nation, or any nation so conceived, and so dedicated, can long endure. We are met on a great battlefield of that war. We have come to dedicate a portion of that field, as a final resting-place for those who here gave their lives, that that nation might live. It is altogether fitting and proper that we should do this.

consecrate: make sacred

hallow: worship

But, in a larger sense, we can not dedicate—we can not consecrate—we can not hallow—this ground. The brave men, living and dead, who struggled here, have consecrated it far above our poor power to add or detract. The world will little note, nor long remember what we say here, but it can never forget what they did here. It is for us the living, rather, to be dedicated here to the unfinished work which they who fought here have thus far so nobly advanced. It is rather for us to be here dedicated to the great task remaining before us—that from these honored dead we take increased devotion to that cause for which they here gave the last full measure of devotion—that we here highly resolve that these dead shall not have died in vain—that this nation, under God, shall have a new birth of freedom—and that government of the people, by the people, for the people, shall not perish from the earth.

Abraham Lincoln, Second Inaugural Address (1865)

Delivered in March 1865, only a month before the end of the Civil War, Lincoln's Second Inaugural Address was intended to reunite the nation. His address stressed the similarities between the North and the South—that they "both read the same Bible, and pray to the same God"—and it cautioned the North against feeling superior. "Let us judge not," he says, "that we be not judged." Speaking to an audience deeply familiar with the Bible, Lincoln asked Northerners and Southerners to regard the war as atonement for the sin of slavery. Since both Northerners and Southerners had tolerated slavery, both sections had to pay the price for their sin in blood. Lincoln closed his address with a plea for harmony and a commitment to care for all the war's victims.

Fellow Countrymen:

At this second appearing to take the oath of the presidential office, there is less occasion for an extended address than there was at the first. Then a statement, somewhat in detail, of a course to be pursued, seemed fitting and proper. Now, at the expiration of four years, during which public declarations have been constantly called forth on every point and phase of the great contest which still absorbs the attention, and engrosses the energies of the nation, little that is new could be presented. The progress of our arms, upon which all else chiefly depends, is as well known to the public as to myself; and it is, I trust, reasonably satisfactory and encouraging to all. With high hope for the future, no prediction in regard to it is ventured.

expiration: end

engrosses: takes up all of

On the occasion corresponding to this four years ago, all thoughts were anxiously directed to an impending civil-war. All dreaded it—all sought to avert it. While the inaugural address was being delivered from this place, devoted altogether to saving the Union without war, insurgent agents were in the city seeking to destroy it without war—seeking to dissolve the Union, and divide effects, by negotiation. Both parties deprecated war; but one of them would make war rather than let the nation survive; and the other would accept war rather than let it perish. And the war came.

One eighth of the whole population were colored slaves, not distributed generally over the Union, but localized in the Southern part of it. These slaves constituted a peculiar and powerful interest. All knew that this interest was, somehow, the cause of the war. To strengthen, perpetuate, and extend this interest was the object for which the insurgents would rend the Union, even by war; while the government claimed no right to do more than to restrict the territorial enlargement of it. Neither party expected for the war, the magnitude, or the duration, which it has already attained. Neither anticipated that the cause of the conflict might cease with, or even before, the conflict itself should cease. Each looked for an easier triumph, and a result less fundamental and astounding. Both read the same Bible, and pray to the same God; and each invokes His aid against the other. It may seem strange that any men should dare to ask a just God's assistance in wringing their bread from the sweat of other men's faces; but let us judge not that we be not judged. The prayers of both could not be answered; that of neither has been answered fully. The Almighty has His own purposes. "Woe unto the world because of offences! for it must needs be that offences come; but woe to that man by whom the offence cometh!" If we shall suppose that American Slavery is one of those offences which, in the providence of God, must needs come, but which, having continued through His appointed time, He now wills to remove, and that He gives to both North and South,

impending: coming soon

avert: avoid

insurgent: rebelling against the government

colored: African American

perpetuate: make last

magnitude: greatness

duration: length of time

invokes: calls forth

providence: divine direction

this terrible war, as the woe due to those by whom the offence came, shall we discern therein any departure from those divine attributes which the believers in a Living God always ascribe to Him? Fondly do we hope—fervently do we pray— that this mighty scourge of war may speedily pass away. Yet, if God wills that it continue, until all the wealth piled by the bond-man's two hundred and fifty years of unrequited toil shall be sunk, and until every drop of blood drawn with the lash, shall be paid by another drawn with the sword, as was said three thousand years ago, so still it must be said "the judgments of the Lord, are true and righteous altogether."

With malice toward none; with charity for all; with firmness in the right, as God gives us to see the right, let us strive on to finish the work we are in; to bind up the nation's wounds; to care for him who shall have borne the battle, and for his widow, and his orphan—to do all which may achieve and cherish a just, and a lasting peace, among ourselves, and with all nations.

discern: recognize

ascribe: see as belonging

scourge: great suffering

bond-man: slave

unrequited: unpaid

malice: a desire to harm others

The Fifty States

Alabama
Population 4,779,736*
State capital Montgomery
Statehood December 14, 1819
State bird Yellowhammer
State flower Camellia
State tree Southern pine
Land area 50,744 square miles

Alaska
Population 710,231
State capital Juneau
Statehood January 3, 1959
State bird Willow ptarmigan
State flower Forget-me-not
State tree Sitka spruce
Land area 571,951 square miles

Arizona
Population 6,392,017
State capital Phoenix
Statehood February 14, 1912
State bird Cactus wren
State flower Saguaro (giant cactus)
State tree Palo verde
Land area 113,635 square miles

Arkansas
Population 2,915,918
State capital Little Rock
Statehood June 15, 1836
State bird Mockingbird
State flower Apple blossom
State tree Pine tree
Land area 52,068 square miles

California
Population 37,253,956
State capital Sacramento
Statehood September 9, 1850
State bird California valley quail
State flower Golden poppy
State tree California redwood
Land area 155,959 square miles

Colorado
Population 5,029,196
State capital Denver
Statehood August 1, 1876
State bird Lark bunting
State flower White and lavender columbine
State tree Colorado blue spruce
Land area 103,718 square miles

Connecticut
Population 3,574,097
State capital Hartford
Statehood January 9, 1788
State bird Robin
State flower Mountain laurel
State tree White oak
Land area 4,845 square miles

Delaware
Population 897,934
State capital Dover
Statehood December 7, 1787
State bird Blue hen chicken
State flower Peach blossom
State tree American holly
Land area 1,954 square miles

Florida
Population 18,801,310
State capital Tallahassee
Statehood March 3, 1845
State bird Mockingbird
State flower Orange blossom
State tree Sabal palm
Land area 53,927 square miles

Georgia
Population 9,687,653
State capital Atlanta
Statehood January 2, 1788
State bird Brown thrasher
State flower Cherokee rose
State tree Live oak
Land area 57,906 square miles

Hawaii
Population 1,360,301
State capital Honolulu
Statehood August 21, 1959
State bird Nene (Hawaiian goose)
State flower Yellow hibiscus
State tree Kukui
Land area 6,423 square miles

Idaho
Population 1,567,582
State capital Boise
Statehood July 3, 1890
State bird Mountain bluebird
State flower Mock orange
State tree Western white pine
Land area 82,747 square miles

Illinois
Population 12,830,632
State capital Springfield
Statehood December 3, 1818
State bird Cardinal
State flower Native violet
State tree Oak
Land area 55,584 square miles

Indiana
Population 6,483,802
State capital Indianapolis
Statehood December 11, 1816
State bird Cardinal
State flower Peony
State tree Tulip tree
Land area 35,867 square miles

Iowa
Population 3,046,355
State capital Des Moines
Statehood December 28, 1846
State bird Eastern goldfinch
State flower Wild rose
State tree Oak
Land area 55,869 square miles

Kansas

Population 2,853,118
State capital Topeka
Statehood January 29, 1861
State bird Western meadowlark
State flower Sunflower
State tree Cottonwood
Land area 81,815 square miles

Kentucky

Population 4,339,367
State capital Frankfort
Statehood June 1, 1792
State bird Kentucky cardinal
State flower Goldenrod
State tree Kentucky coffee tree
Land area 39,728 square miles

Louisiana

Population 4,533,372
State capital Baton Rouge
Statehood April 30, 1812
State bird Brown pelican
State flower Magnolia
State tree Bald cypress
Land area 43,562 square miles

Maine

Population 1,328,361
State capital Augusta
Statehood March 15, 1820
State bird Chickadee
State flower White pine cone
and flower
State tree White pine
Land area 30,862 square miles

Maryland

Population 5,773,552
State capital Annapolis
Statehood April 28, 1788
State bird Baltimore oriole
State flower Black-eyed Susan
State tree White oak
Land area 9,774 square miles

Massachusetts

Population 6,547,629
State capital Boston
Statehood February 6, 1788
State bird Chickadee
State flower Mayflower
State tree American elm
Land area 7,840 square miles

Michigan

Population 9,883,640
State capital Lansing
Statehood January 26, 1837
State bird Robin
State flower Apple blossom
State tree White pine
Land area 56,804 square miles

Minnesota

Population 5,303,925
State capital St. Paul
Statehood May 11, 1858
State bird Common loon
State flower Pink and white
lady slipper
State tree Norway pine
Land area 79,610 square miles

Mississippi

Population 2,967,297
State capital Jackson
Statehood December 10, 1817
State bird Mockingbird
State flower Magnolia
State tree Magnolia
Land area 46,907 square miles

Missouri

Population 5,988,927
State capital Jefferson City
Statehood August 10, 1821
State bird Eastern bluebird
State flower Hawthorn
State tree Flowering dogwood
Land area 68,886 square miles

Montana

Population 989,415
State capital Helena
Statehood November 8, 1889
State bird Western meadowlark
State flower Bitterroot
State tree Ponderosa pine
Land area 145,552 square miles

Nebraska

Population 1,826,341
State capital Lincoln
Statehood March 1, 1867
State bird Western meadowlark
State flower Goldenrod
State tree Cottonwood
Land area 76,872 square miles

Nevada

Population 2,700,551
State capital Carson City
Statehood October 31, 1864
State bird Mountain bluebird
State flower Sagebrush
State tree Pine nut
Land area 109,826 square miles

New Hampshire

Population 1,316,470
State capital Concord
Statehood June 21, 1788
State bird Purple finch
State flower Purple lilac
State tree White birch
Land area 8,968 square miles

New Jersey

Population 8,791,894
State capital Trenton
Statehood December 18, 1787
State bird Eastern goldfinch
State flower Purple violet
State tree Red oak
Land area 7,417 square miles

New Mexico

Population 2,059,179
State capital Santa Fe
Statehood January 16, 1912
State bird Roadrunner
State flower Yucca flower
State tree Pine nut
Land area 121,356 square miles

New York

Population 19,378,102
State capital Albany
Statehood July 26, 1788
State bird Bluebird
State flower Rose
State tree Sugar maple
Land area 47,214 square miles

North Carolina

Population 9,535,483
State capital Raleigh
Statehood November 21, 1789
State bird Cardinal
State flower Flowering dogwood
State tree Pine
Land area 48,711 square miles

North Dakota

Population 672,591
State capital Bismarck
Statehood November 2, 1889
State bird Western meadowlark
State flower Wild prairie rose
State tree American elm
Land area 68,976 square miles

Ohio

Population 11,536,504
State capital Columbus
Statehood March 1, 1803
State bird Cardinal
State flower Scarlet carnation
State tree Buckeye
Land area 40,948 square miles

Oklahoma

Population 3,751,351
State capital Oklahoma City
Statehood November 16, 1907
State bird Scissor-tailed flycatcher
State flower Mistletoe
State tree Redbud
Land area 68,667 square miles

Oregon

Population 3,831,074
State capital Salem
Statehood February 14, 1859
State bird Western meadowlark
State flower Oregon grape
State tree Douglas fir
Land area 95,997 square miles

Pennsylvania

Population 12,702,379
State capital Harrisburg
Statehood December 12, 1787
State bird Ruffed grouse
State flower Mountain laurel
State tree Hemlock
Land area 44,817 square miles

Rhode Island

Population 1,052,567
State capital Providence
Statehood May 29, 1790
State bird Rhode Island red
State flower Violet
State tree Red maple
Land area 1,045 square miles

South Carolina

Population 4,625,364
State capital Columbia
Statehood May 23, 1788
State bird Carolina wren
State flower Carolina jessamine
State tree Palmetto
Land area 30,109 square miles

South Dakota

Population 814,180
State capital Pierre
Statehood November 2, 1889
State bird Ring-necked pheasant
State flower American pasqueflower
State tree Black Hills spruce
Land area 75,885 square miles

Tennessee

Population 6,346,105
State capital Nashville
Statehood June 1, 1796
State bird Mockingbird
State flower Iris
State tree Tulip poplar
Land area 41,217 square miles

Texas

Population 25,145,561
State capital Austin
Statehood December 29, 1845
State bird Mockingbird
State flower Bluebonnet
State tree Pecan
Land area 261,797 square miles

Utah

Population 2,763,885
State capital Salt Lake City
Statehood January 4, 1896
State bird Seagull
State flower Sego lily
State tree Blue spruce
Land area 82,144 square miles

Vermont

Population 625,741
State capital Montpelier
Statehood March 4, 1791
State bird Hermit thrush
State flower Red clover
State tree Sugar maple
Land area 9,250 square miles

Virginia

Population 8,001,024
State capital Richmond
Statehood June 25, 1788
State bird Cardinal
State flower Dogwood flower
State tree Dogwood
Land area 39,594 square miles

Washington

Population 6,724,540
State capital Olympia
Statehood November 11, 1889
State bird Willow goldfinch
State flower Coast rhododendron
State tree Western hemlock
Land area 66,544 square miles

West Virginia

Population 1,852,994
State capital Charleston
Statehood June 20, 1863
State bird Cardinal
State flower Rhododendron
State tree Sugar maple
Land area 24,078 square miles

Wisconsin

Population 5,686,986
State capital Madison
Statehood May 29, 1848
State bird Robin
State flower Wood violet
State tree Sugar maple
Land area 54,310 square miles

Wyoming

Population 563,626
State capital Cheyenne
Statehood July 10, 1890
State bird Meadowlark
State flower Indian paintbrush
State tree Cottonwood
Land area 97,100 square miles

*population statistics based on 2010 U.S. Census

Presidents of the United States

	Born–Died	Years in Office	Political Party	Home State	Vice President
1 George Washington	1732–1799	1789–1797	None	Virginia	John Adams
2 John Adams	1735–1826	1797–1801	Federalist	Massachusetts	Thomas Jefferson
3 Thomas Jefferson	1743–1826	1801–1809	Republican*	Virginia	Aaron Burr George Clinton
4 James Madison	1751–1836	1809–1817	Republican	Virginia	George Clinton Elbridge Gerry
5 James Monroe	1758–1831	1817–1825	Republican	Virginia	Daniel D. Tompkins
6 John Quincy Adams	1767–1848	1825–1829	Republican	Massachusetts	John C. Calhoun
7 Andrew Jackson	1767–1845	1829–1837	Democratic	Tennessee	John C. Calhoun Martin Van Buren
8 Martin Van Buren	1782–1862	1837–1841	Democratic	New York	Richard M. Johnson
9 William Henry Harrison	1773–1841	1841	Whig	Ohio	John Tyler
10 John Tyler	1790–1862	1841–1845	Whig	Virginia	None
11 James K. Polk	1795–1849	1845–1849	Democratic	Tennessee	George M. Dallas
12 Zachary Taylor	1784–1850	1849–1850	Whig	Louisiana	Millard Fillmore
13 Millard Fillmore	1800–1874	1850–1853	Whig	New York	None
14 Franklin Pierce	1804–1869	1853–1857	Democratic	New Hampshire	William R. King
15 James Buchanan	1791–1868	1857–1861	Democratic	Pennsylvania	John C. Breckenridge
16 Abraham Lincoln	1809–1865	1861–1865	Republican	Illinois	Hannibal Hamlin Andrew Johnson
17 Andrew Johnson	1808–1875	1865–1869	Democratic (nominated for vice president on the Republican ticket)	Tennessee	None
18 Ulysses S. Grant	1822–1885	1869–1877	Republican	Illinois	Schuyler Colfax Henry Wilson
19 Rutherford B. Hayes	1822–1893	1877–1881	Republican	Ohio	William A. Wheeler
20 James A. Garfield	1831–1881	1881	Republican	Ohio	Chester A. Arthur

*The Republican Party of the early 1800s evolved into the modern Democratic Party. Today's Republican Party was founded in 1854.

	Born–Died	Years in Office	Political Party	Home State	Vice President
21 Chester A. Arthur	1829–1886	1881–1885	Republican	New York	None
22 Grover Cleveland	1837–1908	1885–1889	Democratic	New York	Thomas A. Hendricks
23 Benjamin Harrison	1833–1901	1889–1893	Republican	Indiana	Levi P. Morton
24 Grover Cleveland	1837–1908	1893–1897	Democratic	New York	Adlai E. Stevenson
25 William McKinley	1843–1901	1897–1901	Republican	Ohio	Garret A. Hobart Theodore Roosevelt
26 Theodore Roosevelt	1858–1919	1901–1909	Republican	New York	Charles W. Fairbanks
27 William Howard Taft	1857–1930	1909–1913	Republican	Ohio	James S. Sherman
28 Woodrow Wilson	1856–1924	1913–1921	Democratic	New Jersey	Thomas R. Marshall
29 Warren G. Harding	1865–1923	1921–1923	Republican	Ohio	Calvin Coolidge
30 Calvin Coolidge	1872–1933	1923–1929	Republican	Massachusetts	Charles G. Dawes
31 Herbert Hoover	1874–1964	1929–1933	Republican	California	Charles Curtis
32 Franklin D. Roosevelt	1882–1945	1933–1945	Democratic	New York	John Nance Garner Henry Wallace Harry S. Truman
33 Harry S. Truman	1884–1972	1945–1953	Democratic	Missouri	Alben W. Barkley
34 Dwight D. Eisenhower	1890–1969	1953–1961	Republican	Kansas	Richard M. Nixon
35 John F. Kennedy	1917–1963	1961–1963	Democratic	Massachusetts	Lyndon B. Johnson
36 Lyndon B. Johnson	1908–1973	1963–1969	Democratic	Texas	Hubert H. Humphrey
37 Richard M. Nixon	1913–1994	1969–1974	Republican	California	Spiro T. Agnew Gerald R. Ford
38 Gerald R. Ford	1913–2006	1974–1977	Republican	Michigan	Nelson A. Rockefeller
39 James Earl "Jimmy" Carter	1924–	1977–1981	Democratic	Georgia	Walter F. Mondale
40 Ronald Reagan	1911–2004	1981–1989	Republican	California	George H. W. Bush
41 George H. W. Bush	1924–	1989–1993	Republican	Texas	J. Danforth Quayle
42 William J. Clinton	1946–	1993–2001	Democratic	Arkansas	Albert Gore, Jr.
43 George W. Bush	1946–	2001–2009	Republican	Texas	Richard Cheney
44 Barack Obama	1961–	2009–	Democratic	Hawaii	Joseph Biden

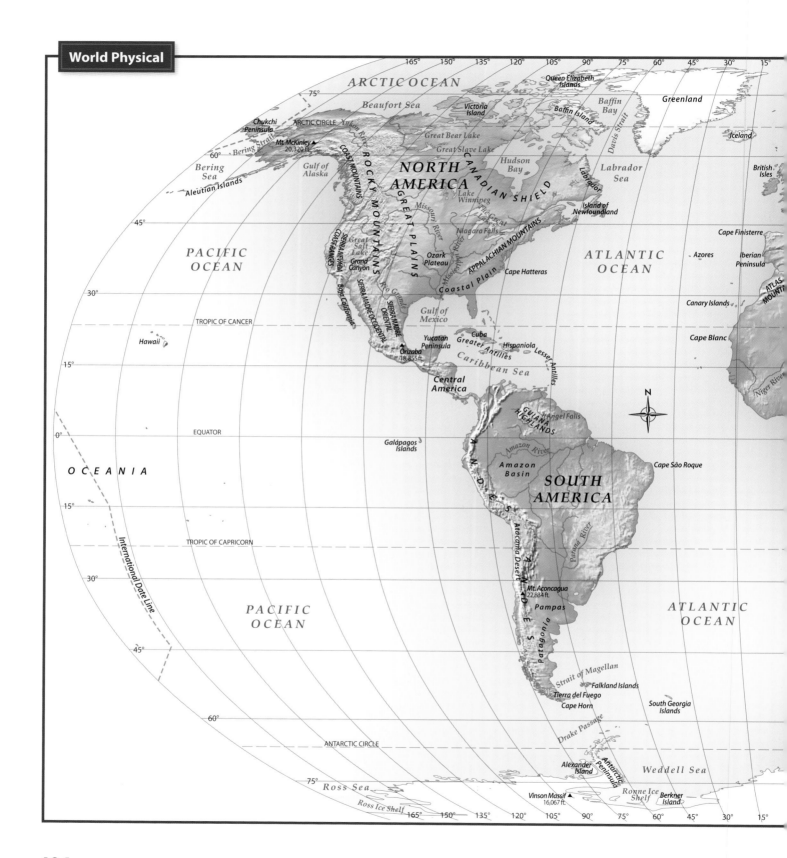

ARCTIC OCEAN

Beaufort Sea

Queen Elizabeth Islands

Baffin Island

Baffin Bay

Greenland

Davis Strait

Iceland

Chukchi Peninsula

ARCTIC CIRCLE

Victoria Island

Great Bear Lake

Great Slave Lake

Mt. McKinley ▲ 20,320 ft.

Yukon River

Bering Strait

Bering Sea

Gulf of Alaska

Hudson Bay

Labrador Sea

British Isles

Aleutian Islands

COAST MOUNTAINS

ROCKY MOUNTAINS

CANADIAN SHIELD

NORTH AMERICA

Lake Winnipeg

Labrador

Island of Newfoundland

PACIFIC OCEAN

GREAT PLAINS

Missouri River

Niagara Falls

Great Lakes

ATLANTIC OCEAN

Cape Finisterre

Azores

Iberian Peninsula

Great Salt Lake

SIERRA NEVADA

COAST RANGES

Grand Canyon

Mississippi River

Ozark Plateau

APPALACHIAN MOUNTAINS

Cape Hatteras

ATLAS MOUNTAINS

TROPIC OF CANCER

SIERRA MADRE OCCIDENTAL

Rio Grande

Coastal Plain

Canary Islands

Baja California

SIERRA MADRE ORIENTAL

Gulf of Mexico

Cape Blanc

Hawaii

Yucatan Peninsula

Cuba

Greater Antilles

Hispaniola

Lesser Antilles

Orizaba 18,855 ft.

Caribbean Sea

Niger River

Central America

N

15°

EQUATOR

OCEANIA

Galápagos Islands

GUIANA HIGHLANDS

Angel Falls

Cape São Roque

ANDES

Amazon River

Amazon Basin

SOUTH AMERICA

TROPIC OF CAPRICORN

International Date Line

Atacama Desert

Paraná River

PACIFIC OCEAN

ANDES

Mt. Aconcagua 22,884 ft.

Pampas

ATLANTIC OCEAN

Patagonia

ANDES

Strait of Magellan

Falkland Islands

Tierra del Fuego

Cape Horn

South Georgia Islands

ANTARCTIC CIRCLE

Drake Passage

Alexander Island

Antarctic Peninsula

Weddell Sea

Ross Sea

Vinson Massif ▲ 16,067 ft.

Ronne Ice Shelf

Berkner Island

Ross Ice Shelf

15°   30°   45°   60°   75°   90°   105°   120°   135°   150°   165°

ARCTIC OCEAN

Svalbard

Barents Sea

North Land

Laptev Sea

East Siberian Sea

75°

Norwegian Sea

Novaya Zemlya

Kara Sea

Yenisey River

ARCTIC CIRCLE

Chukchi Peninsula

Scandinavia

Kola Peninsula

Northern European Plain

URAL MOUNTAINS

Ob River

S I B E R I A

Central Siberian Plateau

60°

Sea of Okhotsk

Bering Sea

Kamchatka Peninsula

Date Line

EUROPE

Volga River

West Siberian Plain

ASIA

45°

Sakhalin

CARPATHIAN MOUNTAINS

The Steppes

Danube River

Mongolian Plateau

Hokkaido

ALPS

Elbrus 18,510 ft.

Aral Sea

Gobi

Sea of Japan

Balkan Peninsula

Black Sea

CAUCASUS MOUNTAINS

TIAN SHAN

Honshu

PACIFIC OCEAN

Anatolia

Mt. Ararat 16,854 ft.

Taklimakan Desert

KUNLUN MOUNTAINS

Huang He River

Kyushu

Mediterranean Sea

Syrian Desert

ZAGROS MOUNTAINS

K2 28,251 ft.

Plateau of Tibet

Yangtze River

East China Sea

30°

Sinai Peninsula

Arabian

HIMALAYA

Mt. Everest 29,035 ft.

TROPIC OF CANCER

S A H A R A

Libyan Desert

Nile River

Red Sea

Peninsula

Great Indian Desert

Ganges River

Taiwan

Arabian Sea

Deccan Plateau

Bay of Bengal

Philippine Sea

15°

S u d a n

Cape Gwardafuy

Cape Comorin

Indochina Peninsula

South China Sea

Philippine Islands

AFRICA

ETHIOPIAN HIGHLANDS

Somali Peninsula

Malay Peninsula

Borneo

EQUATOR

0°

Congo River

Lake Victoria

Kilimanjaro 19,340 ft.

Sumatra

Celebes

New Guinea

Congo Basin

Lake Tanganyika

INDIAN OCEAN

Java

Arafura Sea

O C E A N I A

Katanga Plateau

Lake Malawi

Coral Sea

15°

Victoria Falls

Madagascar

Mozambique Channel

Great Sandy Desert

Namib Desert

Réunion

TROPIC OF CAPRICORN

Western Plateau

Kalahari Desert

AUSTRALIA

Great Victoria Desert

Darling River

GREAT DIVIDING RANGE

30°

Cape of Good Hope

Murray R.

Tasman Sea

New Zealand

North Island

Kerguelen Is.

0   1000   2000 mi
0   1000   2000 km
Scale at equator

Tasmania

South Island

45°

60°

ANTARCTIC CIRCLE

TRANSANTARCTIC MOUNTAINS

75°

ANTARCTICA

Ross Ice Shelf

15°   30°   45°   60°   75°   90°   105°   120°   135°   150°   165°

ATLAS **405**

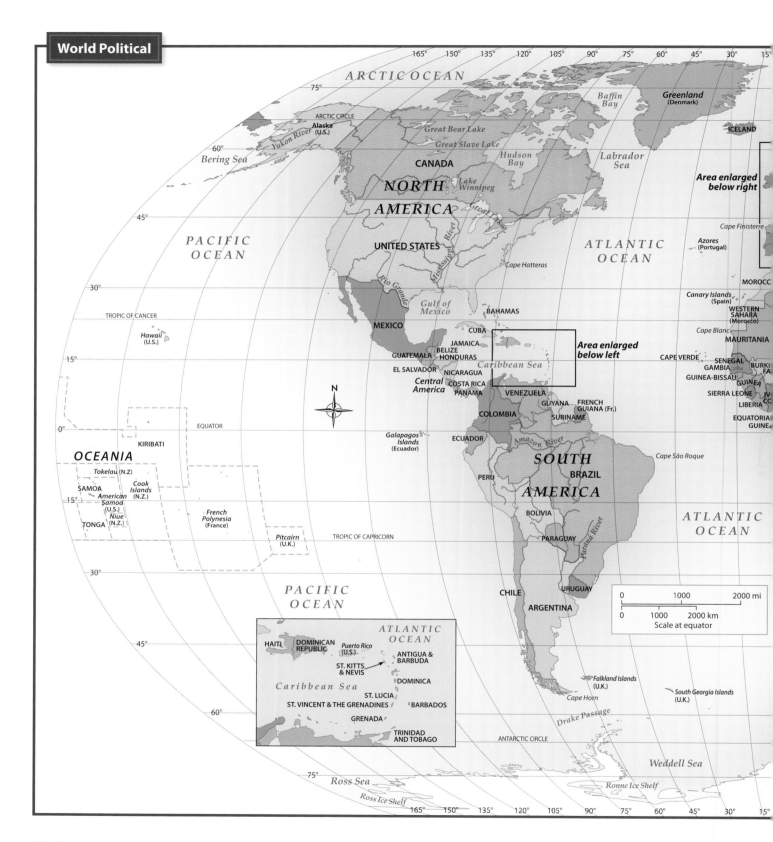

ARCTIC OCEAN

75°

ARCTIC CIRCLE

Yukon River

Alaska
(U.S.)

Bering Sea

60°

Great Bear Lake

Great Slave Lake

Baffin
Bay

Greenland
(Denmark)

ICELAND

CANADA

*Hudson
Bay*

*Labrador
Sea*

NORTH
AMERICA

*Lake
Winnipeg*

45°

**Area enlarged
below right**

PACIFIC
OCEAN

UNITED STATES

Mississippi River

Great Lakes

ATLANTIC
OCEAN

Cape Finisterre

Azores
(Portugal)

Cape Hatteras

30°

Rio Grande

*Gulf of
Mexico*

MOROCC

TROPIC OF CANCER

Hawaii
(U.S.)

MEXICO

BAHAMAS

CUBA

JAMAICA

Canary Islands
(Spain)

WESTERN
SAHARA
(Morocco)

Cape Blanc

MAURITANIA

15°

GUATEMALA
EL SALVADOR

BELIZE
HONDURAS
NICARAGUA

Caribbean Sea

**Area enlarged
below left**

CAPE VERDE

SENEGAL
GAMBIA

BURKI
FA

Central
America

COSTA RICA
PANAMA

VENEZUELA

GUYANA

FRENCH
GUIANA (Fr.)

GUINEA-BISSAU

GUINEA

SIERRA LEONE

IV
CO

0°

COLOMBIA

SURINAME

LIBERIA

EQUATOR

KIRIBATI

*Galapagos
Islands
(Ecuador)*

ECUADOR

Amazon River

Cape São Roque

EQUATORIA
GUINE

OCEANIA

SOUTH

Tokelau (N.Z.)

PERU

BRAZIL

15°

SAMOA
American
Samoa
(U.S.)

Cook
Islands
(N.Z.)

AMERICA

ATLANTIC
OCEAN

TONGA

*Niue
(N.Z.)*

*French
Polynesia
(France)*

BOLIVIA

*Pitcairn
(U.K.)*

TROPIC OF CAPRICORN

Paraná River

PARAGUAY

30°

PACIFIC
OCEAN

CHILE

URUGUAY

0   1000   2000 mi

0   1000   2000 km
Scale at equator

ARGENTINA

45°

HAITI

DOMINICAN
REPUBLIC

*Puerto Rico
(U.S.)*

*ATLANTIC
OCEAN*

ANTIGUA &
BARBUDA

ST. KITTS
& NEVIS

*Falkland Islands
(U.K.)*

*South Georgia Islands
(U.K.)*

Caribbean Sea

DOMINICA

Cape Horn

60°

ST. LUCIA

ST. VINCENT & THE GRENADINES

BARBADOS

Drake Passage

GRENADA

ANTARCTIC CIRCLE

Weddell Sea

TRINIDAD
AND TOBAGO

75°

Ross Sea

Ronne Ice Shelf

Ross Ice Shelf

165°   150°   135°   120°   105°   90°   75°   60°   45°   30°   15°

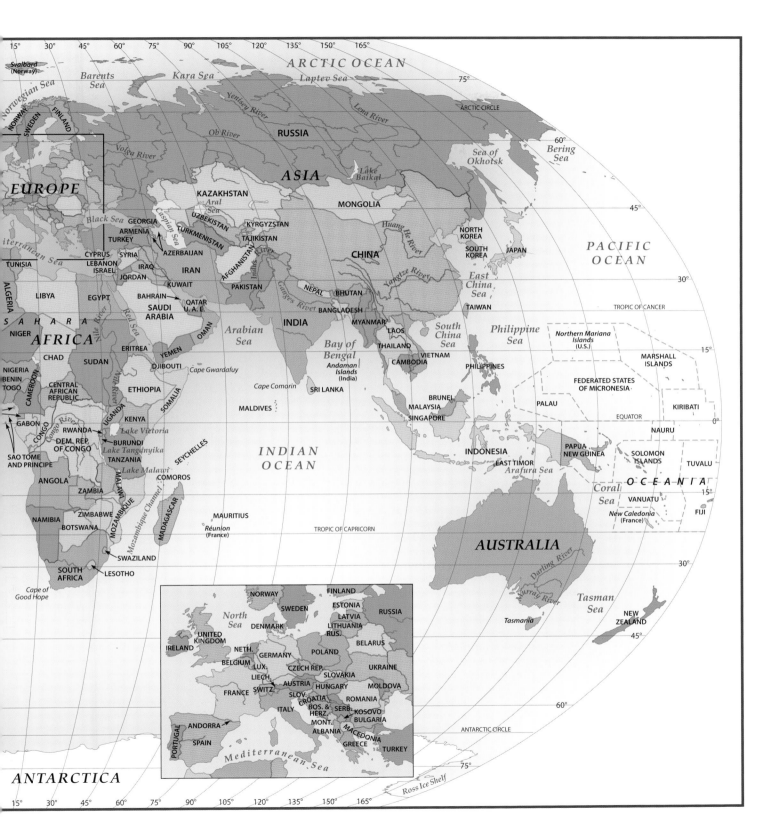

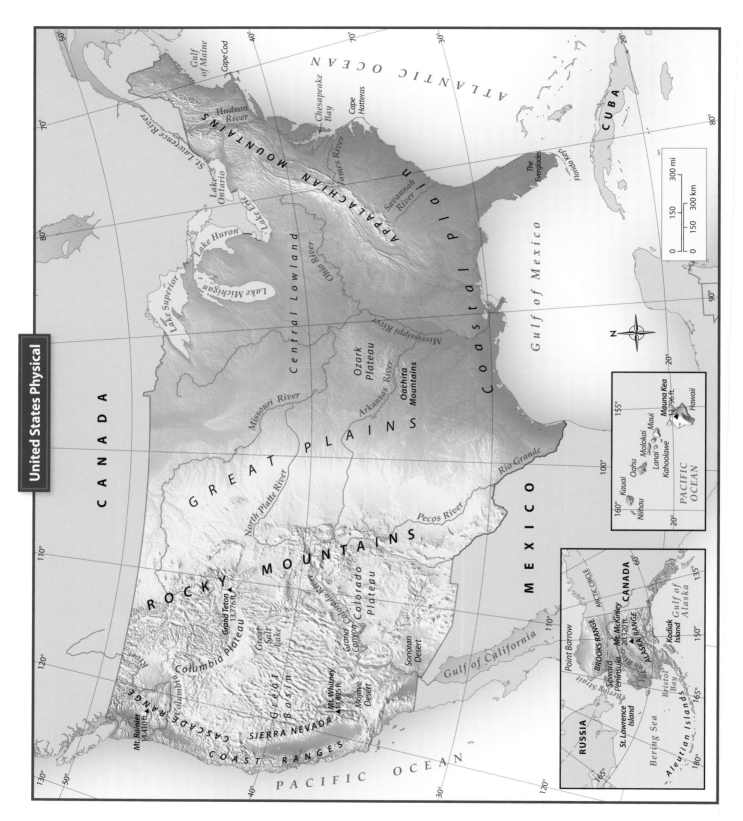

United States Physical

CANADA

Gulf of Maine
Cape Cod
Hudson River
St. Lawrence River
Lake Ontario
Lake Erie
Lake Huron
Lake Superior
Lake Michigan
APPALACHIAN MOUNTAINS
Chesapeake Bay
James River
Cape Hatteras
Savannah River
Ohio River
Central Lowland
Coastal Plain
ATLANTIC OCEAN
The Everglades
Florida Keys
CUBA

Missouri River
Mississippi River
Ozark Plateau
Arkansas River
Ouachita Mountains

GREAT PLAINS

Gulf of Mexico

North Platte River
Rio Grande
Pecos River

ROCKY MOUNTAINS

MEXICO

Grand Teton 13,766 ft.
Columbia Plateau
Great Salt Lake
Colorado River
Grand Canyon
Colorado Plateau
Sonoran Desert
Gulf of California

Columbia River
Great Basin
Mt. Whitney 14,495 ft.
Mojave Desert

Mt. Rainier 14,410 ft.
CASCADE RANGE
SIERRA NEVADA
COAST RANGES

PACIFIC OCEAN

N

300 mi
150
0
300 km
150
0

PACIFIC OCEAN
Kauai
Niihau
Oahu
Molokai
Lanai
Maui
Kahoolawe
Mauna Kea 13,796 ft.
Hawaii

RUSSIA
St. Lawrence Island
Bering Sea
Aleutian Islands
Point Barrow
ARCTIC CIRCLE
BROOKS RANGE
Seward Peninsula
Bristol Bay
ALASKA RANGE
Mt. McKinley 20,320 ft.
CANADA
Gulf of Alaska
Kodiak Island
Bering Strait

408 ATLAS

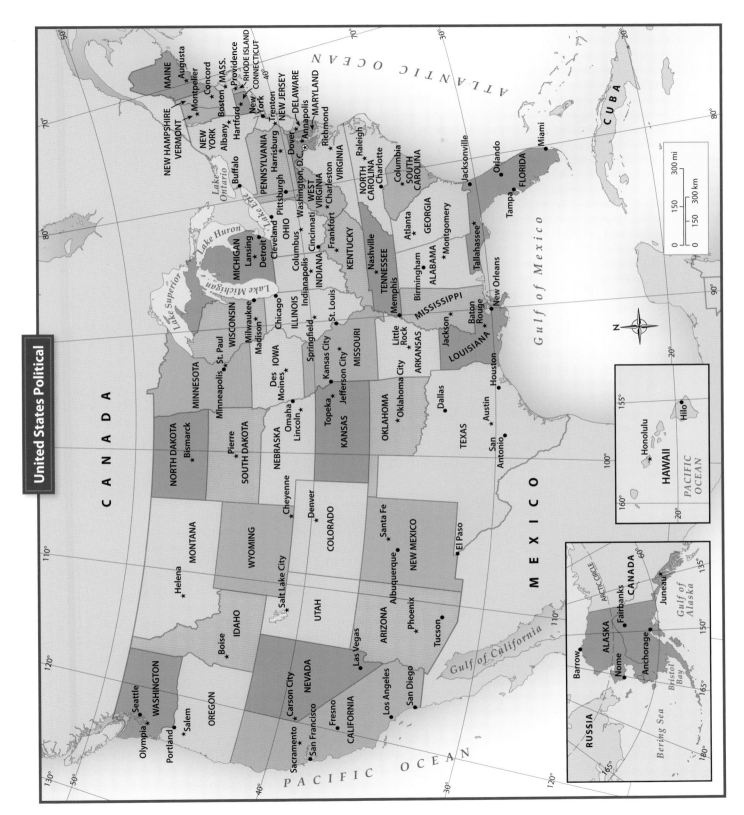

United States Political

CANADA

MAINE
Augusta ★
Montpelier ★
Concord ★
NEW HAMPSHIRE
VERMONT
MASS.
Boston ★
Providence
RHODE ISLAND
CONNECTICUT
New York
Hartford ★
Albany ★
NEW JERSEY
Trenton ★
Harrisburg ★
DELAWARE
Dover ★
Annapolis ★
MARYLAND
Washington, D.C. ⊛
Richmond ★

NEW YORK
Buffalo ●
Lake Ontario
Lake Erie
PENNSYLVANIA
Pittsburgh ●
WEST VIRGINIA
Charleston ★
VIRGINIA

Lake Huron
Lake Superior
Lake Michigan

MICHIGAN
Lansing ★
Detroit ●
Cleveland ●
OHIO
Columbus ★
Cincinnati ●
Frankfort ★
KENTUCKY
Nashville ★
TENNESSEE
Memphis ●

NORTH CAROLINA
Raleigh ★
Charlotte ●
Columbia ★
SOUTH CAROLINA
Jacksonville ●
Orlando ●
Miami ●
Tampa ●
FLORIDA
Tallahassee ★

Atlanta ★
GEORGIA
Montgomery ★
ALABAMA
Birmingham ●

INDIANA
Indianapolis ★
ILLINOIS
Springfield ★
Chicago ●
St. Louis ●

WISCONSIN
Milwaukee ●
Madison ★
MINNESOTA
Minneapolis ●
St. Paul ★

IOWA
Des Moines ★
Omaha ●
Lincoln ★
NEBRASKA

NORTH DAKOTA
Bismarck ★
Pierre ★
SOUTH DAKOTA

Cheyenne ★
Denver ★
COLORADO

MISSOURI
Jefferson City ★
Kansas City ●
Topeka ★
KANSAS

Little Rock ★
ARKANSAS
Jackson ★
MISSISSIPPI
Baton Rouge ★
New Orleans ●
LOUISIANA

Oklahoma City ★
OKLAHOMA
Dallas ●
Houston ●
Austin ★
San Antonio ●
TEXAS

El Paso ●
Santa Fe ★
NEW MEXICO
Albuquerque ●
Phoenix ★
Tucson ●
ARIZONA

MONTANA
Helena ★
WYOMING
IDAHO
Boise ★
Salt Lake City ★
UTAH
NEVADA
Carson City ★
Las Vegas ●

WASHINGTON
Seattle ●
Olympia ★
Portland ●
Salem ★
OREGON

CALIFORNIA
Sacramento ★
San Francisco ●
Fresno ●
Los Angeles ●
San Diego ●

MEXICO

Gulf of Mexico
Gulf of California
ATLANTIC OCEAN
PACIFIC OCEAN
CUBA

N

300 mi
150
0
300 km
150
0

HAWAII
Honolulu ★
Hilo ●
PACIFIC OCEAN
155°
160°
20°

ALASKA
Barrow ●
Nome ●
Anchorage ●
Fairbanks ●
Juneau ★
CANADA
RUSSIA
ARCTIC CIRCLE
Gulf of Alaska
Bristol Bay
Bering Sea
60°
135°
150°
165°
180°
165°

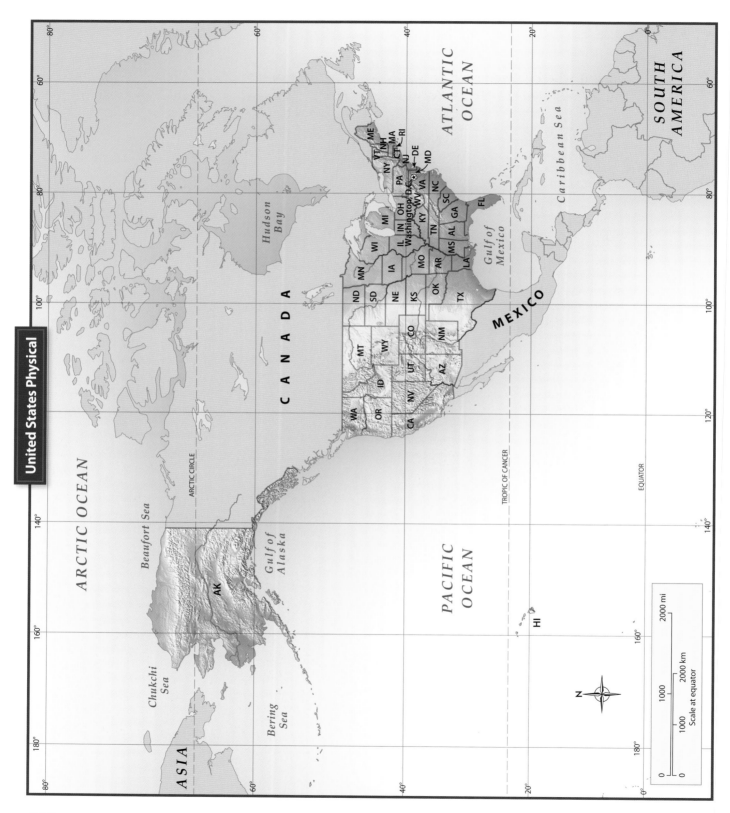

ARCTIC OCEAN

ASIA

Chukchi
Sea

Bering
Sea

Beaufort Sea

Gulf of
Alaska

AK

ARCTIC CIRCLE

PACIFIC
OCEAN

HI

TROPIC OF CANCER

EQUATOR

CANADA

Hudson
Bay

WA

OR

CA

NV

ID

UT

AZ

MT

WY

CO

NM

ND

SD

NE

KS

OK

TX

MN

IA

MO

AR

LA

WI

MI

IL

IN

OH

KY

TN

MS

AL

GA

Washington, D.C.

PA

WV

VA

NC

SC

FL

NY

VT

ME

NH

MA

CT

RI

NJ

DE

MD

MEXICO

Gulf of
Mexico

ATLANTIC
OCEAN

Caribbean Sea

SOUTH
AMERICA

N

2000 mi

1000

2000 km

1000

1000

2000 km

0

0

Scale at equator

Glossary

abolitionist   person who believed slavery was wrong and tried to stop it in the United States

agrarian   related to farming

alien   person who lives in a country but is not a citizen of that country

amendment   change or addition to the U.S. Constitution

antebellum   before the Civil War

aristocracy   people who have inherited wealth and social position; also government by those people

bigotry   intolerance, prejudice

Bill of Rights   first 10 amendments to the U.S. Constitution

black codes   laws passed by Southern states after the Civil War to limit the rights of former slaves

blockade   closing off a place (such as a harbor or port) to prevent entering or leaving an area

Cabinet   officially chosen group of advisers to the president

capital   money for funding a business or other venture

carpetbaggers   derogatory name used by Southerners to label people from the North who went to the South during Reconstruction

census   official count of people

citizen   someone with all the rights, protections, and responsibilities guaranteed under a nation's government

civil rights   rights guaranteed to all citizens by the Constitution and acts of Congress

Compromise of 1850   plan to deal with differences between slave states and free states

confederation   alliance of states

congress   group of representatives who come together for discussion, voting, and action

Constitution   the document that outlines the plan of government in the United States

Declaration of Independence   statement declaring American colonial independence from Britain, signed on July 4, 1776

democracy   government of the people

depression   time of severe economic decline, including high unemployment and falling prices

despotism   complete power over others

emancipation   granting of freedom

Emancipation Proclamation   document written and signed by President Abraham Lincoln that freed all slaves living in Confederate states during the Civil War

emigrant   person who leaves one country to settle in another

equality the state of having the same rights, privileges, and status

executive branch the branch of government that carries out the laws; in the United States, headed by the president

faction division of a larger group made up of people who share common views

farm economy system in which people grow their own food, taking care of their own needs and rarely use money

Federalists people who believed in strong central government during the early history of the United States

forty-niners people who moved to California during the Gold Rush of 1849

free enterprise an economic system allowing private industry to operate with little government control

Freedmen's Bureau an organization set up by Congress to help ex-slaves

Free-Soilers a group of Northerners who wanted to keep slavery from spreading into Western lands in the mid-19th century

Fugitive Slave Act a law passed in 1850 that made it illegal to help runaway slaves

Great Awakening Christian religious revival in the American colonies during the 1730s and 1740s

guerrilla a soldier who fights by using surprise tactics to bring down the enemy

haciendas large ranches in Spanish-speaking areas where cattle and crops were raised

hawks people who advocate war or the use of force against other nations

illiteracy the inability to read and write

immigrants people who move to a new country or region

impeach to charge a public official with crimes or misconduct

inauguration ceremony that ushers a new president into office

indict to charge with a crime

Industrial Revolution in the 18th and 19th centuries, great changes in the way goods were produced and the way people lived, brought about by the reorganization of work using machines and factories

industrialization the process of going from an agricultural system to one based on factories and machines

investor a person who funds a business hoping to make a profit

Jim Crow a system of laws beginning in the late 1800s that segregated blacks and forced them to use separate and inferior facilities

judicial branch the part of government charged with interpreting the laws; in the United States, consists of the Supreme Court and the lower federal courts

judicial review the power of the U.S. Supreme Court to decide if laws are constitutional

Kansas-Nebraska Act a law passed by Congress in 1854 that allowed settlers in Kansas and Nebraska to choose whether to allow slavery there

Ku Klux Klan an organization formed in the South in 1866 that used lynching and violence to intimidate and control blacks and others

labor unions associations of workers formed to promote and protect the rights of members

legislative branch the branch of government that makes the laws; in the United States it is composed of the Senate and the House of Representatives

lynching kidnapping and execution of a person by a mob

Manifest Destiny belief held by many Americans in the 19th and 20th centuries that it was God's will that the United States expand its borders

market economy a system in which people earn wages and provide for their needs by buying goods and services

martyr someone who chooses to die rather than give up a religious belief or political principle

Mexican War fought from 1846 to 1848, it ended with the United States gaining California and New Mexico

militia a body of citizen (not professional) soldiers

Minutemen farmers in colonial America who trained to fight the British

mission local headquarters of a religious group that provides services to local people as it tries to convert them

Missouri Compromise agreement that allowed slavery in Missouri and made it illegal in Maine and most of the rest of the Louisiana Purchase lands

monarchy government headed by a single ruler, especially a king or queen

Monroe Doctrine warning issued by President James Monroe in 1823 that European armies should keep out of the Americas

Native Americans the first peoples of North America, including those called Eskimos and Indians

nativism the practice of favoring native-born citizens over immigrants

neutral not favoring one side or another

Northwest Ordinance a law passed in 1787 that set out rules for how new territories should govern themselves and how they could eventually become states

nullification a state's refusal to recognize or uphold a federal law

ordinance law or regulation

peninsula a piece of land almost entirely surrounded by water

petition a written, formal statement requesting something

Pilgrims English colonists who arrived in Plymouth in 1620 on the *Mayflower*

pioneer   person who is among the first to settle in an unpopulated area

poll tax   tax that has been found to be unconstitutional that people in some states used to have to pay before they were allowed to vote

popular sovereignty   belief that people can and should govern themselves

precedent   act or decision that is used as a model in later cases

prejudice   dislike of another ethnic group, gender, race, or religion based on stereotypes and ignorance

presidio   fort, in Spanish

pueblos   Indian villages built of sun-dried clay mud

Quakers   a Christian group, officially called the Society of Friends, that opposes war and believes in respecting the rights of other people

radical   someone who favors extreme changes in existing laws or conditions

rancheros   owners of big ranches in Mexican America

ratify   to formally approve a suggested action

Rebels   nickname for Confederate soldiers during the Civil War

Reconstruction   the period from 1865 to 1877 when the federal government controlled the former Confederate states

reformer   someone who wants to make the world better by improving social conditions

republic   system in which people elect representatives to govern them according to law

reservation   public land set aside for special use, especially land set aside for Indian peoples after European Americans took over Indian land

scalawags   Southerners who cooperated with the North during Reconstruction

secede   to formally withdraw from a political organization

segregation   the practice of separating one racial, ethnic, or religious group from another, especially in public places

shaman   an Indian religious leader

sharecroppers   people who live and raise crops on land that belongs to other people

siege   the surrounding of a city or a fort by an army trying to capture it

speculation   financial risks taken in order to make a large profit

Stamp Tax   1765 tax that required American colonists to buy a British stamp for every piece of paper they used

states' rights   theory that each state has the right to nullify acts of the federal government

strike   work stoppage to protest low wages or bad working conditions

surrender to give up

system of checks and balances system of government in which the power of each of the branches of government is limited by that of the others

tariff tax on imports or exports

tax money that citizens and businesses are required to contribute to pay for the cost of government and the services it provides

technology use of scientific ideas for practical purposes

temperance movement campaign against alcohol consumption

Trail of Tears the forced march of 15,000 Cherokees from the Southeast to reservations in the West from 1837 to 1838

transcontinental railroad a railroad completed in 1869 that spanned North America

treaty formal agreement between nations

tyranny absolute power, especially when it is unjustly or cruelly used

Underground Railroad network offering help to slaves as they escaped from South to North

Union the United States of America as a political unit, especially during the Civil War; the North and its forces in the Civil War

urban of a city

vaqueros Spanish American cowboys

veto refusal to approve

Whig in 18th-century England, member of an English political party that generally believed the colonists should be allowed to govern themselves; in 18th-century America, Patriot; also, an American political party from 1834 to 1854

wilderness undeveloped land

Yankee nickname for a Union soldier in the Civil War

Illustrations Credits

Key: t=top; b=bottom; c=center; l=left; r=right

Front cover: © Corbis

Back cover: (l) W. Langdon Kihn/ National Geographic Stock; (cl and cr) © Corbis; (r) Dirk Anschutz/Getty Images

iii © Corbis
v © 2011 Sara Tyson c/o theispot.com
vi-1 (l) © Richard Wozniak/iStockphoto
vi-1 (r) © Mateusz Koc/iStockphoto

Part 1: 2 (t) © SuperStock/SuperStock; (frame) ElementalImaging/iStockphoto; (b) A View of Mount Vernon, Gift of Edgar William and Bernice Chrysler Garbisch, courtesy National Gallery of Art, Washington. **3** © Collection of the New-York Historical Society, USA/The Bridgeman Art Library. **4** © SuperStock. **5** Scala/Art Resource, NY. **6** The Granger Collection, New York. **7** © SuperStock; (frame) © ElementalImaging/iStockphoto. **8** The Granger Collection, New York. **9** (l) © Huntington Library/SuperStock; **9** (r)–**12** The Granger Collection, New York. **13** (l) © Corbis; (r) Copper pattern dollar, 1794. National Numismatic Collection, National Museum of American History. **14** © Photri/TopFoto/The Image Works. **15** (t) The Granger Collection, New York; (b) © History/Alamy. **16** (detail) White House Historical Association: 1426. **17** (t) Library of Congress, Prints and Photographs Division, LC-USZ62-48564; (b) The Granger Collection, New York. **18** (t) National Portrait Gallery, Smithsonian Institution/Art Resource; **18** (b)–**24** The Granger Collection, New York. **25** National Portrait Gallery, Smithsonian Institution/Art Resource; (frame) © Photodisc. **26** The Granger Collection, New York. **28** © Bettmann/Corbis; (frame) © ElementalImaging/iStockphoto. **29** © North Wind Picture Archives/Alamy. **31** (t) The Granger Collection, New York; (b) © Bettmann/Corbis. **32** (r) Everett Collection; (l) © Topham/The Image Works. **33** Peter Newark American Pictures /The Bridgeman Art Library. **35** © Visions of America/ SuperStock. **36** (t) The Art Archive/Given in memory of Henry H. Rogers and his daughter Mai Rogers Coe/Buffalo Bill Historical Center, Cody, Wyoming/24.62; (b) © Minden Pictures/SuperStock. **37** (t) © Franz-Marc Frei/Corbis; (b) The Granger Collection, New York. **38** SuperStock/ Getty Images. **39** Tim Fitzharris/Minden Pictures/National Geographic Stock. **40** National Portrait Gallery, Smithsonian Institution/Art Resource, NY. **41** The Granger Collection, New York. **42** (t) Peter Newark American Pictures/ The Bridgeman Art Library; (b) The Bridgeman Art Library. **43** The Granger Collection, New York. **44** (t) Bridgeman-Giraudon/Art Resource; (b) © The Gallery Collection/Corbis. **45** The Granger Collection, New York. **46** © Bettmann/ Corbis; (frame) © ElementalImaging/ iStockphoto. **47** (t) Maria Stenzel/Getty Images; (b) SuperStock/Getty Images. **48** The Granger Collection, New York. **49** (t) William Woodward/The Montpelier Foundation; (c) The Granger Collection, New York; (b) Library of Congress, Prints and Photographs Division, LC-USZC4-405. **51** (t) © Smithsonian Institution/Corbis; (b) Eon Images. **53–54** Peter Newark American Pictures/The Bridgeman Art Library. **55** (t) The Granger Collection, New York; (b) Library of Congress, Prints and Photographs Division, LC-USZC4-2398. **56** (t) The Granger Collection, New York; (b) National Portrait Gallery, Smithsonian Institution/Art Resource, NY; (frame) © Jupiterimages. **57** US Senate Collection. **58** © North Wind/North Wind Picture Archives. **59** (t) The Bridgeman Art Library; (b) The Granger Collection, New York. **60** St. Louis Art Museum, Missouri, USA / The Bridgeman Art Library. **61** The Art Archive/The Granger Collection. **62** Smithsonian American Art Museum, Washington, DC/Art Resource, NY; (frame) © ElementalImaging/iStockphoto. **63** (t) The White House Historical Association (White House Collection); (b) © Bettmann/Corbis. **64** (t and cl and r) The White House Historical Association (White House Collection); (bl and br) The Granger Collection, New York.

Part 2: 65 (l) © Richard Wozniak/ iStockphoto; (r) © Mateusz Koc/ iStockphoto. **66** Art Resource, NY. **67** PhotoObjects.net/Thinkstock. **68** (l) Armed Forces History, National Museum of American History, Smithsonian Institution; (r) © Christie's Images/The Bridgeman Art Library. **69** (t) fotoIE/ iStockphoto.com; (b) The Granger Collection, New York. **70** (l) © Bettmann/ Corbis; (r) Peter Newark American Pictures/The Bridgeman Art Library. **72–73** The Granger Collection, New York. **74–75** © North Wind/North Wind Picture Archives. **76** Federal Highway Administration. **77** © North Wind/ North Wind Picture Archives. **78** Library of Congress, Prints and Photographs Division, LC-DIG-pga-03254. **79** Science & Society Picture Library/Getty Images. **80** © Collection of the New-York Historical Society, USA/The Bridgeman Art Library. **81** © Bettmann/Corbis. **82** The Granger Collection, New York. **83** Dave King/Getty Images. **84–85** The Granger Collection, New York. **87** © SuperStock/SuperStock. **88–92** (t) The Granger Collection, New York; (b) © Everett Collection Inc./Alamy **93** © Collection of the New-York Historical Society, USA/The Bridgeman Art Library. **94** The Granger Collection, New York; (frame) © ElementalImaging/iStockphoto. **95** © North Wind Picture Archives/Alamy. **96–98** The Granger Collection, New York. **99** © Bettmann/Corbis. **100–101** The Granger Collection, New York. **102** Dover Publications. **103** © Corbis. **104** (t) © SuperStock/SuperStock; (b) The Granger Collection, New York. **105** (l) © Bettmann/ Corbis; (r) Smithsonian American Art Museum, Washington, DC/Art Resource, NY. **106** National Geographic Image Collection/The Bridgeman Art Library. **107** Woolaroc Museum, Oklahoma, USA/ Peter Newark Western Americana/The Bridgeman Art Library. **109** The Granger Collection, New York. **111** (l) © North Wind/North Wind Picture Archives; (r) The Granger Collection, New York. **112** Private Collection/Index/The Bridgeman Art Library. **113** (r) Private Collection/

Peter Newark American Pictures/The Bridgeman Art Library; (l) James L. Amos/National Geographic Stock. **114** (t) Dover Publications; (b) Christian Heeb/Aurora Photos. **115** (t) Missouri History Museum, St. Louis; (frame) louoates/BigStock; (b) Dover Publications. **116** Peter Newark Western Americana/The Bridgeman Art Library. **117** The Granger Collection, New York. **118** Property of the Westervelt Collection and displayed in The Westervelt-Warner Museum of American Art in Tuscaloosa, AL. **119** (t) Dover Publications; (b) © Darren Bennett/Animals Animals. **120** (t) Dover Publications; (b) Michael S. Lewis/National Geographic Stock. **121** The Art Archive/Gift of Ruth Koerner Oliver/Buffalo Bill Historical Center, Cody, Wyoming/6922.1. **122** De Agostini Picture Library/Getty Images. **123** © North Wind/Nancy Carter/North Wind Picture Archives. **124** © Christie's Images/The Bridgeman Art Library. **125–126** Peter Newark Western Americana/The Bridgeman Art Library. **127** The Granger Collection, New York. **128** (t) Peter Newark American Pictures/The Bridgeman Art Library; (b) © sodapix/age fotostock. **129** © Gary Crabbe/age fotostock. **130** (t) © North Wind Picture Archives/Alamy; (b) The Bridgeman Art Library. **131** (t) Dover Publications; (b) © 2011 Photos.com/Getty Images. **132** (t) © Panoramic Images/R Watts 2011; (c) © Paul A. Souders/Corbis; (b) Everett Collection. **133** National Gallery of Art, Washington DC, USA/The Bridgeman Art Library; (frame) ElementalImaging/iStockphoto. **134** The Granger Collection, New York; (r) Peter Newark American Pictures/The Bridgeman Art Library. **135** © Bob Turner/age fotostock. **136** © Mary Evans Picture Library/Grosvenor Prints/The Image Works. **137** © Christie's Images/Corbis. **139** (t) Dover Publications; (b) The Granger Collection, New York. **140** Architect of the Capitol. **141** The Granger Collection, New York. **142** Tim Fitzharris/Minden Pictures/National Geographic Stock. **143** Dover Publications. **144** The State Preservation Board, Austin, Texas. **145** The Granger Collection, New York. **146** Peter Newark American Pictures/The Bridgeman Art Library. **147** © Bettmann/Corbis. **148** © Nic Taylor/

iStockphoto. **150** The Granger Collection, New York. **151** Library of Congress, Prints and Photographs Division, LC-USZC4-2439. **153** The Granger Collection, New York. **154** (l) © Mary Evans Picture Library/The Image Works; (r) Sutter's Gold, Division of Work and Industry, National Museum of American History, Behring Center, Smithsonian Institution. **155** The Granger Collection, New York. **156** The Stapleton Collection/The Bridgeman Art Library. **157** (t) Peter Newark American Pictures/The Bridgeman Art Library; (b) © Minnesota Historical Society/Corbis. **158** Courtesy of the California History Museum, California State Library, Sacramento, California. **159** The Granger Collection, New York. **160** Autry National Center; 93.99.4. **161** (l) The Granger Collection, New York; (r) © Bettmann/Corbis. **162** The Granger Collection, New York. **163** (t) Peter Newark American Pictures/The Bridgeman Art Library; (b) Dover Publications. **164** (l) Hulton Archive/Getty Images; (frame) © bubaone/iStockphoto; (r) National Museum of American History-Electricity Collections, Smithsonian Institution. **165** Federal Highway Administration. **166–167** The Granger Collection, New York. **168** St. Louis Art Museum, Missouri, USA /The Bridgeman Art Library. **169** (t) The Art Archive/Culver Pictures; (c and b) The Granger Collection, New York. **170** Fotosearch/Getty Images. **171** (t) © Lebrecht Music and Arts Photo Library/Alamy. **171**(b)–**173** The Granger Collection, New York. **172** (frames) louoates/BigStock. **174** (t) Museum of the City of New York/Getty Images; (b) © Everett Collection/SuperStock. **175–176** The Granger Collection, New York. **177** (t) Kean Collection/Getty Images; (c) National Portrait Gallery, Smithsonian Institution/Art Resource, NY; (frame) © Jupiterimages; (b)–**178** The Granger Collection, New York. **179** Library of Congress, Prints and Photographs Division, LC-USZC4-6165. **180** The Granger Collection, New York. **181** (t) © Lebrecht Music and Arts Photo Library/Alamy; (frame) louoates/BigStock; (b) © PoodlesRock/Corbis. **182** (t) Hulton Archive/Getty Images. **182** (c)–**183** (b) The Granger Collection, New York. **183**

(b) The Granger Collection, New York; (c) (frame) © ElementalImaging/iStockphoto; (b)–**183** (t) © Bettmann/Corbis; (frame) © Jupiterimages. **184** © Bettmann/Corbis; (frame) louoates/BigStock. **185** The Granger Collection, New York. **186** (t) © Interfoto/Alamy; (b) © Blue Lantern Studio/Corbis. **187** The Granger Collection, New York. **188** National Portrait Gallery, Smithsonian Institution/Art Resource, NY. **189** The Granger Collection, New York. **190** (t) National Portrait Gallery, Smithsonian Institution/Art Resource, NY; (b) Smithsonian Institution, Washington DC, USA/The Bridgeman Art Library. **191** The Granger Collection, New York. **192** (t) Smithsonian American Art Museum, Washington, DC/Art Resource, NY; (b) Dover Publications.

Part 3: 193 (l) © Richard Wozniak/iStockphoto; (r) © Mateusz Koc/iStockphoto. **194** The Granger Collection, New York. **195** (c) Jerry Pinkney/Gerald and Cullen Rapp, Inc. **196** © Wilberforce House, Hull City Museums and Art Galleries, UK /The Bridgeman Art Library. **197** © SuperStock/SuperStock. **198** (t) Jerry Pinkney/National Geographic Stock; (b) The Historic New Orleans Collection, accession no.1975.93.1 and 1975.93.2. **199** © Massachusetts Historical Society, Boston, MA, USA/The Bridgeman Art Library. **200– 201** (t) The Granger Collection, New York; (b) MPI/Getty Images. **202** (t) Wood Ronsaville Harlin, Inc.; (b) Schomburg Center/Art Resource, NY. **203** Smithsonian American Art Museum, Washington, DC/Art Resource, NY. **205** (t) The Granger Collection, New York; (b) © SSPL/The Image Works. **206** Library of Congress, Prints and Photographs Division, LC-USZC4-2523. **207–208** (t) The Granger Collection, New York; (b) © Christie's Images/SuperStock. **209** HIP/Art Resource, NY. **211** (l) The Granger Collection, New York; (r) Schomburg Center/Art Resource, NY. **212** (t) © Massachusetts Historical Society, Boston, MA, USA/The Bridgeman Art Library; (b) The Granger Collection, New York. **213** American Antiquarian Society, Worcester, Massachusetts, USA/The Bridgeman Art Library. **214–215** The Granger Collection, New York.

216 © Bettmann/Corbis. 217 (t) The Granger Collection, New York; (b) © Bettmann/Corbis. 218 (t) Robert E. Whitechurch after Peter Frederick Rothermel/US Senate Collection; (b) The Granger Collection, New York. 219 Arthur E. Schmalz Conrad/US Senate Collection; (frame) © Jupiterimages. 220 Texas State Preservation Board, Austin, Texas; (t) (frame) © bubaone/iStockphoto; (b) Private Collection/Peter Newark American Pictures/The Bridgeman Art Library; (b) (frame) ElementalImaging/iStockphoto. 221 Courtesy of the Boston Art Commission. 222 Delaware Art Museum, Wilmington, USA/Gift of Helen Farr Sloan/ The Bridgeman Art Library. 223 Theodore Augustus Mills/US Senate Collection. 224 (t) © AF archive/Alamy; (b) © DreamWorks SKG/Courtesy Everett Collection. 225 C.P. Cushing/Classicstock.com. 228 James Henry Wright/US Senate Collection 229 James M. Edney Jones and Clark/US Senate Collection. 231 The Granger Collection, New York. 232 (l) © North Wind Picture Archives/Alamy; (r) Library of Congress, Washington DC, USA/The Stapleton Collection/The Bridgeman Art Library. 233 The Granger Collection, New York. 234 Barbara Cushing/Everett Collection. 235–236 The Granger Collection, New York; (frame) louoates/BigStock. 237 (t) Frederick Douglass National Historic Site, Washington, USA/The Bridgeman Art Library; (b) Private Collection/Courtesy of Swann Auction Galleries/The Bridgeman Art Library. 238 (t) The New York Public Library/Art Resource, NY; (b)–239 (t) The Granger Collection, New York. 239 (b) © SuperStock/SuperStock. 240 (l) © North Wind Picture Archives/Alamy; (r) © Getty Images. 241 Smithsonian American Art Museum, Washington, DC/Art Resource, NY. 243 The Granger Collection, New York. 244 © Corbis; (frame) louoates/ BigStock. 245 Felix Koch/Cincinnati Museum Center/Getty Images. 246 The Granger Collection, New York. 247 (l) © Paul Collins/collinsart.com; (r) The Granger Collection, New York. 248 National Geographic Image Collection/ The Bridgeman Art Library. 249 MPI/Getty Images. 250 (t) The Granger Collection, New York; (b) © Corbis. 251–252 © Bettmann/Corbis. 253 Schomburg Center/

Art Resource, NY. 254 John Steuart Curry/ Kansas State Historical Society. 255 © Everett Collection/SuperStock. 256 Private Collection/Peter Newark American Pictures/The Bridgeman Art Library. 258 The Granger Collection, New York. 259 © Walter Bibikow/Corbis. 260 © North Wind Picture Archives/Alamy. 261 The Granger Collection, New York. 262 © Bettmann/ Corbis. 263 Peter Newark American Pictures/The Bridgeman Art Library. 264 (t) © The Corcoran Gallery of Art/ Corbis; (frame) © Jupiterimages; (b) Private Collection/The Bridgeman Art Library. 265 (t) © Bettmann/Corbis; (b) Art Archive/ National Archives Washington, DC.

Part 4: 266 (l) © Richard Wozniak/ iStockphoto; (r) © Mateusz Koc/ iStockphoto. 268 Library of Congress, Prints and Photographs Division, LC-DIG-pga-01841. 269 © National Maritime Museum, London/The Image Works. 270 Library of Congress, Prints and Photographs Division, LC-DIG-cwpb-01005. 271 (l) © Bettmann/ Corbis; (r) Library of Congress, Prints and Photographs Division, LC-B8184-10087. 272 (t) The Granger Collection, New York; (b) © North Wind Picture Archives/Alamy. 274 © The Metropolitan Museum of Art/ Art Resource, NY. 275 © Bettmann/Corbis. 276–277 © North Wind Picture Archives/ Alamy. 278 The Granger Collection, New York. 279 (t) Library of Congress, Prints and Photographs Division, LC-DIG-pga-01843; (b) Private Collection/The Bridgeman Art Library. 280 The Granger Collection, New York. 281 © North Wind Picture Archives/Alamy. 282 The Art Archive. 283 The Granger Collection, New York. 284 Library of Congress, Prints and Photographs Division, LC-DIG-cwpb-01600. 285 Museum of Fine Arts, Boston, Massachusetts, USA/ Gift of Martha C. Karolik for the M. and M. Karolik Collection of American Paintings, 1815–1865/The Bridgeman Art Library. 286 The Granger Collection, New York. 287 MPI/Getty Images. 288 (t) The Granger Collection, New York; (b) © Tria Giovan/Corbis. 289 Library of Congress, Prints and Photographs Division, LC-DIG-pga-01847. 290 © North Wind Picture Archives/Alamy.

291 (t) MPI/Getty Images; (b)–293 The Granger Collection, New York. 294 Dover Publications. 295 © Classic Image/Alamy. 296 (l) MPI/Getty Images; (r) The Granger Collection, New York; 297 The Granger Collection, New York. 298 (t) © Corbis; (b) ullstein bild/The Granger Collection, New York. 300 (t) Library of Congress, Prints and Photographs Division, LC-USZC2-2804; (b) Dover Publications. 301 (t) © Minnesota Historical Society/ Corbis; (b) The Granger Collection, New York; (frame) louoates/BigStock. 302 (t) © Bettmann/Corbis; (b) Gregory Manchess/National Geographic Stock. 303 (t) Peter Newark Military Pictures/ The Bridgeman Art Library; (b) The Art Archive. 304 © Francis G. Mayer/Corbis. 305 Dover Publications. 306 Library of Congress, Prints and Photographs Division, LC-DIG-cwpbh-03384. 307 (t) The Stapleton Collection/Art Resouce; (b) Dover Publications. 308 (t) © Civil War Archive/The Bridgeman Art Library; (c) Confederate Memorial Hall, New Orleans, Louisiana, USA/© Civil War Archive/The Bridgeman Art Library; (b) © Christie's Images/The Bridgeman Art Library. 309 © AA World Travel Library/ Alamy. 310 Library of Congress, Prints and Photographs Division, LC-DIG-cwpb-01872. 311–312 (l) The Granger Collection, New York. 312 (r) The Art Archive/Culver Pictures. 313 © Massachusetts Historical Society, Boston, MA, USA/The Bridgeman Art Library; (frame) © ElementalImaging/iStockphoto. 314 MPI/Getty Images. 315 National Guard Bureau. 316 (t) © The Metropolitan Museum of Art/Art Resource, NY; (b) Armed Forces History, National Museum of American History, Smithsonian Institution. 317 (t) Library of Congress, Prints and Photographs Division, LC-DIG-cwpb-01663; (b) Library of Congress, Prints and Photographs Division, LC-USZ62-66616. 318 Gettysburg National Military Park Museum, Pennsylvania, USA/© Civil War Archive/ The Bridgeman Art Library. 319 Library of Congress, Prints and Photographs Division, LC-USZC4-12532. 320 The State Museum of Pennsylvania, Pennsylvania Historical and Museum Commission. 321 (t) Dover Publications; (frame) ©

Jupiterimages; (b) The Granger Collection, New York. **322** © Geoffrey Clements/Corbis. **323** (t) Peter Newark Military Pictures/The Bridgeman Art Library; **323** (b)–**324** (t) The Granger Collection, New York. **324** (b) © Corbis. **325** Delaware Art Museum, Wilmington, USA/Bequest of Jessie Harrington/The Bridgeman Art Library. **326** Smithsonian American Art Museum, Washington, DC/Art Resource, NY. **327** The Granger Collection, New York. **328** © The Metropolitan Museum of Art/Art Resource, NY. **329**–**330** © Corbis. **331** Norman Rockwell Digital Collection. Works by Norman Rockwell. Printed by permission of the Norman Rockwell Family Agency. Copyright © 1943 Norman Rockwell Family Entities. **332** © gchutka/iStockphoto. **333** The Granger Collection, New York. **334** Peter Newark Military Pictures/The Bridgeman Art Library. **335** (t) Library of Congress, Prints and Photographs Division, LC-USZC6-48; (b) Everett Collection. **337** Library of Congress, Prints and Photographs Division, LC-DIG-cwpb-03379. **338** The Granger Collection, New York. **339** © Corbis. **340** The Art Archive/Culver Pictures. **341** The Granger Collection,

New York. **342** Everett Collection. **343** (l) Library of Congress, Prints and Photographs Division, LC-USZC2-2298; (r) © Chicago History Museum, USA/The Bridgeman Art Library. **344** © Medford Historical Society Collection/Corbis. **345** Virginia Historical Society, Richmond, Virginia, USA /The Bridgeman Art Library. **347** Peter Newark American Pictures/The Bridgeman Art Library; (frame) © Jupiterimages. **348** Dover Publications; (frame) © bubaone/iStockphoto. **349**–**350** The Granger Collection, New York. **352** (t) Library of Congress, Prints and Photographs Division, LC-USZ62-13017; (b) © Bettmann/Corbis. **353** (t) Library of Congress, Prints and Photographs Division, LC-DIG-ppmsca-37192; (frame) © Jupiterimages; (b)–**354** (t) The Granger Collection, New York. **354** (b) Louie Psihoyos/Getty Images. **355** © Thinkstock/Photos.com/Getty Images. **356** (t) The Granger Collection, New York; (b) National Portrait Gallery, Smithsonian Institution/Art Resource, NY. **357** The Granger Collection, New York. **358** Library of Congress, Prints and Photographs Division, LC-USZ62-89342. **359** (l) The Granger

Collection, New York; (c and r) P. F. Cooper/George Eastman House/Getty Images; (c and r) P. F. Cooper/George Eastman House/Getty Images. **360** (t) © North Wind Picture Archives/Alamy; (b) The Granger Collection, New York. **361** Library of Congress, Prints and Photographs Division, LC-USZ62-119565. **362** The Granger Collection, New York. **363** (t) Architect of the Capitol; (b) © Bettmann/Corbis. **365** Library of Congress, Prints and Photographs Division, LC-USZC4-2399. **366**–**368** The Granger Collection, New York. **369** Kean Collection/Getty Images. **370** Library of Congress, Prints and Photographs Division, LC-USZ62-63460; (frame) © Jupiterimages. **371** © North Wind Picture Archives/Alamy. **372**–**373** The Granger Collection, New York. **374** US Senate Collection. **375** (t) US Senate Collection; (b) The Granger Collection, New York. **376** CartoonStock.com. **377** The Granger Collection, New York. **378** MPI/Getty Images. **379** The Granger Collection, New York. **380** © Bettmann/Corbis. **381** The Granger Collection, New York. **382** Private Collection/The Bridgeman Art Library.

Index

Flying Cloud (ship), 163
food, 5, 13, 66, 101, 110, 214, 244, 256,
    275–276, 288, 299, 307, 317, 327,
    335, 337–338, 343, 357, 359, 367
    see also agriculture, plants
    of immigrants, 160
    in mining camps, 156
    of pioneers, 33, 35, 113, 122,
        130–131, 136
Ford's Theatre, 349–350
forests, 41, 109, 125, 237, 337, 366
    see also natural resources
Fort Laramie, Wyoming, **129**
Fort Mandan, North Dakota, **34**
Fort McHenry, Maryland, 50–53
Fort Sumter, South Carolina, **336**, 349
    as beginning of war, 271, 276, 278,
        301, 344
    Confederate demands for, 276
Fort Wagner, South Carolina, 315
Forten, James, 200
Forty-niners, 157 *see also* gold
Founding Fathers, 7, 57, 63, 332
Fourteenth Amendment, 347, 364–365,
    371
Fox Indians, **108**, 110
France, 6, 31–32, 141, 180, 188 *see also*
    French Revolution
    naval warfare, 21
    as U.S. ally, 20
    War of 1812 and, 44–46
    war with England, 20–22
Franklin, Benjamin, 20, 22, 79, 165,
    191, 206
Fredericksburg, Battle of, 319
Free African Society, 201
free enterprise system, 13
Free Soil Party, 63, 228, 232, 271
Freedmen's Bureau, 357, 359, 367,
    372
freedom of religion, 9, 144
freedom of speech, 23–24
freedom of the press, 9, 23–24
Freeman, Elizabeth, 198–199
Frémont, John Charles, 141, 294
French immigrants, 188
French Revolution, 5, 22, 44
frigates *see* boats and ships
frontier, 8, 25, 93–94, 96, 99, 105, 107,
    147, 159, 185–186, 188–189, 190,
    192, 203–204, 218, 261–262
Fugitive Slave Law, 173, 227–228, 230,
    238–239, 241–243, 265–266, 271
Fuller, Elizabeth, 67
Fulton, Robert, 83–84
fur trade, 94, 119, 192

G

Gallatin, Albert, 30, 35
games, 273–274, 310
Garrison, William Lloyd, 212, 271, 349
Gatling, Richard, 288
Georgia, 8, **34**, **50**, 57, 70, 106–108,
    108, 109–110, 146, 195, **210**, 211,
    227, **230**, 235–237, 242, **269**, 272,
    280, **336**, 337, 339, 341, 368
German immigrants, 105, 114, 117, 335
Germany, 94, 117, 180
Gettysburg, Pennsylvania, 284, 295,
    319–332, 370
gold, 29, 106, 143–144, 154, 156,
    162–163, 198, 295–296
    mines, 157–160
Golden, Colorado, 158
Goliad, 145–146
Goodyear, Charles, 88
Gordon, James, 91
government, 3–8, 11–13, 15, 17,
    20, 25–27, 29, 62, 77, 106–107,
    110–111, 113, 138, 144, 146, 158,
    168, 183, 217, 221–222, 226, 230,
    232, 241–242, 249, 255, 265–266,
    270–272, 275–276, 278, 287, 298,
    311, 314, 332, 340, 347, 351, 354,
    361–364, 366, 368–369, 373, 381
    see also Congress, House of
    Representatives, presidency, Senate
    Hamilton on, 9–10, 21, 30
    Native American, 105
Graham, Mentor, 263
grain, 8, 66, 75, 82, 187, 299
Grand Ronde River, 125
Grant, Ulysses S., 153, 314
    background, 295
    correspondence with Lincoln, 294,
        348–349
    described, 294, 347, 378–379
    end of war, 343, 345–346, 361
    military tactics, 294, 327–328,
        333–335, **336**, 336–337, 341
    shortcomings of, 378–379
Graybeard Regiment (Iowa), 287
Great Awakening, 168
Great Barrington, Massachusetts, 199
Great Basin, 135
Great Britain *see* England
Great Lakes, 81
Great Plains, 119, 141
Great Potato Famine, 117
Great Salt Lake, 39, **129**, 132, 135–136
    see also Salt Lake City, Utah
Great Spirit, 40, 43
Greek immigrants, 117, 355

Greeley, Horace, 91, 158, 363
Green, Samuel, 253
Greenhow, Rose O'Neal, 296
Gregory, John H., 258
Grimké, Angelina, 172–173
Grimké, Sarah, 172–173
Griswold, Roger, 22–23
Guadalupe Hidalgo, Treaty of, 153–154
Guerrière (ship), 47
guillotine, 44

H

"Hail to the Chief," 54, 350
Haiti, 188, 207
Halleck, Henry W., 294
Hallet, Etienne, 17
Hamilton, Alexander, 6, 21
    Burr and, 28, 31
    as conservative, 11
    death of, 31
    on democracy, 20
    rivalry with Jefferson, 7, 9, 11–12,
        21, 28, 30–31, 56
    as secretary of the treasury, 7–8, 13,
        30
    on strong central government, 10, 21
Hammond, M. B., 292
Hampton, Virginia, 358
Hampton Institute, 363
Hampton Roads, Virginia, 304–305, **336**
Hancock, Winfield Scott, 284, 324–325
Hanks, Dennis, 260
Hanks, Nancy *see* Lincoln, Nancy Hanks
Harding, Rebecca, 96–98
hardtack, 317
Harpers Ferry, Virginia, 255–257
Harrisburg, Pennsylvania, 308
Harrison, William Henry, 42–43, 63–64
Harvard College, 58, 60, 75, 170,
    180–182, 184, 312, 329, 358
Haudenosaunee *see* Iroquois Indians
Havana, Cuba, 224
Hawaiian Islands, **152**
Hawthorne, Nathaniel, 181, 185
Hayes, Rutherford B., 379–380
Hayne, Robert Young, 221, 223
Haynes, Lemuel, 200
Henry, Joseph, 165
Henry, Patrick, 138, 221
Henry, William, 83
Henson, Josiah, 201
Hicks, Edward, 192
Higginson, Thomas Wentworth,
    186–187
Hoban, James, 16
Holmes, Oliver Wendell, 47